W9-BSP-728

A Prophet for Our Time

A Prophet for Our Time

An Anthology of the Writings of
RABBI MARC H. TANENBAUM

Edited by Judith H. Banki and Eugene J. Fisher

Fordham University Press
New York
2002

Library of Congress Cataloging-in-Publication Data

Tanenbaum, Marc H.
   [Selections. 2002]
   A prophet for our time : an anthology of the writings of Rabbi Marc H. Tanenbaum / edited by Judith H. Banki and Eugene J. Fisher.—1st ed.
   p. cm.
   Includes bibliographical references and index.
   ISBN 0-8232-2230-6 (cloth : alk. paper)—ISBN 0-8232-2231-4 (pbk. : alk. paper)
   1. Judaism—Relations—Christianity.   2. Christianity and other religions—Judaism.   I. Banki, Judith Herschcopf.   II. Fisher, Eugene J.
   III. Title.
BM535 .T342   2002
296.3—dc21   2002007657

Printed in the United States of America
02 03 04 05 06   5 4 3 2 1
First Edition

CONTENTS

ACKNOWLEDGMENTS AND DEDICATION

THIS BOOK represents the fulfillment of a dying wish of the author, Rabbi Marc H. Tanenbaum, of most blessed memory. It was made possible by the generous grant from Howard and Edward Milstein and their Foundation, who have through their gift left a precious legacy for all humanity.

As editors, we wish to acknowledge especially two people whose efforts were, in reality and each in their own ways, at least as significant as our own. First, Dr. Georgette Bennett, Rabbi Tanenbaum's widow, whose vision and tenacity not only made this project possible but carried it through to reality. Second, Patrick Hayes, whose fine work in judiciously pruning our original manuscript has made this volume much more "user-friendly" and, therefore, enduring than it might otherwise have been.

Finally, we wish to dedicate this volume to Rabbi Tanenbaum's son, Joshua-Marc, who will go his own, unexpected, and surprising way of life, enriching all whose lives he touches. We wish him well in life's journey. As the old Irish blessing has it, may the road rise to greet him, and may the sun be ever at his back!

FOREWORD:
"AS A MAN AND AS A RABBI . . ."

The Reverend Dr. Joan Brown Campbell, General
Secretary Emerita, National Council of the
Churches of Christ in the U.S.A.

MANY OF US NOW FIND the memory of the mid-twentieth century beginning to fade. Among those images that now blur is the America of the old Protestant cultural hegemony. Although America has always had rich religious diversity, a half century ago it was not as apparent as it is today. Now religious pluralism is an ever-present fact of American life. How we respond to its challenges is still shaped, in part, by the wisdom of Rabbi Marc Tanenbaum, whose insights are collected in this volume.

Just as Marc Tanenbaum stepped forward in the postwar era to instruct and enable Jews and Christians to come to new understandings of each other, so, too, do his words ring from these pages with a clarity and fidelity to timeless, immutable truths. As a man and as a rabbi, Marc was dedicated to justice for all persons, but also to the dignity of all people as a precondition for that justice. In this anthology, one can almost hear again the cadence of his speech—the laughter of his quick wit.

Those who knew Marc Tanenbaum, and they are many, will find in this collection a pleasant reunion with his thoughts on the large and small issues of faith in the nation and the world. Those who never knew him will find here a pastoral approach, thoughtful analysis of interfaith relations, and acute comment on issues that seem to linger with us even at the century's end.

Rabbi Marc Tanenbaum died in 1992. His friends and colleagues Judith Banki and Eugene Fisher have preserved a sampling of his intellectual, ethical and spiritual life in this collection. For Marc's friends of long standing and for those yet to be, I am grateful.

FOREWORD:
A PIONEER AND FRIEND

His Eminence Johannes Cardinal Willebrands,
President Emeritus, Commission for
Religious Relations with the Jews

I

ONE OF THE GREATEST spiritual events of the twentieth century, and not only for Catholics and Christians of the whole world, was the Second Vatican Council (1962–1965). Doubtless it has been of decisive importance for a new relationship between the Catholic Church and the Jews. After centuries of polemics between Christians and Jews, leading sometimes even to persecution of the latter, the church, gathered in an ecumenical council, adopted and proclaimed a declaration that decided to establish "newness of attitudes" of reconciliation and *teshuvah,* of dialogue and cooperation in the *tikkun olam* (the healing of the world) for the Kingdom of God.

We shall never forget righteous Christians like Pope John XXIII and Cardinal Augustin Bea, who led the church to this "change of heart" in obedience to God "according to the abundance of his steadfast love" (Isa. 63:7). Nor shall we forget our brothers and friends like Abraham Heschel and his disciple Marc Tanenbaum, who have given a great contribution to the response to Vatican II on the part of many Jews.

From his studies at the Jewish Theological Seminary, Rabbi Tanenbaum received solid principles on Jewish identity, an essential condition for interreligious dialogue, particularly with Christians. With this preparation he was able to participate, together with other Jews, in the first unofficial relations with Cardinal Bea and his staff. This would lead in December 1970, after the Council, to the establishment of a permanent International Liaison Committee between the Catholic Church and the International Jewish Committee on Interreligious Consultations. From October 1974, at the initiative of Pope Paul VI, these contacts were being fostered on behalf of the Catholic Church by the Commission for Religious Relations with the Jews. In the creation of the dialogue between the two bodies, the wisdom and tenacity of Dr. Gerhart Riegner played a decisive role. From the beginning Rabbi Tanenbaum was among the participants. We worked closely together during a quarter of a century, particularly in the plenary sessions of the International Liaison Committee.

I met Rabbi Marc Tanenbaum for the first time in New York on a Sunday afternoon, March 31, 1963, on the occasion of a meeting of Jewish scholars with Cardinal Bea. Rabbi Marc Tanenbaum was Director of the Department of Interreligious Affairs of the American Jewish Committee and convened the meeting that was chaired by Rabbi Abraham Joshua Heschel.

I shall never forget this meeting, not only the setting and the historical happening, but especially the atmosphere, characterized by Cardinal Bea as "excellent and fraternal." The Jews present were fairly representative of the various existing religious currents within Jewish life. Rabbi Tanenbaum told Father Schmidt, Cardinal Bea's private secretary: "It is a miracle, not that these people met with the cardinal, but that they met with each other." Nevertheless it was the person of Bea and the hope that the Vatican Council would lead the Catholic Church to a new insight and attitude regarding the relations between the church and the Jewish people that brought the Jewish dignitaries together. I felt a sense of awe for the presence of God among us. To me it was clear that we had broken new ground, that a new era had begun in the relations between the church and the Jewish people.

Rabbi Joseph B. Soloveitchik had also been expected at this meeting. He was not able to come because of the serious illness of his wife. I had the privilege and the joy to meet with him privately on the evening of the same day. This convinced me definitively: If the Vatican Council fulfilled its intention concerning the Declaration on the Jews, we would have a dialogue of a spiritual nature with the Jews.

This was surely not for the immediate future. Our secretariat had first of all the responsibility and the task to convince the Fathers of the Council of the necessity—historically and as a matter of principle—to adopt the Declaration on the Jews.

I had the impression that Rabbi Tanenbaum gathered from the New York meeting the same hope and conviction about the future of our relationships. The opposition in the Council, although coming from a minority, was obstinate and persistent. Rabbi Tanenbaum followed the debates in the Council closely and reported every development in press comments, in speeches, and in reports. After the creation of a special secretariat for relations with Non-Christian Religions, many felt relations with the Jews should be transferred to that secretariat. Rabbi Tanenbaum approved the decision of the Holy See that the relations with the Jews should remain with the secretariat directed by Cardinal Bea. He reassured his colleagues in the United States that "the generally positive development between the Vatican and the Jewish people was largely attributable to the great confidence that the Jews have for Cardinal Bea and the members of his Secretariat." To this very positive statement he added a personal note: "I have had the privilege of corroborating with Cardinal Bea and his Secretariat and I have been greatly impressed by the profound theological sensitivity and scholarship that they bring to their understanding of Christian-Jewish relationships." In this context, I should note the positive role of Father Cornelius Rijk, who in that period served our office as the first advisor and staff member responsible for relations with the Jews.

Rabbi Tanenbaum was very much aware of the importance of quick and reliable public information. Often our office was his source of information and sometimes we were irritated by his rapid use of publicity, which he judged useful and even necessary in order to avoid misleading and tendentious information.

During the last phase of the discussions on the final version of *Nostra Aetate*, much of the debate turned around two points: the rejection of the charge against the Jews of "deicide" and the "condemnation" of anti-Semitism. Rabbi Tanenbaum reported the tension, nervousness, confusion as we approached the end [of the Council]. Many spoke of "watering down." The secretariat, responsible for the presentation of the final text, removed the

words "deicide" and "condemnation." This was a free and deliberate decision. We found that the term "deicide" was a theologically questionable expression, not right or worthy of an official
text of the Council and, in accordance with the general intention
of the Council, we wanted to avoid the term "condemn" or "condemnation."

In a letter to Cardinal Bea, Rabbi Tanenbaum expressed his
"profound and heartfelt appreciation for his brilliant leadership"
and for his "heroic patience and unflagging dedication to this
cause." It is my conviction that the close relationship of Rabbi
Tanenbaum with Cardinal Bea, myself, and other members of our
staff found its origin in the meeting in New York on March 31,
1963, with representatives of the Jewish people in the United
States of America.

II

One of the most significant and moving events of my life occurred
on a Saturday evening when I had already made my prayers for
the preparation of the Sunday. The bell rang. I was not expecting
any visit, and was very surprised to see Rabbi Tanenbaum. He had
come right from the celebration of the Sabbath in the synagogue.
In my study he embraced me, opened an embroidered cover from
which he took out his tallith and put it over my head and shoul-
ders. I could not say a word. By this gesture he wished to share
with me and to involve me in his prayer. For a moment I remained
silent and embraced him. Our relationship was not only one of
common study and interest, but it included our relation to God.
We wanted together to stay before God and to invoke His blessing, His grace.

When some voices suggested that the church should rewrite
some passages of the gospels, Rabbi Tanenbaum wrote: "Let it be
said categorically that no informed or responsible Jewish leader
has ever suggested the revision of Scripture which Christians hold
sacred. Jews who have an understanding of Scripture and religious tradition are no more prepared to ask Christians to re-write
their Gospels than Jews could be prepared to accept any suggestion from non-Jews that the Hebrew Scriptures or the Talmud be

rewritten or modified for reason of good will." He asked that responsible instruction should be provided for an "appropriate interpretation of those passages in Christian Scripture which are most easily open to distortion." To meet this need, the Commission for Religious Relations with the Jews, created by Pope Paul VI in 1974, published two documents: *Guidelines and Suggestions for Implementing the Conciliar Declaration* Nostra Aetate (1974) and *Notes on the Correct Way to Present the Jews and Judaism in Preaching and Catechesis in the Roman Catholic Church* (1985).

Until the end of his life, Rabbi Tanenbaum cultivated his relations with us in order to improve and deepen them. In 1986, he called Jews "to develop a theology of Christians and Christianity that is consonant with the realities of an emerging 'new Christian' society that is struggling in unparalleled fashion to uproot anti-Semitism and to resolve her tradition to biblical modes of thought and practice."

When I consider his example of life, I remember what Maimonides said of a person who serves God not because of the promise of reward, "rather such a person does what is true because it is true, and goodness and truth are his only desired compensation." (*Sefer ha-madal* 10,2).

May 18, 1996

BIOGRAPHICAL SKETCH

Judith H. Banki

RABBI MARC H. TANENBAUM made a difference, not only for his lifetime but also for succeeding generations. There are young Christian and Jewish men and women who have grown up free of poisonous religious bigotry, free from fear of the other, respectful of one another's spiritual legacy, involved in collaborative efforts across religious lines on behalf of human and civil rights who do not know how much of the groundwork he laid. There are Africans and Southeast Asians—Vietnamese and Cambodians—alive today because of his activism and mobilization of interreligious resources on behalf of refugees and against world hunger. "If I were to die tomorrow," he told an interviewer in 1980, "I have the sense that I've done something useful with the time I've had here."

His early interests in medicine, law, and commerce could have been put to many uses. But his talents seemed particularly apt for the field in which he gained the most distinction, the field he helped create and then led for more than three decades: the field of interreligious affairs.

The distinction of Marc H. Tanenbaum's achievements and the range of his influence from his self-described beginnings emerge from the commanding presence that moved presidents and popes alike; the resonant voice, eloquent in defense of Jewish dignity and human rights, recognized in every part of the world; the writer and radio personality whose weekly comments reached millions of readers and listeners for more than a quarter of a century, a man designated in a national poll as "one of the ten most influential and respected religious leaders in America," and by *New York* magazine as "one of the foremost Jewish ecumenical leaders in the world today."

He was born in 1925 of Russian parents, both practicing Orthodox Jews, who had emigrated from the Ukraine and who operated
a small grocery store in Baltimore. He grew up in grinding poverty
in the only Jewish home in an ethnic Irish, Italian, and German
neighborhood. He was a middle child, with an older brother and
a younger sister, each separated from him by three years. He attended the Talmudic Academy of Baltimore—he called it the
"Jewish Parochial School"—and City High School. He won a
scholarship to Yeshiva University at the age of fourteen and a half,
started college at fifteen, and graduated at nineteen. The scholarship to Yeshiva was arranged by his mother, in concert with the
principal of his parochial school. Both hoped that he would become a rabbi. His father, on the other hand, was determined that
he become a doctor. "People will always be sick," his father said,
"and doctors will always be necessary."

Genuinely interested in science and biology, he looked into the
prospects of The Johns Hopkins University and its medical school,
only to discover that there was a quota for Jews at this prestigious
institution. He was torn between his parents' ambitions for him.
"They worked out their conflicts over my body," he said later.
He accepted the scholarship to Yeshiva, reserving the option of
medical school, and followed a two-track curriculum: pre-med
and science courses along with the traditional religious studies.
In addition to this rigorous course of study, he was interested in
writing and became editor of the school paper. He was elected
president of his class.

While profoundly committed to Judaism, what he called an increasingly "narrow and repressive" Orthodoxy convinced him
that he could never become an Orthodox rabbi. After graduating
from Yeshiva with a Bachelor of Science degree, he applied for
and was admitted to Essex County Medical School. He went to
medical school for one day. "I was accepted," he recalled. "I
walked into the school. I went into the cadaver room. I looked
around and I said, 'My God, what am I doing here?' . . . I walked
out and never came back."

He was nineteen years old, a college graduate, alone in New
York City. Having rejected the only two options he had considered at school, he turned to writing and editing, and found a job
as assistant to the editor of a weekly newsletter called *Current*

Events. The job was intellectually rewarding, but not otherwise. With a salary of about $35 a week, living in a rented room in a rough neighborhood, with a window facing a brick wall and within earshot of a nightly drunken wife-beater, his life was "dreadful." One day, he ran into a fellow Yeshiva graduate, and learned that several of his classmates were in a similar career bind. They had rejected Orthodoxy but were strongly committed to Judaism. Where to go? This particular classmate was on his way to take the entrance examination for the Jewish Theological Seminary of America, the rabbinic school of Conservative Judaism. On the spur of the moment, he accompanied his friend. Both took the examination; both were admitted. The other party of that chance encounter is the distinguished Rabbi Harold Schulweiss.

The congenial and intellectually free atmosphere of the Jewish Theological Seminary tolerated at the time a remarkable range of views: radical socialists, philosophers, literary types, traditionalists and skeptics. In later years, Rabbi Tanenbaum recalled with pleasure the all-night debates, the intellectual jousting, and the intensity of the arguments. It was an enormously liberating and invigorating culture for him.

In seminary, he found himself drawn to certain subjects: Jewish history, philosophy, and literature. During this period, he became a research assistant for *The Eternal Light,* a popular weekly radio program sponsored by the seminary. Here, and later writing for several Jewish journals, he honed the communication skills that distinguished his career.

One important relationship forged in the seminary that would profoundly influence the shape and direction of interreligious dialogue in the years ahead began as a chance encounter between the young Marc Tanenbaum and Abraham Joshua Heschel. In his senior year at the seminary, Tanenbaum learned one morning that his father had just suffered a heart attack. Overcome with grief, concern, and guilt that his mother and sister were left alone in Baltimore to cope, he encountered Heschel in the elevator. Heschel, recently arrived from Europe, already famous as a scholar and teacher, noted his distress and said, "Something is troubling you. Come into my office." When the young rabbinical student broke down and cried, Heschel immediately called his mother, offering solace and support. Rabbi Tanenbaum never forgot that act of kindness. A genuine friendship and affection developed between the two.

Tanenbaum was ordained in 1950. He knew he wished to serve the Jewish community, but was uncertain as to how: as a congregational rabbi, as a writer, administrator, or organizational staff member. After a stint in the religion department of *Time* magazine, he used the following summer to write fiction. An attempted novel was never completed, and a number of short stories earned only "an extraordinary collection of rejection slips." Then a position in publishing allowed him to arrange for the publication in 1950 of Heschel's first English-language book in the United States, *The Earth is the Lord's: The Inner World of the Jew in Eastern Europe* (New York: H. Schuman, 1950). He also suggested that Reinhold Niebuhr review another book by Rabbi Heschel, whose positive reception helped advance Heschel's reputation in America.

In 1952, he became director of the Synagogue Council of America, the coordinating body of Orthodox, Conservative, and Reform rabbinic and congregational associations in the United States. Officially, the Council claimed to be the voice of religious Judaism, but it was underfunded and weakened by internal disagreements and tensions among its three constituent branches. Rabbi Tanenbaum set out to make it a vital organization, and, despite resistance from many in his own community, began reaching out to the Christian community. He arranged for dialogues between the National Council of Churches and the Synagogue Council. He befriended Bishop Fulton Sheen, the immensely popular television evangelist, and later, Dr. Billy Graham, who recalled "[Marc's] warm smile and always-affectionate greeting from the very beginning of our three decades of friendship." Based on a theological position that Jews were "God's chosen people through whom we had received the writings of Holy Scripture and the Messiah," Dr. Graham and his wife had been quietly helping to bring Jewish people out of Russia and sending them to Israel at a time when Soviet policy was officially opposed to Jewish emigration. Rabbi Tanenbaum found out about this activity and asked to meet with Graham. "Out of that meeting," Graham wrote, "came one of the warmest friendships of my ministry. His years of friendship and counsel to me remain one of the greatest treasures in my memory."

He reached out to the Orthodox community as well. At a dinner honoring Archbishop Iakovos and the memory of Ecumenical Patriarch Athenagoras on October 2, 1986, he called the primate a "beloved friend of many years." "Hellenism and Hebraism, in all their complexities, are the foundation-stones of Western civilization," he continued, "no person, no force can ultimately succeed in severing those profound bonds nor in alienating Greeks from Jews, nor Jews from Greeks." Recalling that twenty years before Archbishop Iakovos sought to enlist Rabbi Tanenbaum's support for a Congressional resolution that would recognize Greek Orthodox Christianity as one of the "Four Major Faiths of America," Rabbi Tanenbaum gave his hearty consent. The resolution was adopted unanimously.

Contacts with Christian leaders broadened into Washington connections, and in 1960, he served as vice president of the White House Conference on Children and Youth, where he invited Rabbi Heschel to deliver a major paper. This move further boosted Heschel's public recognition, and at the same time confirmed Tanenbaum's intuition that Heschel's framing of underlying moral issues and his prophetic language and appearance would strike a responsive chord. The intersection of religion and public policy had a particular appeal for Marc Tanenbaum, and he saw it as a fertile field for interreligious cooperation.

In his judgment, Jews "had an obligation to really move in and be present as a major force in American life. Otherwise, it's always Christian America." He believed that Jews must be seen, not just as three percent of the population, but as one-third of the major religious communities of America. To change the status of Jews, he believed it was necessary for the Jewish religious community to play a more active role in defining national values and priorities.

From a more defensive perspective, he was also concerned about Jewish security: his personal experience of anti-Semitism in the streets of Baltimore; his encounter with social and educational quotas; his conviction that a long-entrenched Christian hostility to Jews and Judaism helped prepare the way for the Holocaust; his discovery that "Judaism was an unknown religion to most Christians," and that much of what was "known" was negative stereotyping; all of this convinced him that an outreach to inform the Christian community about the reality of Jewish history, culture, and religion was worth the gamble.

Two vivid recollections from his childhood also undoubtedly shaped these directions of his mature life. One was a story passed on to him from his parents, about a family member who had been a tragic victim of anti-Semitic violence—an uncle in the Ukraine who had been attacked by a mob on Good Friday, forced into a river, and drowned. The mob, he was told, was led by an Orthodox priest carrying a cross. The other was the memory of his mother preparing Christmas baskets for Christian neighbors even poorer than his own family, because she wanted them to have something with which to celebrate their holy day. As a small boy, he accompanied her on these excursions of charity. At one pole, the haunting family memory of anti-Semitic violence; at the other, the personal encounter of neighborly outreach and goodwill. Both experiences shaped his attitudes and informed his choices for the future.

During his ten years at the Synagogue Council of America, Rabbi Tanenbaum strengthened and increased funding for the organization, but he found the work increasingly frustrating. In 1961, Pope John XXIII called for an Ecumenical Council—the first in nearly a century—to renew the Roman Catholic Church and reach out to other religions. Rabbi Tanenbaum saw the Ecumenical Council as a historic opportunity to mend the church's troubled relationship with the Jewish people. He hoped to relate himself and the Synagogue Council to the forthcoming event, but was forestalled by the SCA's rigid ban on religious dialogue with Christians. The American Jewish Committee (AJC) was one of the few Jewish organizations that took the Ecumenical Council seriously. It had already mounted an active program based on scholarly research into religion textbooks that the Committee had initiated over many years. In 1961 Marc Tanenbaum became its director of Interreligious Affairs in a situation where his inclinations and creative energy found organizational respect and support. He had found his niche!

Rabbi Tanenbaum threw himself into the American Jewish Committee's initiative on behalf of what eventually emerged from the Second Vatican Council as *Nostra Aetate*. He supervised an initiative that included three AJC memoranda sent to Cardinal Augustin Bea: one documenting the negative and hostile portrayal of Jews and Judaism in Catholic textbooks; the second noting anti-Jewish elements in the liturgy; and the last, written by Abraham Joshua Heschel, suggesting concrete steps that the church could take to redress past injustices. When Cardinal Bea visited the United States, Rabbi Tanenbaum arranged for him to meet off-the-record with a group of Jewish religious leaders, including Heschel; the two biblical scholars struck off a personal friendship that withstood the tensions of the months to come. One of the crowning moments of Rabbi Tanenbaum's professional life was that he was present at the fourth and concluding session, at which the Council Fathers voted to adopt *Nostra Aetate* after many delays and—from a Jewish perspective—some watering down of the original text.

He was instrumental in the establishment of the International Jewish Committee for Interreligious Consultations (IJCIC), and was elected its chairman in 1987. IJCIC was formed to represent the Jewish community in dialogues with international Christian church bodies such as the Vatican and the World Council of Churches. He was the first rabbi to address the latter organization, speaking before some 4,000 delegates at the WCC's Sixth Assembly in Vancouver in 1983. He was critically, but always diplomatically, responsive to documents intended to elaborate upon and clarify *Nostra Aetate,* such as the 1974 Vatican *Guidelines* and the 1985 *Notes on the Correct Way to Present the Jews and Judaism in Preaching and Catechesis in the Roman Catholic Church,* and was quick to challenge any anti-Israeli bias in church policies and publications.

In 1983, he moved from Director of Interreligious Affairs to International Affairs Director of the American Jewish Committee. He served as a member of the Human Rights Research Committee of the Foreign Policy Association's Study of Priorities for the 1980s. He testified before the Senate Foreign Relations Committee and the House Foreign Affairs Committee on "Moral Imperatives in the Formation of American Foreign Policy." He also testified before Congressional committees on world refugee and world hunger problems, and played a key role in organizing White House conferences on Foreign Aid and Energy Conservation. He was a trailblazer and activist on behalf of the human rights of immigrants and refugees, and made three trips to Southeast Asia as part of a fact-finding delegation of the International Rescue Committee investigating the plight of Vietnamese boat people. At the Cambodia-Thai border, he joined Nobel laureate Elie Wiesel in the recitation of the Kaddish—the Jewish prayer for the dead—for the millions of Cambodians who died at the hands of the Khmer Rouge.

His counsel was sought by Presidents Jimmy Carter, Ronald Reagan, and George Bush, as well as religious leaders of many faiths. In reflections dated July 26, 1979, he explained how he was called up on a day's notice to the Diplomatic Room in the White House. From there, he boarded a helicopter with other religious leaders, flew across "the strikingly beautiful Catoctin Mountains," and then landed at Camp David.

> We were greeted by President Carter, Rosalyn Carter, and the senior members of the White House staff: Hamilton Jordan, Jody Powell, Gerald Rafshoon, Pat Cadell, Ann Wexler, chief speechwriter Rick Hertzberg, and others. Promptly at 7 p.m., the President invited us to join him, Mrs. Carter, and the staff around the large conference table. Most of us, Christians and Jews, had met with the President before at the White House to discuss and collaborate on other issues of concern facing our nation and the American people. As a result of those shared experiences in seeking to serve our nation and to help save human lives, there prevailed an easy, relaxed, even informal atmosphere which was conducive to frank and probing conversation. The President began the discussion with a brief statement. He spoke to the religious leaders, as he had to others who had preceded us at Camp David, about his concern over the "malaise of America," the restlessness, the anxieties, the uncertainties, the crisis of confidence, the decline of morality, the violence.

Part of his capacity to inform the nation's civil leaders grew from his experience talking to people of other faiths. He was one of the architects of the field now known as interreligious dialogue. A genuine humanitarian, he was concerned for the human plight and religious liberty of all people, but always rose first and foremost in defense of his own people. His universal concerns remained firmly rooted in a very particularist Jewish base. In his almost thirty years at the American Jewish Committee (1961–1990), he forged a career that gave expression to his particular and outstanding skills: rhetorical, analytical, conceptual, and diplomatic. After retiring from the AJC, he served as a consultant.

In the course of a rich professional life, he served on the boards of various institutions, including American Jewish World Service, the International Rescue Committee, the Overseas Development Council, the United Nations Association, the National Peace Academy, the Bayard Rustin Institute, and Covenant House. He was founder and Chairman of the National Interreligious Task Force on Soviet Jewry, which, under the directorship of Ann Gillen, S.H.C.J., vigorously pursued the cause of oppressed Jews and Christians in the Soviet Union. He was awarded fifteen honorary degrees, and was honored by the International Council of Christians and Jews and the New York Board of Rabbis.

However, many people who never met him or read his scholarly papers remember him vividly from his radio broadcasts. Beginning in 1965, he broadcasted a weekly religious commentary on *WINS*-Westinghouse Broadcasting, a news radio station in New York. Brief, pungent, and timely, his commentaries were enormously popular. He also wrote regular guest editorials for the Religious News Service, the Jewish Telegraphic Agency, and the Worldwide News Service. In most of these commentaries, he addressed some newsworthy event, an underlying issue of interreligious significance, or some upcoming Jewish or Christian observance. In many ways they are a gallop through history. These include reflections on Apollo 11 (*WINS* Religion Commentary, July 20, 1969), which he called a scientific adventure: "but our satisfaction over this triumph must be tempered by the sober realization that the times now demand that we devote comparable ingenuity and craftsmanship to the pressing human demands on inner space. We will not be able to justify to our own conscience and before mankind the continued spending of billions for futuristic experiments in outer space when in our midst some 30 million Americans live below the poverty line; while 10 million Americans are chronically malnourished, and hunger, disease, and illiteracy stalk among the millions of human beings who constitute the two-thirds of the human family not in our Western world."

As with his other forms of communication, the responsibility for others was a major theme in these brief reflections. For instance, in a short piece for the *Canadian Jewish News* (May 2, 1991), aptly titled "Jews Must Help Relieve Suffering Wherever It Occurs," Rabbi Tanenbaum confronted those who would not assist in relief efforts for the Shi'ite minority suffering under the Iraqi regime of Saddam Hussein. "We have no moral alternative to aiding in the relief of the hunger, disease, and suffering of these unfortunate people," he said. "*Tikkun olam* (repairing the world) and saving human lives are primary, fundamental Jewish values. If Judaism is taken seriously, it can only be interpreted as conferring an inescapable obligation to reduce human suffering and salvage human beings from destruction."

This biographical sketch of Marc H. Tanenbaum has focused on his professional career, but it should be noted that Rabbi Tanenbaum's first marriage, in 1955 to Helga Weiss, ended in divorce in 1977. Two daughters, Adina and Susan, and a son, Michael, remain from that marriage. A second marriage in 1982 to Dr. Georgette Bennett, an author, broadcast journalist, criminologist, and business consultant, brought joy and warmth once more into his personal life. "My magnificent, beautiful, and brilliant wife," he declared at a ceremony marking his departure from the American Jewish Committee, "has made me possible." Their son, Joshua-Marc Tanenbaum, was born seven weeks after his father's death from heart failure on July 3, 1992, at the age of 66.

Despite his speaking prowess and organizational skills, in his own mind, Marc Tanenbaum remained primarily a writer. When he died in 1992, he left behind an enormous collection of written materials. Most of these were papers and articles prepared for major public presentations or journals. Although he co-edited or contributed chapters and essays to a number of important volumes, he never completed a book entirely of his own. Therefore, these writings constitute an enduring record of his contribution to a field he helped to create and define. Many were prescient, even daring, in their time.

He did not often commit his criticisms of other Jewish positions to print—perhaps because he feared that exposure of internal differences would be exploited by anti-Semites, or perhaps because his early Orthodox upbringing made him chary of offending Orthodox colleagues. As chairman of IJCIC he tried to achieve consensus on policies and positions through the logic of his arguments and the force of his personality. In this he was generally successful, and he retained the respect of his Orthodox colleagues even when they disagreed with him. It was very important to him.

Many Jews and Christians have been nourished by the fruits of Rabbi Marc Tanenbaum's labors. May this collection of his reflections and arguments do justice to his memory.

EDITORS' NOTE

ALTHOUGH THIS COLLECTION of Marc H. Tanenbaum's writings is arranged chronologically, the major issues of Jewish-Christian relations do not divide neatly into decades. Many theological, historical, and pedagogical questions have persisted over the more than thirty years encompassed by these writings. Indeed, some have resisted resolution for over 1,900 years! The chronological approach was chosen as the simplest means of mining this rich lode. We have tried to eliminate, so far as possible, repetition in the selections from Rabbi Tanenbaum's work (some published here for the first time). However, the reader will find that because Tanenbaum addressed different groups over time, he returned more than once to important topics, though often in the context of a different set of larger issues of the day. In the absence of clear footnote annotations, the editors have at times made an educated guess of where in the text the references belong. As in the archaeology of Israel, we are usually close, but sometimes may be off by a line or two. We hope any mistakes will be forgiven. The editors wish also to thank Fr. Gerald Fogarty, S.J., for assistance with historical references and certain pesky Latin phrases.

Some papers have been shortened for purposes of readability or reducing redundancy. However, the editors have intruded as little as possible into the texts themselves. They assume they need not explain, for example, why the author would have used the term "Negro" in the 1960s and "Black" in the 1980s, or why he used the terms "man" and "mankind" when today's sensitivity to women's concerns would indicate "humanity" and "humankind." We know he would have been among the first to pick up on these evolutions of our language, just as he was among the first to replace "B.C." with "B.C.E." and "Old Testament" with "Hebrew Scriptures." Similarly, the editors have let his statistics stand—with the occasional introduction of an editor's note for clarification—as an indication of the substantive background against which Rabbi Tanenbaum forged his arguments at the time.

We do not claim to be disinterested parties. Both of us were professional colleagues of Rabbi Marc H. Tanenbaum who worked with him over many years, and we both considered him a friend. We have found the task of narrowing the vast collection of his writings to manageable size daunting, but necessary. We are honored to bring his voice to life again in this anthology.

Judith H. Banki
Eugene J. Fisher
Shavuoth/Pentecost 2002

1

The 1960s: The Interreligious Agenda and Selected Texts

In the decade of the 1960s a number of events impacted the Jewish community, such as the election of the first Roman Catholic President of the United States (Jewish voters gave John F. Kennedy a higher percentage of their votes than did Roman Catholic voters); the civil rights movement; and the capture and trial in Jerusalem of the Nazi war criminal, Adolf Eichmann. However, two dramatic pieces of history stand out as of intense concern to Jews, with special consequences for Jewish-Christian relations: the adoption of *Nostra Aetate* at the Second Vatican Council—and the intense and sometimes ugly struggle around that document—and the Arab-Israeli "Six Day War" of June 1967.

While some Jewish spokesmen opposed any Jewish advocacy or involvement in Vatican Council II as unseemly or undignified, Marc Tanenbaum believed that the Council convened by Pope John XXIII offered an extraordinary opportunity for the Roman Catholic Church to repudiate, at the highest level of authority, the "Christ-killer" (deicide) charge and other poisonous roots of anti-Semitism against the Jewish people. The World Council of Churches had already done so. It had condemned anti-Semitism as a "sin against man and God" in 1948, and again in 1961. Rabbi Tanenbaum had to coax two constituencies: Jews themselves and Christians engaged in a new rapprochement.

If the post-Vatican Council II warmth nurtured a host of Jewish-Christian dialogues and celebrations, the 1967 Arab-Israeli war threatened to end them all. In the wake of what was perceived in the Jewish community as a widespread failure of the organized churches to respond to what Jews feared might well be another Holocaust, there were many calls for an end to Jewish-Christian dialogue. The disappointment was very deep. Again, in a balancing act of *inter*- and *intra*-religious skills, Rabbi Tanenbaum criticized the instances of anti-Israeli bias he found embedded in the institutional churches, but also reminded American Jewish leadership that it had not sufficiently communicated to Christians the importance and centrality of Israel; that, in fact, Jews had perhaps not realized that importance themselves until the prospect of a combined Arab attack seemed imminent. He argued that the attitudes of the majority of Christians toward Israel were more sympathetic and supportive than the Jewish community acknowledged, and that Jews should not jeopardize hard-won gains by hasty and faulty accusations. Finally, he stressed that the survival and security of Israel would be issues central to Jewish-Christian relations from that point on.

Rabbi Tanenbaum cultivated interreligious activities by engaging his dialogue partners seriously and with a deft diplomatic touch. These years put him in contact with the highest echelons of the Roman Catholic Church and placed him in a mediating role for the Jewish community. He insisted on giving credit where credit was due, whether in praising Pope John XXIII's encyclical *Mater et Magistra* or the World Council of Churches' statement denouncing anti-Semitism as "a sin against God and man" (terminology the Catholic Church would only officially adopt under Pope John Paul II more than two decades later). He encouraged a Catholic television series on NBC aimed at combating anti-Semitism, supported efforts in the Catholic press and by the National Catholic Interracial Council to do the same, and finally, utilized the self-studies of Catholic, Protestant, and Jewish religion texts initiated by the American Jewish Committee beginning in the late 1950s. These now-classic studies by Bernhard Olson of Yale University and Rose Thering, O.P., of St. Louis University were judiciously transmitted to the Holy See at the request of Cardinal Bea, and served as a crucial empirical base for the Second Vatican Council's declaration, *Nostra Aetate* (In Our Age), redefining the church's theological relationship with the Jewish people. Rabbi Tanenbaum's fingerprints are on each of these endeavors.

In addition, he developed criteria for judging American textbooks as anti-Semitic using the self-studies. First, there was the notion that over the centuries had served as a rationale for so much persecution and even massacres of Jews in "Christian" Europe: the "deicide" charge. This was a notion that could be read back into the New Testament by putting together fragments from one gospel with those of others, if one so wished. This created a charge of collective guilt, theological transmission of that guilt was taught in Christian religion classes for centuries, with tragic consequences for Jews. In support of his criterion, Rabbi Tanenbaum cited the Roman Catechism of the Council of Trent, which rightly and clearly stated the Catholic doctrine that the sins of humanity, and especially of Christians, bear the theological responsibility for the death of Jesus. Interestingly, this passage was cited again by the

1985 Vatican *Notes on the Correct Way to Present the Jews and Judaism in Preaching and Catechesis in the Roman Catholic Church* and again by the recent universal *Catechism of the Catholic Church* (1994, the first such universal catechism issued since the Council of Trent) as a culmination of its lengthy section devoted to arguments showing that "the Jews are not collectively responsible for Christ's death."

Secondly, Rabbi Tanenbaum looked at language used in the textbooks to describe Jews and Jewish realities. It is always both effective and helpful for Christians to begin to hear in a fresh way what they have been saying by rote. The result was to check the pernicious effects of scapegoating Jews. Rabbi Tanenbaum noted that the dynamic of de-Judaizing the Jews of the Bible carried into lessons on the "Old Testament" as well, omitting any reference to the Jewishness not just of Mary and Joseph, but also of Abraham and the prophets. "Israelites" was used when the context was negative, for example in the scene in which the Israelites worship the golden calf. Rabbi Tanenbaum also zeroed in on the extremely negative stereotyping of "the Pharisees," to whom are ascribed all sorts of beliefs they never actually held. Today, the 1976 and 1992 textbook analyses show that, as Rabbi Tanenbaum put it, Catholic teaching materials are virtually free of any of the "blatant" polemical dynamics and stereotyping of Jews and Judaism which the St. Louis study uncovered three decades ago.

While the textbook studies offer crucial data in the continuing reflection on Christian and Jewish identity, their later analysis must be seen in light of the event of the Second Vatican Council. Moreover, the theme of Jewish-Christian relations as a confrontation with the past came about because of Rabbi Tanenbaum's involvement with the Council. Only by looking soberly at history could the future look brighter. On October 28, 1965, 2221 bishops joined Pope Paul VI in signing the declaration *Nostra Aetate*, fifteen sentences of which were devoted to overturning centuries of negative Christian teaching about Jews and Judaism. In an address at the North American College in Rome in September of that year, Rabbi Tanenbaum anticipated the declaration as "the turning of a cycle of history." He then added a further caution: "While it is recognized that anti-Semitism arises out of multiple phenomena—political, social, economic—Christians cannot allow Christianity to be exploited by anti-Semites and bigots to advance this teaching, which is anathema to the church."

Rabbi Tanenbaum also helped mediate these positions to his Jewish constituents. *Nostra Aetate* was received by three main groups: the impatient, who noted the lack of any statement of repentance, arguing that the Council had asked forgiveness from Protestants, Eastern Orthodox, and Muslims but not from the Jews; the indifferent, who argued that "it was too little too late," and asked where was the church during the Holocaust when it would have mattered; and the disappointed, who felt that the final version was a watered-down compromise from what they felt to be a stronger 1964 draft. All of these Jewish responses were placed on the dialogue table and had a real impact on the formulation of subsequent documents issued by the Holy See in 1974 and 1985, so that many of the "holes" the critics of the document saw in 1965 have been filled in, theologically, in the intervening 30 years.

While sympathetic to and even sharing some of these less than enthusiastic Jewish responses, Rabbi Tanenbaum was able to look at the whole picture of how the document was likely to influence the attitudes, over time, of the then 600 million Roman Catholics in the world (today there are over a billion). On this level, he saw clear commitment to make the conciliar dream a reality. The American bishops had already established a subcommittee and secretariat to work on the matter full time. Surveying what was already taking place, Rabbi Tanenbaum concluded, "I am deeply persuaded that a vast and irreversible tide of self-purification and self-correction with regard to the portrayal of Jews and Judaism in the teaching process of the Catholic Church . . . is under way."

Finally, noting the continuing "ignorance" of most Christians, even educated Christians, about elementary facts concerning Judaism from the first century to the present, Rabbi Tanenbaum isolated "three decisive areas of scholarship" that needed urgent attention. These included critical biblical commentaries "to remove any possibility for bigots to exploit certain expressions in the Gospels for anti-Semitic purposes"; historical studies to return to Christian memory what Father Edward A. Flannery called the "pages torn out" of Christian history books, for example, on the Crusades and the Inquisition, ritual murder libels, and conspiracy theorizing; and further theological studies on the implications of

taking seriously Paul's assertion that God's "gifts and call are irrevocable." Pope John Paul II fueled the latter when he advanced the
idea in an address in Mainz, Germany, in 1980: God's covenant
with the Jewish people is a "covenant never revoked by God." The
texts that follow have helped to ground these sentiments.

Judith H. Banki and Eugene J. Fisher

1

Paths to *Agape*

AGAPE IS THE GREEK WORD for love. As used by the Christians of
the early church, it was the name given to the "fraternal love
feast" which normally accompanied the religious service of the
Eucharist (thanksgiving over the bread and wine). While possibly
based on the *chaburah*, a type of solemn fraternal banquet held
among Jewish religious societies in ancient Palestine, the *agape*
became for early Christians a formalized act of personal goodwill and assumed a semi-liturgical character. Only those who were
members of the church shared in the love feast which—according
to Church Father Tertullian (ca. 165–245 C.E.)—included, in addition to a modest meal, a general discussion, the reading of Biblical passages, the singing of Psalms, or "unfettered speech."

On January 14, 1962, an *agape* was held in Rome, virtually under
the eaves of the Vatican. Arranged by the Pro Deo University for
Social and International Studies, this *agape* was a significant demonstration, both symbolically and substantively, of the new openness and outreach that increasingly characterizes the present-day
relationships among religious leaders. For the first time in history,
representatives of fifteen non-Roman Catholic religious groups
took part in a Roman Catholic-sponsored "fraternal *agape*." Present were Anabaptists, Anglicans, Baptists, Buddhists, Calvinists,
Confucians, Coptic Orthodox, Hindus, Jews, Lutherans, Methodists, Muslims, Presbyterians, Russian Orthodox, and Waldensians.

The assembly commenced with celebration of a Mass, which
the non-Catholic representatives attended as observers. There followed a dinner that began with a non-sectarian prayer asking for
Divine help "so that each one of us, overcoming and repudiating
our differences and the adversities which poison human relations,

Reprinted from the *AJC Reporter,* November 1962. Rabbi Tanenbaum here describes a scene that presaged by a quarter of a century the global interreligious
gathering called together by Pope John Paul II in 1986 in Assisi.

will spread all around us the seeds of goodness and become messengers of love and life."

One of the highest-placed churchmen in the Vatican, Augustin Cardinal Bea, delivered the keynote address. Cardinal Bea is President of the Secretariat for Christian Unity, one of the fifteen commissions designated by Pope John XXIII in preparation for the forthcoming Ecumenical Council and the secretariat that is concerned with Catholic-Jewish relations. Before this pluralistic group, Cardinal Bea declared that "there is a basic unity among all believers" and that "all men have the same dignity and value before God." He said that "the great challenge to our generation is the problem of group antagonism" and that "it is the primordial duty of all groups of mankind to unite for the purpose of overcoming hatreds of the past."

Among those who were invited to comment on the Cardinal's address were Dr. Elio Toaff, Chief Rabbi of Rome, and Zachariah Shuster, director of the American Jewish Committee's European office. Both Dr. Toaff and Mr. Shuster asserted that Jews have a particular stake in this manifestation of solidarity, for they were the greatest victims of prejudices and antagonisms through the ages, and particularly during the recent Holocaust. Dr. Toaff and Mr. Shuster supported Cardinal Bea's appeal, as did other non-Catholics, to form a common front to overcome racial and religious hostilities and to promote greater understanding and mutual acceptance.

Archbishop Ettore Cunial, Deputy General to the Vicar of Rome, concluded the meeting, saying, "a similar *agape* forty years ago would have been inconceivable. This would mark the beginning of increased interreligious collaboration."

To observers of the interreligious scene on both global and national levels, this steady march during the last half century toward progressively increased cooperation and solidarity among the major religious communities has been little short of astounding. Conditioned to a reading of interreligious history that has been dominated from its earliest days by power rivalries, heresy hunting, and mutual oppressions, some continue to regard all the ecumenical talk and activity with skepticism. To these skeptics, the new extension of the *agape* spirit to all believers is mainly a defensive response to a vast complex of threatening forces: the massive threat of Communism, the competitive missionary enterprises of renascent Oriental religions, the rejection of Christianity as an outpost of Western imperialism on the part of the newly emerging nations of Asia and Africa, and the corrosive influences of materialism and secularism on church adherents.

Indeed, it is evident that these global geo-political and social forces constitute some of the factors that have brought religious leaders to a radical self-examination. However, close association with Catholic and Protestant leaders as well as a careful scrutiny of their literature are persuasive beyond argument that the churches are experiencing an ecumenical revolution that is profoundly spiritual, and is reflected in biblical, liturgical, and theological reformations. These internal religious reforms are providing a radically new basis for dialogues between Catholics, Protestants, and Jews.

Christian leaders are seeking to overcome the formalisms and archaisms that have accumulated over the centuries in order to relate the teaching and institutions of the church to the realities of the nuclear age and the pluralistic world. They have begun to examine deeply the history of the early church in Palestine and in the Dispersion. What were the sources of the apostolic strength of the first four centuries of the "original" church that enabled it to convert an empire and to subdue a paganism as powerful in its own day as Communism is in ours? That search into history has inevitably brought present-day Christian scholars and thinkers into an unprecedented confrontation with such questions as the relations of Jesus to the Jewish people, the early church to the synagogue, the church fathers to the synagogue fathers, and the Jewish understanding of the Bible and the Prophetic tradition.

The growing consciousness of indebtedness to the Jews as "elders in the faith," joined with a recognition of responsibility for the prevalence of anti-Semitism in the Christian cultures of the Western world, have resulted in a unique receptivity to the Jewish people, and a desire to eliminate anti-Semitism in Christian teaching and behavior.

Conscious that this is a special moment filled with opportunity to advance intergroup understanding, the American Jewish Committee has been an active partner in seeking to advance this new spirit of interreligious *agape*. In many instances, the Committee has responded to approaches made to us by the highest authorities in the Catholic and Protestant worlds. In other instances, we have taken the initiative where we felt the need to present a particular AJC human-relations concern.

Thus wind the paths to *agape*. . . .

2

What Is a Jew?

It is an act of *chutzpah,* audacity, on my part even to suggest that I can within the compass of thirty minutes or so answer the question: What is a Jew? How can one deal seriously in one half of one hour with four thousand years of history spread across all the continents of the world, ranging the full spectrum of human experience from tragedy to triumph, through heroism and destruction, from Mount Sinai through Babylonia, Bergen-Belsen, Brooklyn, and Beersheba reborn, all of which have forged the complex destiny, the mysterious and yet marvelous survival of the Jew in the salvation history of mankind. To seek to reduce that to "a talk" really borders on blasphemy. And yet, as the rabbi said to the parishioner who came to him saying that he felt that he was not adequate to pray, had great fear of it, "My son, have fear and pray."

So with fear and trepidation, I embark prayerfully on a suggestive statement regarding, "What is a Jew?" I should like to approach this in something of the biblical and Prophetic tradition, which is to say, that this is to be a non-speculative statement. I seek to address myself to the perceptions that many of you may have about the Jew in your concrete human situations and to see whether I can help to clarify your understanding of the Jew on this reality level, perhaps raise some questions and, hopefully, even try to answer some.

Anyone who travels in interreligious circles can give you, on quite short notice, a checklist of Catholic perceptions or misperceptions about Jews, Judaism, Jewish history, the Jewish people.

This text emerged from *Encounter: Catholic-Jewish Confrontation,* the proceedings of a conference at Rockhurst College, Kansas City, Missouri, January 29, 1963. In addition to Rockhurst College, the Jewish Community Relations Bureau and the Ratisbonne Center were co-sponsors. It was reprinted in an important collection of essays—one of the first such efforts after the Second Vatican Council—edited by Katherine T. Hargrove, *The Star and the Cross: Essays on Jewish-Christian Relations* (Milwaukee, WI: Bruce, 1966), p. 12–23.

And I am sure, as Robert Hoyt has already made impressively clear, that on the other side of the coin one can point to similarly Jewish misperceptions of Catholics. But instead of improvising such a list, instead of giving you my impression of what I think these perceptions are, let me rely on something more substantial in terms of what is a Catholic understanding of the Jew.

Recently, a prominent Catholic educator traveled around the country addressing students in Catholic colleges and universities about the problem that we are discussing here today. And as a result of her discussions with Catholic students, she came away with a list of the questions that Catholics asked her most frequently about Jews and Judaism. The following is a verbatim report of the questions asked of this lecturer by Catholic students. I leave it to the judgment of our Catholic friends in this audience as to whether these views are peculiar to students or whether they are more broadly representative of Catholic opinion about the Jewish people and their tradition. My impression is that the latter is probably the case.

These questions fall into four categories, and these provide the framework for my discussion of "What is a Jew?" The first category deals with the problem of "The Jews in the Business World." These are some of the questions that were asked:

> "Don't you think that in this country we are antagonistic to Jews because they are too successful in business?"
> "Why are all Jews rich?"
> "Why are the Jews better than anyone else in business?"
> "I have heard it said that Hitler had to do what he did because the Jews held all the money in Germany."
> "Why did the Jews in the Middle Ages have money to lend people . . . ? You said that it was the only profession that they were allowed to exercise, but where did they get the money in the first place?"

Category number two, roughly entitled, "Jews Are Secular," and these are the questions:

> "Why do Jews who do not go to the synagogue, even atheists, insist that they are still Jews? A fallen-out Catholic does not still consider himself a Catholic; why does an irreligious Jew still consider himself a Jew?"

Third category, which Philip Scharper dealt with so extraordinarily this afternoon, "The Role of the Jews in the Crucifixion":

"If the Jewish people did not kill Christ, who did?"

"You said that the high priest and the elders and not the Jewish people had a share of responsibility in Jesus's condemnation. That is not true. The gospel says that the people clamored for his death."

"I am a Catholic and I know what I have been taught when I went to catechism, and that is that the Jews killed Christ. This is what my church teaches. I don't like it. I have several friends who are Jewish, but what can I do? I have to believe my church."

"My church teaches that the Jews are no longer the chosen people since they killed Christ. I don't hold it against my Jewish friends; that would be silly. Yet I cannot help remembering that they are not chosen anymore and I guess it does make a difference. What can I do?"

Fourth category, "New Approach to Jewish-Christian Relations:"

"You said that we Christians have a deep conscious or a subconscious contempt of the Jews, but the Jews have a deep contempt for us, too, believe me; so that's 50–50. Don't you think that the Jews should also meet us part of the way in this new approach?" "I do understand that we cannot hold present-day Jewish people responsible for Jesus's death; I don't think I ever did. Yet, my Jewish friends do not become Christians. Why?"

There were several other categories of questions, such as religious freedom in the State of Israel, the Dead Sea scrolls, the threat of Communism to Christianity and its impact on the Christian response to the new world situation. But these questions would carry us far afield. I have selected these four categories out of six or seven as the basis for my remarks.

Now it should be evident at the outset that these questions are formulated in sometimes rather naïve or gross terms, but that is a matter of language and should not detract from the substance of the questions raised. It is also necessary to keep in mind that there were other questions asked that reflected a more positive understanding of and orientation toward the Jew. But these questions that I have just read to you must be taken for what they are, namely, an indication of the mode of perception of the Jew by many Catholics, and to this fact I seek to address myself this afternoon.

Let us seek first to dispose of, at least to try to understand, this popular and negative perception of the Jew as a business man, the Jew as a merchant, because it is one of the most persistent myths and one which Christians, and Catholics in particular, encounter most frequently. Catholics encounter it most frequently because the sociology today of Catholic-Jewish relationships brings Catholics and Jews into greater contact in the major urban centers of America more than any time in the past. Now this myth has deep and ancient roots. A spirit of charity, it would seem to me, requires a genuine effort to try to understand the sources of this sinister view of the Jew as the economic conspirator, a view that is not far removed from the Kremlin's caricature of American capitalists as a collective breed of "Wall Street robber barons."

In seeking to achieve such understanding, hopefully we will gain some insight into the larger process of myth-making and stereotype, confusing truth with half-truths, leaping from the particular to "generalysis," all of which are the surest barriers to mutual trust and to love of neighbor as one's self.

The Jews in Western Europe, going back to the fourth century, were not business people. The Jews were predominantly a farm community, and on the continent, and in particular in Rome, Sicily, in France and Germany, they earned their livelihood as farmers, artisans, and as petty tradesmen. But through the pressures of history, as is known to many of you, Jews were perforce driven from the farms and were compelled to become merchants. The entire farm economy of the Roman Empire was based on slave holding. By virtue of the social arrangement that prevailed at that time, the slave generally adopted the religious practices of his master, and so many slaves owned by Jews became Jews. Adolf Harnack, the eminent historian, adduced evidence that by the fourth century, there were at least two million Roman converts to Judaism, many of them slaves in the household of Jewish masters. When Constantine established Christianity as the official religion of the Roman Empire, Jews were forbidden on the penalty of death to convert pagans, heathens, non-Jews, to Judaism. Thus the basis of the slave economy, and, therefore, of the farm economy, was destroyed for the Jew, and he had to find other ways of subsisting.

During the period of the Muslim-Christian conflict in the seventh and eighth centuries, trade was mainly in the hands of Syrian Christians, and the Muslims, on rising to power, prevented the Syrian Christians from having commerce with their brothers in the Levant. The Jews were then encouraged both by the Christians and the Muslims to become the tradesmen of that world, bridging East and West. Very often, the Jews were indentured as the merchants of princes and popes. Consequently, the only profession open to Jews were those of banker or usurer. In a number of instances, the Church turned to the Jews for funds with which to build the magnificent churches and cathedrals that are the glory of Europe.

Consequently, this history of the Jew as merchant goes back to the earliest days. It is a complex story and cannot, in respect to truth, be explained simplistically as the sinister plot of the Jew to infiltrate the financial power centers of the Christian West. Rather the force of events of history, in most cases not of his own making, cast the Jew into a mercantile role, and throughout the entire period of the Middle Ages, he was given no other option that would enable him to survive. Parenthetically, it may well have been an act of Providence that the Jew's properties were in liquid assets because the expulsions and the persecutions that overtook him demanded that he be able to move swiftly, taking his possessions with him overnight, across foreign borders. It is no accident today that on 47th Street in New York City, the Jews who have come recently from Eastern Europe, from the ghettos of Poland and Russia still wearing beards and side curls, dressed in caftans and gabardines, trade in jewelry and diamonds. A pocketful of pearls or precious stones can be the ransom price for buying one's safety and the security of one's family from border guards. Even in the freedom of America, many of these immigrants act on Old World memories.

The fact that America has beckoned to Europeans precisely because it was the pre-eminent mercantile society doubly served to enhance its appeal for Jewish immigrants who were uniquely prepared by their histories for the great American dream of success and security through commerce and industry. A marriage of the

Jew's past and the pressing needs and opportunities presented by a dynamically expanding America encouraged the Jew to concentrate his energies and creativity in the world of business, trades, and professions. The ancient and inherited Jewish reverence toward Torah as learning, the pursuit of intellectual perfection, provided the internal motivation and the mental orientation that enabled the Jew to respond successfully to the challenges of an industrialized technological society that has placed a premium on the kinds of educational and allied skills that Jews have come by over the centuries. Thus, it is factual to state, as did the college students, that Jews have been successful in business, but the reasons one holds in making such an observation spell the difference between empathy and bigotry.

I was privileged to serve as Program Chairman of the National Conference on Religion and Race, held in Chicago in 1963. One revelation for me that came out of that meeting, far and beyond others, was the failure of the white man—the white Christian, the white Jew—to understand and to feel genuinely the depth of the predicament of the Negro. James Baldwin gave us but a foretaste of what became disturbingly evident at this historic conference, namely, the widespread Negro resentment toward the white man because of the failure of the white man to come to grips with the truth that the Negro is the creature of the white society and he is blamed and abused for being the product that that society has made him. I felt something of a mystical communion taking place over and again between Negro and Jew throughout the conference. Undoubtedly, there was a profound sharing of feeling of common plight; the Negro and Jew alike have suffered from a dominant society which proclaims self-righteous principles of spiritual and democratic equality, but which persists in a relative insensitivity and hard-heartedness to the pain and insult to the human dignity of these minority peoples. The Negro, like the Jew, understands in very personal terms the comment of Heinrich Heine, "My friends, first you cripple the Jew and then you blame him for limping."

What bothers the Jew when he finds his Catholic neighbor espousing such unsympathetic stereotypes is that his understanding of Catholic beginnings in this country leads him to expect the very opposite. The similar immigrant and ghetto phases of their respective American pasts, the discriminations and hurts their communities suffered should have led, at least theoretically, to greater mutual empathy. And certainly the Catholic teaching of charity would lead non-Catholics to a certain expectation in attitude and behavior on the part of those who belong to the faithful. But perhaps what the Jew has not understood is that it is precisely the distinctive character of the Catholic immigrant experience that had predisposed many Catholics to be negative if not hostile to the Jew. The heaviest Catholic immigration to this country came after the Irish potato famines. The immigrants came here penniless, ravaged. The Jewish immigrants, who also fled from dire circumstance, nevertheless brought abilities as shopkeepers, petty tradesmen, and business competence. The encounter between Catholic and Jewish immigrant, therefore, in the early days of this century began in numerous instances as a merchant-customer relationship, a form of relationship that under the best of conditions is attended by resentments, claims and counterclaims, and bruised feelings.

As the American Catholic and Jew today leave behind their immigrant pasts and enter simultaneously into the urban middle-class societies and cultures in which they share increasingly the same values and aspirations, the same levels of education and opportunities for status employment, it is to be devoutly hoped that the stereotypes of the past, which crudely served to compensate for depressed and unequal life situations, will collapse in the face of new social realities which will bring Catholic and Jew together increasingly as human beings and not as abstractions or gargoyled myths.

Even as we confront and try to explode "the social myths" about each other, we will need to be on guard to see through some of the "ideological myths" which time and unreflective habit have allowed to be conjured up to our mutual disadvantage. Perhaps the most vexing "ideological myth" that many Catholics continue to hold about the Jew is that reflected in the students' second category of questions, namely, "The Jew as secularist."

The most complex challenge that the Jew has been faced with since the Emancipation is that of his own self-definition. Is the Jew to be defined solely in terms of religion? Are the Jews a people? Are they a race? A nation? It is no great wonder that Catholic students asked perplexed questions about Jews who do not attend the synagogue and yet insist on identifying themselves with the Jewish people. By all conventional categories, the Jew is an anomaly. It has taken a French Catholic priest, Father Paul Demann, to penetrate into the deeper meaning of Jewish identity. Writing in his most perceptive book, *Judaism* (New York: Hawthorne Books, 1961), Father Demann has avoided the easy way of tagging a label on the Jew, but has sought to understand his human complexity and reality:

"What does it mean to be a Jew?" writes Father Demann.

> Perhaps the least inadequate answer would be something like this: To be a Jew is to belong to a community, a special destiny, which is defined only by history, and this unique history and destiny, with a concrete human condition which flows from them, are closely bound up with the bible history, the history of salvation in the eyes of the believer. With some this belonging will be expressed by loyalty to the tradition of Judaism and the conscious acceptance of a destiny founded on divine election. In others it will take the form of an attachment, whether willing and accepted or almost instinctive, and of the feeling of solidarity founded on a common descent, tradition, education, and condition. Clearly, then, there are several ways of being a Jew. But this does not prevent the Jews from forming an entity whose cohesion, permanence, and personality stand out with extraordinary vigor.

May I respectfully comment that I think it is inherent in the Christian situation that the Jew will never be entirely understood to the satisfaction of Christians. The neo-Platonic and Scholastic categories which are the basis of Catholic thought preclude any precise definition of the Jew in his existential reality. These categories perceive all reality, all of nature, as falling within the duality of the sacred and the secular. To these dualities are attached values, the sacred being associated with the divine and holy, and therefore superior, and secular being associated with an inferior and "unredeemed" order of nature. Therefore, when the term "secular" is used in the Christian tradition, and in particular in the sense of medieval scholasticism, it must perforce bring to mind a negative association.

Christian humanists such as Erasmus and Thomas More sought to close the gap between the secular and the sacred in their conception of the *Res Christiana* penetrating the *Res Publica*—a conception closer in many ways to the Hebrew view of the Biblical categories of reality than to Thomas Aquinas. But up to this day at least, Thomism and the secular-sacred dualism remain as orthodoxy in Catholic thought, and the Christian humanists are referred to still somewhat critically as *Erasmismo.*

We need to face the fact that the conception of the secular, and all that it implies, is a tradition that is uniquely Western. The *métaphysique* of sacred and secular does not exist in the Orient; this dichotomy is unknown to the Muslim, the Buddhist, the Hindu traditions. And the Jew is more the theological child of the East than of the West. The Jewish community emerged out of the Mediterranean world, out of near-Eastern traditions. And the dichotomy of sacred and secular in the scholastic sense is essentially alien to the Jewish experience and thought, and therefore the Jew resists and resents having to define himself in terms which are inherently not Jewish, especially when those terms are employed for polemical purposes of intimidation or coercion.

The Jewish religious experience reflects the Semitic background that viewed religion as the praxis of a particular people; religion was the way of life, the *paidea* of a destined community. The Jew, by virtue of being born into this community, is committed both as a member of its polity as well as of its religious tradition, and the degree of his religious observance or lack of observance does not remove him from his natural society, the most ancient form of human association. (I suggest you read W. Robertson Smith's classic study, *The Religion of the Semites* [New York: Meridian Books, 1956], to perceive the distinctiveness of Semitic religions.) The Rabbinic sages of the Talmud gave a religious interpretation of this ethnic factor in Judaism indirectly in their injunction, "An Israelite even though he has sinned remains an Israelite. Until the day of his death he is able to repent."

The foregoing hardly begins to do justice to the complex question of secularism, both in its general meaning and in its Jewish significance. (A fuller discussion, for example, would have to confront the issue of why there is virtually no anticlericalism in Judaism, while Catholicism, with its traditional opposition to secularism, has been beset by anticlerical movements, very often the most powerful expressions of secularist movements in history.) What I have been trying to suggest is the need for a psychological Mercator's globe of adjustment in our perceptions of each other. Our Western *hubris* (intellectual pride) combined with our American swagger and superiority hinder us from accepting people as they are, in their own terms; prevent us from respecting them in their full integrity and uniqueness. There is some tragic truth in "The Ugly American" insensitivity to the preciousness of other human beings, cultures, and ways of living; but for religious people to wear such "ugly" spectacles is to fall into a heresy that blasphemes the very image of God.

Profoundly related to the problem of Catholic perception of the Jew sociologically ("the merchant") and ideologically ("the secularist") is the theological ground on which the Christian first confronts the Jew. The third category of questions asked by the students regarding "The Role of the Jew in the crucifixion is in fact the most important influence in the shaping of the Christian's attitude toward the Jew." Philip Sharper has already stated with characteristic perception and scholarship how the misinterpretation of the role of the Jew in the Passion, contrary to the authoritative teaching of the church in the Council of Trent catechism which he described, has contributed to the historic use of the Jew as a scapegoat for one's own sins, "the mask" which hides one from one's self.

More than one study has revealed that the predisposition on the part of many Christians to think the worst of the Jew is related to that distorted teaching of the dramaturgy of the Crucifixion in which the Jew is portrayed as the villain, banished and rejected forever, and deserving of his persecution. A study of Protestant religious textbooks, recently published as *Faith and Prejudice* by Bernhard E. Olson (New Haven: Yale University Press, 1963), and the Catholic textbook study conducted at St. Louis University, with which I have been privileged to be associated through my work with the American Jewish Committee, support this thesis.

At the same time, the studies indicate that Protestant and Catholic teachings contain resources, "anti-ethnocentric antidotes" that allow the noblest teachings of charity, truth, and justice to be set forth in a way that is not contradicted by misrepresentations and inadequate formulations about Jews—as well as about Protestants, Negroes, and others that are more reflective of history than of theology. The recognition on the part of His Holiness Pope John XXIII and Cardinal Bea of the primary need to separate the essential teaching from the nonessential—those accidental accretions of changing cultural, political, and social conditions of the past—represents one of the most heartening developments in relations between the faith communities since the earliest centuries of this era. Pope John's removal from the Good Friday liturgy of "the perfidious Jew" reference and Cardinal Bea's condemnation of the charge that Jews are responsible for "deicide" are historic contributions to the improvement of relations between Christians and Jews.

I come now to the fourth category of questions, "The New Approach in Christian-Jewish Relations." Despite the impressive growth in ecumenical understanding, suspicion continues to hover on both sides. Not all Catholics are aware of the great strides that have been made, especially in recent years, toward improving radically the basis of understanding between Catholics and Jews; and among those who are aware, there are some who are not necessarily happy about it. Somehow to view the Jew and Judaism sympathetically calls into question cherished childhood antipathies which have been hallowed by time into dogmas. There are also many Jews who are totally ignorant of the Christian outreach to the Jew as a genuine expression of Christian love and charity. And among those who have heard of the "new approach" there are some who are suspicious of its genuineness and of its motive. Are Christians changing their tactics, substituting "honey for vinegar" in order that Jews lower their defenses and become easier candidates for conversion, or are they prepared to love Jews as they are, as loyal sons of the Covenant between God and Israel?

These resistances reveal the degree to which we are victims of the polemical readings and conditionings of our histories. If the world is not to give up altogether on the now-tired yearning that the forces of religion translate into reality their professions of respect for human dignity based on love of God, that they become in fact agents of reconciliation and harmony in the social order as contrasted with their past histories so outrageously pockmarked with religious wars, heresy hunts, and bloody persecutions, then upon us, each of us, rests the hearty but inescapable obligation to become pedagogues of the new *kerygma* of Christian-

Jewish fraternity. Pedagogues in the specific as well as in the general meaning. We need to examine with meticulous care what we teach our children about each other in our textbooks, catechisms, liturgy, in our Sunday schools, religious schools, and in our homes. We need to train our teachers to be sensitive to the intergroup factors in their classroom presentations. We need to make our parents aware that if our homes are truly altars to the Divine Presence, that anti-Catholic, anti-Jewish, anti-Protestant, anti-Negro attitudes, either as intentional barbs or as unreflective jokes, are in fact violations of the sanctity of the home, of their stewardship of God's children.

Without touching our doctrinal and dogmatic truths, we can reinterpret in our history textbooks, our social science textbooks, and in all our relevant curricula the irenic view of the relationship between Christian and Jew as contrasted with the polemical presentations which now predominate in the majority of our teaching materials. In my studies of the interaction between Christians and Jews from the first four centuries onward, even through the Middle Ages, I have found literally hundreds of episodes which bespeak the warmest and mutually helpful ties between the religious leaders of Christianity and Judaism, as well as on a daily level between "the common people." This is not to minimize for a single moment the tragic fact that the contemporaries of these Christians and Jews were engaged in the most horrible mutual antagonisms and violence, with, let the record be kept clear, Jews being the victims in the majority of instances of this sad history. But Christian textbooks, both Catholic and Protestant, have a far road to travel before they portray adequately and empathetically the Jewish people and Judaism as a living, vital, relevant community in Western civilization. Similarly, Jews are a far cry from dealing adequately and sympathetically with Christians and Christianity. While there are Jews who feel that the persecutions of the past, and in particular the Nazi Holocaust which took place in a nation that boasted of its ancient Christian culture, does not obligate them to meet the Christian halfway, there are also many of us who feel that our obligations to future generations of Jewish children require us to help prepare them to live humanely and fraternally with their Christian neighbors.

The cycle of mutual recrimination, suspicion, and hostility has run long enough. It is time to set into motion a cycle of benign relations, mutually trusting and loving, as befits noble sons and daughters of the Sovereign of the universe. I, as a Jew and as a rabbi, and together with me thousands of my coreligionists here and the world over, are prepared to join hands with you, our Catholic neighbors, to work together unceasingly toward the realization of that goal so simply but compellingly enunciated by Pope John XXIII in his encyclical, *Ad Petri Cathedram:* "Let every man tend to do that not which divides one from another, but let every man do that which unites one to another."

3

Pope John XXIII: "One of the Righteous Among the Peoples of the Earth"

SINCE BIBLICAL TIMES, there has been a vital Jewish tradition which holds that the highest tribute the Jewish people can bestow on a non-Jew is to regard him as *echad m'chasidei umot ha'olam,* "one of the righteous among the peoples of the earth." Such "righteous" ones, according to The Ethics of the Fathers, are regarded as blessed and are "vouchsafed a portion in the world to come." Their lives of piety and righteousness are seen as crucial in helping "to sustain the world." For such noble spirits, the Talmud enjoined Jews to praise God and to thank Him: "He who sees the sages of the nations of the world says, 'Blessed be He who has given of wisdom to flesh and blood.'"

The religious practice is well known among Jews, dating back to the Pharasaic and Rabbinic period, who when they talked of a devout Christian added: "God be with him, God help him, may God prolong his life." When recalling deceased pious Christians, they add the words: "Blessed be his memory, may his soul be received in the host of the blessed."

During the anxious weeks of illness preceding his death, the name of Pope John XXIII became synonymous with *hasid,* the "righteous one," the "pious one," and on the lips of hosts of Jews were these traditional words of prayer and benediction. On May 28, when the newspapers grimly proclaimed, "Pope Worse," the New York Board of Rabbis—representing Orthodox, Conservative, and Reform rabbis serving the largest Jewish community in the world—made a public appeal to its members to offer prayers to God for the pope's recovery. Similar appeals were made by

Reprinted from *Ave Maria National Catholic Weekly,* June 15, 1963 major Jewish religious bodies, national Rabbinic and Synagogal, as well as civic and social action groups such as my own, the American Jewish Committee.

These were unprecedented expressions of concern and tribute from Jews in all walks of life, and from throughout the inhabited world, for a Pontiff of the Catholic Church. Jews have held a number of popes in especial esteem, beginning with the great Pope Gregory I of the sixth century who inaugurated the far-reaching papal bull, *Sicut Judaeis*, which guaranteed the Jewish people their right to unhindered worship and protection from forced conversion. But no pope that I know of throughout the history of the Church has communicated such a clear and consistent attitude of friendship and profound understanding toward the Jewish people and Judaism as had John XXIII. To paraphrase a Presbyterian's comment, "He is the best pope the Jews ever had."

While they shared with many non-Catholics the general regard for Pope John's warm human qualities, Jews had additional reasons for their friendly attitudes.

Actions and pronouncements of the pope had impressed Jews with his serious desire to improve relations between Catholics and Jews. Many were deeply moved by reports that toward the end of World War II, the pope, then serving as the apostolic delegate in the Middle East, made available baptismal certificates that enabled the rescue of thousands of Jewish men, women, and children from Nazi death camps. He had reacted to the appeal for aid spontaneously, and he had made no conditions.

Shortly after ascending the papal throne, the Pontiff ordered the removal from Catholic liturgy of several references regarded as offensive to the Jews. During this year's Good Friday worship services, when the celebrant of the Mass repeated the phrase "perfidious Jews" either out of habit or as a result of using a missal that had not been brought up-to-date, the pope, according to newspaper reports, halted the *Triduum* rite and caused the passage to be repeated with the offensive phrase left out.

His reaffirmations of Christianity's rootedness in Judaism had also strengthened Jewry's positive feelings. The Pontiff's confirmations of this historic bond were repeated on a number of occasions, and perhaps nowhere more clearly than in his seventh encyclical, *Paenitentiam Agere* (To Do Penance), in which he appealed to Catholics throughout the world to fast and offer penance for the Second Vatican Council. He pointed out that the practices of fasting and penance are based on Jewish traditions, the teachings of the Old Testament, of Moses and the Prophets.

Little wonder then that shortly after his election to the papacy in October 1958, the Chief Rabbi of Venice, Dr. Leone Leoni, flew to Rome to deliver a special greeting on behalf of the Jewish community in the city where the new Pontiff had spent five years as Patriarch. Or that in 1960, 102 Jewish leaders returning from a refugee mission in North Africa and Israel made a special stopover in Rome for an audience with Pope John, who received them with the now-celebrated embrace, "I am Joseph, your brother!"

These sympathetic attitudes of Jews toward the pope had been extended toward the Ecumenical Council that he had summoned. Jews generally recognized that the Council was a Christian meeting convoked to consider doctrinal and organizational problems confronting the church and also to explore questions of unity with the "separated brethren" of Protestantism and Eastern Orthodoxy. To the extent that the Council dealt with questions of theology and doctrine of significance to the Catholic faithful and to other Christians, it was evident that Jews were not involved. This feeling for propriety explains why responsible Jewish groups, religious and lay, did not seek invitations to send observer delegates to the Council.

At the same time, Jews felt involved in the Council in fundamental ways. First, in exploring interfaith relations with Protestants, it was theologically inevitable that consideration be given to the heritage of the Hebrew Bible, which all branches of Christianity share in common. And significantly, Pope John's Council during its first session led to increased consultation and dialogue between Catholic and Jewish scholars on the continent and in America, recalling the fruitful exchanges between St. Jerome and Jewish Bible authorities in Palestine where the church father spent forty years translating the Vulgate based on midrashic traditions.

Second, Jews had hoped that the Council's examinations of the relations between Catholics and other groups in a growing pluralistic world would lead to a forthright clarification of the church's position on religious liberty, the separation of church and state, and religious pluralism. Authoritative declarations on these issues would help Jews, as well as Protestants and Orthodox, to overcome lingering mistrust and suspicion.

Third, foremost among the steps that Jews had wished the Council to take to advance the specific end of Catholic-Jewish relationships was that of a re-examination of the sources of anti-Semitism that grew out of the polemical period of early church and synagogue history, the themes of contempt and the system of degradation. Many Jews believed that the Council could literally start a new cycle in Christian-Jewish relationships by condemning vigorously all manifestations of anti-Semitism, as did the World Council of Churches in New Delhi in November 1961.

Despite the catechism of the Council of Trent, which affirms the doctrine that Jesus died for all humanity and that all humanity shares the responsibility for his death, the concept of collective Jewish responsibility persists and finds expression and reinforcement in certain prayers, passages of the liturgy, and in a great many Catholic textbooks. As already indicated, Pope John had demonstrated his personal aversion to the perpetuation of these distorted teachings about the Jews, and many had thought the Council might confront seriously the problem of anti-Semitism in this spirit and set into motion an effective program to combat this complex evil.

Catholic friends tell me that there is now some question as to whether the second session of the Ecumenical Council will be convened. While high hopes of as many non-Catholics as of Catholics have been pinned on the September 8 session, should it not come off, there is real comfort to be found in the tremendous and historic legacy that Pope John bequeathed to his church and to "all men of good will," namely *Pacem in Terris*.

The chorus of enthusiastic praise from Jewish leaders, which formed but part of a vast symphonic endorsement of the encyclical on the part of Protestant, Orthodox, Oriental leaders, even communists, was climactic testimony as much to the universal esteem and trust that were lodged in the person of Pope John as in the fundamental propositions that he had set forth to promote "the universal common good."

For many Jews, as undoubtedly for other non-Catholics, a number of those basic questions which they had looked for resolution by the second session of the Vatican Council were answered by Pope John in *Pacem in Terris*. In moving accents of Christian humanism, Pope John established the commitment of the church to uphold and to foster "the natural rights" of every human being, and what is of decisive importance, in those areas of human freedom and conscience in which the church had heretofore appeared to non-Catholics to be ambiguous, if not a threat to a pluralistic, democratic society.

"By the Natural Law," Pope John declared with penetrating clarity and moral earnestness,

> every human being has the right to respect for his person, to his good reputation; the right to freedom in searching for truth and in expressing and communicating his opinions . . . he has the right to be informed truthfully about public events. Every human being has the right to honor God's upright conscience, and therefore the right to worship God privately and publicly. . . . From the fact that human beings are by nature social, there arises the right of assembly and association. Every human being has the right to freedom of movement and of residence within the confines of his own country; and when there are just reasons for it, the right to emigrate to other countries and take up residence there . . . racial discrimination can in no way be justified . . . injustice is even more serious if . . . sinful projects are aimed at the very extinction of these (minority) groups. . . . The doctrinal principles outlined in this document provide Catholics with a vast field in which they can meet and come to an understanding also with human beings, who are endowed with the light of reason and with a natural operative honesty.

Of such basic and radical importance are these declarations—which are the fruit of the five years of Pope John's papacy although prefigured by his predecessors—that I would presume to say that the church will never be the same again. Nor will non-Catholics who have allowed themselves to be open to the extraordinary spiritual presence of this holy man. Perhaps his greatest gift to all of us has been his compelling us to confront the new realities of the world in which we live: a world in which we white Jews and Christians are already a minority; in which by the year 2000 Catholics will be nine to ten percent of the global population as contrasted with eighteen percent today; in which the rising nations of Africa and Asia and the resurgent Oriental religions will force us to abandon our Western monopolies and hegemonies and accommodate ourselves to a genuine global pluralism, which is another way of speaking of the interdependent human family. *Pacem in Terris,* Pope John's gift, is both a curriculum and a Baedeker preparing us paternally for that world that is already upon us. But the greatest service that Pope John has performed for all of us has been to thrust before the consciousness of the world the realization that it teeters on the brink of thermonuclear destruction, and that the only alternative to this apocalyptic horror—in which East and West can today "overkill" each other at least 125 times!—is the biblical alternative of Deuteronomy, to choose life, to love peace, and to pursue it.

Among the earliest responses to *Pacem in Terris* were those of three Orthodox Chief Rabbis: Dr. Izhak Nissim, the Sephardic Chief Rabbi of Israel; Dr. Jacob Kaplan, Chief Rabbi of France; and Dr. Elio Toaff, Chief Rabbi of Rome, as well as those of Jewish religious and lay leaders in America and in other parts of the world. Dr. Nissim expressed the sense of all the Jewish responses in his statement, "Every man of faith and conscience who believes in divine justice and in freedom must endeavor to bring about the realization of the pope's sublime words."

The fact that the Chief Rabbis publicly associated themselves with the appeal of Pope John is in itself an act of unprecedented and historic significance; I know of nothing similar to this occurrence in 1,900 years of relationships between Christians and Jews. Thus, I take this to be both a tribute to the spiritual greatness of the late Pontiff as well as a response to the frightful challenges of the nuclear-missile age which he sought so vigorously to bring before the human family.

In the middle of the eleventh century, the Catholic Church sought to enforce a "Truce of God," which greatly restricted the time when it was permissible to carry on warfare. Through his brilliant and compassionate encyclicals and the Ecumenical Council, Pope John labored to help achieve a twentieth-century "Truce of God" before the world destroys itself in a thermonuclear holocaust, almost tragicomically, either through mechanical error or human miscalculation.

Perhaps the most significant memorial that we could erect to Pope John, and the most relevant instruction that we could take from his ministry on this earth, would be to undertake at once those steps that would help advance the goals of his latest encyclical which all of us share. To this end, I would propose that appropriate leaders of the three faith communities who share a consensus on world community and world peace take the initiative as early as possible to convene on the American scene a "National Conference on Religion and World Peace."

The recent conference on "Religion and Race," with which I was privileged to be associated as program chairman, is testimony to the great impact that such a combined religious witness can make. Based on the success of such an enterprise, one could then visualize the possibility of a world-wide meeting of a similar character. When leaders of the world's major faith communities will come together at one table to pursue justice, charity, liberty, and peace in freedom, we may well be witness to the beginning of the translation into reality of the prophetic vision of messianic peace for all mankind, *Pacem in Terris.*

4

An Interfaith Reexamination of Christian-Jewish Relations

IN AN EXCELLENT ARTICLE in the April 1960 *Social Order,* Donald R. Campion, S.J., associate editor of *America* magazine, wrote: "Each of the major (religious) traditions cherishes among its most fundamental tenets a set of absolutes which are at odds with bigotry. . . . What nourishes prejudice and foments intergroup tensions is the culture-bound non-essential which has become identified with the substance of religious belief and conduct."

Catholics, Protestants, and Jews consider themselves under divine injunction to practice love of neighbor, seek brotherhood and mutual understanding, banish bitterness and hatred. We have seen appalling fruits of bigotry, from its mildest manifestations, such as stereotypes and misconceptions about other groups, to its most violent and ugly expressions, culminating in the pinnacle of twentieth century brutality—the death camp. Although our religious traditions are different, and the differences should not be ignored or minimized, all of us profoundly believe that religious faith provides the corrective for the spiritual arrogance that expresses itself as prejudice and bigotry. It is all the more shocking, therefore, to be informed that religious institutions, instead

---

Lecture delivered before the *Sister Formation Workshop* at Marquette University in August 1963. Rabbi Tanenbaum challenged women religious based on the results of the St. Louis University analyses of Roman Catholic textbook portrayals of Jews and Judaism conducted by Sisters Mary Linus Gleason, Rita Mudd and, for religion texts themselves, Rose Thering. The latter study provides a measure of progress in the Jewish-Christian encounter. Eugene J. Fisher's own doctoral dissertation for New York University amplified and updated the Thering study in 1976. It has now been updated by Dr. Philip Cunningham as a dissertation for Boston College in 1992. Rabbi Tanenbaum rightly realized very early that the church's "delivery system" with regard to how it shapes the attitudes of its adherents toward Jews and Judaism is to be found in its pulpits and its classrooms. At the Marquette Conference, he had before him a prime audience of leading Catholic educators of the United States.

of counteracting prevailing prejudice and stereotyped conceptions about other people, may actually transmit and bolster them.
In the words of the Rt. Rev. James A. Pike, Episcopal Bishop of
California: "The sad and shocking truth is that the roots of bias
often reach back to the pulpit and the Sunday school class; the
seeds of hatred frequently are planted by the churches themselves
by what they teach, what they fail to teach, and what they are."

How can this be? How can the institutions of our great religions, which are committed to the teaching and practice of love
of God and neighbor, support negative and distorted attitudes
toward other groups? Noted psychologist Gordon Allport has suggested, "The chief reason why religion becomes the focus of prejudice is that it usually stands for more than faith—it is the pivot
of the cultural tradition of a group." Or, put another way, we are
all somewhat the victims of polemical histories. At critical periods
over the past 2,000 years, our separate religious communities have
clashed in serious conflicts, both theologically and historically
rooted, often accompanied by great bitterness, persecution, and
bloodshed. In the heat of argument, many hostile or negative
comments were made regarding one another, and, unfortunately,
these have become embedded in our historic traditions, uncriti-
cally carried forward from generation to generation, and may still
be found in religious teaching. This, plus a somewhat defensive
tendency to view our own group as the victim of persecution and
oppression inflicted by others, can lead to totally polarized and
polemical views of one another. Read a typical Catholic Church
history textbook, for example, on the Crusades. They are almost
invariably presented as noble and chivalrous efforts on behalf of
a holy cause. If slaughter is mentioned, it is the slaughter of the
Christians by Turks. Seldom will you find the information that
for Jews, the Crusades meant a blood bath, the first systematic
massacres of Jews in Europe. On the occasion of the capture of
Jerusalem in 1099, a glorious victory in Christian textbooks, Jewish textbooks will relate that the Jews of Jerusalem were driven by
the victorious Crusaders into a synagogue and burned alive.

Similarly, read Protestant and Catholic lessons dealing with the
Reformation, or with certain areas of contemporary competition.
The same thing happens—not only vulgar name-calling ("obsti-
nate heretics" or "Luther's unrestrained passions" from the

Catholic side, and the Catholic Church "teeming with legalism like a filthy kitchen teems with vermin" from certain Protestants)—but something much deeper and more difficult to correct because less obvious to see: a refusal to identify with the plight of others, a defensiveness which sacrifices charity and sometimes justice to the interests of an unreflective group loyalty. When this happens, as William James puts it, "piety is the mask, the inner force is tribal instinct." The task of freeing the vital core of faith from the cultural and temporal encrustations that have accumulated around it over the centuries is not an easy one. It requires honest self-criticism, diligence, and skill on the part of all our religious communities. But it is a task that must be accomplished. Otherwise, we will find that our professions of noble moral teaching about the brotherhood of man under the fatherhood of God, when contrasted against the daily behavior and entrenched biased attitudes of "religious" people will sow the seeds of skepticism and secularism.

Fortunately, the process of purification has long since begun here in the United States. There is evident a new openness, a willingness to examine educational materials, teacher-training procedures—the total process through which the religious message is promulgated and transmitted to young and impressionable minds. Responsible Protestant, Catholic, and Jewish scholars have undertaken serious and objective studies of the religious education materials used in their respective communities to see how other racial, religious, and ethnic groups are portrayed in these materials, where the problems lie, and what improvements must be made. I am pleased that my own organization, the American Jewish Committee, has stimulated and encouraged these impartial research projects. The Protestant self-study, undertaken over a seven-year period at Yale Divinity School by Dr. Bernhard E. Olson, was published last year by Yale University Press under the title *Faith and Prejudice* (New Haven: Yale University Press, 1963). The Catholic research, undertaken at St. Louis University under the direction of Father Trafford Maher, S.J., includes an analysis of literature materials used in Catholic schools by Sister Mary Linus Gleason, social studies textbooks by Sister Rita Mudd, and religion textbooks by Sister Rose Thering. The findings of the latter study have recently been made public. The Jewish self-study, carried on at Dropsie College for Hebrew and Cognate Learning, under the direction of Dr. Bernard Weinryb, has just been completed and its findings will be announced in the near future.

Obviously, textbooks are not the only, and perhaps not even a decisive, influence in forming attitudes. The role of the teacher is vital, both in the way she interprets the written material and in the way she communicates her own deepest feelings and values. The influence of parental attitudes, which are in turn affected by adult education, is also critical. But textbooks are at least accessible to measurable content analysis, and such analysis can help us by clarifying the problem areas for teachers, parents, religious educators, preachers, writers, and all who are engaged in the vocations of communicating the religious truths and message. Thus, these studies provide us with important insights regarding the way we teach about one another. First of all, they indicate that our religious textbooks are very favorably disposed toward racial and ethnic groups. Bias and distortion occur when other religious groups are written about. As might be expected, the negative and hostile references tend to intensify around certain critical conflicts between our various faith communities. Thus, Protestants and Catholics tend to write negatively—and sometimes with shocking distortions—about Jews in lessons dealing with the Crucifixion, the Jewish non-acceptance of Christianity, the struggle between Jesus and the Pharisees, etc. While all of our textbooks stress charity and love of neighbor in general terms, and include many expressions of general goodwill, this charitable and loving attitude is often forgotten in writing about specific groups and particular situations. Since I am a rabbi, and honestly believe that the Jewish people, beyond any other group, have suffered throughout history from the consequences of distorted and unreflective Christian teachings, I would like to direct my remarks to the question of Christian teaching about the Jews, and to point to some of the more serious problems as I see them.

THE ST. LOUIS STUDY

In reviewing the findings of the St. Louis study, and in much of my own reading of Catholic education materials, it seems to me that there are certain repeated patterns and themes which are prejudicial. I should like to identify and illustrate these problems for you.

First and foremost, there is a very strong tendency in Catholic textbooks to place upon the Jews exclusive and collective responsibility for the Crucifixion of Jesus. I need not tell you that the cry of "Christ killer" against the Jews has been used by anti-Semites throughout the ages to excuse or justify the most violent and brutal persecution. Moreover, authentic Catholic teaching on this question is clear and forthright. I refer you to the words of the Fourth Catechism of the Council of Trent (1545–1563):

> It was the peculiar privilege of Christ the Lord to have died, when He Himself decreed to die, and to have died not so much by external violence, as by internal assent . . . Should any one inquire why the Son of God underwent His most bitter passion, he will find that besides the guilt inherited from our first parents, the principal causes were the vices and crimes which have been perpetrated from the beginning of the world to the present day and those which will be committed to the end of time. . . . In this guilt are involved all those who fall frequently into sin; for, as our sins consigned Christ the Lord to the death of the cross, most certainly those who wallow in sin and iniquity, crucify to themselves again the Son of God, as far as in them lies and makes a mockery of Him. This guilt seems more enormous in us than in the Jews, since according to the testimony of the same Apostle: If they had known it, they would have never crucified the Lord of glory; while we on the contrary, professing to know Him, yet deny Him by our actions, seem in some sort to lay violent hands upon Him. . . . Men of all ranks and conditions were gathered together against the Lord, and against his Christ. Gentiles and Jews were the advisers, the authors, the ministers of His passion; Judas betrayed Him, Peter denied Him, and the rest deserted Him . . .

Despite this splendid and authoritative teaching, despite the statement of Father Louis Hartman, C.Ss.R., general secretary of the Catholic Biblical Association of America, that, "historically speaking . . . there is no basis for the claim that the Jews of that time as a people were guilty of the death of Christ and obviously there is not the slightest reason for bringing this accusation against their descendants of 2,000 years later," and despite many similar statements by contemporary Catholic authorities, a number of Catholic teaching materials persist in stating or implying that the Jews as a people are responsible for the death of Jesus and are consequently condemned and rejected by God. Let me give you some verbatim examples from textbooks used in Catholic secondary parochial schools:

> "The Jews wanted to disgrace Christ by having Him die on the cross."
> "Show us that the Jews did not want Pilate to try Christ but to give permission for His death."
> "When did the Jews decide to kill Christ?"
> "The Jews as a nation refused to accept Christ and since that time they have been wandering on the earth without a temple or a sacrifice and without the Messiah."

In a Lenten missal we read the following:

> His Jewish nation was suffering an exile of seventy years. In captivity they were atoning for the worship of false gods. In these modern days the Jews are still dispersed in every nation in a condition worse than exile. They have been atoning these nineteen hundred years for the greatest of all crimes, committed when an entire nation rejected, crucified, and shed the blood of the Son of God. Among such Christians they are witnesses of a lost vocation, without prince or prophet or sacrifice or a temple in Jerusalem. Divine punishment hangs over them until the end of time, when God, because of His promises to the prophets, will, in some extraordinary way, bring them to believe and live in Jesus Christ.

Statements like these are likely to instill the conviction that the Jews bear a collective guilt and somehow deserve the suffering and persecutions that have marked their long history. This concept is extraordinarily invidious because it cuts off the Jews from the common body of humanity and may make Catholics indifferent to the fate of their fellow human beings.

PARTIALITY IN TERMS

A second problem I have noted in the textbook materials is partiality in the use of the term "the Jews." In many instances, the enemies of Jesus are consistently identified as "the Jews," while his friends and followers, who were also Jews, are not. Contrast the following sets of excerpts:

"Altogether numbering well over five thousand they listened to the Master all day, forgetting even to eat."
"In the beginning of His public life Jesus was held in great admiration by the people."
"The Jews stirred up the rabble against Him."
"With what words of His did the Jews attempt for the second time to stone Him?"

A particularly vivid example of this kind of partiality is found in the following statement: "It was on the day Christ raised Lazarus from the tomb that the Jews decided to kill Him. Nevertheless, they were afraid of the people." Who were "the people?" Martians? Jesus lived his entire life among his own people, and scarcely addressed a word to a non-Jew. "The people" who loved, revered, and followed him, as well as the specific religious authorities who opposed him and plotted against him were all Jews.

Another example of partiality is the frequent use of the generic term "the Jews" applied to situations where only a few individuals, comprising an insignificant proportion of the population, were involved. Unfortunately, expressions such as, "the bloodthirsty Jews," "the carnal Jews," "the envious Jews," "the blind hatred of the Jews" do not make these distinctions. I ask you to consider the impact on young and impressionable minds of the repetition of such phrases without proper distinctions and interpretation of the material. Is it not possible for students to associate these evil characteristics with all Jews?

Another interesting example of partiality in terminology—and I do not think this is deliberate, but is a question of style rather than intent—is that Jews are often referred to differently in New Testament and Old Testament contexts. In Old Testament lessons, where Jews are presented in a very positive fashion, they are often designated "Hebrews" or "Israelites." In the New Testament lessons, "the Jews" appears to be more frequently used. In a recently published textbook for children—and I wish to emphasize strongly that it is one of the best textbooks I have seen—there is an example of this. One passage goes approximately:

God chose a country for the Savior . . . It is the country of Palestine. God chose a Mother for the Savior . . . Her name is Mary. God chose a people for the Savior . . . He called Abraham. . . .

Of course God chose Abraham. But Abraham is not a people. The people are the Jews. Christian students must never lose sight of the fact that "the Jews" of the New Testament lessons are the same people to whom God revealed Himself, who upheld even through martyrdom the faith in the One living God which made Christianity possible.

Another sore point in much of the teaching matter is the treatment of the Pharisees. Naturally, we cannot expect that Christianity must share our views of the Pharisees as, for the most part, saintly, devout, and courageous men on whose moral and scholarly interpretations of the Law and Tradition normative Judaism rests today. In recent years, outstanding Christian scholars have presented a more balanced and affirmative view of the Pharisees, but we must understand and accept that the Jewish evaluations of this group will continue to be different. But all too frequently, the Pharisees are described as absolutely inhuman. No true religious motivation is ever ascribed to them. Seldom if ever is it suggested that some of them might have acted out of sincere conviction. The student is given a picture of a group of people utterly debased, completely hypocritical, motivated by nothing but blind hatred and vengeance. The words of Father Paul Demann, the French Catholic scholar, are particularly relevant here:

> The manner and spirit of approach with which we judge the Pharisees would seem to constitute a true test of the spirit of our teaching. Too often instead of seeing in them, and in the reproaches that Jesus directed to them, the mirror of our hypocrisy, our own narrowness, our own formalism, we are tempted to take exactly the same attitude toward them which they were tempted to take toward the sinners and publicans. To present the Pharisees in a historically and theologically accurate way means to show the very temptations, the sins, the reproaches directed to them are to be taken, not in a collective sense, but rather in a permanent and universal sense. It means to understand and to make it understood that the question is not they as against us, but we besides them.

In expounding Christianity, unjust and inaccurate comparisons with the Jewish faith are often made. Occasionally, gratuitous slurs at Judaism are introduced to heighten the contrast to Christianity. In consequence Judaism emerges as a legalistic religion concerned with external observances, devoid of love, mercy, and compassion. For example: "The Jews believe that one should hate an enemy but Christ taught the opposite." (It might be noted that St. Paul's injunction, "If your enemy is hungry feed him" [Romans 12:20], is a direct quote from Proverbs 25:21.)

Similarly, consider the following statement from a textbook: "Little progress has been made in the conversion to any form of Christianity of groups who regard their race or religion as the antithesis of Christianity, such as the Jews and Mohammedans. Both of these large bodies are more anti-Christian than they are pro-something."

How uncharitable, to say nothing of inaccurate—a generalization! I practice my religion for its own values and in full appreciation of the richness and depth of its tradition, not in opposition to another faith. And I do not consider Judaism the antithesis of Christianity. What is left out of a lesson may be as important in forming attitudes and values as what is put in. By ignoring certain facts—either intentionally or under the influence of unconscious prejudice—authors of educational literature may stimulate or abet bigotry. For example, it would be true to state that in the Middle Ages many Jews were money lenders. But the statement would be misleading unless it were explained that Jews had few other ways of supporting themselves, being barred from guilds and forbidden to own land.

PROBLEMS OF OMISSION

Some omissions likely to foster prejudice also illustrate how textbook materials can be misleading. For example, the Jewish background of Christianity is often ignored. Many Catholics are largely unaware of Christianity's Jewish roots. Some passages give the impression that the Bible did not exist previous to the Catholic Church. Here is a passage to consider: "[God] inspired men whom He chose to write the different smaller books which comprise it. There can be no doubt that the world must thank the Catholic Church for the Bible."

There are few, if any, references to Judaism as a religion after the birth of Christianity. Jewish religious practices, holy days, etc., are described only in the context of the ancient past. The Catholic student is given the impression that Judaism as a faith ceased to exist with the founding of Christianity, or with the destruction of the Temple. The Jews of later ages thus may appear, by implication, as an irreligious people. Even though Catholics believe Christianity to be the fulfillment of Judaism, is there not a responsibility to make clear that Judaism continues as a living faith?

Through omission of facts, later phases of Jewish history are presented in a false light. For example:

> The Jews, as religionists, were not subject to the Spanish Inquisition, but only as baptized Christians, known as Marranos. Jews who practiced their own religion were not molested. Jewish scholars admit that many Jews, of their own free will, embraced the Catholic Church, were baptized, followed Catholic practices, yet were insincere.

It is not mentioned that Jews who practiced their own religion were severely molested by the civil authorities if not by the church. Most Marranos converted, not of their own free will, but under pressure and the threat of expulsion.

WE MUST WIN THIS WAR

I hope you realize that I have not drawn attention to these problems in any spirit of indictment. No one religious, racial, or ethnic group has a monopoly on prejudice or a perfect record of understanding and identifying with the plight of his brothers. All of us need that open-hearted and open-minded process of self-critical examination that I understand to be meant by the expression *aggiornamento*. I am aware that my very presence here today—a rabbi, invited to speak candidly to Catholic teaching sisters—is an example of that process in action. With God's help we can melt down the ancient barriers of misunderstanding and mistrust that have cast us for far too long in a "dialogue of contempt." We are learning to talk to one another and listen to one another, and we must learn better how to teach about one another. As Cardinal

Spellman so movingly stated in an address to the American Jewish Committee's Annual Dinner, "By every means at our disposal we must wage war on the old suspicions and prejudices and bigotry which have set brother against brother and have spawned a brood of evils threatening the very existence of our society. Definitely we must win that war."

It is one of those distorted and terribly harmful notions that somehow gain currency and, like a cancer, spread among certain people who wish to justify their own bigotry. In direct reference to the proposed Council declaration on the Jews, His Eminence explained: "Responsibility for the crucifixion of Jesus as an event of history belongs only to those individuals who were present at the time and who cooperated in His death. It is simply absurd to maintain that there is some kind of continuing guilt which is transferred to any group and which rests upon them as a curse for which they must suffer."

"The Christian faith, on the other hand, does teach that Christ Our Savior died for all of us, in expiation for the sins of all mankind. In this sense we do believe that we are all mystically implicated in His death—but all without exception and in the same way. And His dying for us must never be thought of as a curse upon anyone, but rather as a blessing upon all."

In summary, the Cardinal said: "Anti-Semitism can never find a basis in the Catholic religion. Far from emphasizing the differences which divide Jews from Christians, our Faith stresses our common origins and the ties which bind us together. It is high time to stress the bonds of brotherhood which should characterize our relationship."

5

The American Negro:
Myths and Realities

I

GUNNAR MYRDAL ASSERTS in his now-classic study of the Negro problem in America, *The American Dilemma,* "It should be clear by this time that it is the popular beliefs (the numerous myths, legends, and stereotypes) that are of primary importance in interracial relations."

Recent surveys of the changing attitudes of the white population toward Negroes have tended to agree that there has been a marked improvement. "Most white Americans," Louis Harris, the opinion sampler, has reported in his recently widely publicized surveys, "are willing to have far more day-to-day contact with Negroes than they experience now. On the job, in schools, and in public accommodations, white society appears ready to move a long distance toward meeting Negro demands for integration. Much of the white people in the South," Harris adds, "are also increasingly ready to go along with these demands."

Similarly, an interesting study by Herbert H. Hyman and Paul

In addition to the religious relationships he sought to foster, Rabbi Marc Tanenbaum also had an eye on the large social questions of his day. His work on race relations is typical. Along with other Jewish and Christian activists, he was committed to spurring the religious community into engagement with the civil rights movement. In 1963, he helped organize and served as program chair of the National Conference on Religion and Race. Once again, he invited Abraham Joshua Heschel to speak and there used the occasion to introduce Rabbi Heschel to the Rev. Dr. Martin Luther King Jr. Rabbi Heschel's galvanizing effect on the audience helped enlarge his influence and brought him more squarely into the struggle for equality in America. He later marched side by side with Martin Luther King Jr. in Selma, Alabama. This essay, written for the journal *Religious Education* (Jan–Feb 1964), represents a topic to which Rabbi Tanenbaum would return. It demonstrates that his concern and passions were not only for his own people, but for all peoples.

B. Sheatsley that compares white Americans' attitudes concerning Negroes in 1963 with those held in 1942, twelve years before the Supreme Court decision on school integration, concludes: "The 1963 study shows conclusively that the long-term trend toward acceptance of integration has not halted or reversed itself but rather has continued, and even accelerated."

For the first time, a majority of all white Americans believes that "white students and Negro students should go to the same schools." The idea of a Negro with the same income and education as you, moving into your block, is also more acceptable now. Belief that Negroes can learn things just as well as white people if they are given the same education and training is characteristic of majorities in all parts of the nation.

These reports (based on elaborate data and percentages of opinion samplings, which can be studied with profit and interest but for which there is not enough room here) are obviously encouraging. But there are also reported the contradictory tendencies of "widespread and deeply rooted anti-Negro prejudice," which exist in a profound state of tension in "the divided conscience" of these interviewed. This leaves one wondering as to whether the nation, and in particular, the religious communities, have begun to face up adequately to the seven-eighths of the iceberg beneath the surface.

There is some point at which most white Americans draw the line at the prospect of closer association with Negroes. One conclusion that can be drawn from the patterns of prejudice is that the greater the suggestion of physical contact, the greater the white antipathy—and even revulsion. One reason seems to be that the image of the Negro in the white mind is a complex of unflattering stereotypes. 3 out of 4 whites, for instance, believe that Negroes, as a race, are less ambitious than whites; 71 percent think they "smell different"; 69 percent say that Negroes have looser morals; 49 percent, that they want to live on handouts; 44 percent, that they breed crime. One in three say Negroes are an inherently inferior race (*Newsweek*, October 21, 1963).

The keystone issues around which the civil rights struggle rages are those of providing equal opportunities in the areas of employment, housing, education, and public accommodations. The considerable progress that has been made in each of these areas can be attributed primarily to the alliance of forces exerted by official government agencies either in concert with or challenged by the Negro protest movement and the civil rights revolt. Generally, progress has been achieved against the tide of much public sentiment. (Hyman and Sheatsley note, "In areas where some measure of integration has taken place, official action has preceded public sentiment and public sentiment has then attempted to accommodate to the existing situation.")

If one examines the public rationales for resisting the movement toward racial equalitarianism, whether articulated in the hate-filled outcries of the White Citizens' Councils or in the gradualist pleas of many white moderates, one cannot but help find himself sorting out the "given" reasons from the "real" reasons. And the "real" reasons, those which are expressed with greatest emotion when their nerve-endings are touched, are grounded in misperceptions, distortions, and stereotypes about the Negro, which are as much the product of our "national illiteracy" about the social, cultural, and religious history of the Negro as they are the expressions of our twisted psychological fears and anxieties about blackness as a symbol of violence.

James Baldwin, Louis Lomax, and Malcolm X have made the white society painfully conscious of how wide is the gulf that separates the white man's true understanding of the Negro's psyche and social predicament from that of the Negro's understanding of his self, his situation, and his real relation to the white majority. (The fact that the "big six" civil rights leaders, who, I have no doubt, are very much representative of their people, have increasingly edged their public declarations with something of the desperation and urgency of the "militant" Negroes is an insight into the state of the mentality of the Negro masses as much as of the leaders). The most well-intentioned white civil libertarians, in the majority of instances, have not begun to grasp the full visceral reality of the Negro's daily plight, and the conventional liberal rallying cries for "justice" and "freedom" and "equal opportunity," when uttered in that vague, abstract and principled way, fail to find response and trust in the Negro soul.

II

At the root of the problem is the failure of the majority of white people to begin to comprehend the magnitude of the tragedy of the Negro in America. It has taken a foreign observer to state the true moral size of this primordial American tragedy. The Dutch historian J. W. Schulte Nordholt spent four years of study and research examining the history of the Negro people in America across three and a half centuries, and epitomized his perception of our race relations in these words: "A crime had been committed which has never been equaled in size and intensity and is perhaps comparable only with the persecutions of our own times under National Socialism."

In describing the notorious slave trade—in which the English and Dutch exploited African Negroes as much as did the Americans, both of North and South—Nordholt declares: "A migration of nations had taken place on a scale so vast that it dwarfed completely the migration of nations in ancient times."

The migration began with the importation to this country of nine hundred thousand Negro men, women, and children in the sixteenth century; and then increased to 2.75 million in the 1600s; to 7 million in the 1700s; and then declined to 4 million in the 1800s. The slaves were driven on board the cargo ships by whipping and caning, and were branded by a hot iron, which caused painful swelling in their cheeks, arms, or flanks. Many thought they were going to be eaten by the white man, and in their terror, "stabbed, hanged, or drowned themselves."

In the colonies, they were treated as merchandise by the plantation barons, who washed their investments (a sturdy male sold for about $1,800 during a good market), polished and oiled them to enhance their sales appeal in the slave market. Families were torn apart. Women were sold as "breeders" and drew a high price if they were particularly fecund. Eight-year-old children worked from sunrise to sunset on the Southern cotton plantations under the whiplash of the brutal overseers. In the wild west violence that reigned in the South, any attempt at rebellion was put down by lynchings, the burning alive in the streets of the slave rebels, and public whippings.

In the midst of this repression and persecution of the Negroes, in 1850 a historian was able to report that the men of the white society had sired four hundred thousand children, the offspring of miscegenation! This turbulent society, filled with contradictions, afflicted by a huge racial guilt complex, constantly sought to over justify itself. By the early 1800s, the South was in an overwrought mental condition. Every slave uprising spelled danger to the plantation system. The community could no longer afford differing opinions. The South had grown from a strange and chaotic wild west into a police state.

I rehearse briefly this history because I think it is important that we try to understand what must happen to a thoughtful Negro of today who reads of the pilgrimage of his ancestors through the American wilderness. It occurs to me that he must have a reaction akin to that of the Jew of today who reads of what happened to his forebears in Western Christendom—the chain of persecutions, pogroms, expulsions, autos-da-fé, and finally genocide. The vast majority of Jews make the necessary distinctions between the Christians of the current liberal world and their persecuting ancestors. But the "old world" memories die hard. Even to third generation American-born Jews there is a frightening response to the thought: "The people of the cross have made the Jews the cross among the peoples."

In somewhat parallel ways, I find Negroes reacting to the "old world" memories of their ancestors in slavery. And to those who are deeply knowledgeable of their pasts, and who are close to the feelings and experiences of deprivation that their grandfathers underwent, it does not seem too farfetched for them to call for things like "compensation," and "preferential treatment." While privately they may recognize that these claims are strategies or bargaining points for equality, the mercurial reaction of their white allies and the swiftness with which the civil libertarian becomes estranged are another indication to the Negro that he, although an American who believes in Myrdal's "American Creed," continues to live in two civilizations—one of which remains *terra incognita* to the white American.

III

To return the relationship of the myths to the practical issues of civil rights: Heine could have meant the Negroes of 1963 when he referred to the Jews of the 1700s, "First, you cripple the Jews and then you blame them for limping." In education, we have crippled the Negro and then we blame him for a limping performance. The crippling process began a long time ago. In the 1830s all the Southern states passed laws prohibiting the Negro from learning to read or write. (The plantation barons feared that literacy would lead to dissatisfaction and rebellion). The first schools that were established for Negroes were segregated in Boston, New York, and New Jersey in the 1800s. What is truly remarkable is that despite these handicaps, a number of slaves learned secretly how to read and write, and that the Negroes gave rise to numerous gifted scholars, poets, writers—whose names mean practically nothing to the white American!

In employment, Negroes could not be expected to be enthusiastic workers when for roughly 300 years they were used as doormats. They were prohibited by the slave laws of owning any property or personal possessions and therefore had no reason for incentive or ambition. The stereotype of laziness and passivity more appropriately describes the conditioned response to a repressive condition of the environment and has obviously no justification in attributing this to the character or inborn traits of the people.

In housing, the fear of many white people of integrated housing stems in large measure from the myths of loose morals of Negroes, weak family life, and personal dirty habits, as much as from the presumed loss of property values. Given the history of enforced separation of families of Negroes by white people in the South, the Negro family today in the lower classes is undoubtedly less stable. But evidence is clear that the middle class Negro families are as reliable, conventional, and responsible as any other middle class of any other color. Housing segregation, observes Myrdal, is a rationalization of the view that the Negro is a menace to orderly society unless "kept in his place" by the caste system.

In public accommodations—or a form of social equality—the prevalent belief in a peculiar odor of the Negro is useful to deny social intercourse and the use of public conveniences that would imply close contact. Myrdal observes: "It is remarkable that it (odor) does not hinder the utilization of Negroes in even the most intimate household work and personal services."

If there is any summary instruction that may be derived from this statement, it is in the sense, "that the fault is in ourselves and not in our stars," nor as much in our Negro fellow-citizens. The new frontier in race relations, I firmly believe, beyond the struggle for achieving equality in the legal, political, and social spheres, is that enunciated by the historian Nordholt; namely, that of discovering "a relationship between white man and Negro which does not belittle the human dignity of either" and which enables both together to realize their common sonship under God.

6

The Role of the Church and Synagogue in Social Action

A FEW YEARS AGO, a Hebrew book, published by American Jews in Israel but written in Soviet Russia, was called to my attention. This book, *Torah and Gospel in Soviet Russia,* was an exchange of correspondence between two rabbis—one the Rabbi of Bobruisk, the other the Rabbi of Pavlograd in the south of Russia.

The topic they had been discussing for a number of years in their correspondence was "Whither Soviet Jewry?" What is the future of Russian Jews?

In one of his first letters to the older rabbi, the Rabbi of Pavlograd asked whether or not he should remain in the rabbinate. Why this question? He says, "We have a Synagogue—it's empty. We have no Talmud Torah (Jewish religious school). We have no *heder* (elementary school). We have nothing. But somehow a cou-

---

Reprinted from Philip Scharper, ed., *Torah and Gospel: Jewish and Catholic Theology in Dialogue* (New York: Sheed and Ward, 1966). The importance of scholarly contributions was witnessed again in January 1965, when one of the most significant of the early theological dialogues between Catholic and Jewish scholars was held at St. Vincent's Archabbey in Latrobe, Pennsylvania. Participants included Rabbis Solomon Grayzel, Solomon Freehof, Samuel Sandmel, Robert Gordis, Jacob Agus, Arthur Gilbert, and, of course, Marc Tanenbaum on the Jewish side, and Bishops John Wright and William Connare, and the Reverends John Sheerin, C.S.P., Aidan Kavanagh, O.S.B., Roland Murphy, O.Carm., John F. Cronin, S.S., and Gerard Sloyan on the Catholic side. The prior of the abbey at the time was Abbot Rembert Weakland, O.S.B., who later became Archbishop of Milwaukee. Rabbi Tanenbaum's own paper on the role of church and synagogue in social action is included here. He notes briefly those reforms then underway in Catholic circles, leaving the bulk of this analysis to his dialogue partner, Father Cronin, then Associate Director of Social Action for the National Catholic Welfare Conference, the organization that became the present United States Conference of Catholic Bishops. Significantly, however, Rabbi Tanenbaum also demonstrates a broad awareness of the aims and history of Protestant theology and ethics, which continue to serve as resources for mutual understanding and collaboration.

ple hundred of Jews living in Pavlograd are afraid of remaining without a Rabbi. But I have nothing to do.

Wouldn't it be more desirable to resign and become a factory worker in Russia and at the same time remain a pious, traditional Jew as I am?"

The other rabbi advised him not to resign. The line of the argument he used and the criterion he applied to what a rabbi is or should be is very interesting. A rabbi should be in his world an almost functionless person. His only function is to study and to pray, and his house should be open to other people; that is the only function of a rabbi.

I tell you this story about the book not because I want you to adopt on the American scene that criterion for the rabbi—or, by inference, for the priest or minister—but because the Rabbi of Bobruisk referred to something else.

In his semi-rabbinical language, the rabbi referred to an idea about cycles in history. There are various cycles in human history, the rabbi writes in one of his letters. Fundamentally, there are only two—the naturalistic cycle and the metaphysical cycle. Now we are in the midst of a new naturalistic cycle, as the rabbi said, a materialistic, secularistic, and naturalistic cycle in highly industrialized countries, in countries with a technological civilization, or in countries aspiring to create a technological civilization. And our duty "is to be patient and wait. This new naturalistic cycle is going to commit suicide."

"I see already the germs of death in this cycle, in this new naturalism," wrote the Rabbi of Bobruisk. "And then a new wave of the metaphysical outlook will seize Soviet Russia; not only Russia, the world as a whole; and the Jew will again find his place in the world and his language will be more understood than it is today. But in order to welcome the emergence of the new metaphysical cycle we must have you in Pavlograd and you must have me in Bobruisk, and there must be hundreds of others like us in other places. That is your task."

This Dostoievskian midrash might well be viewed as a parable on the situation of the Church and Synagogue in the twentieth century. Without subscribing to the conclusions of the Rabbi of Bobruisk, nor to his overly simplified and apocalyptic views on "the cycles of history," I cite this episode because it is suggestive, symbolically and metaphorically, of these three larger themes with which I should like to deal in this paper:

1. The existential situation of the church and synagogue at this moment in history, and some implications of the present condition for social action;
2. Some of the theological and historical factors that have formed the relations of the church and synagogue with the social order;
3. The challenges, the dilemma, and the possibilities in social action for the religious communities.

THE EXISTENTIAL SITUATION

A virtual revolution has taken place over the past two decades within the religious communities—within them as well as between them. The impressive record that Father John S. Cronin documents of the accomplishments in such social-action areas as race relations, anti-poverty campaigns, civil liberties, and the pursuit of peace (with some qualifications) is a decisive testimony to this growth of collective social consciousness and witness on the part of denominations, singly and cooperatively. More than one Congressman and civil-rights leader has publicly testified that the collective action of the Catholic, Protestant, Orthodox, and Jewish leadership was a crucial factor in passage of the 1964 Civil Rights Act.

Nevertheless, the term "revolution" should not be used unqualifiedly. In the face of the glaring moral corruptions and social injustices that pockmark our society; in the wake of the even more overwhelming problems of potential nuclear holocaust and of poverty, disease, and illiteracy that afflict most of that two-thirds of the human family so callously called "underdeveloped"; in confronting the fantastic challenges of the "triple revolution" of cybernation, weaponry, and human rights, it is evident that the Kingdom of God is far from being realized and that a posture of (cf. "The Church, the Synagogue, and the World," Father Cronin's contribution to this Colloquy) denominational or inter-religious triumphalism is unwarranted, and, worse yet, dangerous because it creates an illusion of achievement which is the greatest enemy of growth and development, the fruits of realism.

In point of fact, the social action enterprises of the churches and synagogues cannot be adequately comprehended apart from a recognition of the transcendent reality of this time; that is, the contradictory existential situation in which the West, and, in particular, the Western religious communities find themselves.

The ultimate contradiction, quite obviously, is that posed for the entire human family by the nuclear age itself. The science and technology that hold out the possibility, for the first time in man's recorded history, of banishing the scourges of poverty, disease, and ignorance are, at the same time, a Pandora's box of apocalyptic terror that enables modern man to "overkill" himself at least 125 times!

In the middle of the eleventh century, the Catholic Church was in a position to enforce a "Truce of God" that greatly restricted the time when it was permissible to carry on warfare. By means of the "Truce of God," the church prohibited warfare between contending parties from Wednesday evening to Monday morning of each week, and during the period of church festivals. Thus, there were, at least theoretically, only eighty days for fighting in each year, never extending over more than three consecutive days. The difference between the unitary, feudal society of the Middle Ages, in which the church held effective political power, and the relative impotence today of all the churches combined to affect, for example, the decisions for the prevention of the proliferation of nuclear bombs is too obvious to require comment. Nevertheless, this paramount "social action" question must be confronted with a new seriousness as to whether the prophetic, moral, and spiritual resources of the world's major religions cannot be asserted at this critical hour to help achieve a twentieth-century "Truce of God" before the world destroys itself in a nuclear-missile holocaust, almost tragicomically, either through mechanical error or human miscalculation.

There are other decisive factors that have undergirded the renewal and reform of religious communities, and foremost among them has been the recognition on the parts of Pope John of blessed memory, Pope Paul, and other Catholic, Protestant, Orthodox, and Jewish leaders of the radically altered new realities which confront all Western religions, and the West itself. (There is substantial evidence that certain forms of *aggiornamento* are taking place among the major Oriental religions—Islam, Buddhism, Hinduism—but this paper is confined primarily to a survey of the church and synagogue of the Occident.)

For the first time since the emergence of Christianity in the fourth century as an established, organized religious community, Christians—and allied with them Jews and all others who count themselves as citizens of the West—find themselves at one and the same time as a minority and a majority. Father Karl Rahner's insistence on the "Diaspora" situation of Christians takes on concrete human meaning and is not just a charming Biblical metaphor to be taken abstractly. (It takes on meaning for Jews, too, but apparently Jews are veterans of the Exile and suffer less trauma, having come to grips with the condition some time ago at Babylon.)

The "diaspora" situation of Christianity (and Judaism) is profoundly shaped by the rise of nationalisms in Africa and Asia. In many of these countries, Christianity is regarded as the "white man's religion," the handmaiden of Western imperialism and colonialism. The tragic massacres of missionaries in the Congo and Angola reveal the depths of the hostility of the African toward peoples of the West, even if the European was at one time considered a Christian benefactor. The harassment and banishment of Christian missionaries in the Sudan is only one of the more recent of a long series of acts in many parts of Asia and Africa that have reduced Christians to tolerated minorities.

Accompanying the rise of nationalism is the resurgence of the Oriental religions, once regarded as moribund. Islam has the most aggressive missionary outreach in Black Africa. Islam converts seven Africans for every one African converted either to Catholicism or Protestantism. Similarly, Buddhism, Hinduism, and Confucianism have been undergoing a renaissance, are rapidly developing a political sophistication, which reflects itself in effective-social organization, and have become increasingly competitive with Western Christianity.

The "contradictory" aspect of the existential situation grows out of the fact that at the moment when Christians and Jews are becoming collectively a "minority" living in the "diaspora," they are at the same time experiencing an unprecedented growth and strength as a "majority" in the United States. The churches and synagogues in America, and their auxiliary bodies, today have the highest rate of growth, the highest levels of per-capita contributions, the most extensive building programs, the highest rate of attendance at religious services and of enrollment of children in religious schools, the most carefully developed social welfare programs for youth and the aged—the highest in comparison to their growth in the past and in contrast to churches and synagogues anywhere else in the world. This growth has taken place—not coincidentally—in a free, voluntary, pluralistic society, and not in a confessional church-state arrangement. But this very growth and this very strength have given many Christians and Jews—and other Americans—a "buffered" vision of the world-at-large. The description of the American state of mind by Bishop Fulton J. Sheen is tragically accurate: "Americans live in a sumptuous palace in the midst of a vast slum."

The problems of religious liberty, freedom of conscience, the question of proselytization or witnessing, freedom of movement, the relationship of church to state, racial and religious discrimination—once regarded as the preoccupation of Westerners and Christians in the internal relationships between Catholics and Protestants, on the one hand, and Christians and Jews on the other, have now been catapulted onto the world scene. In an age in which there is instantaneous global communication and rapid transportation and mobility, it is no longer possible either to "keep under wraps" for long or to withhold from the judgment of a restive and interdependent human family any acts or attitudes which reflect contempt for the human person or which deny him his "natural rights."

An attack on a Negro in Birmingham today will tomorrow be condemned editorially in a Ghana newspaper. The harassment of Christian missionaries in Jerusalem will be protested at once on the front pages of Christian newspapers and the general press in various parts of the world. The denial of the religious rights of a Protestant or Jew in Spain or in Colombia will become the subject of a consultation within hours in New York or Geneva. The banishment of priests and nuns from Indonesia results in immediate protests from far-flung parts of the world.

From the foregoing I would here summarize three conclusions:

1. A world, teetering on the brink of nuclear destruction, can

little afford the perpetuation of an atmosphere of hatred, division, and suspicion.

2. The human society, both East and West, threatened by moral decay and materialism, needs every human and spiritual resource to meet the overwhelming needs and challenges of our age. Repressive, mutually antagonistic religious, racial, and ethnic group conflicts will paralyze mankind in its effort to meet the challenges of survival. The monopolies and hegemonies of the past must give way to a global pluralism in which, in the words of Pope John's *Pacem in Terris,* "the universal common good, that is, the common good of the entire human family" is promoted.

3. Religion itself will be irrelevant if it continues to perpetuate the glaring contradiction between preaching high moral principles of love, sympathy, and charity, and allowing the undisciplined practice of the opposite in the forms of race prejudice, anti-Semitism, anti-Catholicism, anti-Protestantism, and other ethnocentric blasphemies.

THEOLOGICAL AND HISTORICAL FACTORS

"Are the churches (and synagogues) exerting even as much as 10 percent of the influence which they could—or should—be exerting in the fields of peace and social justice? Are they tooled for such a task by intention, declaration, organization, program, finance, staff?"

E. Raymond Wilson of the Friends Committee on National Legislation posed this question in his article, "Are We Serious about Social Action?" (*The Christian Century,* February 10, 1965). On the basis of a sampling of Protestant denominational social action, Wilson comes to several striking and chastening conclusions (which, I would argue, are virtually applicable without much qualification to that of the Catholic and Jewish communities as well). First, "through the past two decades there has been considerable growth in church social action programs at national, state, and local levels, but that growth has been slight in comparison with the many opportunities available for effective action." For example, Mr. Wilson writes, "What is needed now is enlightened and continued support, backed by testimony that is competent, relevant, and effectively presented, of such objectives as wider development of United Nations operations; more far-reaching steps toward disarmament; enlarged but more discriminating mutual aid and technical assistance projects to overcome world hunger, ignorance, disease, and poverty; and expansion of programs for population control. Such issues get no appreciable supporting mail from churchmen, in contrast to the stream of letters inspired by the isolationists, the 'fright peddlers' and others who would have our national concern limited to the part of the human race labeled 'American.'" He adds that in the area of negotiations dealing with the ending of the spiraling arms race, "it is disheartening that, so far as I know, no religious organization has a full-time staff person dealing with disarmament problems."

Secondly, "There is with all of us a temptation to confuse resolutions and pronouncements with social action. Such statements do serve to register a certain degree of consensus, but they are not self-executing."

Thirdly, an appraisal committee of the National Council of Churches' Division of Christian Life and Work has reported that "only one-third of the member churches have assigned full-time staff members to the specific task of supplying local congregations with pertinent information and helping them engage in social action endeavors." He asks: "How can we hope to achieve goals as disarmament, world peace, or racial justice when the average church member's annual sacrifice to keep his denomination at work in those areas on the national level is no greater than his expenditure for one candy bar, one soft drink?"

How does one explain such relatively limited action on social issues? Mr. Wilson seeks to offer several reasons. One is financial: "yet throughout the nation expensive new buildings are being constructed by congregations whose social budgets are starved for funds or are nonexistent." Another is the fact that "conservative boards and ecclesiastical hierarchies" are frequently unwilling to approve new endeavors that compete for funds and attention with entrenched programs." A third reason is "theological," and he explains it in these words: "For far too many, Christian religion is merely a personal matter having no relation to the unsolved problems of national and international life. If a wider horizon exists, it is likely to be confined to the foreign mission enterprise;

if ethical concerns intrude, they are often limited to the effect on the public of smoking, gambling, and drinking." Related to that, he adds, is the view that "the church shouldn't 'get into politics.' Lobbying is something nice people don't do . . . The church should stay out of controversy."

At the very heart of the question of the relation of the church and synagogue to social action is the theological and philosophical issue of the orientation of the religious traditions to the world. A good deal of the behavior of the religious communities in response to contemporary social challenges can be understood primarily in light of theological positions whose origins stem back to the foundations of the faith communities.

In his perceptive study, *Christ and Culture* (New York: Harper Collins, 1952), H. Richard Niebuhr set forth the five main ways in which Christians have understood the relationship between the church and the world: Christ against culture (e.g., Tertullian); Christ of culture (e.g., Locke, Ritschl, Barton); Christ above culture (e.g., Thomas Aquinas); Christ and culture in paradox (e.g., Luther); and Christ the transformer of culture (e.g., the "conversionism" of F. D. Maurice).

Thus, four of these historic formulae involve a separation of religion from the public domain—if not a separation, then certainly a primary emphasis on personal salvation or otherworldly concerns. The views of St. Augustine are most frequently cited as the proof texts of the classic Christian view that the ideal world is always above and not at the end of human history.

"Two loves," says St. Augustine in *De Civitate Dei*, "have made two cities, love of self unto contempt of God, the Earthly City; love of God unto contempt of self, the Heavenly City," the City of God. The *Civitas Dei* is a "mystical society" of all the elect, past, present, and future. The *Civitas Terrena*, the Earthly City, is identical neither with the earthly State, nor with any particular earthly State such as the Roman Empire, nor with any merely human society; it too is a "mystical society," that of the impious, the damned.

In an essay on "Aspects of Medieval Thought on Church and State," Gerhart B. Ladner (*The Image of Man in Medieval Art* [Latrobe, PA: The Archabbey Press, 1965]) writes: "St. Augustine's concept of the City of God is a specifically Christian ideal of community life . . . It is only natural that notions of such perfection as that of the City of God or of the Church itself which in one of its aspects is 'the only human society engaged in building the City of God' tended to depreciate the state as conceived by pre-Christian antiquity. St. Augustine is indifferent towards the state as community and territory." Ladner adds that Augustine's view was "rather generally held in the patristic period and was an important factor in the development of early medieval political theory."

An eminent Protestant church historian, A. C. McGiffert, in his introduction to *Protestant Thought Before Kant*,[1] traces mainstream Christian ideas about human nature and temporal society back to the teachings of St. Paul.

The theological system of the Middle Ages was, in its controlling principles, as old as the Apostle Paul. He was led by his own experience to draw a sharp distinction between the fleshly man, who is essentially corrupt, and the spiritual man, who is essentially holy. The one is natural, the other supernatural. The one is doomed to destruction; the other is an heir of eternal life. The spiritual man does not come from the natural by a process of development and growth, but is a new creature born directly from above. Wherever Paul may have got the suggestion which led him to interpret his experience in this way, his low estimate of man and his contrast between flesh and spirit revealed the ultimate influence of Oriental dualism which was profoundly affecting the Hellenistic world of the day. A sense of moral evil, a conviction of human corruption and helplessness, and a recognition of the worthlessness of the present world were becoming more and more common, and men everywhere were looking for aid and comfort to supernatural powers of one kind or another. The later Platonism, from which the theological thinking of the great fathers chiefly drew its sustenance, was completely under the sway of this spirit.

With the traditional view of human nature was correlated the notion of the present world as evil, sharing in the curse of man and doomed to destruction as he is. To escape from it was the one great aim of the serious-minded man. Salvation meant not the

---

[1] A. C. McGiffert, *Protestant Thought Before Kant* (New York: Harper and Row, 1963), 24.

salvation of the world itself, its transformation into something better and holier, but release from it in order to enjoy the blessedness of another world altogether. The dominant spirit was that of other-worldliness. To be a Christian meant to belong to another sphere than this, to have one's interest set on higher things, to live in the future, and to eschew the pleasures and enjoyments of the present. Asceticism was the Christian ideal of life.

The practical implication of this theological worldview, according to McGiffert, was that "social service on a large scale was postponed to modern times." It was not a mere accident that this was so, he explains; "rather, it was because of an altogether different ideal, and an altogether different estimate of the present world."

The emergence of Protestantism, particularly in a certain tradition of Martin Luther's teaching, it would seem, represented a radical break with this line of Pauline and Catholic teaching. Luther's conception of salvation as being wholly a matter of divine forgiveness (man is saved by faith and not by works, as developed in *The Liberty of the Christian Man*) led to the belief that the Christian is free from the necessity of earning his salvation by engaging in particular religious practices and performing works of special merit; this, in turn, also meant the sacredness of all callings, even the most secular and the most humble, and the possibility of serving God in worldly profession, business and trade as truly as in monastery and priesthood.

> It looks like a great thing when a monk renounces everything and goes into a cloister, carries on a life of asceticism, fasts, watches, prays, etc. . . . On the other hand, it looks like a small thing when a maid cooks and cleans and does other homework. But because God's command is there, even such a small work must be praised as a service of God far surpassing the holiness and asceticism of all monks and nuns. For here there is no command of God. But there God's command is fulfilled, that one should honor father and mother and help in the care of the home (Luther's *Primary Works* V, p. 100, as quoted by McGiffert).

But Luther, a complicated man, often contradicted himself, and his views on the relation of salvation to moral and ethical responsibility were no exception. The Protestant historian McGiffert quotes Luther's contradiction as it appeared in his essay,

Against Latomus, "As wrath is a greater evil than the corruption of sin, so grace is a greater good than the perfect righteousness which we have said comes from faith. For there is no one who would not prefer (if this could be) to be without perfect righteousness than without the grace of God." McGiffert observes: "It was a religion and not an ethical motive which controlled him; not to attain moral purity, but to be on good terms with God was the supreme need of his being. To claim that the Protestant Reformation was due primarily to ethical considerations, and was the result of dissatisfaction with the moral state of the world, and of the desire to raise the moral tone of society, is nothing less than a travesty upon the facts."

John Calvin, the great formulator of the Reformed theology whose *Institutes of the Christian Religion* (1536) became "the theological textbook of all Western Protestantism," was even more rigorous than Luther in conceiving of man in terms of his "corruption and depravity" as a correlative of his doctrine of unconditional predestination and God's omnipotent will. As Calvin says in his *Institutes* (Book 3, chapter 9), "With whatever kind of tribulation we may be afflicted, we should always keep this end in view, to habituate ourselves to a contempt of the present life that we may thereby be excited to meditation on that which is to come."[2] "There is no medium between these two extremes, either the earth must become vile in our estimation, or it must retain our immoderate love. Wherefore if we have any concern about eternity, we must use our most diligent efforts to extricate ourselves from these fetters."[3]

Protestant scholasticism as expressed in the *Formula of Concord* (1580), which was widely adopted as the official doctrinal standard of the Lutheran churches, served to stereotype this view of human nature and the negative relation of religion to life. As in all Scholasticism, according to McGiffert, the importance of a

---

[2] *Triple Revolution,* Information Service, Department of Research, National Council of Churches, New York, May 22, 1965.

[3] Cf. *The Challenge to Change* by Abbé François Houtart (New York: Sheed & Ward, Inc., 1964) for an excellent summary of global change from a sociological and religious perspective; also my articles: "The New Realities," in *Worldview* magazine, published by the Council on Religion and International Affairs, 170 East 64 St., New York, N.Y.; "Confronting the New Realities of the Nuclear-Space Age," *Sister Formation Bulletin* 10, no. 2, (winter 1963–64).

particular doctrine came to depend upon its place in the closed system rather than upon its practical relation to life.

In response to the rigidities of Scholasticism, the emphasis upon formal orthodoxy, the absorption of leading churchmen in theological controversies, and also in reaction to the depressed religious and moral life that ensued on the heels of the Thirty Years' War (1618–48), there emerged in Germany under the advocacy of Philip Jacob Spener (1633–1705) the Pietist movement that became a dominant force in German religious life down to the eighteenth century, even influencing the reconstruction of theology at the beginning of the nineteenth century. Both in his organization of Bible reading groups, commonly known as *collegia pietatis,* and in his introduction to the mystical work, *Pia Desideria,* Spener emphasized the practical nature of Christianity, which consists not in the knowledge, but in the conduct and, particularly, in the exercise of mutual love and service. Spener, an orthodox Lutheran, insisted that personal piety, the bent of the heart and life, the feelings and will at the expense of the intellect, personal faith, and growth in Christian perfection were more important than doctrinal soundness.

Spener interpreted Christian conduct in otherworldly terms. His ideal was not, as with Luther, victory over the world, but escape from it. Piety was to show itself in devotion to spiritual and supernatural things, and in the transfer of affection and interest from this world to another. As McGiffert profiles the movement: "The pietism of Spener and his followers was essentially medieval in its estimate of man and the world. Distrust of human nature and despair of the salvability of society were both characteristic of it. Salvation meant escape from an evil world for a few elect souls who banded together for spiritual communion and mutual edification, and these elect souls were not the Christian Church but a small circle within the larger body."

The vitalizing of Christian piety, the breaking of Scholasticism's control, the recognition of religious experience as the chief basis of theology, the emphasis of the will instead of the intellect in religion, the prominence given to the emotions, above all the individualism given to the whole movement and its hostility to ecclesiasticism, sacramentarianism, and sacerdotalism, meant much for days to come. Pietism was one of the forces that brought the modern age in the religious life of Germany.

Without succumbing to the temptation of employing history as the "imperialism of the present," one can understand the warrant which justified Franklin Littell, in his examination of the moral collapse of the Lutheran churches under Nazism, to conclude that "a sentimental and degenerate personal piety pervaded the established churches of Europe, secure in the stagnant swamp of culture-religion."[4]

German pietism, in turn, influenced English Evangelicalism through the impact of the Moravians on John Wesley (1738), founder of British Methodism. Calvinist and Arminian evangelicalism, through Wesley communions and the preaching of Wesley's associate, George Whitefield, influenced the New England theology of America, especially through the revivalist activity of Jonathan Edwards. Like the German pietists, the Evangelicals were ascetic in their tendency. Their ideal was to live with heart set constantly upon the future, and natural human interest in the present world was condemned as irreligious. "Friendship with the world," Wesley said, "is spiritual adultery." But, as church historian McGiffert points out:

> The Evangelicals were not as consistent and thoroughgoing as their medieval prototypes; they did not advocate retirement from the world and seclusion in a monastery. But they denounced many of the ordinary pursuits and pleasures of society, commonly looked upon as indifferent matters, and insisted that they ought to be eschewed by the Christian. Card-playing, dancing, gaming, horse-racing, theater-going, elaborate dressing, and frivolity of all kinds came in for most vigorous condemnation. To be a Christian very commonly meant above all to turn one's back upon such employments. Thus there grew up an externality of religion and an artificiality of practice even more complete than anything witnessed in medieval Catholicism.[5]

Both in England and in the United States (in the former under the impact of the industrial revolution and in the latter under the

---

[4] For an insightful analysis of revivalism and its relation to nativism and American political pietism in the form of radical-right movements, see Franklin Littell, *From State Church to Pluralism*.

[5] McGiffert, *Protestant Thought Before Kant*, 168.

force of pressures exerted by a frontier society) evangelicals and revivalists did not overlook responsibility for the welfare of one's fellows. Love and service were an important part of Christian virtue, and the evangelicals gave themselves to humanitarian and social labor on a large scale and with great effectiveness. It meant much for the future that not rationalists, and deists, and unbelievers alone were fired with a growing enthusiasm for humanity, but that the great representatives of a revived Christianity shared the same spirit.

This survey of some of the theological factors which have helped shape the contemporary stance of religious communities toward the social order has concentrated mainly thus far on the Hellenic, that is, Platonic, dualistic element in Christian tradition. But there has been another formative influence at work, namely, the Hebraic, which requires comment.

In an essay entitled, "The Present Heritage of the Long Encounter between Christian Faith and Western Civilization," Reinhold Niebuhr asserts that "the civilization of Europe has been created by a culture in which the Christian faith has been a chief component." Among the "distinctive qualities" which he regards as "possible ultimate causes of unique aspects of European culture," Professor Niebuhr cites three that have their origins in Jewish religious thought and tradition:

1. The hazardous affirmation that history is meaningful and the temporal process is not merely a corruption of the eternal.

2. The emphasis on the value and dignity of the life of the individual and the equally important affirmation that the unique freedom of the individual is the source of evil as well as of virtue. [Niebuhr cites Pascal's phrase of "the grandeur and misery of man" as affirming Augustinian realism as reflected in the emphasis that "the freedom of the self is the root of both the creative and the destructive possibilities of human action."]

3. The attitude toward the whole temporal process, which is not regarded as divine (as in systems of cosmic pantheism), or as evil or illusory because it is not divine (as in systems of acosmic pantheism), the Hebraic component of Western culture contributed this sober attitude toward the temporal and the natural, making it possible for Western man to regard nature, in Santaya-

na's phrase, as "man's stamping ground and system of opportunities."

In *Moral Man and Immoral Society* (New York: Charles Scribner's Sons, 1932), Niebuhr elaborates his view:

> It was the peculiar genius of Jewish religious thought that it conceived the millennium in this-worldly terms . . . Whenever religion concerns itself with the problems of society, it always gives birth to some kind of millennial hope, from the perspective of which present social realities are convicted of inadequacy, and courage is maintained to continue in the effort to redeem society of injustice. The courage is needed, for the task of building a just society seems always to be a hopeless one when only realities and immediate possibilities are envisaged.

In his Harvard essay, Niebuhr observes that the Jewish idea of the Messiah, "the hope in a future fulfillment of history in which, under a Messianic king, power and virtue would be perfectly coordinated, was the most potent . . . of the various solutions to the problems of historical meaninglessness." He adds, however, that "the radical transformation by New Testament faith of Old Testament messianism was one of the two greatest revisions of the Hebraic faith (the other being the emphasis on grace, rather than law, as a saving power). The revision was expressed in viewing the Messianic fulfillment in the crucified Christ, rather than in the triumphant Messiah," and this view assumed "a perennial variance, even contradiction, between historical achievements and the divine."

But this radical revision, Niebuhr observes, did not completely suppress the original messianic or eschatological vision. The early church was dominated by the imminent *parousia* of the promised triumphant Messiah, at the price, says Niebuhr, of the lack of a responsible attitude toward all the proximate solutions of the communal problems of a sinful world. He continues: "An historical religion must have the tension supplied by an eschatological vision. But the vision must not be so pure or so determined as to destroy responsibility for proximate goals, a fact which Karl Barth evidently does not understand."

From the point of view of Jewish concerns about the social order, this tendency of Christian thought toward a "neutralism" or irresponsibility for historic tasks in this world has been one of the fundamental departures from the prophetic view, and has stood in radical contrast to a mainline emphasis in Judaism. In the judgment of Rabbi Abraham Joshua Heschel, there has been a tendency on the part of Christian theologians to affirm mystery at the expense of history, but Christianity is both proclamation and event.

It may be worthwhile to recall that the characteristic Jewish experience of God is the awareness of His presence in human events. Every aspect of the Jewish tradition is pervaded by the memory of His redemptive act in the exodus from Egypt. Almost the whole of the religious calendar is an act of recalling the past experience of the Jewish people as a record of God's relationship to it. The emphasis of Jewish faith is therefore neither on metaphysical speculation nor on dogma, but on human action. Life is the arena of moral choice, and man can choose the good. He can make himself worse than the beast or he can ascend to but little lower than the angels. Every man plays his role, for good or ill, in the redemptive history of mankind, for man is God's partner in the work of creation. In *Imitatio Dei,* the Jew is obligated to seek justice and pursue it, to care for the widow and orphan and the stranger at the gate.[6]

This is not to say that rabbinic Judaism denies dualism altogether. The concept of the *yetzer hara* (the evil inclination) in constant tension with the *yetzer tov* (the good inclination in man's nature), of Kodesh (holiness) and of *chol* (this-worldliness) are intimations of a recognition of the *homo duplex.* But it is characteristic of rabbinic thought that these are *experienced* as "value-Concepts" by the individual alone or in community, rather than "congealed in a static, hierarchical system of thought."

The growth of involvement in social action on the part of the Christian community has, indeed, been a radical response to external forces of the twentieth century, such as those elaborated earlier in this chapter: population explosion, anxieties of the nu-

---

[6] For a fuller development of the basic ideas, values, and religious life of Jews and Judaism, see *Judaism* by Rabbi Arthur Hertzberg (published by George Braziller), *The Rabbinic Mind* by Rabbi Max Kadushin (published by Jewish Theological Seminary Press), and *The Prophets* by Rabbi Abraham J. Heschel (published by Harper and Row).

clear space age, Communism, emerging new nations, resurgent Oriental religions, secularism, and pluralism. But it owes whatever deeper meaning it possesses to interior forces at work in the life of Christianity and Christendom, namely, the biblical, liturgical and theological renewals. In its concerted effort to recover the Hebrew mode of thought by restoring the Scriptures to a more central place in study and worship, the church has moved decisively to overcome the bifurcating and "abstractifying" of life that was one of the byproducts of Scholasticism.

The emphasis in Vatican Council II's schema on *De Ecclesia* (On the Nature of the Church) which speaks of the Catholic Church ("while on earth it journeys in a foreign land away from the Lord . . . like an exile") and its conception of itself as "the people of God" related providentially to "Israel according to the flesh" finds resonance in the non-Catholic ear.

Especially compelling have been the declarations of several council fathers at the Ecumenical Council during the third session as they discussed Schema 13, "The Church and the Modern World." Bishop Remi Joseph De Roo of Victoria, British Columbia, said, "Christians achieve their total vocation when they engage themselves in the structures of the world, share in its struggles and commune with the inner dynamism of humanity. A Christian must immerse himself in the world. He dare not consider himself as foreign to or above the world, belonging to a church which condescendingly imparts gifts reserved to her by God alone."

The late Cardinal Meyer of blessed memory, whom I was privileged to know both in connection with my work as program chairman of the National Conference on Religion and Race as well as in Rome during the third Council session in September 1964, in commenting on Schema 13, said that he missed in the draft "a sound theological basis for joyful acceptance of the world and a correction of the false dualism which would separate soul and body, the church from the world, spirit from matter." In essence, said Cardinal Meyer, all creation goes together. Men must realize that their daily work is a part of the plan of salvation. The Redemption was total. It was not a snatching of man's blithe spirit from the weight of his body, nor did it imply a hopeless break between the world of the spirit and world of flesh, matter and physical energy. In the divine economy, redemption meant much more than the salvation of souls; it meant also the resurrection of bodies and indeed the resurrection of the universe itself.

That this reorientation of the church toward the world and its values is profound, more than a matter of perfunctory or isolated ecclesiastical statements, is reflected in a survey of current Catholic and Protestant theological thought contained in an article by Thomas E. Clark, S.J. (*America*, May 29, 1965), whose subtitle significantly is: "Christian secularity finds positive values outside the institutional Church." Father Clark identified the two movements of modern Christian thought, immanence and secularity, as today "coming into vital confrontation in our effort to adopt a new Christian posture before the world and its values."

Citing the contributions of such Catholic thinkers as Maurice Blondel, Henri de Lubac, Hans Urs von Balthasar, Karl Rahner, Jacques Maritain, Pere Chenu, E. Schillebeeckx, and John Courtney Murray, as well as of such Protestant thinkers as Dietrich Bonhoeffer, John Robinson, Paul Van Buren, and Harvey Cox, Father Clark stresses that "for over a half century now . . . the insistence has been on the *unity* rather than on the distinction of natural and Supernatural orders, the immanence of the Christian in the human (rather than on its transcendence of the human)." In a revelatory exploration of the meaning of "secularity" for modern Christianity, Father Clark makes many assertions that will startle conventional ears, but what he affirms has a greater ring of relevance than has been heard for a very, very long time from religious quarters: Christian secularity excludes instrumentalization. The goodness of the creature (and not merely its non-evilness), of the world, of time and temporal institutions, is a central conviction of Christian secularity. Any purely instrumental approach to the world—that is, any attitude that would see in it merely a tool for Christian evangelization, that would neglect its innate values, its own immanent dynamisms and finalities—is incompatible with Christian secularity. The world is to be taken seriously. As Father Robert Johann has put it: "Whatever ultimate meaning life may have . . . life is a call to share in the world's making."

Why do I, and probably a great many other Jews, welcome this profound reorientation in Christianity and Christians? First—and I must ask you to indulge me here if this smacks of Jewish triumphalism, but you will grant that two millennia of "grandeur and misery" in the diaspora is a long time to wait—the very Jewishness of Christendom's posture today seems to confirm the mission of the Jews to serve as a light unto the nations. Perhaps all our witnessing across the millennia to the Covenant and to the mandates of the Prophets is getting through after all. More seriously, it helps make sense and give reality to the teachings of Maimonides and other Jewish sages who regarded Christians (and Muslims) as the missionary outreach of Judaism, charged by Providence to bring the idea of God and of obedience to His word to the heathen of the world.

Secondly, in light of their history, Jews have a special stake in a peaceful social order, in concretizing justice and freedom. The Catholic Church, and many Protestant bodies, have become major agencies of social reform. As citizens of the Western world, Jews see themselves increasingly as allies with their Catholic (and Protestant) neighbors in social reconstruction.

Thirdly, involvement in social action is providing Jews and Judaism with new opportunities of service beyond their own group. This is a test of our Prophetic universalism. Heretofore, Jews have been preoccupied with helping to defeat the Nazis and Fascists, rescuing refugees, building and securing the State of Israel, combating anti-Semitism (which still preoccupies our community for we are deeply concerned about anti-Semitic discrimination in Soviet Russia and in parts of Latin America).[7] As these problems have diminished, Jews have become increasingly free to make contributions to the resolution of problems that are not specifically Jewish—problems such as are related to race relations, the war against poverty, and international affairs. In this sense, Rabbi Louis Finkelstein has formulated this challenge: "Our ancient teachers were right in their admonition that there is a great contribution to be made only by those without power, who are few in number, always a minority, uncertain of their ability to meet alone

---

[7] Cf. *CIF Reports*, studies of developmental programs in Latin America published by the Center for Intercultural Formation, Cuernevaca, Mexico, under the direction of Msgr. Ivan Illich. Also *Profile of Latin America*, a Protestant analysis by Dr. Stanley Rycroft, research specialist on Latin America for the National Council of Churches, New York, N.Y.

the challenges of the world . . . We are a pledge to remind the world of its true goal."

RELIGION AND SOCIETY: DILEMMA AND POSSIBILITIES

The context in which the present shape of social action is being forged is that of a voluntaristic society within which the Federal Government is assuming ever-increasing initiatives and responsibilities in the achievement of social-welfare purposes. Prescinding from the debate over whether this is good or bad for America, it is one of the overarching facts of the life in our nation that the government, in building the "Great Society," is calling upon voluntary agencies (conceived as large blocs of influence over substantial constituencies) in order to help advance the goals of health, education, welfare, civil, and human rights. Religion, along with labor, business, farm, and education, is unblinkingly conceived of as another of the major blocs. This development has obvious advantages for "religion," for it means that religious institutions are taken into serious account in the affairs of our nation. At the same time, this development brings the church and synagogue face to face with acute predicaments.

The first dilemma centers on bureaucracy. In an age of bureaucracies, can a group of "amateurs," joined in small units, still be heard? If the answer is no, the trend toward bureaucratization of the church and synagogue would seem to be justified. But when these institutions become just one more bureaucracy, will they say anything worth hearing? Bureaucracy can threaten religion with impersonalism, and when the church and synagogue fall victims to impersonalism, the vitality of society and one of the chief sources of a nation's moral strength is affected.

The second dilemma involves the use of power by religious groups. The individual is guided by the higher ethics of selflessness in personal relations; but social cooperation requires coercion. Social organization is structured power, for, as Reinhold Niebuhr has pointed out, "only a romanticist of purest water could maintain that the national group ever arrives at a 'common mind' or 'general will' without the use of force or the threat of force." However, "power is poison," as Henry Adams has said—a poison that blinds the eyes of moral insight and lames the will of moral purpose. The church and synagogue can forswear all use of power in order to remain true to a biblical and prophetic imperative. But this would render their efforts ineffectual in the social order and may contribute to anarchy or to a moral order based on naked power. (Most forms of social order are better than anarchy, and an order only partly imbued with morality is better than one of no morality at all.) Or the church and synagogue can seek power for the sake of the prophetic imperative which demands realization; however, they must recognize the real possibility of becoming compromised in the use of that power. Religious motivation is no protection against such compromise. Experience shows, in fact, that power, wielded in the name of God, is subject to special perversions, one of the most destructive of which is the fanaticism "occasioned by attributing ultimate validity to historically relative norms, purposes, and ends." The only palliative for either religious fanaticism or the secular fanaticism of political religions, as Niebuhr points out in his Harvard essay, "is an open society, as it has developed in the last three centuries, which grants no immunity from criticism or review to any authority proclaiming the truth, whether in the political, the religious, or the scientific realm."[8]

This discussion raises a number of basic questions for which there are no easy answers and which have not yet been adequately examined by church and synagogue leaders. For example, what are the theological justifications for the involvement of the *corporate* church and synagogue in influencing the public order? And, as indicated above, in what ways are church and synagogue to exercise their power? Are the limitations that we would put on church involvement a result of theological conviction or, rather, of prudential judgment based on certain convictions concerning the nature of the democratic process?

To be specific, if church and synagogue leaders can lobby vigorously—literally buttonhole Congressmen—as they did with such effective strategy for the enactment of the Civil Rights bill, why should they not lobby also for a measure that would curb pornography? If synagogue and other Jewish leaders can threaten con-

---

[8] Harvard Divinity Bulletin (October 1961).

gressmen with the loss of votes on an issue that affects the economic welfare of a Jewish Sabbath-observer or that impinges on the welfare of the State of Israel, is it wrong for a bishop to exercise the same threat on such issues as bus transportation for parochial school children or the revision of the divorce law?

What are the rightful areas and responsibilities of the state and church, together and separately, in their effort to achieve and maintain standards of private and public morality? What is the particular role of the corporate church and synagogue—as against that of the individual clergyman and in contrast to that of the layman—as they seek to make religion a significant force in life? How can the church and synagogue wield their power and yet maintain respect for those of other faiths who differ? How, too, can they wield their power while maintaining respect for those within the faith community who differ with the church or synagogue on those political issues which contain spiritual or religious significance? Where do the political and moral meet? Where do they separate?

As one attempts to respond to what, to this writer, is the most crucial of these questions, namely, the exercise of corporate power by church and synagogue, I would submit that, on the one hand, those committed to the Prophetic tradition cannot escape the responsibility of moralizing power; on the other hand, they must resist all temptations to make a bid for direct power. The religious groups, as I view it, should seek to make effective use of indirect methods of pressure, namely, exhortation and persuasion. Of all the steady contributions which religion makes to American life, its creating of a moral atmosphere and consciousness, within which social and political decisions are made, is more significant than that of supplying the basis for these decisions. It is more a policy of the church and synagogue indirectly shaping a whole pattern of national thinking than of supplying precise doctrines.

Religious institutions made their most significant contributions by remaining true to their vocations as judges of society, as centers of independent criticism insisting that the nation live up to its own ideals and general standards of morality. Churches and synagogues that fail to rebuke people when they worship themselves or fall down before nationalistic idols are, by their own standards, guilty of betrayal. By following the example of those saints and sages who cried out against injustice, complacency, and spiritual torpor, religious spokesmen exercise liberty for the benefit of all. By keeping alive before the nation a sense of the Absolute as man's highest ethical aspiration (which eliminates partial perspectives) and a sense of the Divine as Benevolent Will by condemning selfish actions and desires, so that no position of power in the community remains unchecked, the church and synagogue contribute to justice and to rendering responsible the exercise of every kind of political power.

Toward working out such generalized positions as these in a concrete situation, Dr. Gibson Winter (*Christianity and Crisis,* May 31, 1965) gives a valuable illustration in his article, "The Churches and Community Organization." In a perceptive analysis of "the political character of community organization" whose purpose is to help the dehumanized and impoverished masses of the ghettos to "regain dignity and independence through self-determination," Dr. Winter raises the question of what is "the method of participation appropriate to the situation and to the nature of the Church." One of the conclusions suggested by Dr. Winter is that "the churches have a servant role to fulfill—not leading but encouraging community organization where possible. They also have a prophetic role to play, not letting community organizations settle for token reprisals but pushing on to a new political and cultural vision for metropolis."

At the same time, the nation has a right to expect religious groups, whatever their theological claims, not to impose their special truths on others by special coercion, by use of economic pressures, political threats, boycotts, or blacklists. A religious absolutist position that attempts to translate beliefs into laws or public practices binding on all represents a genuine threat to freedom.

A third problem of critical seriousness is the lack of communication between religious and secular culture. As William Clancy has written in *Religion and American Society* (Santa Barbara, CA: Center for the Study of Democratic Institutions, 1961), "The forces of religion and the forces of liberal culture seem increasingly to be addressing and describing different worlds."[9] Liberal deafness toward theology deprives them of a wealth of humane wisdom; on the other hand, religious leaders often speak in formulas that no longer have meaning for those to whom they are addressed. The absence of communication between religious and liberal culture should be taken as one of the most serious problems of our time. Contrary to the eschatological vision of our Rabbi of Bobruisk (which many religionists share either consciously or unconsciously), the secularistic cycle is not on its way to suicide and will likely be with us for the duration of our civilization.

We are in a new era in man's history, the age of urban secularization, which Harvey Cox describes with shocking power in his book on "technopolis," called *Religion in the Secular City: Toward a Postmodern Theology* (Reprinted, New York: Simon and Schuster, 1984). The secular city (which supersedes not only early tribal society, but also the town culture that has shaped the world since the time of the Greek *polis*) requires not only a renewed message from the church and synagogue, but also a renewed language. "We must not define our 'spiritual' resources too narrowly in traditional religious terms," Reinhold Niebuhr asserted in the UNESCO pamphlet, "Our Moral and Spiritual Resources for the International Order." We cannot forget, he adds, that the very creation of our free society was the joint achievement of religious and secular forces. The American consensus has been kept alive over centuries through combined efforts of the church, law, university, press, and the learned professions.

The secular disciplines, frequently so defective in their ultimate frames of reference, nevertheless provide the discriminating judgments which made it possible for modern man to analyze complex problems of social, economic, and political justice and to puncture the pretensions of religious people who sought to make religious faith an instrument of political power and self-aggrandizement.

---

[9] Cf. *Religion and American Society* issued by the Center for the Study of Democratic Institutions. This section of the paper is much indebted to this and related Center publications.

In summary, the church and synagogue can make effective contributions to America not by putting themselves at the disposal of the nation, or by blessing whatever our society does or hopes to do, but

1. by providing a source of values;
2. by enlightening and inspiring the individual citizen to have courage and patience;
3. by helping the individual and society to become sensitive to the injustices and petty tyrannies that exist in our midst;
4. by providing the individual with motivation for responsible life in our society and with stable standards of moral judgment;
5. by calling men to self-knowledge and personal humility and bidding them to be aware of the unfathomable depths of human personality, keeping the sense of transcendence alive.

7

Vatican II: An Interfaith Appraisal: A Jewish Viewpoint

IT SHOULD BE SAID at the very outset that there is considerable confusion in the use of the term "ecumenical," confusion both within Christendom, as well as confusion between Christianity and Judaism. In its strictest technical sense, the term "ecumenical" applies to relationships among Christians—Catholics, Protestants, and Eastern Orthodox; and the ground of ecumenism is the shared Christology which is particular to Christendom. In this sense it is, therefore, a misnomer and a misapplication of the term "ecumenism" to apply it to relations between Christians and Jews. One can apply it, of course, to Christian-Jewish relations in

In this address to the International Conference on Theological Issues of Vatican II at the University of Notre Dame in March 1966, Marc Tanenbaum presents a major Jewish response to *Nostra Aetate* while also contextualizing the contemporary situation with a sweeping social analysis of American life. The text is reprinted from John H. Miller, ed., *Vatican II: An Interfaith Appraisal* (Notre Dame, IN: University of Notre Dame Press, 1966). At this conference, he joined Catholic theologians like Yves Congar, Karl Rahner, Henri de Lubac, and John Courtney Murray. Among key Protestant attendees were George Lindbeck, Albert Outler, and Robert McAfee Brown. Recalling the disputations and traumas of past centuries, Rabbi Tanenbaum contrasts them with the reasoned and passionate appeals in favor of the text from some "thirty-five cardinals and bishops from around the world" during the heated debate on the text, not missing, however, the equally impassioned screed of one Italian bishop who argued that the Jews really are collectively responsible for Jesus's death. This last failed to gain votes, needless to say, as the "Jewish declaration" passed overwhelmingly. A somewhat revised version of this essay appeared in a book edited by Rabbi A. James Rudin and Eugene J. Fisher, *Twenty Years of Catholic-Jewish Relations* (Mahwah, NJ: Paulist Press, 1986). In that context, Rabbi Tanenbaum gave the substance of the remarks printed here as a counterpoint to a Catholic retrospective by Monsignor George G. Higgins. He also added an extended quotation from the audience with Pope John Paul II in February 1985, at which time the pope acknowledged the significance of the American Jewish Committee and his hopefulness in future joint endeavors. Together with his loving and insightful memoir of Rabbi Heschel, included in the section from the 1980s, this text presents Rabbi Tanenbaum's most thorough analysis of the debates at the Second Vatican Council.

its broadest, most generic sense; but in its authentic theological meaning, it is a term specifically applicable to relations within Christendom. In this application, it deals with the activities of Cardinal Bea's Secretariat relating to the reunion of the "separated brethren." Yet having said that, at the same time one cannot really explore or exhaust the full meaning of what ecumenism means in its ultimate reaches without its application to relations between Christians and Jews, since the Hebrew Bible is the foundation of all monotheism. But for reasons of clarity, it is probably wise and prudential that we use the term "interreligious relationships" to describe the relations between Christianity and Judaism and between Christians and the Jewish people.

It is appropriate, I think, to ask why it is that "the Jewish declaration," introduced at the second session of Vatican II, November 1963, and promulgated [as chapter 4 of *Nostra Aetate*] October 28, 1965, has elicited such widespread universal attention.

As Cardinal Bea said in his *relatio* September 25, at the time of his introduction of the "Jewish declaration,"

> I can only begin with the fact that this Declaration certainly must be counted among the matters in which public opinion has shown the greatest concern. Scarcely any other schema has been written up so much and so widely in the periodicals. . . . Many will judge the Council good or bad by its approval or disapproval of the Declaration.

This decree has engaged the concern and the attention of 2,300 Council Fathers in Rome over a period of three years. It has involved the attention of the Protestant and Orthodox observers. Why is the issue of the relationship of Christianity to Judaism and the practical relations between Christians and Jews on a daily level of such central significance?

It is my thesis that the issue of relations between Christians and Jews has reached the point of ripeness, of maturation, in a way that can be seen analogously in terms of the ripeness and the fullness which relations between the Negro and white societies have reached. The moment of crisis, or the moment of truth, in relations between Negro and white are being tested and resolved to the degree to which we overcome the contradictions between our professions of love, charity, and justice, and our practices

which have often stood in flagrant opposition to our pious verbal-
izations. In the process of being confronted by Negroes with a
challenge to our moral claims, and our negative attitudes and
behavior toward them, we have begun to find it necessary to face
truthfully the fact that we have been dealing with Negroes in the
main as abstractions, as mythic perceptions, but not as real people, not as persons who have a human dignity that demands a
certain response from us as brothers. One of the facts that has
become very clear to us is that we have evaded our moral duties
to the Negro by substituting a series of myths for genuine confrontation. These myths have buffered us from encountering the
reality of the Negro. As we dig beneath the surface of our attitudes
and feelings in all the issues of the civil rights struggle, we find
that in each instance we have developed a mythology that has
crippled us from coming to grips with realities. Thus, we have
told ourselves, literally for 350 years, that Negroes are illiterate;
Negroes have weak family life; Negroes are lazy and unreliable,
and perhaps the most diabolic myth of all, Negroes have a bad
odor.

We have told ourselves that Negroes are illiterate, refusing to
face up to the fact that by the year 1830, every state in the South
had passed a law proscribing Negroes from learning to read or
write because of the fear that literate, educated Negroes would
rise up in rebellion against their white masters, the plantation
barons. And so now we justify our segregation in schools by saying
the Negro never learned to read or write; he is illiterate and therefore he cannot have equal education opportunities. We have broken up Negro families, used Negro women for breeding purposes,
sold them "down the river," destroyed the foundations of Negro
family life, and now we use this as an excuse for saying that Negroes cannot live next door to us because of their family habits.
We have prevented this by saying that they are lazy, shiftless, unreliable. Then we have kept Negroes away from public accommodations because of their supposed "bad odor." But as Gunner
Myrdal said in *The American Dilemma* (New York: Harper and Row,
1962), "This has never prevented us from using Negroes as por-
ters or as people who run our houses for us as maids."

Now in many ways the mythology, the unreality, the capacity to
abstract human relationships and to empty them of solid human

meaning and feeling, finds its analogy in the relations between Christians and Jews. What we have begun to confront in the relationships between Christianity and Judaism and between Christendom and Jewry is the fact that there is a fundamental ambivalence historically and theologically within Christian teaching and with Christian social practice that has never been confronted before in any serious and systematic way in the past nineteen hundred years of the Christian-Jewish encounter. Just as the social revolution of the Negroes today has caused us to confront the race issue in a way that we cannot escape, so certain revolutionary facts of the twentieth century have made the Christian-Jewish confrontation inescapable.

I believe that the Nazi Holocaust and all that that has meant for the Christian conscience, as well as the tremendous needs of a new world of the twentieth century in which Christians and Jews together find themselves increasingly a minority in relation to a non-white, non-Judeo-Christian world, are compelling us to confront the deep realities of the relationship between Christians and Jews. Fundamentally, Christianity has never made up its mind as to where it stands in terms of its common patrimony with Judaism and its daily attitudes and relationships and behavior toward Jews. We find as we look into the history of the Christian-Jewish encounter for the greater part of the past two millennia that there have been teachings and episodes betokening the greatest of mutual respect and esteem between Christians and Jews. Thus, we find in St. Athanasius, one of the early church fathers at the beginning of the fourth century, who said that "the Jews are the great school of the knowledge of God and the spiritual life of all mankind." St. Jerome, who lived in the fifth century and who spent forty years in Palestine where, in Caesarea with Jewish scholars and biblical authorities, he studied the Holy Scriptures and the Masoretic traditions—and from whom he obtained insights on which he based his translation of the Scriptures into the Vulgate—declared that "the Jews were divinely preserved for a purpose worthy of God."

This side of the affirmative attitude of the Church toward the Jews reflected the tradition of St. Paul in Romans 9 to 11, which speaks of Christians being engrafted onto the olive tree of Israel (11:7) planted by God. This tradition also found expression in positive behavior of popes even in the Middle Ages. Thus Callistus II issued a bull in 1120 beginning with the words *Sicut Judaeis* in which he strongly condemned the forced baptism of Jews, acts of violence against their lives and property, and the desecration of synagogues and Jewish cemeteries. Gregory IX issued the bull *Etsi Judeorum* in 1233 in which he demanded that the Jews in Christian countries desire to be treated with the same humanity as that with which Christians desire to be treated in heathen lands.

Side by side with that tradition there existed a tradition of hostility and contempt which the late French historian, Professor Jules Isaac, has written about in his various studies. This tradition was perhaps most explicitly embodied in the eight sermons of St. John Chrysostom, who in the year 387, spoke from the pulpits of the city of Antioch to the first congregations of early Gentiles who became Christians, saying:

> I know that a great number of the faithful have for the Jews a certain respect and hold their ceremonies in reverence. This provokes me to eradicate completely such a disastrous opinion. I have already brought forward that the synagogue is worth no more than the theatre . . . it is a place of prostitution. It is a den of thieves and a hiding place of wild animals . . . not simply of animals but of impure beasts . . . God has abandoned them. What hope of salvation have they left? They say that they too worship God but this is not so. None of the Jews, not one of them is a worshipper of God. . . . Since they have disowned the Father, crucified the Son and rejected the Spirit's help, who would dare to assert that the synagogue is not a home of demons! God is not worshiped there. It is simply a house of idolatry. . . . The Jews live for their bellies, they crave for the goods of this world. In shamelessness and greed they surpass even pigs and goats. . . . The Jews are possessed by demons, they are handed over to impure spirits. . . . Instead of greeting them and addressing them as much as a word, you should turn away from them as from a pest and a plague of the human race.

Now, if one enters into the historic background and the context within which St. John Chrysostom made these remarks, perhaps one can understand a little better—one can explain if not excuse—what led St. John Chrysostom to make these anti-Jewish remarks. It may be useful to take a moment to observe that the church in the first four centuries of this era was struggling for its existence as an autonomous, independent faith community. In the minds of the Roman Empire the early Christians represented another Jewish sect. Judaism was the *religio licita* (a favored religion), and for early Christians to achieve any status, including the right to conduct Christian ceremonials, they had to come as Jews to achieve recognition from the Romans. And so the early church fathers found it necessary to separate Christians from the Jews. The early Christians felt very close to Jews; observed their Sabbath on the Jewish Sabbath, their Easter on the Jewish Passover. At the time of the Council of Elvira (ca. 300) many Christians in Spain thought the Jews had a special charism as the People of God and therefore invited them to bless their fields so that they would be fruitful. To separate Christians from their associations with Judaism, to create a sense of autonomy and independence for Christianity, apparently in the wisdom of the early church fathers it became necessary to embark on a drastic effort to break the bonds between church and synagogue and to give Christians a consciousness of difference from the Jews. In the process of this disidentification, however, the pattern of anti-Jewish attitudes and of anti-Jewish behavior became so entrenched, that by the time the church became the established religion of the Roman Empire, these attitudes were reflected increasingly in ecclesiastical legislation. These laws subsequently led to the establishment of ghettoes, the forcing of Jews to wear yellow hats and badges, and in general, this legislation reduced Jews to the status of pariahs throughout the Roman Empire. As the church became the major institution integrating the whole of medieval society, the perception of the Jew within medieval Christendom became the perception of the Jew within Western culture and civilization.

Lest one think that these attitudes are mainly of academic or historic interest, one needs to confront the following facts. A prominent Catholic educator has recently traveled around this country to various Christian seminaries and universities, to speak of the new understanding between Christians and Jews. As she sought to elaborate her thesis of the historical and theological factors that helped shape the conception of the Jew in the Western world, she received many questions from students at the end of her lectures. These are some of the questions that were asked of her by students in Catholic and Protestant seminaries and universities, and also on some secular campuses:

> If the Jewish people did not kill Christ, who did?
>
> You said that the high priest and the elders and not the Jewish people had a share of responsibility in Jesus's condemnation. That is not true. The gospel says the people clamored for his death.
>
> I am a Catholic and I know what I have been taught when I went to catechism, and that is that the Jews killed Christ. This is what my church teaches. I don't like it. I have several friends who are Jewish, but what can I do? I have to believe my church.
>
> Don't you think that in this country we are antagonistic to Jews because they are too successful in business?
>
> Why are all Jews rich?
>
> Why are the Jews better than anyone else in business?
>
> I have heard it said that Hitler had to do what he did because the Jews held all the money in Germany.

The St. Louis University study, in its examination of Catholic parochial school textbooks, found that there are echoes and resonances of this tradition of contempt in materials used even to this day. Thus, for example, to cite some of the teachings that have an unerring echo from the teachings of St. John Chrysostom, it is written in some of the religious textbooks studied by Sr. Rose Albert [Rose Thering, O.P.]:

> The Jews wanted to disgrace Christ by having him die on the cross.
>
> Show us that the Jews did not want Pilate to try Christ but to give permission for his death.
>
> When did they decide to kill Christ?
>
> The Jews as a nation refused to accept Christ and since that time they have been wandering on the earth without a temple or a sacrifice and without the Messiah.

The findings of the Yale University Divinity School study, published in book form as *Faith and Prejudice* (New Haven: Yale University Press, 1963) by Dr. Bernhard E. Olson, have revealed analogous results in some of the denominational textbooks used in Protestantism. There have been significant revisions, as well as improved portrayals of Jews and Judaism, in Catholic and Protestant teaching materials since the publication of the St. Louis and Yale studies. Nevertheless, there is still a heavy residuum from the polemical histories of the past in far too many textbooks, and, above all, in sermons, religious radio broadcasts, seminary manuals, bible commentaries, liturgical missals, catechisms, passion plays, and, in fact, in the daily attitudes of many professing Christians.

These studies, which are of interest, I think, to people who have professional religious and educational responsibilities, do not begin, however, to make us aware of the consequence of these generations of teachings in terms of the impact they have had on the attitudes toward Jews in Western society and culture. These views which began in a theological and religious matrix have penetrated into the marrow of Western civilization and continue to influence the Western world's attitudes toward Jews to this very moment.

When you go home to your studies, if you will open any unabridged dictionary and look up the definition of a Jew, you will find the following:

> *Webster's Universal Dictionary:* "Jew—to cheat in trade; as to Jew one out of a horse. To practice cheating in trade; as he is said to Jew. To Jew down."
>
> *Funk and Wagnalls:* "Jew—(slang) to get the better of in a bargain; overreach: referring to the proverbial keenness of Jewish traders."
>
> *Merriam Webster:* "Jew—adjective, Jewish, usually taken to be offensive. Jew—verb, to cheat by sharp business practice, usually taken to be offensive. Jew—noun, a person believed to drive a hard bargain."

Contrast this with the dictionary's definition of "Christian":

> *Webster's Universal Dictionary:* "Christian—colloquial, a decent, civilized, or presentable person, characteristic of the Christian people, kindly."

If one looks at the general social reality in terms of the way the Jew is perceived by and large (with significant changes in recent years growing out of greater contact with each other), one finds, for example, a striking double standard of evaluation of the behavior of the Christian and the Jew in the world of commerce. When a Jewish businessman is successful in a given business or industry, in the parlor rooms and in the bars where the "man-to-man talk" is made (and all of us have heard this enough to know that it is true and not a figment of one's imagination), one hears the "explanation": "Well, he's a Jew." There's something sharp, there's something cunning about his practices. It is the Jewishness of the man that leads to his success. But if a Christian or a Gentile engaged in the same industry, using virtually the same business practices, achieves the same kind of success, then in the American mythos this is the result of "Yankee ingenuity." This is living out the Horatio Alger myth of rags to riches in American life. It is a consequence of living out the "Puritan ethic."

One must confront ultimately how as recently as the past twenty-five years in a country—which, when it vaunted its great values and its great moral traditions, spoke of itself as a country of ancient Christian culture, which was in fact the seat of the Holy Roman Empire for almost a millennium beginning with Charlemagne—it was possible for millions of Christians to sit by as spectators while millions of human beings, who were their brothers and sisters, the sons of Abraham according to the flesh, were carted out to their death in the most brutal, inhuman, uncivilized ways. And one must confront as one of the terrible facts of history of this period, the conversation that took place between Adolf Hitler and two bishops in April 1933, when they began raising questions about the German policy toward the Jews and Hitler said to them, as reported in the book, *Hitler's Table-Talk* (London: Weidenfeld and Nicolson, 1973), that he was simply completing what Christian teaching and preaching had been saying about the Jews for the better part of 1,900 years. "You should turn away from them as a pest and a plague of the human race," said St. John Chrysostom, and 1,500 years later thousands of his disciples implemented his teachings, literally.

One must compel oneself to face these hard facts in our own time because there is a tendency to want to evade the reality of this problem, since in America both for Christians and Jews anti-Semitism is not much more than a social nuisance. It is not a serious problem of human deprivation, of human discomfort, or a clear and present danger. But to this very day in the city of Buenos Aires, for example, where four hundred thousand Jews live, Jewish merchants are packing guns into their business places, synagogues are being stored with armaments because in the past three or four years the Neo-Fascist, ultra-nationalist movement called TACUARA, consisting entirely of young, well-to-do Catholic students, have been tramping through the streets of Buenos Aires spraying machine gunfire at synagogues and throwing bombs into Jewish businesses. In June 1963, the TACUARA apprehended a Jewish girl, Graciela Sirota, as she came home from the university in the evening, kidnapped her, and carved a swastika in her breast. The chaplain of this TACUARA movement is Father Julio de Meinvielle, who has claimed that he bases his "ministry" to these students in the TACUARA movement on the fact that the tradition of St. John Chrysostom's views toward the Jews and Judaism and those who have repeated that tradition, represent *the* authentic view of the church toward the Jewish people and to Judaism.

Within the past four to five years all of us have lived through what in fact may be the most revolutionary period in the history of the Christian-Jewish encounter over the past two millennia. As in race relations, the churches have begun to seek to reconcile the ambivalences and the contradictions between theology and history. The Catholic Church, through Vatican Council II's approval of a declaration dealing with Catholic-Jewish relations, the World Council of Churches, in its very forthright resolution at New Delhi in December 1961, and American Catholic and Protestant bodies have all contributed dramatically to the powerful assault against anti-Semitism. Their wide-ranging programs of textbook and curriculum revision, teacher training, seminary education, retreats and adult education have been confronting increasingly the issues of responsible portrayal of Jews and Judaism.

If nothing else came out of Vatican Council II other than what took place in Rome on September 28 and 29, 1964, the Council more than justified its existence in terms of Jewish interests. On Friday, September 25, 1964, Cardinal Bea arose in the aula of St. Peter's Basilica to read his *relatio* to the "Jewish Declaration." After indicating the importance of this decree to the life of the church, the importance of the church's understanding of her true relationship to Israel, to the Bible, to the Jewish people, ancient and present (an understanding upon which is founded the whole future and prospect of the biblical, liturgical and theological renewals of the church), Cardinal Bea declared before 2,300 Council Fathers, "There are many historical instances from various nations which cannot be denied. In these instances this belief concerning the culpability of the Jewish people as such has led Christians to consider and to call the Jews with whom they live the "deicide" people, reprobated and cursed by God and therefore to look down upon them and indeed to persecute them." The moment of truth, as those of us who were privileged to be in Rome were able to observe, occurred on those two days when thirty-five cardinals and bishops from twenty-two countries arose on the floor of St. Peter's, and one after another, in terms more powerful and more committed than had ever been heard before, called upon the Catholic Church to condemn anti-Semitism as a sin against the conscience of the church. Thirty-one of the cardinals and bishops from every major continent of the world took positions regarding Catholic attitudes in relation to the Jewish people, Judaism, the role of Israel in salvation history, the synagogue and its continued relevance, conversion, anti-Semitism— positions that have never been heard before in 1,900 years of Catholic-Jewish history, positions articulated with such friendship, indeed, fraternal love, as to make clear that a profound turning point had taken place in our lifetime.

Cardinal Cushing, the first of the American hierarchy to speak out on the declaration on the Jews, called for a denial by the Council of the culpability of the Jews as a people for the death of Jesus. "Rejection of Jesus by the Jewish people is a mystery and is to serve to instruct us not to inflate us," Cardinal Cushing said.[1] He declared that the Catholic Church cannot judge the ancient judges of the Jews, as that is for God to do. At the same time, the cardinal said Christians must be aware of the universal guilt of all men who by sinning crucified and are crucifying Christ.

The late Cardinal Meyer of Chicago stated that "it is not

---

[1] These paraphrases of the interventions of the council fathers are based on the press reports issued by the Press Service of the National Catholic Welfare Conference (see *Council Daybook: Vatican II: Sessions 1–4,* Floyd Anderson, ed. [Washington, D.C.: National Catholic Welfare Conference, 1965–66]), and also on the summaries printed in the *Herder Correspondence.* The publication of the full texts of the interventions would be a valuable contribution, in my judgment, to a fuller understanding of the historic implications of the Council's actions for the future of Catholic-Jewish relations.

enough for the church to deplore any injustices against the Jewish people. It must also point out the close relationship of the church with the Jews." Cardinal Meyer pointed out that St. Thomas Aquinas taught that the Jews were not guilty of deicide.

Cardinal Ritter of St. Louis said that the declaration would repair injustices of past centuries. He said that it is often assumed that God abandoned the Jews, and the Jews were rightly to be accused of condemnation of Jesus. Now he said an opportunity had been offered to remedy these errors and to remove these injustices. Referring to the passage that spoke of the "reunion" of the Jews with the church, Cardinal Ritter said it sounds as if the church envisions conversion of the Jewish people. He pointed out that the text did not speak of the Muslims, Hindus, and Protestants in the same respect. Therefore, he suggested that the final text find less offensive wording and include a paragraph expressing the biblical hope of the union of all men at the end of days.

Cardinal Léger of Canada called the declaration a necessary act of the church's renewal. Cardinal Lercaro of Bologna suggested that the declaration emphasize biblical discussions with the Jews. He said the Jewish people should not be regarded as having value only in the past. But the heritage of Israel, the institution of the Eucharist within the Jewish paschal cycle, the relation between the Passover meal and the Mass, the common fatherhood of Abraham—all these should be emphasized in the declaration, Cardinal Lercaro said, in order to give witness in a pastoral way and to foster piety. He added that the Jews of today should not be called an accursed or deicide people, but rather that we should recognize that all of us "have strayed like sheep."

Archbishop Pocock of Canada said that the Church must acquit the Jewish people of all false accusations made in the past through the abuse of truth and charity.

Bishop Stephen A. Leven of Texas, in rejecting the ancient deicide charge against the Jews, declared:

> Fathers of the Council, we are not dealing here with some philosophical entity but with a word of infamy and execration which was invented by Christians and used to blame and persecute the Jews. For so many centuries, and even in our own, Christians have hurled this word against Jews, and because of it they have justified every kind of horrible excess and even their slaughter and destruction.

It is not up to us to make a declaration about something philosophical but to reprobate and damn a word which has furnished so many occasions of persecution through the centuries. We must tear this word out of the Christian vocabulary so that it may never again be used against the Jews.

During those two days of debate in Rome and in the final text that was promulgated by Pope Paul VI on October 28, 1965, the Catholic Church took a great and historic leap forward in reconciling this ambivalence, affirming on the highest levels of its teaching authority the indebtedness of Christianity and the Christians to Judaism and the Jewish people, the rejection of anti-Semitism, and all unprecedented calls for fraternal dialogue between Christians and Jews.

There is a larger dimension to what took place in Rome at Vatican Council II that should be of as great significance to the Jewish people as the Jewish Declaration itself. The clue to that larger significance is suggested by the letter that Pope Paul VI sent to Cardinal Tisserant, dean of the Council presidency, on November 9, 1965. In that letter, Paul VI announced that Vatican Council II would end on December 8, "on the same date on which in 1869, there was solemnly inaugurated the first Vatican Ecumenical Council." The Pope then said that "our Council can well be considered under many aspects a worthy counterpart" of Vatican Council I. Before this audience, I need not belabor the point of how great an advance, indeed a revolution, Vatican Council II represents in contrast to Vatican Council I. As you well know, most objective, impartial historians have described Vatican Council I as that which marked the decisive victory of ultramontanism. The foundation stones of Vatican Council I were based on the encyclical *Quanta Cura* and the accompanying *Syllabus of Errors* issued by Pius IX in 1864.[2] B. Bury, Regius professor of modern

---

[2] Whether the *Syllabus* possessed dogmatic character is a subject of controversy which Prof. Bury discusses at some length. He cites critics, such as M. Dupanloup and others, who sought to minimize its binding import, but concludes from evidence contained in letters of Cardinal Antonelli "that the *Syllabus* was intended to have dogmatic value . . . on the subject of modern errors." Similarly, there is a deep divergence of views regarding ultramontanism itself. Paul Droulers, S.J., for example, writing in the *Journal of World History*, characterizes the "ultramontanist" movement as one "impelled by the desire for greater purity and fervor" and constituted a "voluntary renunciation of local ecclesiastical par-

history at Cambridge, in his study *The History of the Papacy in the 19th Century* (New York: Schocken Books, 1964) summarizes the contents of the encyclical and the *Syllabus* in this way:

> The leading ideas which are associated closely with modern prog-
> ress are described as *monstrosa opinionum portenta,* and those who
> propagate them are designated slaves of corruption who design to
> demolish society, *civilis societatis fundamenta convellere . . .* He [Pius
> IX] begins his comments on this doctrine (of toleration) by quot-
> ing with approval and the right of each man to practice his own
> religion are described as *deliramentum.* Such liberty, says Pius, citing
> St. Augustine, is *libertaus perditionis.*

Professor Bury concludes (p. 6) that "the general drift of the argument [of the encyclical] is: liberty, toleration, secularism, and democracy are closely bound together, and what they mean is materialism."

Wrapped up in religious phraseology, Bury adds, the encyclical "is really a political document setting forth an ideal of civilization and declaring principles of political import."

> The positive principles which it asserts by means of condemning
> their negations may be summed up thus: The state must recognize
> a particular religion as regnant, and submit to its influence, and
> this religion must be Catholic; the power of the state must be at its
> disposal, and all who do not conform to its requirements must be
> compelled or punished. The duty of governments is to protect the
> church, and freedom of conscience and cult is madness. Not the
> popular will, but religion, that is the papal authority, is the basis of
> civil society, otherwise it will sink into materialism. The church is
> superior to the state, and therefore the state has no right to dictate
> to her, and has no power over religious orders. The family and the
> education of children belong to the church, not to the state. The
> pope can decree and prescribe what he chooses, without the state's
> permission, and his authority is not limited to doctrines and morals
> (p. 8).

---

ticularism. It held up the pope, the head and center of the church, as the visible source of Catholic vitality, while steadily consolidating this practical authority." Looking at the same set of "facts," the Lutheran church historian, Rudolph Sohm, in his book, *Kirchengeschichte im Grundriss* (Leipzig: E. Ungleich, 1890), characterized ultramontanism as "the intolerant doctrinal Catholicism which with its lust for power demands once more the complete subjection of the individual, of the world itself, to the supreme authority of the church."

The Episcopal scholar, the Rev. Dr. Frederick Grant, in his introduction to Professor Bury's study, described the mentality of Vatican Council I and of Pius IX as that which held that "the best safeguard of the Christian faith" against liberalism and modernism was to convert the Catholic Church into "a Maginot line of impenetrable defense." In the face of a series of shocks beginning with the Reformation in the sixteenth century and climaxed by the French Revolution in the eighteenth century, the Church became preoccupied with her own self-preservation and was relatively indifferent to the fate of those who were non-Catholic. This virtual obsession with the preservation of herself and her institutions made it possible for the church to enter into concordats with the blackest forces of reaction, a tradition that led to tragic consequences in the twentieth century.[3]

As one reads the texts of the sixteen declarations promulgated by Vatican II and compares these with both the spirit as well as the rhetoric of the documents of Vatican Council I, there is no conclusion possible other than that the Catholic Church has undergone a revolution in terms of not only her self-perception but in her attitudes toward non-Catholics and her own responsibility for the welfare of other people. Nowhere is this new attitude of concern for others, involvement in their fate and destiny, more clearly reflected than in the *Constitution on the Church in the Modern World*, the *Declaration on Religious Freedom*, the *Decree on Ecumenism*, and the *Declaration on the Relationship of the Church to Non-Christian Religions*. No person of goodwill can fail to be moved by these words contained in the *Constitution on the Church in the Modern World:*

> The joys and the hopes, the grief and the anxieties of the men of this age, especially those who are poor or in any way afflicted, these are the joys and the hopes, the grief and the anxieties of the follow-

---

[3] Paul Droulers, S.J., writing on Roman Catholicism in the *19th Century World* (p. 293), states, "The diplomacy of the Court of Rome . . . was adapted to meet the varying circumstances of the individual countries, striving to obtain the fullest possible measure of civil liberty for the celebration of worship and the exercise of spiritual government . . . the bull *Sollicitudo Ecclesiarum* of August 7, 1831, contains an explicit reminder that in the cause of religion the Holy See will negotiate with any duly constituted government, though this does not imply recognition of its legitimacy before the law.

ers of Christ. Indeed, nothing genuinely human fails to raise an echo in their hearts. For theirs is a community composed of men (article 1). . . . In our times a special obligation binds us to make ourselves the neighbor of every person without exception, and of actively helping him when he comes across our path, whether he be an old person abandoned by all, a foreign laborer unjustly looked down upon, a child born of an unlawful union and wrongly suffering for a sin he did not commit, or a hungry person (article 27). . . . Respect and love ought to be extended also to those who think or act differently than we do in social, political, and even religious matters (article 28).

This emergence from behind something of a Maginot line and the joining of a dialogue with the world was dramatically ratified as much for non-Catholics as for Catholics in the brilliant address of Pope Paul VI before the United Nations at the end of last year [1965]. The Pope renounced for the Catholic Church any pretense to temporal power and then declared, "We make our own voice of the poor, the disinherited, the suffering, to those who hunger and thirst for justice, for the dignity of life, for freedom, for well being and progress." Pope Paul VI gave Catholic support to "the pluralism of states" and to "coexistence" between peoples. He said to the United Nations: "Your vocation is to make brothers not only of some but of all peoples." He then ratified "the formula of equality" saying: "Let no one inasmuch as he is a member of your union be superior to the others; never one above the other." The Pope then decried that "pride" which "disrupts brotherhood." Noting that the United Nations proclaims "the fundamental rights and duties of man, his dignity, his freedom—and above all, his religious freedom," the Pope declared that "the life of man is sacred; no one may dare offend it."

I believe that I speak the mind of most informed Jewish observers when I say that if this mentality had been normative for the popes, the Vatican, and the Catholic and Protestant masses over the past one hundred years, the incredible phenomenon of hundreds of thousands of so-called devout Christians becoming accomplices or passive spectators to the cruel slaughter of millions of men, women, and children who happened to be born Jews—or Gypsies—would not have been possible. The pragmatic significance of this newly-articulated humanitarian mentality has given birth, I have no doubt, to the magnificent involvement of priests, nuns, and Catholic laymen who, together with ministers and rabbis, marched together through the streets of Selma, Alabama, or in the March on Washington as a powerful renunciation of that mentality that echoed in traumatic silence less than twenty-five years ago in the cities of ancient Christian culture of Germany and Austria. The pope cried out, "No more war! War never again!" and moved the world when he pleaded. Vatican Council II has proclaimed to the whole of the human family, "No more indifference, indifference and silence no more!" as long as the dignity of a single human being is offended or exploited.

The promulgation of the *Declaration on the Relationship of the Church to Non-Christian Religions* on October 28, 1965, received a mixed reaction in the Jewish community. As a commonplace pun has it, "Where there are two Jews, there are three opinions"— which is a Jewish self-critical way of describing the deep-seated democracy and pluralism that exists in Jewish life. The Jewish reaction ranged across a broad spectrum. There were those who opposed the Declaration and, in fact, who resented it. There were those who were indifferent to it. There were those, including myself, who welcomed the Declaration as an important contribution to improve the future relations between Catholics and Jews. In my study of the Jewish responses, I became aware of how decisive a role mass media played in influencing relations between groups. A substantial segment of the Jewish community reacted not to the content of the Declaration, as much as to the headlines that reported it. The day following its promulgation, newspaper headlines throughout this country and, in fact, throughout the world, carried such statements as "Vatican Council Exonerates Jews for Death of Christ," or "Catholic Church Absolves Jews of Crucifixion." The so-called Jewish man-in-the-street naturally responded to such presumptive formulations with resentment, if not worse. No Jew in my acquaintance has ever felt guilty for the death of Jesus. Therefore, no Jew ever felt in need of absolution. But it was the newspapers and the radio and television commentators who used those words. The text of the Declaration itself does not use "absolve" or "exonerate" even once. This is not to impute bad motives or incompetence to the mass media. The problem of reducing to headlines a complex historical and theological problem is one that I am glad I did not have to face. But again, the fact that such headlines and such radio and television reports were dinned around the world for days both prior to and following the promulgation led almost inevitably to a negative reaction of so many Jewish people.

A more substantive consideration is the fact that the Vatican Council, for whatever reasons, "backed and filled" over this declaration for some four years. And to many Jews it was as though the Jewish people were being subjected to a trial over this period of time. When you add to that the fact that a number of unfortunate episodes took place during those four years (including the insulting articles and speeches by Bishop Carli of Segni, who said, in fact, the Jews and Judaism today are collectively responsible for the crucifixion and stand under God's reprobation because of it), then one has another insight into how the Jewish patience wore thin. Overriding all, however, was the absence in the Declaration of any note of contrition or repentance for the incredible sufferings and persecutions Jews have undergone in the Christian West. The church's various declarations asked forgiveness from the Protestants, the Eastern Orthodox, from the Muslims, but not from the Jews. Many Jews, especially those who lived through the Nazi Holocaust, asked with great passion, "How many more millions of our brothers and sisters will need to be slaughtered before any word of contrition or repentance is heard in the seats of ancient Christian glory?"

The Jews who are indifferent to the Vatican Council's action believe that it was too little and too late. Within this group there is a strong feeling that the Catholic bishops in Germany and perhaps Pius XII himself could have spoken out decisively, unambiguously, at a time when it would have meant something of profound importance to the Jewish people. That did not happen in terms adequate to the need and, therefore, the loss of confidence in the present usefulness of the Vatican statement is widespread among this group. In the perspective of history this group has also been aware that up until the time of the Enlightenment and the French Revolution, the church contributed to the disenfranchisement of the Jewish people of the Western world and much worse. This group looks to the secular powers of the world for its political and civic salvation. In the view of this group, his-

tory has outdistanced the Christian community, and such statements are only pleasant rhetoric and are really of no significant
effect in terms of the security or fate of the Jewish people in the
twentieth century.

In the view of the third group the text of the final version of
the Declaration represented a compromise document compared
to the text that was introduced at the close of the third session
and which received an overwhelming majority vote of the council
fathers. The earlier version was warmer, more generous, and less
severe: it dealt explicitly with the "deicide" concept, which became something of a symbolic test of goodwill. In that perspective, the failure of the Council to enact the majority will of the
fathers of 1964 was a disappointment. But in the view of this
group, seen in the perspective of 1,900 years of Christian-Jewish
history, this Declaration represents an incredible achievement.

As important as the Declaration itself is, the commitment of
Catholic Church authorities and institutions to translate the
guidelines in this document into reality in the lives of 550 million
Catholics throughout the world was of even greater importance.
That commitment was given decisive expression when the American Catholic hierarchy designated a special sub-commission on
Catholic-Jewish relations charged with the responsibility of implementing the objectives of the Declaration throughout every level
of Catholic culture and society. The determined action of the
Vatican shortly after the Declaration was promulgated which put
an end to the veneration of Simon of Trent—that ritual blood
libel episode which since the fifteenth century has been celebrated by annual procession through the streets of Trent, repeating an insult to the whole of the Jewish people—was another
impressive demonstration of the commitment of the Catholic
Church to express in deeds its new attitude of respect and esteem
for the Jewish people. The instruction given by Cardinal Döpfner
of Munich to the organizers of the Oberammergau Passion Play
to revise the text so that all anti-Jewish references are removed
is another earnest of the Catholic Church's commitment to the
uprooting of the sources of anti-Semitism.

In the face of the agonizing history that many of the people of
the cross had wrought in the transformation of the Jews into a
cross among the peoples, there should not be too great baffle-

ment or wonder over some of the skepticism of a number of the Jewish people in this country and abroad as to the real meaning of the Vatican Council Declaration to them and their children. As long as Father Julio de Meinviele of Buenos Aires is allowed by the Catholic hierarchy to serve as chaplain to a group of young Catholic Fascists, who ruthlessly exploit anti-Semitism for their economic and political purposes; as long as hostile references to the Jewish people, Judaism, and the synagogue continue to appear in Catholic textbooks, missals, liturgical commentaries, theological dictionaries, and sermons, a great many Jews will continue to view the Vatican Council Declaration as a vain and even hypocritical show. Having worked closely with members of the Catholic community both here and abroad, especially in the fields of religious history and religious education, I am deeply persuaded that a vast and irreversible tide of self-purification and self-correction with regard to the portrayal of Jews and Judaism in the teaching process of the Catholic Church—nor should the Protestants be slighted—is under way and that the fruits of this process are already in evidence. That is not to overlook the hard reality that a great deal more needs to be done before the last weeds of anti-Jewish teaching and anti-Jewish poison are removed. But in my judgment, no Jew has a right to belittle the great advances that have been made already. I am persuaded that we are now going through a period of transition which will find both Jews and Catholics fumbling and stumbling as they seek to find appropriate new modes of relating to each other in a growing climate of mutual tolerance and esteem.

During the course of the deliberations of Vatican Council II in connection with the "Jewish Declaration," the contradictory and at times confused views expressed with regard to the inclusion or elimination of a passage in the third version of the text relating the question of the conversion of the Jews brought into sharp focus the fact that the Catholic Church has done very little serious thinking about the place of Jews and Judaism in the divine economy. That episode alone underscored the need for Catholic theologians and scholars to develop a theology of Israel and the synagogue in salvation history that has some correspondence with the historic realities of the present-day living Jewish people. At the same time, the bewildering and bewildered response of many

Jews to Vatican Council II, whose attitudes toward present-day Christians are based on old-world memories of Christians as persecutors, threw into sharp relief the critical need for Jews to develop a theology of Christians and Christianity that is consonant with the realities of an emerging "new Christian" society that is struggling in unparalleled fashion to uproot anti-Semitism and to restore her traditions to biblical modes of thought and practice.

At the heart of Christianity's problem of what to make of the Jew is the Christian's immense ignorance, if not illiteracy, regarding Judaism. If the Jews were supposed to have committed deicide against Jesus, then a great many Christians in fact have committed homicide against him. They have killed Jesus as a Jew and as a man. The weapon was ignorance of Jesus's Jewishness. But Jesus's life, his preaching, his teaching, his vision of the kingdom of God, the very ground of his messianism cannot be accurately or profoundly understood apart from his background in the synagogue, his life of worship and observance as a Jew, and his education with the Pharisaic rabbis of the first century. Indeed, the New Testament itself cannot be fully comprehended as other than a Jewish book, written almost entirely by Jews for Jews, and in the Jewish mode of exegesis, known as *Hagaddah*. Long passages of the New Testament are, indeed, actually nothing less than new and different exegeses of the Jewish Bible, the difference being determined by the belief in the divinity of Jesus, which stands in opposition to the uncompromising monotheism of Judaism.

The significance of this Christian amnesia regarding the Jewishness of the origins of Christianity is that the Christians who live in this ignorance are expressing the Marcionite heresy. Further, God bestowed promises upon the Jews and chastised them with curses, in order that they might repent. But a certain tradition of Christian teaching appropriated the promises for "the new Israel" and imposed upon the "old Israel" the left-over curses. In this way, many Christians found it possible to cease to identify religiously with Judaism and, worse, perceived the Torah and Judaism as "stagnant" and "desiccated." From this conviction it was but a short step to the belief that the church "superseded" Israel—despite St. Paul's admonition in Romans that God's call and promises to the Jews are irrevocable.

When one adds to this ignorance of first-century Judaism the even greater lack of knowledge about post-biblical Judaism, the ground of misunderstanding becomes an abyss. To most Christians, Judaism came to an abrupt end with the close of the canon of the Hebrew Scripture. But Judaism did not come to an end with the Old Testament. Just as a non-Catholic does an injustice to Catholicism by failing to take into account the significance of tradition, church teaching, and canon law, in addition to Sacred Scripture, so do non-Jews distort Judaism by failing to recognize that modern Judaism is the product of a long and rich development of post-biblical thought, devotion and piety that the great rabbis and sages of the Jewish people developed over the past 1,500 years. In the absence of that knowledge, the Christian pedagogues' continued use of the stereotypes of "Pharisees" for hypocritical post-biblical Jews, the false antimony of Judaism as a religion of law and justice versus Christianity as a religion of love, mercy and compassion will only serve to perpetuate bias and know-nothingism in religion.

In this perspective, it has now become very clear that there are at least three major and decisive areas of scholarship that must be vigorously pursued by Catholic and other Christian scholars if the call of Vatican Council II for "biblical and theological studies" is to be translated into "mutual understanding and respect." These are, first, critical commentaries and interpretations of the New Testament that will remove any possibility for bigots to exploit certain expressions in the gospels for anti-Semitic purposes. An excellent example of such studies is to be found in the essay "Anti-Semitism and the Gospel," by Dominic M. Crossan, O.S.M., which appeared in a recent issue of *Theological Studies*. In that essay, Crossan wrote that "the often-repeated statement that the Jews rejected Jesus and had him crucified is historically untenable and must, therefore, be removed completely from our thinking and our writing, our teaching, preaching, and liturgy."

The second area is that of historical studies. If one reads church histories and Jewish histories of the same events, it is as though Christians and Jews are being educated in different universes of discourse. A Christian historian, for example, Philip Hughes, writes of the Crusades of the eleventh and twelfth centuries as holy war to free Jerusalem. "Never before had Europe known such a vast and successful propaganda as the preaching of the

First Crusade, and its success is a most eloquent proof of the reality of the new reform papacy's hold on the average man and of its popularity with him," wrote Hughes in his *A Popular History of the Catholic Church* (New York: Macmillan, 1947). To Jewish historians the Crusades "becomes a gory story of pillaging Jewish settlements, killing Jewish people, looting Jewish wealth. Such serious restrictive legislation as the humiliating garb, ritual-murder charges, host desecration libels, and confinement of the ghetto were not the heritage of the Dark Ages but the heritage of the Crusades" (Max Dimont, *Jews, God and History* [New York: Simon and Schuster, 1962]).

As Edward A. Flannery, author of *The Anguish of the Jews* (New York: Macmillan, 1965), has written, "most Christians have torn out of their history books the pages that Jews have memorized." The time has come, perhaps, for a proposal to be made for Christian and Jewish historians to join together in writing a common history of the Jewish-Christian encounter which will fill in the blank pages.

The third area of much-needed scholarship is that of theological studies in Jewish-Christian relations. Unless and until Christian scholars and people develop theological conceptions regarding Judaism and the synagogue that reflect in some way the vital reality of the existence of present-day Judaism, very little else of significance in Jewish-Christian relations will be possible. Gregory Baum has begun to point the way:

> The apostle tells us that the Jews of the Synagogue remain dear to God for the sake of the fathers (cf. Rom. 11:28). Their election stands. Why? Because God is faithful, his gifts and call are irrevocable (Rom. 11:29). His election cannot ultimately be undone by human decision against it. The scriptural theme is invoked in the conciliar text. . . . What does this mean for the understanding of the Jews of our day? Giving this Pauline theme its weakest possible meaning, it asserts that God continues to be present and to address Jewish believers in their synagogue services. The testimonies of God's mercy in the past as celebrated in the synagogue worship remain a way of divine action, for "His gifts and call are irrevocable." We have here the answer to a question crucial to the Jewish-Christian dialogue. What is the present synagogue worship before God? Is the Christian forced to regard present Jewish worship as an

empty form, as words and gestures without meaning? Or is he able to acknowledge in Jewish worship the presence of the living God? The conciliar text answers this question by its adoption and use of the Pauline theme. God remains present in his gifts to Israel (*Ecumenist*, May–June 1965).

8

A Jewish Reaction to Catholic Positions in Vatican II

MY TALK IS BASED on two texts. One derives from the recently promulgated Vatican Council Declaration on Non-Christian Religions, which asserted, among other things, the following: "Since the spiritual patrimony common to Christians and Jews is thus so great, this sacred synod wants to foster and recommend that mutual understanding and respect which is the fruit above all of biblical and theological studies as well as of fraternal dialogues."

My second text is derived from one of the basic works of Jewish tradition, *The Sayings of the Fathers* (of the Synagogue): "The world is founded upon three pillars, upon *Torah, Avodah,* and *Gemilut Chasadim.*" The very foundations of the earth are reared on Torah, which in its broader meaning, is study or learning; on *Avodah,* which technically means worship, but can mean as well, service of the heart or service of the total person; and on *Gemilut Chasadim,* on righteous deeds, acts, and works of charity.

The Fathers of the Synagogue, it seems to me, have suggested some fundamental approaches which might be considered appropriate for the advancement of objectives which the Fathers of the

Excerpted from a paper delivered before the Twenty-first Annual Convention of the Catholic Theological Society of America, Providence, Rhode Island, June 20–23, 1966. Notable here is Rabbi Tanenbaum's effort to continue a distinctly theological conversation between Christians and Jews, a central element of current dialogues. One suggestion he made then and has yet to be acted upon yet remains a challenge and an opportunity, namely, that Jewish and Christian scholars "sit down together and write a joint history, if not of the entire encounter between Christians and Jews across two thousand years then of sections of it—objective, impartial treatments." While there have been "dialogical history texts" (pairing Jewish and Christian scholars on the same period but in separate papers as in the edited collection by Eugene J. Fisher, *Interwoven Destinies: Jews and Christians Across the Ages* [New York: Paulist Press, 1993]), a truly joint venture has yet to be undertaken. In this selection, Rabbi Tanenbaum takes his own advice which he offered in his speech at Notre Dame University, namely, to provide one element in a framework for mutual history-making.

Catholic Church have proposed—the objectives of mutual knowledge and respect which all men of goodwill, living in the pluralism of America and in a growing interdependent world, must certainly share. In speaking of the tradition of Torah, of understanding, of knowledge, of information, indeed, of scholarship in this context of advancing Jewish-Christian relations, I should like to suggest something which has not been done before, at least to my knowledge, but which sooner or later should certainly be done. Perhaps some of you who hear my voice might consider this a worthwhile subject to explore yourselves.

Before the proposal, the problem. One of the great problems between Christians and Jews has been the breakdown in communication. We have been trained in virtually different universes of discourse and nowhere is this more clearly evident than in the ways, for example, in which we portray each other, in our history books, not just in the elementary and secondary textbooks but in the college and university and seminary levels as well. A Christian historian, for example, Father Philip Hughes, writing in his excellent study, *A Popular History of the Catholic Church* (New York: Macmillan, 1947) describes the Crusades of the eleventh and twelfth centuries as "holy wars" to free the Holy Land in Jerusalem from the infidels. Father Hughes did not refer to the place of the Jews in the Crusades, not even once.

To Jewish historians writing about the same Crusades, scholars such as Heinrich Graetz, Marx and Margolls, Solomon Grayzel, the Crusades are described, in the language of one of these historians, as, "A gory story of pillaging Jewish settlements, killing Jewish people, looting Jewish wealth. Such serious restrictive legislation as the humiliating garb, ritual murder charges, host desecration libels and confinement of the ghetto were not the heritage of the Dark Ages but the heritage of the Crusades."

For the Christian who is raised on the tradition of history contained in Father Hughes's book, the Crusades will be forever seen as a noble, heroic, and by and large holy undertaking. But no Christian who is raised on that version of the Crusades will ever understand the mind-set of his Jewish brother who has been instructed by his reading of the Jewish version of that period.

Two completely different mentalities are developing side by side. The Jew responds to this understanding of his history in the

Christian West with a feeling of some vast, inchoate sense of his victimization and he responds, humanly, with resentment. The Christian who knows nothing about this side of the history of the Jew in the West—the Crusades, the Inquisitions, the pogroms, the exclusions, the ghettos, the yellow badges of shame—often concludes that Jews who seem to get quickly nervous over outbreaks of anti-Semitism are strangely hypersensitive, even paranoid. And many Jews find it difficult to believe that Christians do not know anything about Jewish suffering of this magnitude in the past and conclude that Christians are being hard-hearted and insensitive— and the cycle of misunderstanding thereby proceeds apace.

And so I should like to propose that we face squarely into this issue as one of the major obligations posed by Vatican Council II. As one way of coming to grips with this problem, I should like to see Catholic, Protestant, and Jewish historians sit down together and write a joint history, if not of the entire encounter between Christians and Jews across two thousand years, then of sections of it, perhaps as monographs, research papers, or background documents to be used in college and seminary courses— objective, impartial treatment of the Crusades, of the Spanish Inquisition period, of the portrayal of the Jew and Judaism in patristic literature, of the role and the place of the Jew in the Middle Ages in his relations with a Christian society, of what a trauma the French Revolution meant for the church while for the Jew it meant the civic and political salvation of the Jewish people. The very process of creating such a body of literature will be greatly instructive for all who will be exposed to study, research and writing in this field. Such work, carried out by seminarians together, teachers, scholarly clergy, educated laymen, would help immeasurably to overcome the misconceptions and the misrepresentations that have accumulated across the centuries and which have contributed so much to the distortion of our relations even to this very day. The very least that we might hope for is that we will overcome our ignorance about each other's history books and what they contain.

Another area of study involves that of biblical and theological studies and is suggested by the Vatican Council declaration quite explicitly. The council fathers called for accurate interpretation in precise historical and theological terms of the role of the Jewish people in the crucifixion. The declaration declared, in these words: "What happened in His Passion cannot be charged against all the Jews without distinction then alive, nor against the Jews of today." It added: "The Jews should not be presented as rejected or accursed by God as if this followed from the Holy Scriptures."

A St. Louis University study of religious textbooks used in parochial schools, conducted by Sister Rose Albert [Thering] under the direction of Father Trafford Maher, has disclosed that, in a substantial number of textbooks and teacher manuals, and this has been true as well of sermons, liturgical commentaries, and other forms of catechetical materials, the enemies of Jesus have frequently been identified as, quote, "the Jews," while his friends and followers, who were also Jews, are not referred to in those terms. Thus, in some of the textbooks that were studied, we find the following is written: "It was on the day that Jesus raised Lazarus from the tomb that the Jews decided to kill him. Nevertheless they were afraid of the people." But who were the people that the Jews were afraid of? Martians? They were Jews, other Jews. The historic truth is that Jesus scarcely ever spoke a word to a non-Jew. His whole milieu, the people with whom he lived, with whom he had his daily encounters, were all, friend and foe alike, Jews. And yet this tradition of selective interpretation of scripture continues to this very day.

Now let me be very clear about one point. No informed Jew is asking Christians to revise the New Testament for the sake of good Jewish-Christian relations. Those who have any understanding of Scriptures are no more prepared to ask Christians to rewrite the gospels than Jews would be prepared to accept any suggestions from non-Jews that the Torah or the Talmud be revised for reasons of goodwill. However, since present-day Jews are living descendants of the Jews who are referred to repeatedly in the gospels, and in light of centuries of persecutions of Jews by people who called themselves Christians and who exploited some of these teachings to cover up their bigotry, what many Jews do raise as a question before the conscience of their Christian neighbors, especially biblical and theological scholars and students, is whether there are not resources in biblical exegesis and related scholarship that would enable Christian teachers, priests, and the average Catholic parent to interpret in proper context and in its spiritual meaning those passages of the New Testament which are most easily open to distortion. The need to prepare commentaries on the Scriptures, on the Liturgy and the para-liturgical materials that reflect this ecumenical spirit and the insights of recent biblical scholarship is, in my judgment, an imperative one.

I make bold to raise this issue in this form because I am greatly encouraged by the leadership already given in this direction by eminent Catholic scripture scholars and theologians. One is heartened to find this point of view clearly and concretely reflected in such new textbooks and teacher manuals as the "To Live is Christ" series by Brother Frederick and Brother Albert, for Catholic high schools. The authors write in the teacher's manual:

> We must follow the example of our Lord upon the cross, who did not apply the term God-killers to the Roman powers, nor to those (Judas included) who brought him before the Romans, and certainly did not apply any blanket condemnation upon any group or nation because of the actions of a minority. Rather we should think of the significance the Crucifixion has for us Christians: We should think of the love of God shown for us in this action and the promise of resurrection in union with that of Jesus. We should consider that, when we sin, we are turning our backs on the life work of Christ, and making his death useless in our regard: It is we who condemn him to martyrdom, then, in our own hearts.

Another dimension of this area of biblical and theological concern is that related to the conventional practice of making unjust and inaccurate comparisons between the Jewish faith and Christianity. Occasionally, gratuitous slurs against Judaism are used to heighten the contrast to Christianity. In consequence, Judaism emerges as a legalistic religion, concerned solely with external observances, ritual, legalistic piety, devoid of love, mercy and compassion. For example, as one of the textbooks cited in the St. Louis study says: "The Jews believe that one should hate an enemy, but Christ taught the opposite." It might be noted that St. Paul's injunction, "If your enemy is hungry, feed him," contained in Romans 12:20, is a direct quotation from Proverbs 25:21, with which the Jews had something to do.

Also, in this style of teaching, the Pharisees, who for the most part, were saintly, devout, and courageous men and on whose scholarly and moral interpretations modern Judaism rests today, are frequently described as inhuman, without true religious motivation. As the distinguished Jewish biblical scholar, Dr. Robert Gordis, has declared: "Every competent scholar knows that the Old Testament conceived of God in terms of love as well as of justice, just as Jesus's God manifested Himself in justice as well as in love, for justice without love is cruelty and love without justice is caprice." If anything has brought this lesson home to us, my friends, it is the race struggle which is presently convulsing our nation, which is based on a demand for justice as much as on brotherly love.

The last aspect of biblical and theological concerns that I would like to touch on deals with the problems of omission. Very often, a form of distortion appears in teaching or, for that matter, in everyday discussion, either intentionally or under the influence of unconscious prejudice. For example, because of the general omission of the Jewish background of Christianity, many Catholics and other Christians are unaware of Christianity's deep roots in Judaism and in the Jewish people. Some passages in textbooks, for example, give the impression that the Bible did not exist prior to the Catholic Church. Here is a verbatim quote from one of the textbooks cited in the St. Louis study: "He inspired men whom he chose to write the smaller books which comprise it. There can be no doubt that the world must thank the Church for the Bible."

In such material and in history books, in books that are used in all ranges of education, there are few references to Judaism as a religion in its present form. After the birth of Christianity, Jewish religious practices, holy days, are described mainly in the context of the ancient past. The Catholic student, or the Christian student generally, is given the impression that Judaism as a faith ceased to exist with the founding of Christianity or with the destruction of the Temple. The Jews of later ages thus appear, by implication, as an irreligious people or as some weird phenomenon. What are Jews doing here, since in this view of the Old Testament, it has been fulfilled and the Jews have been superseded? The extreme secularized version of this attitude was expressed by Arnold Toynbee, who thought the Jews were a fossil of an ancient, Syriac civilization. Well, if we want to be rational people, we need to face the evidence of our senses. There are few Jews around who are fossilized and even fewer whom I know who regard themselves as Syriac vestiges.

If one wishes to understand the Jews as they understand themselves today, the People of Israel means the actual living Jewish people who became a people through the covenant made by God with Israel at Mount Sinai and who have been giving living witness to the word of God through centuries of devotion and piety and service, as well as through tragic suffering and martyrdom. This covenant has transformed the Jews into an eternal and permanent people, as the psalmist declared:

> My mercy will I not break off from him, nor will I be false to my faithfulness. My covenant will I not profane, nor alter that which has gone out of my lips. Once I have sworn by my holiness, surely I will not be false unto David. His seed shall endure forever and his throne as the sun before me. It shall be established forever as the moon and be steadfast as the witness in the sky (Ps. 89).

Perhaps this is what St. Paul meant when he declared in the book of Romans that the calls and promises of God to the people of Israel are irrevocable—"for the gifts and calling of God are without repentance."

How does classic Judaism view the election of the Jewish people in its own terms? The noted scholar Hans Joachim Schoeps in his study *The Jewish-Christian Argument* (New York: Holt, Rinehart, and Winston, 1963), pp. 29–30, formulates this traditional view quite accurately in the following words:

> In all ages, the Jewish faith has viewed possession of the Torah as the guarantee of its secure election. For ages, the Jews have expressed their deepest understanding of themselves in the daily Benediction of the Torah: "Blessed art Thou, O Lord, our God, King of the Universe, who hast chosen us from among all nations and hast given us thy precepts." The *Pirke Avot* (Ethical Sayings of the Synagogue Fathers) relates the saying of Rabbi Akiva that the Israelites are called God's children, as was declared to them out of God's special love. And further: "Beloved are the Israelites, for a special instrument has been granted them. Out of special love, it was declared to them that a precious instrument had been granted to them, through which the world was created." For it is written in Proverbs 4:2, "For I give you good doctrine; forsake ye not my teaching." (3,18) One of the Tannaim, a mystic by the name of

Rabbi Simeon ben Yohai, spoke of the nearness of God to his chosen people, the reality of the union of his *shekhinah* (Divine Presence) with Israel even after the destruction of the temple: "Come
and see how beloved to the Holy One, blessed be his name, are the
Israelites. Wherever they were exiled, the *shekhinah* was with them.
So it was in Egypt (there follows a reference to 1 Sam. 2:27), so it
was in the Babylonian *gâlûth* (reference to Isa. 43:14), so it was in
the Edomitic (Roman) *gâlûth* (reference to Isaiah 63:17). Even
when they are finally delivered, the *shekhinah* will be with them, for
it is written in Deuteronomy 30:3: "The Lord thy God will turn thy
captivity." It is not written that he will bring it back, but will turn it
back. This teaches that the *shekhinah* of the Holy One (blessed be
his name) will return with them from the *gâlûth*." (*Megillah* 29a)

This and many other doctrinal statements of the Talmud, or
interpretation of the Midrash (usually verifying the suggested exegesis with suitably selected passages from Scripture), quite obviously must be viewed as replies to Christian polemic. Israel
remains the people of God; the covenant cannot be nullified.
Thus, the scholars reassure the nation. At the moment, the nation
is in travail, but, in the first place, the evidence of such travail is
not an admissible argument, since it is historical impotence which
can demonstrate God's love; in the second place, there is not the
slightest causal relationship between the misery of the nation and
the crucifixion of Jesus, although presumably it is related to the
punishments threatened in Scripture, if the people break the or-
dinances of the covenant and sin obtains the upper hand. In this
other event, the Torah has promised, "the Lord shall scatter thee
among all peoples, from the one end of the earth even unto the
other end of the earth" (Deut. 28:64).

Starting with the ninth chapter of the Epistle to Barnabas and
running through all patristic literature is the assertion on the part
of Christian writers that Israel has been rejected by God because
of the sin of the golden calf. If this is true, Israel replies, "If I
appear so reprehensible on account of this single offence, how
reprehensible must you be" (*Shir ha-Shirim Rabbah* on 1:6, and
elsewhere). But such verdicts are not man's to deliver, for no man
knows God's decree. And the Christians do not have the right (so
the rabbis assure us repeatedly), by means of their allegories, to
interpret Scripture contrary to the sense of the words in order to

"prove" the rejection of Israel, and in this manner claim the election for the church. What is revealed is revealed, and God is a God of truth. It is written in the Torah: "And yet for all that, when they are in the land of their enemies, I will not reject them, neither will I abhor them, to destroy them utterly, and to break My covenant with them; for I am the Lord their God" (Lev. 26:44).

That is the point: punishment, yes—but not rejection. The *gâlûth* is perhaps even a blessing for Israel; it assures the eternity of the nation. That suffering would come upon Israel was predicted by the prophet Isaiah: "I have tried thee in the furnace of affliction" (48:10). The destruction of the temple and the dispersion among the Gentiles have their point of origin in the election, and are compassed within the divine plan. This all came about *umippene hataenu* ("on account of our sins") and will endure until, at a future time, our destiny will be altered by divine mercy. If now the scoffers come and ask, Where is, then, the power of God, seeing as he does not punish the persecutors of Israel? Rabbi Joshua ben Levi (*Amora* of the first generation, about 320) answers: "This is his power, that he restrains his wrath and remains patient with blasphemers. These are his terrible deeds; for without the terrible deeds of the Holy One (blessed be his name), how could Israel continue to exist among all the nations of the world?" (*Yoma* 69b)

In regard to the sufferings which afflict the Israelites here below: as repayment for the afflictions sent by God, they have promised to them in return the divine precepts, the Holy Land, and the world to come (*Mekiltaii* on Exod. 20:3). Knowing this, the same Joshua ben Levi could even dare to say, "Not even a wall of iron can effect a separation between Israel and its Father in heaven" (*Pesahim* 85b). And this deep conviction is paraphrased by another passage: "Even were all the nations of the earth to join together to put an end to God's love for Israel, they could not do so" (*Shemot Rabbah*).

Jews are heartened to find a number of Christian scholars who are beginning to understand and to reflect this basic tradition of Judaism, both present as well as past. Father Henry Renckens has written in his recent book, *The Religion of Israel* (New York: Sheed and Ward, 1966), "Christianity would be unthinkable without Judaism" and "The old Israel is a work of the Holy Spirit, as is the new." "If we take the Church and Holy Scripture seriously," Father Renckens adds, "then we are bound to take Judaism and its literary activity down to this day seriously." Monsignor John Oesterreicher has recently stated it another way:

> It is simply not true that because the synagogue did not accept Jesus as the giver of a new life, she is a dead tree carrying dead leaves. God's grace is at work in the synagogue. The worshiping community of Israel is alive to Him.

The challenge of Jewish-Christian relations is then for the Jew to come to grips with that which God must have intended in the emergence of Christianity out of the soil of the Holy Land, to come to grips with the holiness and sanctity that is found in the lives of so many of the new Christians with whom we have our being today. For Christians, it is to come to know Jews and Judaism in their full, living, present-day reality as a living, worshiping community, striving to be ever the banner of God's fidelity, a kingdom of priests and a holy nation.

9

Israel's Hour of Need and the Jewish-Christian Dialogue

THERE CAN BE no question but that the Israeli-Arab crisis of June 1967 put a severe strain on Jewish-Christian relations. But the exact nature of that strain and its implications for future relations between Jews and Christians and for Israel are far from adequately understood in the Jewish community.

In recent extensive travels around this country, I have been dismayed to find so much misinformation within the Jewish community about "the Christian response" to Israel in her hour of desperate need. Worse still were the conclusions for Jewish policy that derived from this distorted understanding. It is bad enough to come to wrong conclusions; to come to wrong conclusions on the basis of wrong information is reckless, irresponsible, and dangerous for Jewish well-being and security.

Shortly after the June hostilities, a number of Jewish personalities made big bold headlines in the nation's press with blanket

---

Excerpted from *Conservative Judaism* 22:2 (winter 1968). The outbreak of hostilities between Arab states and Israel in June of 1967, and the lack of public response to the crisis by the Christian churches, as Marc Tanenbaum noted, put "a severe strain" on Jewish-Christian relations. Jews felt that they had been abandoned once again. In this article, and in a paper delivered at the first Southern Baptist-Jewish Scholars Conference in Louisville in August of 1969 (the selection that follows), Rabbi Tanenbaum laid out his own response to the post-1967 Jewish-Christian crisis and delineated for Christians what Israel means to the Jewish people. Against charges within the Jewish community that the dialogues had broken down or were ineffectual, Rabbi Tanenbaum noted polling data in support of Israel by most Americans. Secondly, he pointed out that "not all Christians were silent." Numerous Catholic and Protestant leaders and groups had, indeed, spoken out to support Israel and condemned aggression, although he also points out that some of the Christian rhetoric, for example asking for "a crusade of prayer for peace," revealed something of a Christian tin ear when it came to communicating with Jews! Rabbi Tanenbaum did accept as valid the concern of the Orthodox Jews that the dialogue not become an "exchange of ignorance," and urged that competent experts be involved on both sides. He argued that the crisis was an opportunity for further dialogue.

condemnation of the Christians [who], by and large, were silent. Several Jewish leaders, including some of my colleagues in the rabbinate, publicly declared that this silence was proof positive that "the Christians are morally and spiritually bankrupt" and that Jewish-Christian dialogue is a farce. The same leaders demanded that Jewish groups withdraw from dialogues with Christians because they have proven to be "obviously inadequate" in influencing Christian attitudes toward Israel and the Jewish people.

Given the state of anxiety and tension among all Jews during those days in late May and early June when the Arabs were threatening to exterminate the Jews of Israel, it is altogether natural that a number of our spokesmen expressed themselves in highly emotional terms. But the emotional response that was appropriate in those charged circumstances is hardly appropriate today; and it is certainly inadequate for coming to grips with the present problems of Jewish statesmanship. Our hard choices of policy and program—including Jewish-Christian relations—that best serve the interests of the Jewish people, of Israel, and of world peace, will have to be based on a rational and dispassionate grasp of realities. What are some of these realities?

First, the generalization that the Christians failed the Jews of Israel by their silence, and implied lack of support, is inaccurate, misleading, and not substantiated by the evidence. On July 10, Louis Harris published the results of a survey that indicated that key Israeli concerns meet with this kind of overwhelming approval by Americans:

> Eighty-two percent believe that Israel's existence as a sovereign state should be formally accepted by the Arab nations.
> Eighty-eight percent believe Israel should be guaranteed passage through the Gulf of Aqaba.
> Eighty-six percent feel that Israel should also have freedom of passage through the Suez Canal.
> Almost eighty percent oppose any UN condemnation of Israel as the aggressor in the war.
> Sixty-two percent of U.S. public opinion rejects Israeli withdrawal from occupied territory as a precondition to negotiations.

In the same poll, 70 percent of the respondents felt that "Jerusalem should become an international city open to all." However, a subsequent Gallup poll released in October disclosed that a dramatic shift had taken place: 56 percent of the American people favored Israel's retaining control over a reunified Jerusalem.

Who are the Americans who feel this way about Israel? That 91.9 percent of the American people chose voluntarily to associate themselves with the Christian community in their replies to census takers is relevant to our concerns, and we need not be sidetracked by philosophical questions about the meaning or depth of their commitment. At the very least, this data indicates that associating oneself with the Christian denominations did not have a negative correlation with support of Israel.

In the face of this evidence, which Louis Harris characterizes as "sweeping majorities (of) the American people who support the principal arguments by Israel for a permanent peace in the Middle East," on what basis and by what justification have Jewish spokesmen made loose charges to the effect that "the Christians" did not support Israel?

To a White House administration that appears to be responsive to consensus politics—at least on some major issues—a persistent rumor that "the Christians" of America did not support Israel could become a dangerous political threat to Israel, for whose security and international position the strong backing of the American government is of such obvious critical importance. I cannot repress the homiletic point made in *Pirke Abash*, "Wise men, be guarded in your words!"

Second, the generalization that "the Christians by and large were silent" must be qualified by the documented evidence that a significant number of prominent and influential Catholic, Protestant, and Orthodox Christian leaders did speak in support of Israel's right to exist, to freedom from the threat of Arab belligerency, and to free access to international waterways. There is not enough space here to quote the full documentation. Those who are interested in precise facts are invited to read a recently published study issued by the American Jewish Committee, *Christian Reactions to the Middle East Crisis: New Agenda for Interreligious Dialogue*. The July 1967 issue of *Christian News From Israel*, published by the Israeli Ministry of Religious Affairs, contains similar documentation.

According to the AJC study—which seeks to provide an objective and balanced analysis of the reactions of Christian leaders, institutions, and journals to the Middle East crisis during the ten-week period from mid-May to the end of July—it is evident that eminent Christian leaders and leading Christian journals of opinion took clear positions in support of Israel's national integrity and her navigation rights during the "tense weeks before the outbreak of hostilities, when it appeared that Israel might become the victim of combined Arab aggression."

Thus, for example, a joint statement published all over the country on May 29 called upon, "our fellow Americans of all persuasions and groupings and on the Administration to support the independence, integrity, and freedom of Israel." The statement was signed by such prominent Christian leaders as the Rev. John C. Bennett, president of the interdenominational Union Theological Seminary; Dr. Reinhold Niebuhr, one of the foremost Protestant theologians; the Rev. Dr. Martin Luther King Jr.; the Rev. Robert McAfee Brown, Professor of Religion at Stanford University; the Rev. Dr. Franklin Littell, President of Iowa Wesleyan (Methodist) College; the Rev. Alexander Schmemann, Dean of St. Vladimir's Russian Orthodox Seminary; and Father John Sheerin, editor of the *Catholic World* and Vatican representative at numerous ecumenical conferences.

In addition, Catholic and Protestant leaders in major communities in the United States issued joint statements of conscience supporting Israel's position both at the height of the war and since the close of hostilities when the struggle had moved from the battlefield to the United Nations. A good example was the "Declaration of Moral Principle" issued on June 7 by Cardinal Cushing and a number of other Catholic and Protestant religious leaders in the Boston area:

> None of us can be indifferent or uninvolved in confronting the moral issues inherent in the current conflict in the Middle East. We cannot stand by idly at the possibility of Israel's destruction, of decimating the two and a half million people. . . . The end of hostilities must be followed by a firm and permanent peace; which will recognize Israel as a viable nation in the community of nations.

Another impressive example came in July from Los Angeles where clergymen of all denominations signed a public declaration of support that was well publicized in the press and other media. Father Charles Casassa, the Jesuit president of Loyola University in Los Angeles, sent a copy of the declaration to President Johnson, [United Nations General Secretary] U Thant, and the State Department, and received a sympathetic response from the Administration.

In the preamble to their document, the Los Angeles clergy indicated that their action grew directly out of their involvement in Jewish-Christian dialogues: "In recent years, great strides have been made in the area of interreligious dialogues and we are now confronted with the need to express ourselves together in terms of the religious and moral implications of the moral crisis."

On July 12, at the height of the United Nations debate about Israel's reunification of the city of Jerusalem, seventeen leading Protestant theologians, professors, and seminary presidents published this advertisement in *The New York Times:* "For Christians, to acknowledge the necessity of Judaism is to acknowledge that Judaism presupposes inextricable ties with the land of Israel and the city of David, without which Judaism cannot be truly itself. Theologically, it is this dimension to the religion of Judaism which leads us to support the reunification of the city of Jerusalem."

The majority of the scholars who signed this remarkable document—including the leading New Testament scholars Professor Krister Stendahl of Harvard and Professor W. P. Davies of Duke University—have been active participants in theological dialogues with Jewish scholars, the latest of which was the International Colloquium on Judaism and Christianity held at Harvard Divinity School in 1968. The value of their declaration was underscored when Israel's Foreign Minister, Abba Eban, quoted the text of their statement before the General Assembly as an authoritative theological reinforcement of Israel's position.

When all the available statements and actions by individual Christian leaders of both national and local prominence are weighed in the balance, it becomes perfectly clear that while the response may not have been overwhelming, it certainly was considerably more substantial, and significant, than is conveyed by the judgment that the Christians by and large were silent. When compared with the support given to Israel by individual leaders of the political left and liberal movements, the response of Christian leaders stands out as even more impressive. See "The American Left and Israel," by Martin Peretz in *Commentary*, November 1967.

THE JEWISH RESPONSE

One can make too much of declarations by individuals; just as one can make too little of them. In the internal Jewish debate thus far, it is puzzling to find that many Jewish spokesmen and commentators have tended to minimize the value of individual commitments by Christian leaders. But why? In 1953, Elmo Roper conducted a national survey in which he asked Americans, which one of these groups do you feel is doing the most good for the country at the present time?

Forty percent of the American people picked religious leaders as the group "doing the most good" and most to be trusted. "No other group—whether government, Congressional, business, or labor—came anywhere near making the prestige and pulling power of the men who are ministers of God," Roper stated. The image of the clergyman among Americans may not be without its ambiguities, but there can be little doubt that clergymen as individuals rank high in the American scale of prestige and public influence. In recent years their leadership in the Vietnam peace effort, in the war against poverty, in community organization in the slums, and in support of aid to underdeveloped countries, has further solidified their moral influence among large segments of the population. Considering this standing in American society, the support of Israel by prominent individual Christian clergymen ought to be valued very highly indeed.

When Christian individuals aligned themselves one-sidedly with the extremist Arab cause, as in the case of the Rev. Dr. Henry P. Van Dusen, a former Protestant seminary president, who wrote a letter to *The New York Times* equating the Israeli victory with the Nazi blitzkrieg, there was quick response. Other Christian leaders, most notably Dr. Roy Eckardt, voiced their distress both at his point of view and at the harm done by his negative influence. Logic and common sense alone should have compelled us to give at least as much weight to the positive influence of declarations by those Christian leaders who unequivocally backed Israel's cause and helped shape affirmative public opinion in America.

When early in June the AJC publicized a survey emphasizing the "widespread support" of Christian leaders and masses (as reflected in the public opinion polls), a representative of the Union of American Hebrew Congregations berated that evaluation in the public press, terming it "exaggerated oversimplification." His comment had little effect other than to tell some of the most distinguished American Christians, including two of the former U.S. Catholic Cardinals, one archbishop, hundreds of Protestant scholars and church leaders, as well as the editors of major Christian journals whose pro-Israel stands were cited in the survey, that their support was not regarded by Jews as terribly important after all. Imagine the situation in reverse. What a pained outcry would have arisen from Jewry had the same group of Christian leaders come out in support of Nasser and the Arab League. One of the lessons to be learned from this experience, it seems to me, is that we need to overcome the self-righteous reflex of rubbing into the dirt the faces of Christians who come to our aid—in frustrated retribution against those who do not.

Third, Jewish leaders directed their most valid, serious, and justifiable criticism at the "establishment" institutions of the Catholic and Protestant churches. As the AJC study puts it: "The reluctance of the two 'umbrella' organizations—the National Council of Churches and the National Conference of Catholic Bishops—to commit themselves unequivocally on the basic question of Israel's survival, especially in the face of Arab threats to annihilate the whole population, came as a surprise to many Jewish leaders. Neither of these two groups issued any clear-cut statement to this effect during the saber-rattling days in May."

Jews, including those who have been engaged in dialogue with these bodies for a number of years, did not expect Christian institutions to accept the Jewish understanding of the religious and cultural significance of Israel and Jerusalem to Judaism. Nor were Jewish leaders looking to Christian institutions for a commitment on political or legal issues relating to Israel's sovereignty—Israel's right to exist was not up for negotiation in any case. It was the moral and human issue of the potential massacre of 2.5 million

Jews that demanded a spontaneous outcry from those authorized to speak for the Christian conscience in the nation.

Those were "the Christians who by and large were silent" on the life-and-death issue of Jewish survival.

The record must show that Catholic and Protestant leaders who hold positions of authority in their respective establishments— notably Monsignor George Higgins, Director of Social Action for the National Conference of Catholic Bishops; Father Edward A. Flannery, Executive Secretary of the U.S. Bishops Sub-commission on Catholic-Jewish Relations; and the Rev. Dr. David Hunter, Associate General Secretary of the National Council of Churches—did take strong public positions on Israel's survival. They did so, however, in their private capacities. Their courageous and independent stands, taken at some personal risk and in the face of some institutional pressures, were a reflection of an understanding of the interior mind of Jews, the consequence of many years of close association and friendship with Jewish leaders.

When the U.S. Conference of Catholic Bishops did issue a statement on June 8, it asked for "a crusade of prayer for peace" and expressed the "fervent hope" that the UN would be successful in halting the conflict. In the face of what appeared to most Jews as the imminent prospect of another Auschwitz for the corporate Jewish body in Israel, this rhetoric, with its echo of the earlier flight into pietism by Christian leaders in Nazi Germany, contributed to a pervading sense of gloom in American Jewry.

Nor were the statements of the National Council of Churches, although formulated in more political terms, a source of great moral reinforcement for Jews or for Israel. In the June 6 telegram to President Johnson, in which they pressed for a cease-fire through the United Nations, they also appeared to equate Israel's right to exist with the need to resolve the Arab refugee problem. In their July 7 resolution, the National Council of Churches contributed to the moral confusion of cause and effect by labeling Israel's retaliation to Arab provocations "aggression" and "expansionism."

Despite the chagrin and distress these positions have aroused in the Jewish community, there is some encouragement in the fact that modifications in stance have begun to emerge, and these are potentially of considerable political importance to Israel and to eventual peace in the Middle East. Some of these changes are demonstrably attributable to marathon dialogues that a number of us have been engaged in with Catholic and Protestant institutional representatives since last June.

The most striking change has been that of the Vatican in relation to Jerusalem. Pope Paul VI, on several occasions, called for the internationalization of the city of Jerusalem, a policy that most members of the Catholic hierarchy in the United States have felt obliged to follow. On July 11, a "dialogue" took place in Jerusalem between Israel's Prime Minister Levi Eshkol and the Vatican's representative, Monsignor Angelo Felici, following which they issued a joint communiqué stating that they had explored formulae for the holy places "in an atmosphere of cordiality and mutual understanding." Since then the Vatican has changed its position, now aligning itself with the views of the World Council of Churches, which from the beginning of the crisis asked of Israel only assurance of free access to Christian holy places.

The July 7 resolution of the National Council of Churches also represents a shift from a one-sided attitude leaning toward the Arab cause, in the direction of a more balanced advocacy of even-handed justice in the Middle-East: "Indispensable to peace in the Middle East is acceptance by the entire international community of the State of Israel . . . Early talks between belligerents with or without the good offices, conciliation, or mediation of a third party are encouraged."

However profound and justified our frustrations with, and criticism of, the Christian institutions, hardheaded realism requires that Jewish policy-makers do not yield to the temptation to break off diplomatic relations with the spokesmen of Christendom and retreat to a fortress Judaica. There are Christian leaders of goodwill within the establishments who are allies or potential allies of the Jewish community, and only by keeping communication with them open and ongoing can we hope to deepen their understanding of our positions, and to win their institutional support.

The counsel of those who have been advising Jews that Christianity is "a sinking ship," that we live in a "post-Christian world," or that dialogue with Christians only "white-washes their criminal past," is the most dangerous kind of nonsense. Jewish leadership must repudiate this diatribe at all costs, because it gives our people a false sense of security, and sets into motion an anti-Christian mood that can paralyze any creative relationship with the majority society. This resort to slogans about a "post-Christian world" obscures a very complex problem that I have dealt with at greater length in another essay; suffice it for present purposes to point out that this cliché encourages many Jews to believe that they can arbitrarily turn their backs on Christian society and establish themselves elsewhere. How misleading! There is no future for Jews anywhere in the Arab-Muslim nations. The illusion of a Jewish future in the proletarian utopia of the Soviet Union has been completely dashed. The elementary fact is that the overwhelming majority of the Jews in the diaspora live in the midst of predominantly Christian communities, in the United States, Western Europe, and Latin America. The security of the State of Israel and of its Jewish community rests heavily on the continued support of the United States Government and its people. The realistic problem for us is not how to escape these facts of our existence, but how to relate to them seriously—which means to recognize the fundamental importance of strengthening cooperation and authentic solidarity with Christians and their institutions. It is they who constitute primary structures in our environment.

Taking the foregoing into account—the generally supportive response of the Christians in American society, the positive reaction of numerous Christian leaders, and the changes that appear to be taking place even in the Christian establishments—one could come to a valid conclusion radically opposite to the one widely expressed in the Jewish community; to the conclusion that "the Christians by and large" did well by Israel. That judgment can be further strengthened when Christian support of Israel is analyzed in relation to other critical issues in the life of the church, such as Vietnam, the race problem, admission of Red China to the United Nations, draft-card burning, conscientious objection, birth control, celibacy, and church-state issues. On each of these major problems the Catholic and Protestant communities are severely divided, and find it exceedingly difficult to obtain a Christian consensus that would include the hawks and the doves, the militant liberals and the white backlash, the conservatives and the progressives. If the Christian masses and the Christian leaders who have spoken out in support of Israel remain stable and steadfast in their present views, it should be a major source of moral stamina to Israel and her people during the long and protracted negotiations that lie ahead.

The foregoing assertion nevertheless raises a critical question: just how deeply rooted are the commitments of Americans who have indicated support of Israel? It has been speculated that this overwhelming popular support of Israel derives from the peculiar American tendency to identify with the underdog. It crystallized during the time when the Israelis were threatened with extermination. For most Americans nurtured on the B-film and soap-opera culture of "cowboys and Indians," "good guys and bad guys," it was natural to back little David surrounded by murderous Goliaths. But the roles have now shifted. Are we to anticipate that this large popular support will shift to the side of the Arabs, who are the new "underdogs"? Certainly the Russian and Arab propaganda campaigns, which have been trying diabolically to portray Israelis as the "New Nazis pursuing the Arabs cast in the role of the new Jews," are striving to bring about such a shift in world public opinion.

The Harris and Gallup opinion polls were conducted respectively in July and October of 1967, and would therefore argue that Israel's victory was not met by a significant shift in public sentiment away from Israel. However, conversations between numerous Jewish leaders and many Christians—clergy and laymen—since the end of the June war lead to the inescapable impression that the majority of Christians who supported Israel did so on the basis of strong humanitarian feelings. Such feelings and expressions of conscience, while they are to be honored for what they are, are inadequate to sustain conviction for the long pull ahead in the Middle East. It therefore seems imperative that Jews help their Christian neighbors enlarge their intellectual grasp of the issues, including the meaning of Israel and Jerusalem to the Jewish people and to Judaism.

And that brings us to the role of the Jewish-Christian dialogue as an instrument for furthering Christian understanding of Jewish peoplehood and its relation to Israel. Those who have downgraded the dialogue or condemned it as bankrupt are no more accurate in their understanding of its achievement than they were in their emotional and imprecise evaluation of "the Christian response" to Israel. From first-hand experience, I know that those who have spoken of such dogmatic terms have either not participated at all in the more serious Jewish-Christian dialogues, or at most have taken part in two or three seminars and institutes. On the basis of this minimal experience, they generalize about a whole movement.

If the same standard of success or failure were applied, for example, to the usefulness in our synagogues of adult Jewish education programs in transforming the congregants' patterns of religions observance and in-depth knowledge of the Talmud and classic Jewish sources, then I fear that many rabbis would be compelled to close down their synagogues and conclude that Judaism has failed. But that conclusion would be as erroneous as the one which some Jewish leaders, especially a few nationally prominent rabbis, are making about the Jewish-Christian dialogue. The dialogue may not have proven to be all that its supporters have claimed, but it is certainly more than the caricature its opponents have made of it.

A value judgment of the Jewish-Christian dialogue requires a fair-minded confrontation of the bald evidence. It is incontrovertible fact for those who have actively participated in dialogues—especially with academicians, theologians, religious school teachers, seminarians, and clergy—that these interactions have helped bring about profound and positive changes in the attitudes and behavior of many Christians toward the Jewish people, Judaism, and the synagogue. The evidence is so clear-cut and palpable that it is difficult to understand assertions to the contrary. Documentation of the changes that have already taken place in Christian thought, teaching, and practice, on all levels of Christian culture, could fill a large volume. (The rates of change are uneven, of course, in this mammoth process.)

How far the dialogue process has helped Christian leadership to overcome the ancient myths and stereotypes about "deicide" (the "Christ-killer" charge), proselytizing, and the permanent worth and value of Judaism is reflected in the official statement of the American Catholic Church issued in March 1967 as the "Guidelines for Catholic-Jewish Relations of the National Conference of Catholic Bishops." These guidelines charge "Catholic educators and scholars" with responsibility to carry out the following program of implementation on all levels of Christian society:

- In keeping with the [Vatican Council II] statement's strong repudiation of anti-Semitism, a frank and honest treatment of the history of Christian anti-Semitism [should be incorporated] in our history books, courses and curricula . . .
- The presentation of the Crucifixion story in such a way as not to implicate all Jews of Jesus's time in a collective guilt for the crime . . .
- A full and precise explanation of the use of the expression 'the Jews' by St. John and other New Testament references which appear to place all Jews in a negative light. (These expressions and references should be fully and precisely clarified in accordance with the intent of the [Vatican Council] statement the Jews are "not to be presented as rejected or accursed by God as if this followed from Holy Scripture.")
- An explicit rejection of the historically inaccurate notion that Judaism of that time, especially that of the Pharisees, was a decadent formalism and hypocrisy, well exemplified by Jesus's enemies . . .
- An acknowledgment by Catholic scholars of the living and complex reality of Judaism after Christ and the permanent election of Israel alluded to by St. Paul (Rom. 2:9–11), and incorporation of the results into Catholic teaching . . .
- It is understood that proselytizing is to be carefully avoided in the dialogue.

THE THEOLOGICAL VANGUARD

Unquestionably the most significant consequence of the Jewish-Christian dilemma has been the emergence of "a new theology of Israel" among a group of influential Catholic and Protestant theologians, the net effect of which is to call upon Christians to give up their designs to convert Jews. This "new theology" is hinted at in the last statement of the Bishops' guidelines quoted above; it appears in more explicit theological form in the following paragraph from an essay by Father Cornelius Rijk, recently appointed advisor on Jewish affairs to Cardinal Bea at the Vatican:

In our time Christian theology has gained a new religious understanding of the people of Israel through the realization that God
continues to be with his people and that the revelation of the Old
Testament is now complete as far as the Jewish people are concerned, even though they have not recognized Jesus of Nazareth as
the Messiah. The Messiah came to fulfill the Old Covenant, but
there is no suggestion anywhere in the New Testament that the
Old Covenant was thereby abolished. Nor is it ever stated that God
rejected his own people and that Christianity came to take the
place of Judaism.

Anyone who knows anything about the past 1,900 years of Jewish-Christian relations is fully aware that these theological affirmations by the highest authorities of the Roman Catholic Church
constitute little short of a revolutionary change in position. This
change is matched by parallel developments among leaders in the
Protestant communities. No Jew needs to turn somersaults in the
street because the Christian world is finally beginning to correct
its errors and misperceptions about us. But what moral, intellectual, or practical purpose is served by acting as though no change
at all is taking place, or by seeking to discredit this healthful development?

There are, of course, many conservative Christians who, ironically, share with some Orthodox Jews a deep suspicion of change,
and who are anxious about the present liberalization process in
the Catholic community. These are mostly the same Orthodox
Christians (also called "conservatives") who, in alliance with the
prelates from the Arab countries, resisted the efforts of progressive churchmen to condemn anti-Semitism and declare a clear
policy of friendship and respect for Jews and Judaism. Do Jews,
wittingly or unwittingly, want to play into the hands of the camp
of Christians whose spiritual ancestors were the source of so much
agony and bloodshed for our people, and so much contumely for
our religion? These are the Orthodox Christians who have found
it theologically intolerable that the Jews have returned to the Holy
Land, and that the holy places are now under Jewish jurisdiction.
These same conservatives can be counted upon to do everything
humanly possible to prevent the recognition of the State of Israel
by the Vatican. (Liberal churchmen who have not been confronted in the dialogue with their liberal bias against Israel make

strange bedfellows with ultra-conservatives and are not exempt from the same criticism.) Is it not paradoxical that Jews who demonstrate such devotion and passion to preserve the State of Israel should continue to press their opposition to the dialogue process which holds out such promise of an understanding that can lead more Christians to the support and recognition of Israel's right to exist?

The Italian historian Benedetto Croce pointed out that an intellectual elite in every society establishes and maintains the new ideas that become the keystone of all social and cultural change. What this elite thinks today, Croce stated, often becomes the thought of the masses in decades to come. Already new elite Christian ideas about Jews and Judaism have begun to percolate down to the Christian masses through new textbooks used in parochial schools and Sunday schools, teacher training institutes for nuns and Protestant teachers, seminars for Christian seminarians, chairs of Jewish studies in colleges and universities, adult education institutes for Christian parents, and the growing use of Christian programs on radio, television, and other mass media.

The notion that these changes would have taken place if Christians simply studied Jewish books, without a living encounter with Jews in dialogue, is an illusion and a fantasy. Vast libraries of Judaica, in all languages, have been available to Christian scholars, clergymen, and teachers for almost 2,000 years. How many significant changes in Christian attitudes toward Jews and Judaism can be attributed to the study of this literature? Indeed, there is plenty of evidence that Christian savants, nurtured on anti-Jewish theological stereotypes, and living in isolation from Jews as persons, read into or read out of Jewish sources texts that confirmed their preconceived bias. Those Jews who advocate just letting Christian scholars study the Judaic literature as a substitute for dialogue must explain how they would deal with such noble fruits of that process as Johann Eisenmenger's *Judaism Unmasked, The Protocols of the Elders of Zion* (1732), and the most recent anthology of vicious anti-Semitism, reputedly published and distributed by Arab sources at Vatican Council II, *The Plot Against the Church*. All these marvelous works were the result of such library studies.

The fact is that the policy of withdrawal from Jewish-Christian dialogue and reliance on theoretical understanding flies in the face of everything we know from social psychology about attitude change. Kurt Lewin, the father of this social science, has demonstrated clinically that changes in attitudes and behavior do not result from cognitive information or abstract ideas alone, but primarily from living human interaction, which transmutes ideas into personal values. The changes that have taken place thus far in Christian attitudes toward deicide, anti-Semitism, proselytization, and the living relevance of Rabbinic Judaism are case histories demonstrating the validity of this approach.

The more recent substitute for religious dialogue that has been vigorously advocated by some Jews, strange to say, is interfaith social action. I know of no proposal more contradictory to traditional, *halachic* Judaism, for in effect, it advocates a separation between religion and life. The late Chief Rabbi Kook of Israel, one of the great sages of traditional Judaism, declared that

> man's physical concerns and spiritual aspirations are inseparable. The sacred cannot exist without the profane. The sacred and the profane together influence the human spirit, and man is enriched "by absorbing from each whatever is suitable. Indeed, the sacred can exist only so long as it rests upon a foundation of the profane" since spiritual sanctity must rest upon the solid base of normal life.

Holiness set up in opposition to nature was described by Chief Rabbi Kook as "the holiness of the exile," a reflection of the long dispersion in which Jews were cut off from normal existence in society.

Not only is this religious social action absurd from the point of view of Judaism, it is impractical as well. To avoid examining the basic religious grounds for social action work, to cooperate with Christians without such examination, can lead to an incredible situation in which Christians and Jews would collaborate to "redeem" the civic society while Christians look upon their Jewish partners as "unredeemed." How strong an alliance in social action do Jews believe they could sustain, while Christians continued to think of Jews as "fallen and faithless Israel?"

To call for an embargo on the discussion of religious issues with Christians and to promote relations solely on the basis of social action would mean that we were presenting Judaism to the Christian world as a secular humanist institution. As Arthur Hertzberg has frequently noted, Jews and Judaism have greater dignity and status in the Bible than they have in any other intellectual construction in the Western world, and traditional Jews who take this "social action only" line appear to be bent on undermining that extraordinary reality.

Rabbis, priests, nuns, and ministers do not come together for social action because they are experts in nuclear non-proliferation treaties, or in the administration of economic development programs in Lesotho, or in city planning. What brings them together is a recognition that they share a moral conscience, which in turn derives from a certain attitude toward Sacred Scriptures and their sacred histories, that they all have a certain explanation for man and society that is shaped by messianic visions of a kingdom to come in which justice and righteousness are consummated. Certainly they will carry out their redemptive work more effectively if they have technical competence, but that is not their primary vocation. If it is not religious principle that binds them together, then the work can be done more honestly and unambiguously under the auspices of the Foreign Policy Association or the American Civil Liberties Union.

Traditional Jews make one very sound criticism of the dialogue that must be taken seriously. That concern is that dialogue may become an arena for trading ignorance. With rare exceptions, our representatives in theological dialogues more than hold their own, and generally convey a deep impression of the vitality and richness of contemporary Jewish scholarship and cultural life. The lay dialogue has taught us that we have tended to overestimate the knowledge among Christians of their own faith and doctrines, and have underestimated the capacity of our intelligent, carefully selected Jewish laymen. We have also learned that Jewish-Christian lay dialogues have become an increasingly strong incentive for our people to know themselves as Jews. As a result, the dialogue has been characterized as "the secret weapon of adult Jewish education."

In summary, the evidence is overwhelming that we have made remarkable, indeed unprecedented progress on the issues we have stressed in the Jewish-Christian dialogue. Can the dialogue be similarly effective in helping overcome Christian ignorance of misunderstanding of Jewish peoplehood (*k'lal yisrael*, the sacred congregation of Israel) and the symbolic meaning of Israel and Jerusalem to Judaism and the Jewish people?

The answer is yes, but with provisions. The first provision is that Jews themselves clarify their own understanding of these complex questions. We are far from anything like a consensus on the meaning of Israel to the Jewish people. Is Israel simply a secular nation-state? Does it represent the fulfillment of messianic expectations that date back to the prophets of Israel? Is it an eschatological reality, pointing to the day of judgment which the prophets foretold would usher in *malkut shamayim,* the kingdom of heaven?

When in recent weeks some of my colleagues in the rabbinate have expressed bitter disappointment over the "Christian silence" about Israel, I asked them, "When did you speak to a Christian minister about the religious significance of Jerusalem to Judaism?" Invariably the answer was "never" or "not very recently." Further, I would ask, "When did you last speak to your congregation about this?" Again, "not very recently," or "we take our relationship to Israel for granted; everyone knows that the ark faces toward Jerusalem, that the glass is broken at each wedding to commemorate the destruction of the Temple in Jerusalem, that our three pilgrim festivals keep alive the memory of the national sanctuary on Mt. Zion," and so forth.

In the main, rabbis and Jewish teachers have not clarified these fundamental issues relating to Israel, neither for themselves nor for their Jewish audiences. How much less have we clarified these questions for our Christian neighbors? Given this enormous lack in theoretical understanding, it is virtually a miracle that Jewish people have behaved as well as they have. It is equally astounding that the Christian leaders and masses responded to Israel's predicament as affirmatively as they did.

Before us, therefore, is a great task of intellectual clarification, and of communication. The Israeli-Arab crisis resulted in a crisis in Jewish-Christian relations. But it is a crisis that is also a great opportunity.

10

The Meaning of Israel: A Jewish View

THE DOMINANT REALITY in Jewish life today is that the Jewish people throughout the world have experienced a profound transformation since the six-day war between Israel and the Arab states in June 1967. No one can truly understand Jews or Judaism today—nor can Jewish-Christian relationships be accurately comprehended—unless one takes into account the magnitude and depth of this transformation, which verges on collective *metanoia.*

The threats of Arab leaders, broadcast daily over Radio Cairo, Radio Amman, and from Damascus during the weeks before the June 1967 war, to annihilate the two-and-a-half million Jews in Israel, were answered by a Jewish unity, Jewish solidarity, and a consciousness of interdependence in fate and destiny, for which I can find no precedent in the past two thousand years of Jewish history.

During the last week of May 1967, just a few days before the Israeli-Arab hostilities broke out, I was called hurriedly to attend

Address to the Southern Baptist-Jewish Scholars Conference in Louisville, August 18–20, 1969. In this address, Rabbi Marc Tanenbaum describes the effects of the trauma of the Holocaust on the "interior life of the Jew today." He finds "a clue to the disorientation among Jews all over the world after the genocide experience" in the "remarkable debate" over Rolf Hochhuth's *The Deputy,* a theatrical presentation on the fate of Jews during the Holocaust. He notes the historical absurdity of the play's premise, namely, that "the pope had the power to stop the Nazi juggernaut just by speaking out." Rabbi Tanenbaum believes that, morally, Pope Pius XII should have spoken out more forcefully than he did, but indicts as "incredible" what he calls Hochhuth's "simplistic thesis." He then turns to an analysis of why so many of his fellow Jews bought into the Hochhuth thesis. This is an unflinchingly candid view of one's own people. Once again, Rabbi Tanenbaum's challenge for a *heshbon hanefesh*—literally "a reckoning of the soul" or rigorous self-examination—this time in his own community, is as urgent now as when first issued. Tanenbaum goes on to describe feelingly and beautifully what Israel means for Jews and, by implication, what it can mean for Christians.

a meeting of Jewish leaders in New York City. Leaders of some twenty-three major Jewish bodies, representatives of all branches of Jewish life—Orthodox, Conservative, Reform, Zionist, non-Zionist, secular, labor, social welfare, Jewish education—listened to a report by a young Israeli who had flown in from Jerusalem the day before. Like the few Jews who escaped from Hungary and Poland during the Nazi occupation and rushed to Paris and London to awaken the conscience of the world to what was happening to the six million Jews in Europe, this young Israeli was driven on his mission of mercy, repeating the ancient Yiddish cry, "Rateveh!" "Help, save us!"

He placed a tape-recorder before this group of Jewish leaders and played off Arab-language broadcasts monitored a few days before, and translated them into English.

The Voice of the Arabs, Radio Cairo: "Destroy them and lay them waste and liberate Palestine. Your hour has come. Woe to you, Israel. The Arab nation has come to wipe out your people and to settle the account. This is your end, Israel. All the Arabs must take revenge for 1948. This is a moment of historic importance to our Arab people and to the holy war. Conquer the land."

Another tape carried a broadcast by the Syrian Defense Minister: "We say: We shall never call for, nor accept, peace. We shall only accept war and the restoration of the usurped land. We resolve to drench this land with our blood, to oust you, aggressors, and throw you into the sea for good."

Then the young Israeli showed us photostatic copies of captured battle orders of the Egyptian army and air force, the Syrian and the Jordanian armies. Jordan, the "moderate" among the Arab states, issued operational orders to seven brigade headquarters instructing them to wipe out the civilian inhabitants of Israeli population centers. These orders, discovered at Ramallah headquarters north of Jerusalem, stated: "The intention of H.Q. Western Front is to carry out a raid on Motza colony (an Israeli village of some eight hundred people three miles west of Jerusalem), to destroy it, and kill all its inhabitants. . . ."[1]

---

[1] *The Record of Aggression,* distributed by the Israel Information Services, New York, July 1967.

Had the Egyptians, Syrians, and Jordanians struck first, carrying out their battle orders, it is estimated that 250,000 to 500,000 Jewish men, women, and children would have been murdered in the first hours of war. As those Jewish leaders listened, one suddenly felt something extraordinary happening in the crowded room. All the man-made distinctions that had separated one Jew from another seemed visibly to evaporate. At that moment they no longer saw themselves as Orthodox, Conservative, Reform, religious or secular, Zionist or non-Zionist. There was one emotion: we were all Jews, all conscious of our being one people, all overwhelmingly convinced of our responsibility to each other.

That transformation did not occur only in the Jewish leadership. It reached into virtually every Jewish heart around the world. The reality and intensity of that "new Jewish being" manifested itself in myriad ways. Five leaders of the anti-Zionist American Council for Judaism, now aware that ideological anti-Zionism was a betrayal of their people at a moment when Arabs were publicly proposing a "final solution" in Israel, resigned from the organization and made substantial contributions to the United Jewish Appeal's Emergency Campaign Fund for Israel. A Jewish taxi-driver stopped in front of the Jewish Agency building in New York City, opened his doors, pointed to his two teenaged sons in the cab, and said to an Agency official, "Here are my two sons. They are all I have in the world. Take them. Let them go to Israel and milk cows, tend the fields, so they can relieve others to go to the battlefields. Our people need help."

It is not hyperbole, in my judgment, to say that this consciousness of Jewish unity and solidarity as a people, of a common fate and destiny across all national and linguistic barriers, is surpassed only by the moment in Jewish history when Moses brought the tribes together at the foot of Mount Sinai where they were transformed through the Covenant into an historic people charged with the task of helping to bring redemption to the world.

How does one explain this phenomenon? Two decisive events in contemporary Jewish experience must be taken into account in any effort to understand the interior life of the Jew today. The first is the Nazi Holocaust. The other is the meaning of the State of Israel to the Jewish people and to Judaism.

THE HOLOCAUST

Discussion of the Nazi Holocaust must be approached as one confronts the sacred—with fear and awe. Less than twenty-five years ago, our people suffered an unbearable trauma, from whose shattering effects we have yet to recover. In his recent book, *The Legends of Our Time* (New York: Holt, Rinehart, and Winston, 1968), Elie Wiesel, who survived three concentration camps and has become an emissary to keep alive the hallowed memory of the six million Jewish victims, described his conversation with a distinguished literary critic: "I asked Alfred Kazin one day if he thought the death of six million Jews could have meaning, and he replied he hoped not." Wiesel adds: "All of us, I believe, in varying degrees must take responsibility for what happened in Europe. . . . We belong to a generation at once lost and guilty, and our collective conscience lies under a weight of humiliation."

A clue to the depth of disorientation among Jews all over the world after the genocide experience can be found in the remarkable debate over Rolf Hochhuth's play, *The Deputy*. That play which, in my judgment, was a Lutheran Reformation morality drama in which Jews as persons were practically incidental, depicted Pope Pius XII as the opposite number to Hitler, implying that the pope had the power to stop the Nazi juggernaut just by speaking out.

I believe firmly that the pope, by his self-definition as the vicar of Christ on earth, had no moral alternative but to make his voice heard, clearly and decisively, in protest against the murderous evil of the Nazis. As Gordon Zahn, the Catholic sociologist, has demonstrated in his study, *German Catholics and Hitler's Wars* (New York: Sheed and Ward, 1962), the absence of clear-cut moral leadership on resistance to collaboration with Hitler's war machine and murder-factories, either from Rome or the German bishops at Fulda, reinforced a mentality among German masses to conform to Nazi demands.

Nevertheless, Hochhuth and the adapters of his play are still responsible for gross oversimplification of the complex political, economic, and social factors that were operating behind the Nazi dynamic and the stand of Pius XII.

As incredible as his simplistic thesis was the uncritical response of so many Jews who affirmed that that was the way it was—Pius XII was mainly responsible. Most contemporary Jews are products of the Enlightenment, have a rational critical faculty and can be expected to understand the issues of the Nazi period in their full complexity. That so many of our people accepted the Hochhuth drama as the whole story reveals and confirms the huge burden of anguish the Nazi experience has placed upon the Jewish psyche and soul. It has been intolerable to live with the knowledge that the Jewish people were singled out for total extermination by an advanced twentieth-century nation. How can one manage to stay sane in the face of that ultimate irrationality and madness? Some answer is necessary to ease the pain of that shattering realization. If Pius XII is an answer, even a partial and least bit rational answer, then so let it be, said the unsettled Jewish conscience. The Jews' preoccupation and agitation—tragically with such good reason— about Christian silence in the face of Nazi savagery must now also be considered in terms of its deep psychic meaning. Perplexity over the almost total conformity of Christian institutions and leaders to the demands of the Nazi regime in Germany, and the silence and indifference of Christians in other countries, has diverted Jews until recently from another gnawing preoccupation, namely, with the inadequacy of their own response to their European brothers who were being prepared "like sheep unto the slaughter." Only now, some twenty-five years later, are Jews able to begin to face the questions: "Where were we? Did we do enough?"

There have been efforts to express this preoccupation constructively. The Jewish community recently organized an emergency relief campaign to provide food, clothing, medicines, and money for the victims of the Nigerian-Biafran struggle. The response was incredible. Within a brief period of months, the Jewish community organizations turned over to Church World Service, Catholic Relief Services, UNICEF, and other relief bodies more than 500 tons of supplies and about $350,000. Also, as is generally known, many Jews have been identified with the struggle for social justice for the black, brown, red, and deprived white peoples of this nation. Jews were prominent in the March on Washington for Jobs and Freedom, in the marches to Selma and Memphis, and in inner city work in the slums and ghettos of the North.

There are no Jews, to my knowledge, in Nigeria or Biafra. Most of the tribesmen are either Muslims, animists, or Christian Ibos. There is very little prospect that they will become Jews, certainly in our lifetime. There are very few Jews among the 21 million Negroes in this country. The unprecedented outpouring of relief aid to the people of Nigeria and Biafra was a genuine act of Jewish identification with them on the basis of their common humanity, assuredly motivated by the prophetic inheritance of Judaism. Similarly, involvement in the social-justice struggle of blacks and other poor people is an authentic Jewish expression of humanitarian conscience. But increasingly I am persuaded that the disproportionate involvement of Jews, and the "surplus of intensity" of the Jewish response, reveals that another force is at work in the Jewish soul. These marches and these instant responses of relief aid to distant Africans are, on the deepest levels, an act of delayed atonement for the marches we did not make in the 1930s and 1940s to Washington, Paris, Berlin, and Warsaw, when it might have made some difference; for the food, clothing, and medicine we were not able to get through to Dachau, Bergen-Belsen, and Auschwitz when it might have brought relief and comfort to our brothers and sisters.

Learning to live in the shadow of the Nazi Holocaust involves thinking not only about the meaning of being a Jew, but the meaning of being human as well. In the unique deposits of historical data inherited by contemporary Jewry is the fact that in the years between 1939 and 1945 of the Christian era, and in Germany, the seat of the Holy Roman Empire and the heartland of the great Protestant Reformation, it was possible for thousands of persons to buy, for twenty-five cents, a phial of Zyklon-B gas that could wipe out the lives of a hundred human beings within minutes. The conclusion from this scientific data is that human life became literally worthless; the value of human existence itself has been called into question. For the Jew who has managed to survive and live in this day, the Nazi Holocaust has impaired the image of God, of man, and of the moral order in the universe. Only since the revelations of what happened in Auschwitz have we begun to hear Jewish theologians speak of the death of God, the *deus absconditus*, who has hidden His face from us. See for instance Franklin Littell, *The German Phoenix—Men and Movements in the*

Church in Germany (New York: Doubleday and Co., 1960); Guenter Lewy, *The Catholic Church and Nazi Germany* (New York: McGraw-Hill Book Co., 1964); Saul Friedlander, *Pius XII and the Third Reich: A Documentation* (New York: Alfred Knopf, 1966); Arthur C. Cochrane, *The Church's Confession Under Hitler* (Philadelphia: The Westminster Press, 1962); Frederick K. Wentz, *The Reaction of the Religious Press in America to the Emergence of Nazism* (Ann Arbor, MI: University Microfilms, Inc., 1954); Richard Rubenstein, *After Auschwitz* (Indianapolis: Bobbs-Merrill, 1966).

When, therefore, Jews heard the rhetoric and themes of genocide and "final solution" in the May and June 1967 proclamations from Cairo, Amman, Damascus, and Baghdad, the sleeper reaction to the Nazi Holocaust was instantly awakened. There were two distinctively new Jewish themes in the overwhelming united response to these threats, both permanent and universal lessons engraved on Jewish consciousness in the wake of the Nazi trauma. In the 1930s, Jews in Germany did not believe Hitler's proclamation that he would exterminate them, even though it was explicitly formulated in *Mein Kampf* (English translation: Boston: Houghton Mifflin, 1943) and in hundreds of other threats. Jews today believe what their enemies say and take it seriously. Second, Jews will never again be silent in the face of persecution and threats of annihilation: the world may find reasons to abandon Jews; Jews will never again abandon Jews, anywhere. This transformed consciousness of the Jewish people and the bonds of solidarity between the diaspora and Israel amount to a refusal to give Hitler and the Nazi murderers a final victory over both Jews and civilized humanity.

THE MEANING OF THE STATE OF ISRAEL

To comprehend the present meaning of the State of Israel to the Jewish people, it is essential that we see it in some historic and theological perspectives, involving the biblical, post-biblical, and contemporary periods. So vast and complex is the literature on this subject that one must limit himself to so many conclusions (and refer the interested reader to available bibliographies).

Before this group of distinguished Christian and Jewish scholars, so many of whom are steeped in biblical scholarship, it is unnecessary, and would be a presumption, to dwell on the biblical bases of the Jewish relationship to Israel as the Holy Land. A few examples of the rich contemporary literature on this subject are R. H. Charles's *Study on Eschatology* (New York: Schocken Books, 1963); Harry Orlinsky on *Ancient Israel* (Ithaca, NY: Cornell University Press, 1963); B. Locker on *Israel: An Echo of Eternity* (New York: Farrar, Straus and Giroux, 1969) by Abraham Joshua Heschel; *The Zionist Idea* (Garden City, NY: Doubleday, 1959) by Arthur Hertzberg; *The Five Roots of Israel* (London: Vallentine, Mitchell, 1964) by James Parkes, among a host of other works.[2]

There is abundant biblical evidence on this central theme: Israel became a nation at the Exodus, but the promises of the ultimate greatness of Israel, and its destiny as a source of blessing to all mankind, were made before to Abraham, Isaac, and Jacob. Central in the covenant with Abraham was God's promise of the land of Canaan (Gen. 17:8), "To thee and thy seed . . . for an everlasting possession."

The bond between the chosen people and the chosen land became inextricable in the minds of biblical and prophetic authors. Palestine was not only the scene providentially chosen for the formation of children of Israel into "a kingdom of priests and a holy nation," but also the *axis mundi*, the center of the prophetic doctrine of the coming kingdom.

Ezekiel, while a captive carried away by Nebuchadnezzar, has good tidings not only for the people of Israel (chapter 37, the vision of the "valley of bones"), but also for the land bereaved of its people:

> But ye, O mountains of Israel, ye shall shoot forth your branches and yield your fruit to my people of Israel; for they are at hand to come. For behold I am for you and I will turn unto you, and ye shall be tilled and sown; And I will multiply men upon you, all the House of Israel, even all of it; and the cities shall be inhabited and the wastes shall be builded; And I will multiply you man and beast; and they shall increase and bring fruit; and I will settle you after

---

[2] A significant body of writing on this subject has begun to appear in such journals as *The Journal of Ecumenical Studies* (articles by Rev. Edward A. Flannery, Rabbi Jacob Agus, etc.).

old estates, and will do better unto you than at your beginnings; and ye shall know that I am the Lord (Ezek. 36:8–11).

Similarly, there is much evidence in post-biblical history and experience to support the Jewish concept that the land of Israel is deeply intertwined with the faith and the destiny of the people of Israel. Let us take this citation from Elias Bickerman's study, *From Ezra to the Maccabees* (New York: Schocken Books, 1962):

> The post-biblical period of Jewish history begins toward the end of 450 B.C.E. (the period of Nehemiah). That period is marked by a unique and rewarding polarity: on the one hand, the Jerusalem center and, on the other, the plurality of centers in the diaspora. The Dispersion saved Judaism from physical extirpation and spiritual inbreeding. Palestine united the dispersed members of the nation and gave them a sense of oneness. This counterpoise of historical forces is without analogy in antiquity. . . . The Jewish Dispersion continued to consider Jerusalem as the "metropolis" (Philo), turned to the Holy Land for guidance, and in turn determined the destinies of its inhabitants. Men who established normative Judaism in Palestine—Zerubabbel, Ezra, Nehemiah—came from the diaspora, from Babylon, and Susa. The diaspora clung to its unique God and to Jerusalem, the unique center of lawful worship. But at the same time, the God of Zion . . . was not only the God of the Jews. He was the sole God in heaven and earth, the so-called deities of the pagans were nothing but vain idols. Hence the polarity of Jerusalem and the Dispersion had its ideological counterpart in the paradoxical combination of universal monotheism and particularism, in the conception that the sole Lord of the universe dwells on the hillock of Zion. This theological paradox held the Jews in the Dispersion together, and from all points of the compass they directed their eyes to the Lord's Temple in Jerusalem.

Bickerman's formulation does justice to the ideational reality that existed in the minds of post-biblical Jewry. The consequences of that relationship between the holy land and the diaspora can be appreciated only by studying its effects in history across the centuries until now. So profound was the hold on the religious imagination of world Jewry of Jerusalem as the holy city and Palestine/Israel as the spiritual center, that in every century there were waves of *aliyah* (immigration) to the holy land. Over the past two thousand years there have been at least thirteen different regimes ruling Palestine, but Jews managed nevertheless to maintain an unbroken stream of pilgrims and settlers in its cities and villages.

Two vital historic footnotes: there has never been an Arab political state in Palestine; the several Arab dynasties that governed Palestine since the rise of Islam in the seventh century ruled the country as a military satrapy from distant centers in Cairo, Baghdad, or Damascus. The only time in which Palestine was organized and governed as a sovereign political state was when it was under Jewish rule.

The religious symbolism of the holy city and the holy land, with their powerful messianic and eschatological motifs, has dominated the entire synagogal, liturgical, and halachic discipline of world Jewry from the time of Ezra and Nehemiah down to this day. No synagogue or temple can be erected anywhere in the inhabited world unless the holy ark and Torah scrolls are planned to face in the direction of Jerusalem, the site of the Holy Temple. Each of the major pilgrim festivals of Sukkoth (Tabernacles), Passover, and Shavuoth (Pentecost) involves the whole of worshiping Jewry in a reenactment of past experiences of redemption relating them to the scene of the Jews' historic origins as a people in the Promised Land, and yearning together for some future Messianic redemption which in some mysterious, providential way will be bound up with the future of the Promised Land.

The daily, Sabbath, and festival prayers of the Jewish people reiterate the constant refrain, "and rebuild Jerusalem speedily in our day," . . . "extend thy canopy of peace over Jerusalem we pray." The theme is repeated throughout the grace after meals. At the climax of the Jewish wedding, the groom breaks a glass recalling the tragic destruction of the religious and national shrine of Jerusalem, and a prayer is chanted looking forward to the bride and groom rejoicing in the streets of Jerusalem. (The text from "the seven marriage benedictions" reads: "Soon may there be heard in the cities of Judah, and in the streets of Jerusalem, the voice of joy and gladness, the voice of the bridegroom and the voice of the bride, the jubilant voice of bridegrooms from their nuptial canopies, and of youths from their feasts of song.") Pious Jews, in their last wills and testaments, insisted that their families purchase soil from the holy land so that it could be placed in their coffins, suggesting some metaphysical, mystical link with the soil on which, tradition asserts, the resurrection of the dead will begin.

Quite obviously, many Jews today do not believe in these religious ideas, and some practice few of the rituals except for the *rites de passage* which inevitably confront them with these traditions. But enough Jews have believed in the truth of these biblical, prophetic, and rabbinic ideas and traditions, and a large enough number continue to be attached to them today, to account for the profound latent emotional, historic, and spiritual attachment to Israel that became manifest when her existence appeared to be threatened in June 1967. Something fundamental in the Jewish religion—despite the unclarity of the messianic and eschatological aspects of contemporary Israel—was at stake: the very continuity of Jewish history in all its paradox was threatened, and its sacrifice in such a savage and ignominious end was intolerable. Jews indeed behaved better than they truly understood.

One additional explanation is necessary to round out an understanding of the meaning of Israel to contemporary Jewry. As one studies the historical literature of the nineteenth and early twentieth centuries, one is struck by the extraordinary preoccupation of the most prominent Christian scholars with the Jewish predicament of marginality in the Christian West. Max Weber, in his monumental study on *Ancient Judaism* (1917–19) describes the status of the Jews in Western Europe in these words: "Sociologically speaking, the Jews were a pariah people, which means . . . that they were a guest people who were ritually separated, formally and de facto, from their social surroundings." The closest analogy that Weber could find for the Jewish situation was that of the "untouchables in the Indian caste system."

Heinrich von Treitschke, historian and high priest of Prussianism, wrote a series of articles in 1879 in the *Preussische Jahr Bucher* in which he declared: "The Jews are our misfortune." Paul de Lagarde, son of a Lutheran minister, authority on the Septuagint, and adherent of German deism, asserted, "To let the Jews into Prussia today . . . is to turn Prussia into Palestine."

Jews found themselves condemned as capitalist and socialist, as primitive religionist and atheist. The intellectual and academic atmosphere was filled with religious and racial anti-Semitism. "The Aryan lives by honest labor, the Semite by management, jobbing, and exploitation. The Aryans are the true creators in philosophy, religion, and science; the Semites are the imitators and plagiarists" (August Rohling and Eugen Duhring). See Peter G. J. Pulzer, *The Rise of Political Anti-Semitism in Germany and Austria* (New York: Wiley, 1964).

In response to these incessant diagnoses of the Jewish predicament by Christian scholars and divines, Jews were determined to provide their own prognosis on putting a decisive end to their pariah status. As in the days of Saul, they now were resolved to become a nation like unto all the nations. Thus Jews in nineteenth-century Europe fused the strains of the inherited spiritual traditions in which Palestine was so markedly central, with the Christian and Western solutions for national normalcy which they learned as active participants in every major movement for national self-determination on the Continent. In Russia, the pogroms of the 1880s, 1903, and 1907 that "convulsed the Pale of Settlement" stoked the fires of Jewish nationalism. Moses Rischin notes: "In the face of unprecedented barbarism, the Zionist impulse, which had remained dormant despite the existence for over a generation of the "Lovers of Zion" and other Zionist groups, acquired life. Jewish youth marshaled courage in an effort to salvage its self-respect and that of fellow Jews. They (Zionists) drew up schemes and programs for the rescue of oppressed Jews that helped sustain morale in these terrible times" (Moses Rischin, *The Promised City*, Hebrew Union Press, 1962).

Thus Israel became a haven for the oppressed Jews from every nation on the Continent. It also became the symbol and reality of the normalization of the Jew. Israel became the most systematic expression of the Jewish presence in the world. Despite the success of Jews in other democratic countries, Israel was the only spatial center in which Jews created out of the distinctive Jewish ethos and their own intellectual, spiritual and moral resources economic, military, political and social institutions. Not to use the word lightly, Israel represents the incarnation of Jewishness in the world.

Despite the richness and vitality of diaspora Jewish religious experience, it is in Israel that the Jewish religious and moral systems are being put to the crucial test. The relation and relevance of the synagogue and rabbinic Judaism to the moralizing of secular power is being tested here as nowhere else in the world. It is in Israel that Jews as a majority society encounter history and shape modernity.

If these expressions of the Jewish reality in the world were to become expendable, then being a Jew anywhere becomes expendable, certainly profoundly diminished. Jews therefore cannot tolerate the prospect of the undermining of the State of Israel, or the weakening of the unique experiment and mission of the Jewish people and society in Israel, for in their survival and destiny there is at stake the success or failure of the nearly 4,000 year-old mission of the people, the faith, and the land of Israel.

March 11, 1987: The Reverend Jessie Jackson contacted Rabbi Marc Tanenbaum to help deal with the backlash against his "Hymie Town" re-
mark. In an effort to repair the damage to the relationship between
blacks and Jews, Jackson and Tanenbaum appeared together at the
Black-Jewish People to People Forum at Queens College at the City University of New York.

August 29, 1991: Rabbi Tanenbaum arranged an appearance of the Reverend Billy Graham before the New York Board of Rabbis. From left to
right: Bishop Fulton Sheen, Rabbi Marc Tanenbaum, and the Reverend
Billy Graham.

February 15, 1985: One of the many audiences that Rabbi Tanenbaum had with Pope John Paul II. At this particular audience, the topic was Vatican recognition of the State of Israel. Over many years, Rabbi Tanenbaum worked for the Vatican–Israel Accords that were signed in 1993. Ironically, they were signed only a few months after his death.

March 1963: A historic meeting at the Vatican. Rabbi Tanenbaum is flanked in this photo by Cardinal Bea and Rabbi Abraham Joshua Heschel, whom Tanenbaum recruited as the American Jewish Committee's spokesman at Vatican Council II. (Rabbi Tanenbaum was the only rabbi present when Vatican Council II adopted *Nostra Aetate*.)

August 1983: Rabbi Tanenbaum holding the baby daughter of a Zim-babwean Christian leader at the World Council of Churches meeting in Vancouver. Rabbi Tanenbaum gave a historic keynote address. It was the first time that a rabbi had been invited to address the World Council of Churches.

December 1960: President Dwight D. Eisenhower receiving the first "Ju-daism and World Peace" Award from the Synagogue Council of America (SCA). Rabbi Tanenbaum was the executive director of the SCA and attended the award presentation in the Oval Office with the SCA leader-ship. Rabbi Tanenbaum served as executive director of the SCA from 1953 to 1961 and opened up the area of interreligious relations during his tenure.

February 15, 1979: Rabbi Tanenbaum being sworn into the President's Commission on the Holocaust. From left to right, Rabbi Tanenbaum, Elie Wiesel, and the Honorable Thomas P. "Tip" O'Neil, Speaker of the House of Representatives. *(The White House)*

November 16, 1989: International Rescue Committee Freedom Award Dinner. From left to right, Leo Cherne, then-President of Poland Lech Walesa, Bob De Vecchi, John Whitehead, and Rabbi Tanenbaum. *(Camera Arts Studio)*

5

April 17, 1985: President Ronald Reagan's plan to visit the Bitburg Cemetery in Germany, which houses the graves of many Nazi SS officers, caused a public-relations disaster for his administration. He called on Rabbi Tanenbaum to come to the White House and help him find a way out of the debacle. Rabbi Tanenbaum suggested some remarks for the president and outlined a course of action that allowed President Reagan to proceed diplomatically without offending the Jewish people or the German government.

2

The 1970s: The Interreligious Agenda and Selected Texts

The 1970s was a decade marked by a number of national and international crises, some of which impacted powerfully on interreligious affairs. These included the emergence of dynamic and sometimes aggressive Christian evangelistic campaigns; yet another Arab-Israeli war, launched by a surprise attack on Israel by the combined armies of Syria, Egypt, and Jordan on the Jewish Holy Day of Yom Kippur (October 1973); and the notorious "Zionism Equals Racism" UN Resolution, pressed through the UN General Assembly by Arab and Communist governments in 1975. Most Jews continued to perceive a widespread and continuing anti-Israel bias within the institutional Christian churches. Although these strained the Jewish-Christian dialogue, they did not end it.

Rabbi Marc Tanenbaum's close friendship with the Rev. Billy Graham, sustained over the years, helped diffuse some of the tensions of the Christian evangelistic campaign. Rev. Graham publicly rejected the targeting of Jews as a group for conversion. During their twenty-five-year association, they worked together to ease the plight of Soviet Jews, obtained military aid for Israel during the Yom Kippur War, and responded to many other pressing issues of the time. Just as Rev. Graham spoke up for oppressed Jews, Rabbi Tanenbaum defended evangelical Christians. Together with Ann Gillen, S.H.C.J., Rabbi Tanenbaum joined Rev. Graham in protesting the treatment of Jews and evangelicals in the former Soviet Union.

These were years of consolidation, marked by programs to institutionalize and regularize interreligious dialogue on some systematic, ongoing basis. A variety of interreligious conferences and dialogues marked these years, bringing together scholars, religious educators, and sometimes seminarians to explore historical and theological issues. In 1968, the Holy See had set up a Pontifical Council for Religious Dialogue with the Jews. In response to this initiative, several Jewish organizations, American and international, came together in 1970 to form a committee that might serve as a counterpart in dialogue to international church bodies such as the Vatican and the World Council of Churches. Rabbi Tanenbaum was instrumental in establishing this ad hoc association, which took the acronym IJCIC (the International Jewish Committee for Interreligious Consultations), and he served as its first chairman. In 1972, the International Liaison Committee—a joint committee of

Vatican and Jewish organizational representatives—was set up to regularize the timing and substance of their meetings.

Social questions also loomed large at the international level. This was the decade of the Vietnamese "boat people," and Rabbi Tanenbaum was drawn into their plight, becoming an eloquent advocate for the rights of refugees and immigrants through his involvement with the International Rescue Committee. During this decade, he made three trips to Indochina. He also became deeply involved in issues of world hunger.

The essays of the 1970s reflect new initiatives to develop organized, ongoing dialogues with Roman Catholics, Greek Orthodox, Lutherans, and Protestant Evangelicals and confront major social domestic and international issues challenging all religious groups in America. Always historically minded, Rabbi Tanenbaum continued to speak on the good times as well as the bad times of Jews living in Christian Europe, the surprising (to some) policy of the papacy that often came to the aid of local Jewish communities suffering persecution from civil or religious leaders, and the fluctuations of tolerance and oppression over time. In a speech on Jewish-Christian relations in historical perspective delivered in the Pope Pius XII Religious Education Lecture Series in Detroit (February 25, 1970), Rabbi Tanenbaum concluded that repression of Jews and Judaism "may have been inherent" in the situation of two organically linked religious traditions living within the same society, but it "was not inevitable."

A historical thread ran through Rabbi Tanenbaum's efforts at making traditional adversaries into partners in dialogue. History was a touch point that was at once universal and transcendent in scope, allowing for the institutionalization of dialogue. On December 20–23, 1970, Rabbi Tanenbaum, along with other Jewish leaders, participated in an historic meeting in Rome with a Catholic delegation from the Holy See led by Cardinal Johannes Willebrands, President of the Vatican Secretariat for Promoting Christian Unity. Earlier that year, Rabbi Tanenbaum had participated in meetings between representatives of Jewish groups to establish the International Jewish Committee on Interreligious Relations, whose five original members were the American Jewish Committee, B'nai B'rith International, the Jewish Council for Interreligious Consultations in Israel, the Synagogue Council of America, and the World

Jewish Congress. The meeting issued a joint *Memorandum of Understanding* that constituted "the first step for the creation of a permanent International Liaison Committee (ILC) between the Roman Catholic Church and the world Jewish community" (see *Fifteen Years of Catholic-Jewish Dialogue, 1970–1985* [Vatican City: Libreria Editrice Vaticana/Lateranense, 1988], p. xv). The ILC has now met formally seventeen times in sites around the world (Paris 1971; Marseilles 1972; Antwerp 1973; Rome 1975; Jerusalem 1976; Venice 1977; Madrid 1978; Regensburg 1979; London 1981; Milan 1982; Amsterdam 1984; Rome 1985; Prague 1990; Baltimore 1992; Jerusalem 1994; Vatican City 1998; and New York in 2000). In between formal sessions, the ILC has provided an important channel of communication for responding to opportunities and crises such as the Auschwitz Convent controversy. It is one of the enduring legacies of the Second Vatican Council "generation" of Cardinal Willebrands and Rabbi Tanenbaum to see the possibility of new relationships given a mutually developed history.

These advances were not strictly between Catholics and Jews. One can find Rabbi Tanenbaum's responses to many Christian communities because he believed in the "rightness" of religious pluralism from a Jewish theological perspective. He emphasized Judaism's teaching about the unity of humanity as well as the particular revelatory basis of Jewish tradition. These were measured remarks, for he cautioned that "a refurbished Western evangelicalism, reinforced by Anglo-Saxon *hubris,* can be the surest way to disaster on a global scale."

This kind of seriousness surfaces in many of the formal dialogues. In January 1972, the Greek Orthodox Archdiocese of North and South America and the American Jewish Committee jointly sponsored a scholarly colloquium on Greek Orthodox-Jewish relations. The topics included the biblical, historical, and contemporary ethical and social ("nationalism and religion") aspects of the ancient relationship. The papers and concluding recommendations were published in 1976 in special issues of the *Greek Orthodox Theological Review* and the *Journal of Ecumenical Studies* devoted entirely to the colloquium and were co-edited by Rabbi Tanenbaum and Rev. Nomikos Michael Vaporis. In a brief statement included in both special issues, Rabbi Tanenbaum noted the historic character of this dialogue and acknowledged, from the Jewish side, "Rabbinic

Judaism is in many ways unthinkable without its absorption of certain basic Hellenistic institutions, legal categories, modes of thought, and styles of language." While emphasizing the need for a "healing process" between the two communities after centuries of "mutual antagonism," he underscored also that "the Greek Orthodox Church has a notable record of helping save Jewish lives under the Nazis, for which we give thanks to God."

Having done so much in the 1960s to establish the agenda for the dialogue between Jews and Christians, Rabbi Tanenbaum was well placed to evaluate its progress in the 1970s. He pointed up crises faced by the Jewish people worldwide, particularly in the Soviet Union and Israel—compelling concerns of the Jews which he felt (rightly) were not yet properly appreciated by Protestants or Catholics. Interestingly, he estimated that since the Second Vatican Council "something like 85 percent of Jewish-Christian dialogue has been Roman Catholic-Jewish," and that only in "the past two years" had he seen a "turn into a new cycle of relationships with Protestant leadership."

Expanding dialogues was vital to eradicating misunderstanding. In a commencement address given in June of 1971 at St. Louis University, a Jesuit institution, Rabbi Tanenbaum set the agenda of Jewish-Christian relations in the context of "world community," and deconstructed three "current mythologies" as "misleading and destructive." The first is that people in the West live in a "post-Judeo-Christian age." To the contrary, he felt that never before have Jewish and Christian perspectives, such as the truly radical views of Genesis on technology and the nature of humanity, been more necessary "to mediate the fruits and benefits of a scientific-technological development to the Third World without the imperialism and triumphalism" of the past. Second, were the myths of anti-institutionalism and "anti-Establishment." The real danger of large institutions, whether governmental or religious, is not their size but the quality of their leaders' "ethical integrity and religious humanism." Finally, he worries about a "fusion" between the American experiment in pluralism and "the evangelical empire."

There were more authentic approaches to broadening dialogue. For example, a July 1973 article for *The Lamp: A Christian Unity Magazine,* published by the Roman Catholic Friars of the Atonement, distills Rabbi Tanenbaum's global ecumenism and Noahide

Covenant themes. It adds an important notion, namely that Maimonides, among others, saw a role for Christianity and Islam "as being *preparatio messianica,* agents in the divine economy who prepare the way for the messianic age by helping to bring the words of the Torah to the distant ends of the earth." The notion of *preparatio messianica* applied by Jews to Christians represents a significant step beyond the generic category, "righteous among the nations," by taking into account something of the very particular character of Christian claims to continuity with Biblical Israel in the past and therefore with the Jewish people's role in the future. Theologically, of course, from a Christian point of view Christians are not Gentiles, but a priestly people called into being by God for a very particular purpose in God's plan of salvation for all, a claim certainly recognizable (if not acceptable) in Jewish tradition.

Reports on updates of the original Protestant, Catholic, and Jewish self-studies were given at a conference at St. Louis University in June of 1974. Eugene J. Fisher's update, then under preparation as a dissertation for New York University, received its first, preliminary airing at this conference. When it was published as a book by Paulist Press in 1977, he received permission to use the conference's title, *Faith Without Prejudice.* Rabbi Tanenbaum introduced the St. Louis Conference, expressing the hope that other areas in a world wracked by inter-ethnic and interreligious conflict might find in the American experience useful lessons on "how to make pluralism work." Religious Americans, he noted, "have learned how to instruct a new generation of Catholics, Protestants, and Jews in how to be faithful to one's own doctrines and traditions and at the same time to develop authentic respect for the faith and religious commitment of others. We have in short developed a model of building community without compromise of our most cherished beliefs, (which) . . . may well be the most valuable 'export' we have to share with other nations, peoples, and non-Western religious communities."

Judith H. Banki and Eugene J. Fisher

11

Jewish-Christian Relations: Issues and Prospects

I AM EXTREMELY GRATEFUL for the opportunity to be here with you, and for the privilege of the invitation. Not the least part of the delight in accepting the invitation was the opportunity that it afforded me to meet once again with a revered and greatly admired scholar, Dr. Albert Outler.

My assignment, as I understand it, is to try to undertake a *tour d'horizon* of Jewish-Christian relations from a Jewish perspective. This presentation is intended as an overview of the major issues and concerns as seen in the Jewish community, both in the academic and intellectual aspects of the Jewish community, as well as in the living experience of the Jewish people that I encounter in a variety of ways in my travels around the country and in other parts of the world. I submit that this will have to be necessarily a somewhat sketchy presentation of themes, each of which would require for any adequate treatment a full lecture. As you will see, each of the subjects which I should like to identify as being central to the current Jewish-Christian agenda has spawned a very substantial literature, and each of the themes could in itself constitute the basis of an entire seminar of not just one day.

At the very outset, I should like to point to at least three areas in which there has been quite substantial progress, growth, development in understanding and in relationships between the Christian and Jewish communities, and particularly the Catholic and Protestant communities in relationship with the Jewish community. I specify that because I believe we have another set of concerns that are emerging out of the present situation in relationship with the Eastern Orthodox churches. And these

Excerpted address, Perkins School of Theology, reprinted from the *Perkins Journal*, fall 1970.

three areas, I would submit, fall under the categories of the increasing and serious attention that has been given by the highest teaching authorities and institutions of the Roman Catholic and the Protestant communities with regard to Christian responsibility for certain traditions of Christian teaching that have nurtured anti-Semitism during the greater part of the past two millennia.

Secondly, I would submit that there has been substantial growth and progress in the Christian development of a "theology of Israel," a theology of the Jewish people in the context of a theology of the people of God. And related to that there has begun to take place a facing up to the historic amnesia that has obtained in church history with regard to the portrayal of post-biblical Judaism, Rabbinic Judaism, in the pedagogic process of Christendom. In this second area—an adequate Christian understanding of the theology of the Jewish people—let me say that there is a companion problem on the Jewish side, namely, the issue of the Jewish community developing an adequate Jewish theological understanding of the place of Christianity and Christians in God's divine plan—which also needs to be examined in terms of the present agenda.

And thirdly, there has been substantial growth and progress in the approach on the part of Christians and Jews to their common concerns as people and as communities to the commanding issues of social justice, world community, and international economic development and related problems. In identifying these problems, it should be noted that progress has been more substantial in some areas than in others, and that in all cases the progress is marked by some ambiguity in terms of the unfinished agenda which is still to be faced.

Now, let me deal in rather summary fashion with the first area of concern, namely, that of the address on the part of Christian leadership to the problem of anti-Semitism, the roots of anti-Semitism in Western culture, and the influence of certain forms of Christian teaching and tradition. We have passed a major landmark in this area of concern, a landmark that must be located in the extraordinary action of Vatican Council II in its adoption of the Statement on the Jews.

I recall the days during which I was in Rome as personal guest of Cardinal Bea and of Cardinal Shehan, who was then chairman of the American Bishops' Commission on Ecumenism and Inter-Religious Affairs. As a Jew who comes out of a rather Orthodox background, and whose family was victimized on my wife's side by German Nazi anti-Semitism and on my parents' side by Russian-Polish anti-Semitism, I recall standing in Rome in St. Peter's Basilica at the time of the intervention of Cardinal Bea as he introduced that particular declaration and I found it simply incredible. There in the presence of some 2,500 Council Fathers from throughout the world, the Roman Catholic Church faced forthrightly the issue of the church's responsibility for the abuse of Scripture and the New Testament teachings as it is developed in certain traditions, and for the basic "themes of contempt," and literally sought to turn the church around in a totally opposite direction. Despite all the ambiguities of the language that existed in the Vatican Council declaration, there can be no question that in the perspective of 1,900 years, this was a major, revolutionary turning point on the part of the Roman Church.

The argument that we in the Jewish community who were involved in relating to the Roman Catholic hierarchy, both here and abroad, sought to make clear to those who were skeptical about that process, was that this was the beginning, the first step, in a process of Christian self-purification. I am persuaded that the events since that time have more than amply justified the involvement of the Jewish community in that cooperative process with the Roman Catholic Church, because what emerged as a result of Vatican Council II was the U.S. Bishops' Guidelines on Jewish-Catholic Relationships that clarified much of the ambiguous language. The guidelines also went on to deal with the basic themes in a very direct way: the problems of teaching that were centered in the misrepresentation of the Pharisees; the conflicts between Jesus and the Pharisees; and the false dichotomy that portrayed Judaism as a religion of harsh legalism in contrast to Christianity as a superior religion of love. These and related questions were faced directly and frontally in the Bishops' Guidelines on the Catholic-Jewish Relationships, which now in fact have become the basis of a major program on many levels in the Roman Catholic community—clergy, teachers, religious education, textbook revision, etc.—a whole new Christian culture with regard to the church's attitudes toward Jews and Judaism has been inaugurated in the wake of Vatican Council II.

In a companion way, the action of the World Council of Churches in 1961, which also sought to face these questions, represented a major contribution to facing the issue of anti-Semitism within the Protestant and Eastern Orthodox communities. But I must confess that there is a strange kind of "out-of-phaseness" that we experience in relationship to much of the national Protestant leadership on this question. Since Vatican Council II, Jewish-Christian dialogue has been, at least until the past two years, something like 85 percent Roman Catholic-Jewish. It is only now beginning to turn into a new cycle of relationships with Protestant leadership. We find ourselves now engaged in growing dialogue with good friends in the Southern Baptist Convention, the Lutheran Churches, the United Presbyterian Church—however, that's a relatively new phenomenon. In terms of this unresolved aspect of the Jewish-Christian agenda, there is reason for very serious concern in the Jewish community as to the depth of the commitment of national Protestant leadership to implementing the insights which have emerged out of contemporary scholarship with regard to the problems of Christian teaching about anti-Semitism. As of this moment, with the exception of the Southern Baptist Convention, there is not a single national Protestant denomination that has a single person working full-time on Jewish-Christian relationships. Not a single national Protestant denomination has a person charged with responsibility to deal with uprooting the sources of anti-Semitism in Protestant culture or to deal with the developing of more affirmative relationships between Christians and Jews.

The reason I begin this presentation with reference to anti-Semitism as the first issue on the agenda of Jewish-Christian relationships today is that there is a tendency on the part of some to feel that there is a peculiar kind of Jewish paranoia with regard to anti-Semitism. I wish there were such a fantasy life of the Jewish community. We could deal with it seriously. Tragically, Jews are deeply preoccupied with the problems of anti-Semitism today because we find ourselves confronting a whole new constellation of anti-Semitism internationally, with spillover nationally, which has made our community considerably anxious these days and weeks and months. The Jewish community has become the object of manipulation by the Soviet Union, which is using anti-Semitism, including classical theological anti-Semitism, on a calculated, systematic basis. The great paradox confronts us of a government committed to uprooting religious teaching in the life of its own society, exploiting classical Russian Orthodox anti-Semitism of the Czarist period as a way of building its relationship with the Arab countries and of suppressing intellectual dissent within its own borders. The Soviet Union has established an official institute on anti-Semitism in the Ukraine, with a professor writing encyclopedia articles of an anti-Jewish character, publishing books on "Judaism Unmasked," demonstrating that the Jews for theological reasons are involved in an international conspiracy—the themes of the discredited *Protocols of the Elders of Zion*. That material is now being imported into Western Europe, Latin America, and the United States primarily by propagandists for the extremist factions of Arab nationalism and their radical left allies. And this nation is being swamped, both in overt and covert ways, with forms of anti-Semitism, including the revival of the ritual blood libels in Islamic versions, whose only parallel is the propaganda activity of the Nazis and their sympathizers in the 1930s.

And so the phenomenon of anti-Semitism today, as we are experiencing it in its political and sociological forms, with a continued appropriation of theological nurturing of anti-Semitism by a variety of sources, makes this question a basic one in the dialogue between Christians and Jews. And indeed, Jews are concerned as they look to Christian colleagues and neighbors for some sympathetic understanding of the seriousness of the problem and an appropriate, concerned response. The potentiality of the resurrection of anti-Semitism in demonic forms is here with us. As we struggle with the crisis of Vietnam and Cambodia, Jews on the one hand are being singled out for attack by the radical right because many Jewish kids are involved in the New Left on the campuses and in protest movements. The radical right is exploiting in this country a theme of the Jewish-Communist-Marxist-Zionist conspiracy to destroy America, and therefore the elders of Jewish kids react humanly by trying to cool it. The parents now find it increasingly difficult to speak out on Vietnam and Cambodia, and then because they are silent, the New Left is now hitting the Jewish establishment for copping out on the moral issues of the war. And so Jews are damned if they do and damned if they don't. Throughout all of this, the themes of anti-Semitism are being incorporated as ways of signaling messages to the Jewish community about its continued marginality to the mainstream of American society.

I move from that area of concern which is existential and deeply significant for the Jewish self-consciousness today to a substantially healthy development in our encounter; namely, the rediscovery by Christians of Judaism and the Jewish people. It is increasingly clear that for internal Christian theological reasons, as the churches go through their own process of renewal and reform, and find it essential to reconceptualize the classic traditional categories within which Christians have done theology, and are seeking to recover the early foundations in which the church constructed her being, her existence, the churches are brought back inevitably to face the reality of the biblical and Hebraic origins of the church, and of the biblical-theological categories. In the process of doing that, many Christian theologians and church historians are becoming aware of the vitality and the continued reality of the Jewish people as a living witness to that tradition which many Christians now are beginning to recover as their own. And I think it is quite clear, as one studies Professor Jules Isaac (*The Teaching of Contempt* [New York: Holt, Rinehart, and Winston, 1964]) or Dr. James Parkes (*The Conflict of the Church and the Synagogue: A Study of the Origins of Antisemitism* [New York: Hermon Press, 1974]), or any of the church historians who have been writing about the early centuries, that this is a relatively new development. In much Christian theological writing and church historical material, Judaism ceased to exist with the destruction of the Temple of Jerusalem in the first century. Post-biblical and Rabbinic Judaism has been considered a rather anomalous kind of thing that somehow you are not able to make sense out of. When Toynbee spoke of the "Syriac fossil" of Judaism, he was reflecting a sentiment that was widespread in much Christian thought.

Out of a commitment to truth, and an effort to understand the realities of living Judaism today, there has now begun to develop a new discipline of thought, both in the Roman Catholic and the

Protestant communities, with regard to formulating a more adequate theology of Israel as a living, vital, dynamic, witnessing, worshiping, praying community. One need only cite the Catholic writings of people like Hans Küng, Gregory Baum, Edward A. Flannery, Cornelius Rijk, Kurt Hruby, John Oesterreicher, Marcel Dubois, and Gabriel Moran; in the Protestant community, scholars such as Krister Stendahl, W. D. Davies, Albert Outler, J. Coert Rylaarsdam, Roy Eckardt, Franklin Littell, Markus Barth, Elwyn Smith. These and others have come to the firm conviction that a fundamentally new Christian theology of the covenant—a new conception of Israel—is required. One of the more recent formulations of such a theology of Israel, which affirms the permanent validity of Judaism and the coexistence of the two covenants, of Israel and the church, is to be found in an essay by Dr. Monika Hellwig in the *Journal of Ecumenical Studies.* "Christianity has been confronted with a logical dilemma in terms of seeing Christianity as superseding Judaism and the fact that the Jews were blind to the revelation of Jesus as the Christ," writes Dr. Hellwig, adding that the

> Christian position on the blindness of the Jews rests rather heavily on the assumption that revelation is a past event and consists of what God told us . . . The process of revelation is seen as communication of fully shaped and immutable concepts in a mechanical and para-experiential model. Today we are at an important moment of truth and opportunity. Not only does this understanding of revelation render the truth claims of the Jewish and Christian communities ultimately irreconcilable, the Christian theologians themselves have found that they can no longer work with this model in attempting to answer contemporary questions about Christian life. Christian theology can no longer remain internally coherent in a two-story universe in which grace is separate from nature in the sense that it operated outside of the sphere of human experience. We are being compelled to rely on our experience and observations of the historical situation for the interpretation of God's intervention in history. We simply cannot answer the questions of contemporary Christians in terms of an understanding of revelation as instantaneous transfer of fully conceptualized knowledge from the realm of non-experiential supernatural to the experiential natural . . . We may be approaching the point of dialogue at which Jewish and Christian thinkers can attempt to express to

each other on behalf of their respective traditions the meaning of those events which have altered their capacity for perception. Such truth-claims need by no means be mutually exclusive. They are far more likely to be complementary, and dependent upon each other for fuller comprehension.

And Dr. Hellwig goes on to elaborate a theology of the complementariness of Judaism and Christianity by building on Romans 9 to 11. Dr. Hellwig comes to a conclusion which Yehuda Halevi forecast in the twelfth century, namely, that despite our human perversity, it is quite conceivable that God in his own plan established one covenant with many branches, and that Judaism, Christianity, and Islam are branches grafted on to the common trunk, rooted in the one covenant. The more appropriate role for them as sons and daughters of the common covenant is to be complementary and supplementary to each other, rather than exclusivistic and polemical in their relationships with one another.

The polemical history that dates back to the first four centuries of our encounter, when the synagogue and church broke with one another, reflects patterns that have determined our history, our fate and destiny across the millennia. One recognizes the magnitude of the problem of fostering mutual understanding as one surveys the way in which church history and Jewish history textbooks continue to support this historiography of misunderstanding each other. As one looks into much of church historical writing and Jewish historical writing, it is evident that by and large we are continuing to develop two different universes of discourse among our young people.

The problem exists on the Jewish side as it does on the Christian side. For example, Jewish historic accounts of the French Revolution and the Enlightenment are at great variance with Catholic histories of the same period. In much of the Jewish accounts of the French Revolution, it is hailed as the salvation of the Jews. The French Revolution enabled the Jews to achieve civic equality for the first time in virtually 1,700 years in the Christian West. The Jewish history books never mention the fact that at the same time the French Revolution was a pogrom against the Roman Catholic Church, and that many of the orders of the sisters and the priests who are here in this country are here as "displaced persons" of the French Revolution. The convents were destroyed, monasteries were uprooted, most of the major universities under Catholic auspices were eliminated by the French Revolution in the process of the disestablishment of the Catholic Church. To many European Christians, who have a guarded feeling about the ultimate redemptive value of the Revolution and the Enlightenment, they speak a language which many Jews do not begin to comprehend. And so here is an area of unfinished business on the Jewish-Christian agenda, which is worthy of further exploration.

In a certain sense, the kind of issues discussed thus far are really very conventional ways of approaching the Jewish-Christian dialogue. They exist without almost any reference to time. In talking about Jewish-Christian relationships over the past 1,900 years, one would have to face all these questions as the central, perennial questions of the dialogue—anti-Semitism, the theology of the people of God, of the people of Israel, the theology of Christianity—as well as the problem of portrayals of both of our respective historic experiences.

But there is a new turn in our relationship which has been transforming, and that involves the Jewish community's understanding of itself, of its vocation, of its selfhood. It is virtually impossible, it seems to me, in terms of any reality-oriented dialogue, for Christians and Jews to talk with each other unless they face the centrality of that new Jewish self-consciousness in the Jewish community. That has very much to do with the experience Jews throughout the world have undergone since the June 1967 war in the Middle East. Now, here, too, it is quite possible to deal with the transformation of the Jewish understanding of peoplehood and the Jewish relationship to the land and the State of Israel also in quite conventional ways. And I daresay that the overwhelming majority of the dialogues between Jews and Christians in which the issue of Israel has emerged, and whatever understandings or misunderstandings have developed between Christians and Jews around the Middle East crisis, have taken place on the basis of these conventional categories. There is great validity to that, and I think every Jewish-Christian dialogue, if it is to be based on an honest understanding of both partners in that dialogue, must go through that process. It is essential that the Jewish partner of the dialogue communicate to the Christian community that Jews reacted almost traumatically in their response to the threats of the annihilation of Israel in May and June 1967, and an awareness of the importance of Israel in terms of its historical, religious, liturgical dimensions. The historic relationship of the Jewish people to the land of Israel literally across 3,000 years is constitutive to the Jewish identity. From the beginning of the promise given to Abraham down through every century there have been Jewish settlements in Palestine.

Whether there was a Jewish state, a Jewish commonwealth, a Jewish sovereignty, or whether the Jews lived in the Dispersion, there were always Jewish communities present in the Holy Land, always communities that sought to retain a commitment and loyalty to the promise given to the forefathers, as well as to retain a community that would point toward the future promise. A very substantial presentation could be made on the depths to which the Holy Land has penetrated Jewish consciousness. Israel is the place of the origins of the Jewish people as a historic community, and that has profound religious meaning to the Jews. Every Jewish prayer book is replete with references to the restoration of Jerusalem to her former glory. The daily prayer services, the Sabbath prayer services, the pilgrim festivals of Passover, Sukkoth (Tabernacles) and Shavuoth (Pentecost) are simply incomprehensible without reference to the centrality of Israel in the Jewish self-understanding of the past, the present, and the future promise. And yet, as one thinks about that method of communication, of what Israel has meant to the Jewish people historically, theologically, religiously, liturgically, one becomes aware of the difficulty that Jews are building into their communication to Christians, because the effect of that interpretation is to suggest, all right, that's a Jewish hang-up. That is your Jewish thing and your Jewish problem, and as a matter of ecumenical friendship, we will seek to understand that this is your difficulty. And one, in fact, sees this in the latest unofficial Vatican declaration on the Jewish people. There is a spirit of extraordinary friendship toward the Jews in that document. And yet, there is almost an unintended confession that we really don't comprehend this whole relationship of the universal religious community and its link to that particular land. The document states that Catholics must simply respect the fact that there is a bond between the Jewish people and the land of Israel, which is to say that we'll shelve that for the time being, until the Messiah comes and works that out for everybody.

There are at least two profound theological, intellectual, spiritual issues that Jews are struggling with in their understanding of the relationship of their adherence to the universal faith of Judaism, and their ties to that particular land. These are not just Jewish questions, I submit, but are of the deepest intellectual and spiritual importance to Christians as well. What Jews are struggling with as they are trying to find the meaning of the restoration of the State of Israel, and the implications for a universal tradition in relation to a holy land, holy places, and holy cities is essentially this: we are engaged in the deepest kind of struggle to try to retrieve some validity for the meaning of religious symbolism in the consciousness of religious man today—of the homo religious. We live at a time which contemporary historians tell us is an age of a highly rational, mechanical culture. We live at a time in which the control of nature has been dominated by scientific, rational thinking. As Cyril Richardson has written in Ernest Johnson's book on *Religious Symbolism* (Port Washington, NY: Kennikat Press, 1969), we are likely to think of symbolism as being something essentially unnecessary. We deal in hard facts that do not lend themselves to the symbolic. We think of a symbol as standing for something else, and we imagine that as soon as we grasp that something else, the symbol has served its turn and is no longer of use. It is the something else to which the symbol points that is the reality, and hence we no longer need the symbol, once we have passed beyond it to the truth that it tells. That is why as a culture we have so few symbols. That is why, incidentally, in America today we find people trying to develop a civil religion with civic religious symbols because the classic, historical, traditional symbol system has collapsed in this rational, technical culture. So we imagine that our control of nature brings us into direct contact with reality which we can manipulate to our own ends and which needs no symbolic expression.

And yet the irony of this moment in which rational man finds symbols to be a kind of buffer against reality and therefore useless is that it takes place at a time in which psychotherapy and psychoanalysis have had their greatest dominance. Psychotherapy is modern Western man's mode for the pursuit of wholeness and spiritual health. Psychotherapy deals in nothing else than the symbol life of the human being, and the whole internal self-understanding and self-consciousness of man is mediated entirely through the symbol system. The whole dream of life of man is the symbol system that articulates the deepest unconscious awarenesses of man. And yet, in public religious life the crisis of faith that exists today is crucially located in the question of the collapse of belief in religious symbol systems.

I have been reading some of the literature about the current debate over the Eucharist and communion, and I have been struck by rather interesting analogies to our subject. The question as to whether the divine presence is present in reality in the two elements of the Eucharist or in the communion, or whether the Eucharist is simply commemorative or the memorial of the past, raises the question of the transcendence and the immanence of spiritual reality in the life of man. How the holy and the sacred are experienced in human existence, in the life of the individual and of the community, are not unlike some of the questions that Jews are struggling with when they probe the meanings of the *shekhinah,* the divine presence, and its mediation in the life of the Jewish people as centered in the "holy" temple and the "holy" city of Jerusalem. And so, I should like to suggest that what Jews are engaged in seeking to articulate some meaningful understanding of the holiness of the Holy Land is the meaning of sacred values, the validity of religious symbols, and the presence of the sacred in the life of all people. If Jews are able to make a valid intellectual case for the articulation of their universal tradition in relationship to that particular historic society and land, then it will not have been without some relevance for others who are engaged in the struggle to try to make some sense out of the present crisis in faith.

Involved also in this question of the relationship of Judaism to the land of Israel is the problem of religious language, indeed, the problem of language altogether. There is the need to make distinctions between factual language, the language of science and rationalism, and poetic, religious, mythic language that deals with reality on another order of existence. And the problem of the universal and the particular has occupied for centuries the most sophisticated philosophers and theologians, and it is not going to be resolved here, not in these waning moments of this presentation.

Much of this discussion of the universal and the particular may be bypassed if we realize that the problem is not answerable in the terms in which it is proposed, simply because they confuse the map with the territory. That is to say, much of the factual language which we use in our conventional discourse today is something like the map which abstracts from the reality of experience, and it has the same relationship to reality that the map has to all of the richness and the depth and the vitality of the terrain. Good and evil are abstract categories, and categories do not perform their function unless they are kept distinct. Therefore, it is perfectly proper that the concepts of good and evil be distinct, dualistic, irreconcilable, and that they be firm and clear as any other measure. But the problem of the duality, or the inherent contradiction between the universal and the particular, arises only when the abstract is confused with the concrete, and when it is thought that these are clearly distinguishable entities in the natural universe. Factual language is never more than a strictly limited symbolism for what is happening in nature. The image, the religious, poetic, or mythic image, is closer than linguistic categories to events themselves.

It is important also to indicate that it is not only a question of language, but as well of the philosophical inheritance of the Western world. I cannot dwell at too great a length on the question of the metaphysical dualism which has come down to us through the Scholastic tradition in which the universal has been, as it were, elevated to a category of superior form of being, and the particular is seen as an inferior form of existence. One needs to read people such as Herbert Richardson, Leslie Dewart, Rosemary Ruether, or some of the other newer theologians today who are engaged in the "de-hellenization of dogma," and are seeking to break down the disparities of the dualism between essence and existence. They now are making the case that one cannot really talk of universalism in abstract ways, especially in the scholastic sense, without seeing that the universal does not exist without its being expressed in the particular, in the concrete experience of man. The particular has no meaning without its being a form of representation of universal meanings.

In much of the newer writings and theology that has been developing in recent years, there is a clue that can help us understand each other on this question. There is a sense in which Jews
can understand themselves as they reflect this through Christian
self-understanding when Christians speak of the church universal.
There is a projection of the conception of the church in its ideal-
typical sense which is messianic, eschatological, and which speaks
of the church universal as an instrument of God's action involving
the whole human family. Jews understand that tension between
the universal and the particular when they speak of the Lord God
of Israel being the Lord God of all the nations. Indeed, one of our
great scholars, Solomon Schechter, spoke of "catholic Israel," as
universal as is the church universal. Yet in terms of the reality in
which the church universal is experienced by its communicants,
that experience is not unlike that with which Jews are wrestling
today. Herbert Richardson in his book, *Towards an American Theology* (New York: Harper & Row, 1967), makes the observation that
if one really wants to understand the Christian situation, one must
understand Christianity as a universal church as it is experienced
in its spatial centers. That is to say, one can really not speak of the
church universal or the universal Christian faith apart from the
various historic forms in which it was experienced by its communicants and continues to be experienced today. Thus he says that
Christianity exists in the modality of Latin-Hispanic culture, and
that is Latin Christianity. And Latin Christianity informed Latin-
Hispanic culture, shaped it, and was in turn shaped by it. But one
cannot speak of the universal church in its Protestant Reformation form without understanding the degree to which the Reformation tradition was deeply implicated in the culture, the society,
the economics, the politics, of northern-western Europe, and the
degree to which the Reformation church cannot be understood
apart from the degree to which the culture, the society, the history shaped the church in its deepest spiritual formation. And
obviously, as one looks at Byzantine culture, one cannot understand the Byzantine Orthodox Church apart from its relationship
to the Byzantine Empire and the degree to which the imperial
form of that culture shaped the imperial theology and the very
hierarchical and ecclesiastical structures of that church. That was
the spatial center of the Orthodox Church. The Latin-Hispanic

world, with its culture, provides the spatial center of Latin Christianity, just as northwestern Europe provides the spatial center for Reformation Christianity. Today, as Richardson says, the spatial center in which whatever really significant, dynamic theology will develop in Protestantism, and perhaps Catholicism, will be the dynamic centers of American culture as Christianity seeks to engage scientific, technological civilization there.

I would submit that the land of Israel represents for the Jewish people the spatial center of Judaism. The experience of Christendom and of Christianity's encounter with history and modernity which has taken place in these variety of spatial centers finds its analogies in the way in which Judaism is seeking to engage modernity and history in the land of Israel. The disparity in our perception of this has more to do with demography, with the quantity of persons than with the essential relationship. Had there been five hundred million Jews in the world with Israel as its spatial center, undoubtedly, there may have been other spatial centers flowing out in the dispersion but related to Israel as the center of Jewish cultural and religious life, historical origins, and messianic promise for the future.

The degree to which Jews are able to resolve the relationship in constructive ways, are able to moralize and spiritualize their relationship to that spatial center, to that degree we are engaged in an understanding which is uniquely Jewish, but hopefully, may have some instruction for others who are concerned about the present spiritual crisis for the whole of mankind.

12

A Survey and Evaluation of Christian-Jewish Relationships since Vatican Council II

THE MOST SIGNIFICANT FACT in Jewish-Christian relations during the past five years that Vatican Council II inaugurated is that meaningful first steps have been taken to create an emergent new Christian culture within which anti-Semitism can no longer find official church sanction, and in which Judaism is beginning to be appreciated as a permanent source of truth and value for the Jewish people. In that emergent new Christian culture, the Jewish people are being perceived in their own terms, rather than as candidates for conversion, and that constitutes the most significant breakthrough which now makes it increasingly possible to have authentic communication between Judaism and Christianity as religious peers.

That period of five years has also witnessed a growing relaxation of suspicion and defensiveness against the Catholic community among many Jews, and in this freer atmosphere Jewish thinkers and leaders are beginning to reevaluate seriously, also for the first time in centuries, the Jewish religious convictions about the legitimacy of Christianity as a valid form of salvation for Christians who stand in some true relationship with the Covenant of Israel. That many Catholics have struggled with integrity and sympathy to comprehend the complex but profound bonds that link Jewry with the land and people of Israel has been a strong motivation to many Jews to explore a reciprocal relationship that

Excerpted from a presentation to "Toward a Theology of Israel" Convocation: Observing the Fifth Anniversary of the Conciliar Statement on the Jews, October 25–28, 1970, Seton Hall University, South Orange, N.J. This paper was presented in cooperation with Sister Rose Thering of the Seton Hall Institute of Judeo-Christian Studies, Mrs. Judith H. Banki, Rabbi A. James Rudin, and Dr. Gerald Strober, Interreligious Affairs Department, American Jewish Committee.

will contribute to genuine human community with Christians in which religious fellowship, cooperative study, and mutual aid can flourish.

The fact that during the four sessions of Vatican Council II some 2,500 Council Fathers from throughout the inhabited world spent hours deliberating, many with utmost seriousness, the relationship of the church to the Jewish people and of Christianity's rootedness in Judaism, and articulated their majority consensus through the adoption of the Statement on the Jews, argues forcefully for the existence of such a new Christian spirit. Those conciliar deliberations represent in fact the most extraordinary "seminar in Jewish-Christian relations" ever held in the past 1,900 years. That is a far more significant reality than the specific final language of the text. An imperfect text that is vigorously implemented on the key substantive issues is to be preferred over a "perfect text" that is ignored.

A survey of the scholarship and studies in Jewish-Christian relations discloses, in my opinion, the urgent need for establishing some effective communications center, well-staffed, well-financed, and of high status, that will help focus and augment the impact of the thinking and writing and research that is already going on or that can be stimulated. Ideally, if you will forgive the borrowed image, a "Manhattan Project" in Jewish-Christian relations (and Islamic relations as well) is required if we are at all serious about moving beyond our present halting, scattered probings in this area. During the past three years, I have been discussing such a proposal with Christian, Jewish, and some Islamic scholars, somewhat in the form of an Institute for Advanced Studies in Jewish-Christian-Islamic Relations that will have both national and international centers, and the response has been quite positive. Failure to provide such instruments for rational, systematic development of the field may well lead to a loss of the precious momentum released by Vatican Council II, or its diversion into pathways that in the end could demean the entire concern for Jewish-Christian-Islamic relations as a priority.

Unless some more effective way is found for establishing direct, ongoing, and effective connections between the "right" ideas about Judaism and Christianity that scholars formulate and the Jewish and Christian communities in which they are rooted, I fear we shall contribute further to perpetuating the crisis in the religious communities of having a group of ecumenical generals who blow their trumpets and find their infantry troops marching off in the opposite direction. We see evidences of such a crisis in the area of religious social action where religious leaders have developed a consensus on liberal social justice causes regarding peace and war, race, anti-poverty, dissent, without having paid adequate attention to forming the consciences of their constituents. [They] are startled to find at moments of decision that they speak only for themselves and their witness to their churches and synagogues, and to the nation-at-large, has become severely weakened. It is not inconceivable that scholars and religious leaders can repeat that error in relation to forming a new culture of Jewish-Christian relations. The obligation of participatory democracy is a two-way street: scholars have an obligation to come close to established religious and communal structures and to infuse their ideas into the vast systems of communication; religious institutional leaders have a parallel obligation to involve the academic community on a serious, systematic and decision-making basis in conceiving programs and implementing them. *The Ethics of the Fathers* spoke of "the raising up of many disciples" as serious a *mitzvah* as the studying of the Torah itself.

There is a major movement in the religious communities, as there is in other levels of government and voluntary activity, toward decentralization of programming toward the local communities. The adoption of guidelines by the dioceses of New York and Brooklyn, of Albany, Cincinnati, Allentown, and a number of other communities suggests that there is emerging a pattern of strong church support, with parallel Jewish support, for growing and deepening interaction between Christians and Jews in most of the major communities throughout the United States. In 1969, the American Jewish Committee was involved in 104 Jewish-Christian programs. From the Jewish side, if you add the parallel programs of the Anti-Defamation League, the Jewish Chattauqua Society of the Union of American Hebrew Congregations, local Jewish Community Relations Councils, and rabbinical groups, you have some idea how extensive a network of interreligious relations has already been developed during the past five years.

These local interreligious dialogues have involved scholars (frequently on a single-lecture basis), clergy, religious teachers, seminarians, men, women, youth, mass media representatives. We must resist the urge in this survey to be encyclopedic, if for no other reason than that the data are far too heterogeneous, ranging over all levels and types of sophistication. The materials also are only in small part measurable since the whole range of human expression and interaction between Christians and Jews is involved—their scholarship, their writing, their speech, their routine social and commercial intercourse, their unorganized as well as their organized sentiments. Suffice it to say virtually an entire new discipline has emerged in Jewish-Christian relations as well as the structures for the creation of a new culture.

In order to enable scholars and religious leaders to assess the impact of Vatican Council II's Statement on the Jews, and to probe its implications for their future work in Jewish-Christian Relations, the American Jewish Committee and the Institute of Judeo-Christian Studies have just completed a detailed, systematic, nationwide survey of the specific changes in educational programming that have taken place during the past five years in response to the call for implementing the objectives of the conciliar statement. The educational categories surveyed cover curricula courses, teaching methods, examination of textbooks and other materials, institutes on Jewish-Christian relations, use of specialized Christian and Jewish faculty, etc. While members of the AJC and the IJCS knew that some changes had taken place because they had themselves been involved in various programs of implementation in the academic and religious communities, at no time had there been any such systematic study to document and to evaluate the efforts to implement the Vatican Statement. This study is designed to meet that need.

DESCRIPTION OF SURVEYS

The surveys were limited to the American scene. Somewhat different surveys were sent to a representative sampling of four key Catholic groups: Catholic seminaries (100); Catholic colleges and universities (227); Catholic high schools (500); and offices of superintendents of diocesan schools (152). No investigation of the elementary curricula was done except that which was covered by the superintendent's office. Obviously, some questions directed to seminaries and universities were inappropriate for high schools, and vice versa. However, some key questions were asked of all four categories: whether courses in Jewish studies were provided in the schools, whether the school curricula dealt with present-day Judaism, whether it covered areas such as the Nazi Holocaust, and the history or the theological implications of the State of Israel. Similar questionnaires were also sent to Protestant colleges (344) and seminaries (210). During this time, a study of Jewish elementary and secondary textbooks was carried out by an Orthodox Jewish educator in consultation with AJC regarding the nature of Jewish teaching about Jesus, Christianity, and Jewish-Christian relations.

The response percentages varied among the Catholic and Protestant groups, and this fact should be kept in mind in any evaluation of these responses. For example, since a smaller percentage of high schools than of colleges and universities responded to the survey, we may assume that only the more interested high schools responded—perhaps those which had already taken some steps to implement the conciliar declaration. Responses to the survey were:

Catholic: 147 out of 227 colleges and universities, or 65 percent
31 out of 100 questionnaires for seminaries, or 30 percent
177 out of 500 high schools, or 35.4 percent
46 out of 152 superintendents of schools, or 30 percent

Protestant: 180 out of 344 colleges, or 52 percent
65 out of 210 seminaries, or 30 percent

Reviewing the survey responses may help to provide an understanding of the ways in which Christian students and seminarians learn about Jews and Judaism, a question related directly or indirectly to the conciliar statement on the Jews. Very few of the institutions have departments of Jewish studies. (For the Catholics, zero percent of the seminaries, and only 1.3 percent of the colleges; for the Protestants, zero percent of the seminaries and 4 percent of the colleges.) Nearly half of the institutions do provide separate courses in Jewish studies (44.8 percent of the Catholic seminaries and 43.2 percent of the Catholic colleges; 30.7 percent of the Protestant seminaries and 37.7 percent of the colleges); 27.3 percent of Catholic high schools treat Judaism in Comparative Religions. A high percentage of all these institutions (68.9 percent Catholic colleges; 82.7 percent Catholic seminaries; 82.1 percent Catholic high schools; 78.4 percent Protestant seminaries; and 81.1 percent Protestant colleges) offer scripture and/or theology courses that specifically treat *the relationship of Christianity to Judaism*. Only 14.1 percent of Catholic colleges offer a course covering the *intertestamental period*, as compared with 50.2 percent of Protestant colleges; 48.2 percent of Catholic seminaries offer a course, as compared with 26.1 percent of Protestant seminaries. 55.3 percent of Catholic high schools teach the Rabbinic background of the New Testament in religion classes. 37.8 percent of Catholic colleges offer a special course on Judaism; 24.1 percent seminaries.

Do these institutions deal with (the meaning of) the Nazi Holocaust? Here the figures for the institutions of higher learning are much smaller, ranging from zero percent (Protestant seminaries), 2.2 percent (Protestant colleges), 1.3 percent (Catholic colleges), to 5.8 percent in Catholic seminaries. (Catholic high schools reported 23.2 percent treated the Nazi period in religion courses, and 13.6 percent did so in Church history courses.)

Courses on the history of Israel? 10.3 percent of the Catholic seminaries and 5.4 percent of the Catholic colleges and universities say yes, but only 1.5 percent of the Protestant seminaries and 6.8 percent of the Protestant colleges. Catholic high schools report 19.6 percent yes.

Courses dealing with the theological significance of the State of Israel are comparatively low: Catholic colleges, 1.3 percent; Catholic seminaries, 10.3 percent; Protestant seminaries, zero percent; and Protestant colleges, 5.1 percent. (Catholic high schools—25.3 percent).

On the question of *whether Jewish scholars are teaching courses in the institutions,* the figures are 7 percent yes for Catholic seminaries; 42.5 percent for Catholic colleges; 12.3 percent for Protestant seminaries; and 20.5 percent for Protestant colleges. Only 5.3 percent of the Catholic high schools responded that they had Jewish scholars teaching courses, but almost 70 percent, a really remarkable figure, responded that they invite a local rabbi to join the class when specifically Jewish subjects are being discussed. Many high schools visit a neighboring temple or synagogue for added lectures or Sabbath services (57.7 percent).

What are some of the implications of these figures and statistics? One possible conclusion is that the two most decisive events that have forged the consciousness of contemporary Jews—the Nazi Holocaust and the rebirth of Israel—are relatively ignored in both Catholic and Protestant seminaries and colleges. It can also be surmised from the responses that Judaism is taught essentially as a "religion" (in the Theology Department or the Department of Religious Studies of Catholic colleges, 75.6 percent; only 29 percent in the History Department) and probably most specifically as background for, or prelude to, Christianity. Of course, this does not mean that Judaism must necessarily be presented in a negative light. But it does seem appropriate to question whether certain aspects of Judaism which are critical to Jews as they understand themselves receive full exploration, such as Jewish historical continuity, the strong sense of Jewish peoplehood, and Jewish religious development in the post-biblical period as reflected in the oral law and the opinions and decisions of the Talmudic and Rabbinic scholars and teachers.

In other words, even a sympathetic treatment of "Old Testament" Judaism in Christian educational institutions will not likely prepare students for an adequate understanding of contemporary Jews and Judaism. Interestingly, Catholic high schools score somewhat better on these grounds. Understandably, a smaller percentage of them offer courses in Jewish studies (27.3 percent), but their responses showed a somewhat fuller treatment of the meaning of the Nazi Holocaust (either in religion or in church history courses). The Catholic high schools also scored a higher percentage on teaching the history of the State of Israel.

The high school responses, incidentally, appeared to be supported by the responses of the diocesan school superintendents. Fifty percent of them responded that the treatment of present-day Judaism was covered in their schools; 55.5 percent indicated their belief that their religious textbooks carried an adequate and positive treatment of Judaism and its relationship to Christianity; 49 percent said that the theology of Judaism was part of the curriculum of the secondary schools; and 18 percent said the schools dealt with the theological significance of the State of Israel.

While these questions may point to some negative findings of the survey, they must also be viewed in the light of the past. There is no pre-Vatican II study with which to compare our present results. Nevertheless we have no reason to doubt that the responses are better today than they would have been five years ago and the increased positive interest in Jewish studies and in institutes on Jewish-Christian relations is reflected in the kinds of comments made by the responding institutions.

Most institutions indicated visible rewards both in the courses on Judaism and in the institutes. Rose Thering, O.P., summarizes these responses:

> Almost every college engaged in an implementation of the conciliar statement stated, in one way or another, that students, faculty, administration, and the community (both Christian and Jewish) surrounding the institution developed a deeper understanding, awareness, and appreciation not only of each other but of their own faith and tradition. Both Testaments of the Sacred Scripture became more meaningful to the Christians. In these classes, there was focusing on Jewish roots that apparently had not even been guessed. A deep appreciation of Jewish spirituality resulted. A deep interest in Jewish thought was generated not only as it related to Christianity and present-day situations, but an appreciation of the grandeur of Judaism itself developed. An awareness of the injustices meted out to Jews throughout history helped remove latent prejudices, and attitudes moved toward real brotherhood.

In general, a high proportion of the respondents felt that the courses and institutes encouraged Jewish-Christian understanding and friendship; moreover, they appeared to evoke especially good responses among students.[1] A number of graduate students

---

[1] Question #27 asked for an evaluation of the institutions' efforts at implementation of the Vatican II statement. Of Catholic colleges and universities, 27 percent responded "very good;" 28.3 percent, "good;" 13 percent, "fair;" 6.7 percent, "poor." Among the "very good" responses were such opinions as these:

"In the excellent atmosphere of Jewish-Christian relations here, we feel we have shown that Vatican II was 'for real.'"

"Our student response is excellent."

"Great progress has been made since Vatican II."

(Seminaries) "This institution recognizes its responsibility to implement Vatican II's statement, and it has taken some significant steps to meet it; much still remains to be done, however."

were stimulated to carry out research projects dealing with biblical, historical, or liturgical aspects of the interrelationships between Judaism and Christianity. In one university, an M.A. comprehensive exam found very knowledgeable responses to the question: "How would you reconcile Matthew's handling of the Jews in the Passion narrative with the Statement of Vatican II?" From the comments of those who answered the questionnaire, it would seem that implementation of the conciliar statement was very rewarding. The sampling of Catholic institutions of higher learning (65.5 percent) shows an overall honest effort to implement the conciliar statement, and perhaps most encouraging, many of the institutions which have made beginnings indicated their desire to do more, and many which have done little have indicated a desire to begin. Lack of qualified personnel, lack of funds, and lack of time in already crowded schedules appeared to be the major impediments, rather than lack of interest or leadership, for programming in Jewish-Christian studies.

RECOMMENDATIONS

In light of the foregoing findings, the authors of this study recommend

1. Colleges, universities, and seminaries should consider including in their curriculum a course related to the Nazi Holocaust, the history and theology of the State of Israel. These areas could very well be covered in a survey course on Jews, Judaism, or Jewish-Christian relations. A well-prepared faculty member could cover this material in a course on the history of Israel.
2. More attention should be given to the intertestamental period, particularly the Rabbinic background of the New Testament for seminary students who will be the future priests preaching homilies.
3. To help prepare faculty in these areas, institutes of Jewish studies—such as those conducted by the American Jewish Committee and the Anti-Defamation League of B'nai B'rith—need to be continued.
4. High school textbooks, even those with good intergroup orientations, need to consider more adequate treatment of the Nazi period and the State of Israel.

5. A high school curriculum for the history of the State of Israel is needed.
6. High school faculties need to be given more opportunities for further preparation in this field of study so as to be able to teach more adequately courses on Jews and Judaism, the Nazi Holocaust, and the State of Israel. Institutes of studies in Judaism and Christianity offered during the summer months at universities and colleges can make possible the necessary education in these areas which many teachers never received when doing their graduate work in theology, sacred scriptures, or history. Teachers should seek in-service programs from their local diocesan or archdiocesan officials. School offices could co-sponsor these programs with the local university or college.
7. The Office of Superintendents should consider taking the initiative in providing in-service education in these areas.
8. The setting up of libraries on Jewish-Christian relations in Ecumenical Institutes and in various schools is greatly to be desired.

13

Statement on "Jerusalem" Before the Near East Subcommittee of the House Foreign Affairs Committee

MY NAME IS Rabbi Marc H. Tanenbaum of New York City. I serve as National Interreligious Affairs Director of the American Jewish Committee. The views that I present in this testimony are my private convictions, although I should like to feel that they represent a broad sentiment within the Jewish community.

In accepting the invitation of the Chairman, Congressman Lee Hamilton, to testify at this hearing, I did so with the understanding that my role is that of a religious spokesman and a student of religious history. I am not here as a political figure from whom formulae or proposals for the political resolution of the status of

---

This excerpted testimony was given before the Congressional Subcommittee on July 28, 1971. As one of the leading religious spokespersons of his time, Rabbi Tanenbaum was sought out often to give testimony on a variety of national and international public policy issues. Significantly, the first we have is on the attachment of Jews to Jerusalem. On other occasions, Rabbi Tanenbaum gave testimony (December 18, 1974) before the Ad Hoc Committee Hearings on World Hunger. There he called on all, and especially the Jewish community, "to take an active part in helping to mobilize maximum American relief support to meet the needs of the millions of impoverished, hungry, and starving peoples throughout the world." Again, in April and May of 1977, the Ninety-fifth Congress held hearings on the implementation of the Helsinki Accords and Religious Liberty and Minority Rights in the Soviet Union. Rabbi Tanenbaum, introduced by Senator Claiborne Pell, sought to "unmask what has been in fact an incredible shell game" played by the Soviet authorities. When the Soviet government allowed the Russian Orthodox Church to join the World Council of Churches, he asserted, they at the same time launched internally a program of suppression in which numerous "seminaries were closed" and "churches converted quietly into museums." Religious liberty, he assured the senators, "is a central issue among many Americans today." Throughout his various Congressional appearances, however, his words reflected a passion captured most eloquently in this selection, an almost poetic reflection on the importance of Jerusalem in Jewish consciousness.

Jerusalem and attendant issues are to be expected. In the last analysis, that responsibility should rest on the principal parties involved whose governments and leaders have the authority and competence to negotiate such mutually acceptable terms. Since the lives of thousands of persons who have their daily existence in the city of Jerusalem are involved in the outcome of such political arrangements, it would be a presumption, and even mischievous, on my part, especially since I am not a citizen of Israel nor of Jordan, to pretend at playing foreign-minister-in-exile.

Nevertheless, it is self-evident that Jerusalem is unique among the cities of the world, with special although differing claims on the religious and cultural sentiments and loyalties of millions of Jews, Christians, and Muslims. Therefore, it should be profitable to seek to clarify the nature and meaning of those commitments and their implications for the adherents of the three great mono-theistic religious communities. As I indicated in my letter of ac-ceptance, I take part willingly in these hearings in the hope that they will contribute in some measure to the depolarization of ten-sions in the Middle East, the overcoming of hostilities and misun-derstandings, and above all, to the building of a common ground on which constructive policies and programs can be shaped for the welfare of all the people—Muslims, Christians, and Jews—in that region, and to their eventual reconciliation as sons and daughters of the Covenant of Abraham. After some 20 years of mutual recrimination and isolation, if the People's Republic of China and the United States now find it possible to begin a ratio-nal dialogue looking hopefully toward coexistence and mutual acceptance, is it too much to hope that such a breakthrough might become possible between the Arab and Israeli nations and peoples?

JERUSALEM IN JEWISH CONSCIOUSNESS

This coming Saturday evening, the Jewish people throughout the inhabited world will observe Tishah B'Av, the ninth day of the Jewish month of Av. Tishah B'Av is the most important of four historical fast days in the Jewish liturgical calendar that commemorate events connected with the destruction of the ancient Temple and of Jerusalem.

According to Jewish tradition, it was on the ninth day of Av in the year 586 B.C.E. that the first Temple was destroyed by the Babylonians. On the same day six hundred fifty-six years later, 70 C.E., the second Temple was burned by Titus and his Roman legions. In the year 135 C.E., the Second War of Independence against the Romans, with the Jewish forces under Bar Cochba and Rabbi Akiva, ended with the fall of fortress Bethar on the ninth of Av. By tragic coincidence, the expulsion of Jews from Spain in 1492 also began on this "black-letter" day of Jewish history, resulting in thousands of Jews seeking refuge in the Holy Land. In our own time, a great catastrophe is bound up with Tishah B'Av; on that day in 1914, Russia ordered the mobilization of her armies, and the World War started. A year later, Czarist Russia evacuated all Jews from the border provinces, and a period of great catastrophe began for East-European Jews, who still remember that their misfortunes began on Tishah B'Av.

The fast of Av is marked by all the rigor of the Day of Atonement. Among traditional Jews, Tishah B'Av is preceded by three weeks of mourning, during which all celebrations are forbidden. At the final meal before the fast, on the eve of Tishah B'Av, some Jews dine on hard rolls and eggs, sprinkling the eggs with ashes, a ritual associated with mourners after funerals.

After the meal, Jews go to their synagogues, which are dimly lighted; they sit on low benches or on boxes; they wear slippers and pray like mourners with bowed heads. They read from The Book of Lamentations, purportedly written by the prophet Jeremiah who foretold and witnessed the downfall of Jerusalem. Then dirges or odes of mourning are recited by the worshipers over the passing of the Temple and the religious and national life of which it was the symbol and the embodiment. The closing section of the ceremony expresses the Jewish people's longing for the Holy Land and contains prayers for her speedy restoration. After midday on this fast, Oriental Jewish women anoint themselves with fragrant oils, for it is believed that this is the birthday of the Messiah, who will arise out of despair and bring consolation to his people.

That ritual, reenacted annually for nearly 2,500 years by Jews dispersed in every part of the world, speaks more persuasively than academic tomes of the centrality of Jerusalem in the religious and folk consciousness of the Jewish people. How does one explain the persistence and tenacity of the attachment of the Jewish people to Jerusalem? The answer in large measure must be looked for in the Jewish religion and Jewish history.

JERUSALEM IN THE BIBLICAL TRADITION

All of the biblical writers looked to Jerusalem as the essence of the meaning of their faith, life, and hope. As Professor Shmaryahu Talmon, a leading biblical scholar now teaching at Harvard University, has observed ("The Biblical Concept of Jerusalem," *Journal of Ecumenical Studies* [fall 1971]): "The city name Jerusalem is mentioned in Hebrew Scriptures some 750 times. Zion appears 180 times. There are several hundred more references to diverse appellations of the city, such as Mount Moriah, City of David, City of Jude, Temple Mount, Holy City, Shalem, etc. Altogether there must be some two thousand mentions of Jerusalem in the Hebrew canon." The number of references is even greater in intertestamental literature and in Rabbinic writings.

"The word count," Professor Talmon states, "reveals to us the locality of Jerusalem in biblical thought. The plethora of references discloses the importance of the city and the ideas connected with it in the minds of the biblical authors and their audience alike" as it developed and grew over a thousand years. Historically, the association of the Jewish people with Jerusalem dates back to the Patriarch Abraham, the founding father of Judaism. Abraham had a two-fold relationship with Jerusalem: one located in a political context arising out of the war against the five foreign kings who had invaded Canaanite territory to fight against the kings of Sodom and Gomorrah (Gen. 14); and one establishing the religious character of Jerusalem through the Patriarch's building of an altar on Mount Moriah (Gen. 22) for the sacrifice of Isaac at God's behest. This two-fold significance of the city was projected into the days of the Davidic kingdom.

Initially, Jerusalem had served as a foreign cult place (Gen. 14:2; 2 Sam. 24:18–25) inhabited by Canaanites, and later ruled by Jebusites. In the late Bronze Age, there was nothing to indicate the city's destiny as a national and religious focus. It was through the actions of David that the "foreign" city was transformed for the first time in its history into the capital—"the metropolis"—of the Jewish kingdom. Jerusalem became a new unifying political center for the Israelite tribes whom David had set out to weld into one nation ("And David and all Israel went to Jerusalem," 1 Chron. 11:4). By transferring the ark of the covenant from Kiryat Ye'arim, the shrine of Shiloh, to Jerusalem, and by laying the foundations for the building in Jerusalem of the Temple dedicated to Israel's God, David endowed the city with the status of the chief sanctuary of Israel, "the place which the Lord Thy God shall choose to put his name there" (Deut. 12:21). David thereby made Jerusalem the cornerstone of the religious and cultic unification of Israel. The concept of Jerusalem as "the holy city" dates from this time.

"It is extraordinary," comments the noted Anglican historian, Dr. James Parkes (*Whose Land: A History of the Peoples of Palestine* [New York: Taplinger, 1971]), "how quickly Jerusalem became in the national thought of the Jewish people not just a symbol of unity but an embodiment of the whole conception of the covenant relationship between God, land, and people." David, who remained for all subsequent history, the ideal of a Hebrew king, and the prototype of the expected Messiah, more than any other individual associated with it, is the father of the city as it has evolved in history. Fittingly, he was buried within its walls, and his tomb remains a venerated shrine.

It will be of some contemporary interest to recall, as Professor Talmon reminds us, that even while Jerusalem was decisively transformed by David into the "cornerstone" of Jewish national and religious unity, "Jerusalem always had a mixed population, knit into one social network" that respected the multiple individual or group identities. "Not only are we told (by biblical writers) that Jebusites, from whom David had captured the city, were permitted to continue to live in it unmolested side by side with the Israelites," Professor Talmon writes, "but our sources also report at great length that the royal court literally was overflowing with foreign warriors (and . . .) advisers, some of whom rose to prominence in the administrative hierarchy of the realm, as, for example, David's and Solomon's ministers. These foreign elements apparently were economically and socially fully integrated and they in fact became a main pillar of support of the Davidic dynasty."

In the period of Israel's unity under David and Solomon, the Jewish nation experienced unprecedented political glory, economic achievement, and religious splendor. It is for this reason that Jerusalem, as the capital of the realm, became a beacon of well-being and success for future generations. Late biblical and post-biblical Judaism made the idealized image of that historical Jerusalem the keystone of their hope for a national and religious renaissance. Ultimately, they perceived in it the prototype of the New Jerusalem, the very fulcrum around which turned their messianic and eschatological aspirations.

The "Holy City"

The depth of Jewish feeling towards Jerusalem as "the holy city" of Judaism is reflected in the fact that in the Midrash of the Rabbinic sages, the terms for the Temple and Jerusalem were used interchangeably. The City, as it were, constituted a broader extension of the Temple itself. It is the whole circumference of the city that is held, and will be held, holy.

Jerusalem acquired a sanctity of its own. Laws were enacted that accorded legal status to the holiness of the city and defined the implications of this status as they affected all of Jewry. To protect the holy city from defilement, practices were instituted which meticulously regulated life within it. The dead were not to be buried within its walls. Streets were swept daily.

In the mind of the Jewish people, as well as in actual practice, Jerusalem became an integral part of the Temple and identical with it. Highly instructive is the fact that a half-shekel was collected each year from every adult male Jew in Palestine and the diaspora, and the proceeds were used for the public sacrifices. But this revenue not only covered all the expenditures of the Temple, such as the remuneration of the judiciary and of the Torah-scroll proofreaders, but also paid for the maintenance of the "city wall and the towers thereof and all the city's needs" (Talmud, Tractate *Shekalim* 4:2).

In distinction from other religions that have invested their reverence for Jerusalem on particular localities or sites that are connected with specific events in their religious histories, Judaism has sanctified the city as such. In doing so, Judaism has kept alive the significance attached to Jerusalem in the Bible, and that has been of decisive importance for the commanding role of the holy city in Jewish tradition until this very day.

To students of comparative religion and *Religionsgeschichte,* Jerusalem is the primordial archetype of supremely sacred space. As Professor Mircea Eleade, one of the leading authorities of comparative religion, has demonstrated in his numerous studies, Mount Zion as "the sacred mountain" and Jerusalem as "the sacred city" symbolically represent in Judaism "the *axis mundi,*" the cosmic axis, which constitutes the center of orientation in the cosmos for Jewish believers. That cosmological significance of Jerusalem to Judaism is reflected in Jewish *aggadic* tradition as exemplified by the following assertion in *Mishna Yoma:* "Traditions relate that in the Temple there was the *Eben Shetiyyah* (the foundation stone) which was so named because upon it the world was founded, and from this as a center the earth was created" (*Yoma* 54b). This legend reflects the view that since the Holy Land was God's chosen country, it must have been first in creation; and because the site of the Temple was the most sacred of all places, the process of creation must have begun there.

THE "HEAVENLY JERUSALEM"

The aspiration to see the Temple in all its purity and splendor and, after its destruction, to witness its restoration which finds expression in the vision of the heavenly Temple, gave rise to the longing and yearning for the heavenly Jerusalem. The idea of a heavenly Temple or city is connected with the idea of ultimate redemption, of the end of the days, and in the deepening of religious feeling awakened by the Temple and the holy city. This is expressed by the Rabbis in the language of the Midrash (*Tanhuma Pekudei* Sec.1): "And so you find the Jerusalem above directly opposite the Jerusalem below. Because of His great love for the earthly Jerusalem, He made another above . . . and so David said, Jerusalem thou art builded as a city that is compact altogether" (Ps. 122:3).

In the wake of enemy incursions, desecrations, and destruction, the concept of the heavenly Jerusalem acquired a new significance for it now constituted a source of consolation and hopeful confidence in ultimate rehabilitation and reconstruction of the nation. In contrast to the concept that the heavenly Jerusalem is to come down to earth, Talmudic literature expresses the view in the remarks of Rabbinic sages that the heavenly Jerusalem will remain forever ensconced above, while the earthly Jerusalem will be reconstructed with human effort. The two cities will, however, maintain a close connection with one another. As Rabbi Johanan said, "The Holy One, blessed be he, declared: 'I shall not enter the Jerusalem which is above, until I enter the Jerusalem which is below '" (*Taanit* 5a). This concept follows logically from the view that the Divine Presence, the *shekhinah,* departs into exile and suffers along with Israel, and that the perfection of the heavenly worlds can only be restored with the redemption of and reconstruction of the earthly Jerusalem by human hands.

The fervent hope for a future restoration of Jerusalem, which signifies the glorious revival of the nation, became the vision of Jewry throughout the exile. Linked with the eschatological picture of the ultimate and final peace for all mankind, the era of eternal peace to be inaugurated in Jerusalem, was the ongoing hope of Jewry for an imminent restoration of Jerusalem as a renewed center of national worship and an imminent source of rejoicing and well-being.

The Three Religions

Thus far, I have concentrated on the meaning of Jerusalem to Judaism and the Jewish people. The Holy Land, and, in particular, the Holy City, have mothered however two religions, Christianity as well as Judaism, which in turn possess a unique relationship to a third, Islam. Though the immense majority of Jews and Christians have long ceased to dwell within its narrow frontiers, and it was never a primary Islamic homeland, yet to none of the three has it become a matter of indifference. But the interests of the three religions differ in both emphases and intensity.

Christianity has become indigenous in many parts of the world. It is represented by strong Christian states. There is nowhere a desire of homeless Christians to return to the original land of their religion. Yet its holy places have been a constant attraction for Christian pilgrims, and their protection and maintenance has been a religio-political interest of Christian powers at many periods of history. For two centuries, there were efforts of Christendom, again half religious and half economic and political, to regain the land by force, and the Crusades have left a permanent mark on the country.

Significantly, the crusaders did not establish a settled agricultural population and did not strike roots in the Holy Land. Once the European presence was drastically reduced, their kingdom collapsed.

The Jewish interest has been both more intense and more complicated. For Jewry has nowhere established another independent national center, and, as is natural, Jerusalem and the land of Israel are intertwined far more intimately with the religion and historic memories of the Jewish people. The connection of the Jewish people with Jerusalem and the land has been of much longer duration; in fact it is continuous from the second millennium B.C.E. up to modern times. Only the defeat by Rome, and the scattering by imperial force of the Jewish population, made a decisive change politically in the history of the land. Nonetheless, the realities of Jewish history during the nineteen centuries of exile are misrepresented without acknowledging the impressive existence of Jewish communities in the land itself throughout the centuries. In Jerusalem itself, as Rabbi Arthur Hertzberg has pointed out ("Israel and Palestine," *IDOC* [October 1970]), "whenever the barest possibility existed, even under hostile powers, enough Jews were to be found to cleave to Jerusalem that, across the centuries, theirs was the largest continuing presence in the city." Thus, according to the *Encyclopedia Britannica*, since 1844, a half-century before the first stirrings of modern Zionism, Jews represented the majority of the population of Jerusalem.

Jewish religious literature is more intimately connected with its history, its climate, and its soil. In the daily prayers of the Jews to this day one of the benedictions of the silent devotion is a prayer for the rebuilding of Jerusalem. In the grace that Jews say after every meal, morning, noon, and night, the third benediction reads: "And rebuild Jerusalem, the holy city, speedily and in our day; blessed art thou, O Lord, who builds Jerusalem."

All synagogues throughout the Jewish world, from the first synagogue in antiquity to those being erected this very day, have been built in such fashion that they face toward Jerusalem. To be buried on the Mount of Olives, no matter where one dies, has been regarded for two millennia as the surest hope of the resurrection, and bodies were being returned from Rome some two thousand years ago for that purpose. To participate in the rebuilding of Jerusalem was the hope of the ages. Jerusalem and the land therefore have provided an emotional center which has endured through the whole of the period of "exile" and has led to constant returns or attempted returns in every century, culminating in our day in the Zionist movement.

Jerusalem and the land is not in the same sense the homeland of the third religion with whose history its own is intertwined. The homeland of Islam is Arabia. In Jerusalem stands the third holiest shrine for Muslims throughout the world. Indeed, Islamic tradition maintains, as Prof. Eleade points out, that "the highest point of the earth is the Ka'aba (in Mecca) because the polar star shows that it is opposite the center of the sky," that is to say, that Mecca is "the center of the universe" in Islamic cosmology.

From the Arab conquest until the British mandate, Palestine and Jerusalem were never even a name on the political map of the world. They were a portion of some larger unity, whether Arab, Mamluk, or Turkish, and their people were never conscious of themselves as a national unit, nor did they ever attempt to form an independent kingdom. During the long period of Islamic rule, with its kaleidoscopic changes of dynasty, no claimant to the throne of caliphs, or even to a separate sovereignty, ever emerged from its population. The land and the city were the alternate prey of dynasties ruling from Damascus, Baghdad, Cairo, or Istanbul. Only in the twentieth century have they resumed a separate identity and that initially by the will of outsiders rather than that of the will of their own population.

Implications and Conclusions

All the major biblical faiths have deep interests and continuing involvements in Jerusalem and the holy land, but they are not exactly parallel. There is need for an objective assessment of the moralities involved in the entire situation, and as Arthur Hertzberg has wisely observed in his essay, "we must get our moral priorities in the right order."

A viable Jewish people in the land of Israel, and the restoration of Jerusalem to its natural condition as a unified city, is indispensable to the survival of the Jewish spirit and ethos in our age. An Arab sovereignty in Palestine, and in particular over that part of post-partition Palestine which is now Israel, accompanied by the unnatural bisection of Jerusalem, is not vitally necessary to the survival and creativity of the whole of Arab national culture and history, or of the Islamic faith. The great centers of Arab continuity and survival are elsewhere. The Christian interest in the holy land, as Professor George Williams of Harvard recently formulated it, involves religiously solely the question of free access to the holy places, and the security and stability of the Christian populations in Jerusalem and in Israel. Once these interests are satisfied, Christians go beyond their religious competence and enter into the realm of politics in which they have no standing as ecclesiastical bodies. As groups of Christian authorities both in Israel and the United States have recently testified, never has there been such free access to the holy places as since 1967 when Jerusalem was reunified under Israeli jurisdiction.

14

Do You Know What Hurts Me?

A HASIDIC RABBI, renowned for his piety and compassion, was unexpectedly confronted one day by one of his devoted, youthful disciples in their house of prayer and study. In a burst of feeling, the disciple exclaimed, "My master, I love you!" The ancient teacher slowly looked up from his books and then asked his fervent disciple, "Do you know what hurts me, my son?"

The young man was baffled. Composing himself, he stuttered, "I don't understand your question, Rabbi. I am trying to tell you how much you mean to me and you confuse me with strange questions."

"My question to you is not at all strange or irrelevant," the Hasidic rabbi stated. "It is the very soul of understanding love and compassion in our tradition. For if you do not know what hurts me, how can you truly love me?"

If Jews and Christians want to consider seriously their mutual relationships, it is not sufficient that they declare to one another generalized sentiments of reciprocal regard. Genuine caring between groups, as between individuals, presupposes a willingness to enter into the life situation of the other, and to be present with concern and support at the moment when the other person or group is hurting.

As human beings, Christians and Jews share a universal agenda. In a growing interdependent "global city," they are both concerned about eliminating wars and establishing peace; about overcoming racial injustices and ending the scourges of poverty, illiteracy, and disease; about ecology and preserving the quality of life; about nation-building and economic development in the Third World; about closing the gap between the "have" and the

Reprinted from *Event* (12 February 1972): p. 4–8. In this article for the magazine published by the American Lutheran Church Men, Marc Tanenbaum is at his most colloquial in relaying an old Hasidic story. From it Rabbi Tanenbaum argued for the delineation of a "universal human agenda."

"have-not" nations (20 percent of the world's population who live in the predominantly white, Western world still control 70 percent of the world's wealth); about reordering our national priorities.

This universal agenda links together Christians and Jews as citizens and as neighbors. That linkage, I would argue, would be inconceivable without a basic commitment to the "Judeo-Christian" value system that orients Jews and Christians in a special, distinctive way toward the universe. While Judaism and Christianity obviously differ in their respective interpretations of Sacred Scriptures, the biblical ground of these monotheistic faiths unites their adherents in a theology of creation which affirms the unity of the human family under the sovereignty of a transcendent Creator-God; a shared reverence for the prophets of Israel who require justice and righteousness and therefore impose an obligation of respect for the dignity of every person and of building a society based on caring and compassion. They also share common approaches to a theology of redemption, which conditions Jews and Christians to a messianic view of history and thereby requires active participation in shaping purposefully the events of history so the kingdom of God on earth—a redeemed world freed of hatred, war, bloodshed—may ultimately be realized by the universal fraternity of the people of God.

The truth of the matter is, however, that humanists and ethical culturists, even Marxists, share in this universal agenda, albeit the ground of their values has been secularized, and most no longer recognize nor acknowledge their indebtedness to the biblical-prophetic sources who shaped decisively Western civilization. From this point of view, Judaism and Christianity have succeeded far better than they have been aware. Their biblical values have become blended imperceptibly into the cultural wallpaper of Western society which now takes for granted ("co-opted" is the current word for it) the revolutionary contributions of ethical monotheism. In turn, the universalization of the Jewish-Christian agenda has had the paradoxical effect of weakening the sense of special vocation of both Christians and Jews, and consequently, has eroded the conviction that their relationship to one another has any further special importance.

But here two crucial points must be made. The first is that universal value systems that are cut off from a vital relationship with their particularized sources of origins have tended to wither and collapse. That is precisely what happened to the "oikumene"— that ecumenical empire of Alexander the Great and his followers—whose Hellenistic civilization lost vital, nourishing contact with the human realities and dynamisms of the Greek city-states. It became a "cut-flower" civilization, an abstract society, and its culture of social fruits died for lack of continuous nurture.

In many ways that is what is happening to the "civic religion" of America, which is becoming an idolatrous caricature of a living authentic biblical religion. A vital Judaism and Christianity whose prophetic impulses are in good working order ought to subject to continuous judgment and constructive criticism these tendencies to manipulate religious symbols for the apotheosizing of distorted nationalism and the "American way of life" as the objects of ultimate loyalty and veneration.

The decline of that lively prophetic consciousness, which at its best convicted as inadequate all self-worship of ego and group and required the loyalty of a faithful people to certain minimal ethical and spiritual norms ("commandments" or "laws"), is nowhere more grotesquely to be seen today than in the widespread and pervasive paganism, hedonism, and self-indulgence of our consumer society, "the people of plenty." How to reverse that new paganism and to restore the sense of self-transcendence and of biblical stewardship of material goods for service to all members of the human family—especially the poor and the deprived—ought to be a high priority on the universal agenda of Jews and Christians today.

Not only would the restoring of such an alliance between Christians and Jews in opposing these anti-biblical tendencies help both communities cease taking each other for granted to their mutual disadvantage, but it would also restore to Judaism and Christianity that authentic vocation of sensitizing and humanizing society, the building of world and national community based on mutual concern and reciprocal trust—which is what the covenanted community of Israel was all about in its truest purposes.

The second point that needs to be made about present-day Jewish-Christian relations is that each community of faith not only participates in the universal agenda but also has its own "particular" agenda that is valid and legitimate in its own terms. Jewish-Christians relations today are crucially determined by the way and to the degree to which we listen to each other's particular agenda and support one another actively when the particular claims of the other do not violate one's own principles.

Thus, for example, the Catholic agenda includes such particular issues as government aid to parochial schools; and public morality positions on abortion, divorce, and birth control. The Protestant agenda involves such concerns as developing a Protestant theological consensus that would bring some order out of the confusion that issues from the death-of-God school to evangelicalism; the racial crisis in the Protestant churches which is the unique scene of racial difficulties since some 17 million of the nation's 22 million blacks are identified in some way with the Protestant community; and ecumenism in all its tendencies and counter tendencies, since Protestantism, to its credit, took the first initiatives and provided the earliest leadership in launching the ecumenical movement.

The Jewish agenda, in its particularity, is concerned about the security and survival of the people and the State of Israel who play such a central and dynamic role in the Jewish religion and in Jewish cultural identity; the achievement of the human rights of the 3 million Jews in the Soviet Union; the liberation from oppression of Jews in Arab countries, especially Syria, who suffer from torture and denial of the right to emigrate; the new forms of virulent anti-Semitism now being fostered as an article of political policy by the Soviet Union, East European Communist parties, and their Arab allies (see "Jews under Communism," by Paul Lendvasi, *Commentary* magazine, December 1971); and the urgent question of Jewish education of our young people who are the basis of any Jewish future.

The Catholic has a right to expect Protestants and Jews, if they are genuine allies, to try to understand the magnitude of the education crisis the Catholic people face. While no one who is deeply committed to the separation of church and state (as this writer is) should be expected to compromise that fundamental position on which the democratic experiment pivots, Catholics do have a moral right to expect that their partners in dialogue search out with them positive ways of alleviating their school crisis, for the simple and self-evident reason that all Americans have a basic stake in the quality education of some 5 million American children who happen to be Catholic (and of some 60,000 Jewish children who attend Orthodox day schools; and of Protestant children in primarily Lutheran parochial schools).

Similarly, Protestants have a right to expect that their ecumenical allies demonstrate empathy and support in meeting the vital needs of their particular agenda, and not to stand aloof in self-righteous smugness, muttering pleasurably over "the theological nervous breakdown of Protestantism" (as some non-Protestants have recently done), or the decline of "WASPism," the latest form of bigoted ethnic stereotyping. Catholics and Jews have a vested interest in the constructive renewal and reform of the Protestant ethos because "the ecumenical moderates" of American Protestantism (to use Martin Marty's term) created those conceptions and practices which made possible pluralism, dialogue, and religious liberty—the foundation stones of an open, voluntary, democratic society.

By the same token, the Jewish community has a moral right to expect that Catholics and Protestants who take seriously their Jewish partners go beyond the conventional pieties and sentimentalities of Christian "charity" and seek genuinely to understand what hurts the Jewish people today. Having lost a third of their flesh-and-blood family in the Nazi Holocaust just twenty-five years ago, Jews are not being irrational, hysterical, or hyper-sensitive when they call upon Christian allies, who claim to be "branches grafted on to the olive tree of Israel," to take an unequivocal stand against those Arab leaders who in May 1967 were threatening "the final solution" of nearly 3 million Jews now living in Israel, or against those Soviet leaders who are engaged in the religious and cultural extinction of Judaism through forced assimilation of Jews who are being denied elementary rights of religious self-determination and of emigration.

Any Christian who truly knows his Jewish neighbors must surely realize that the Jewish people are opposed to the cold war, desire detente between the superpowers, and, above all, pray and yearn for *shalom*, peace, which is the very name of the God of Israel and the God of all the nations. They want peace and justice not only for themselves, but for all people, including the Christian and

Muslim peoples in the entire Middle East. But it is a false consciousness and a defective universalism that pursues a universal
peace that requires the sacrifice of any particular group or its vital
interests. Ultimately, the Jewish-Christian dialogue will make its
greatest contribution when it manages to articulate the vision and
to create the living relationships that make possible the establishment of authentic human community without compromise of the
essential differences and claims to truth and value that Christians
and Jews, and all historic groups, legitimately embody. For that is
the vision of the people of Israel which is as old and as new as
King Solomon's prayer of dedication of the Holy Temple in Jerusalem, "Hear thou in heaven thy dwelling place, and do according to all that the stranger calleth to thee for; that all people of
the earth may know thy name, to fear thee, as do thy people Israel; and that they may know that his house which I have builded,
is called by thy name. . . . That all the people of the earth may
know that the Lord is God, and that there is none else" (1 Kings
8:43, 60).

15

Judaism, Christianity, and Islam: Discovery of Mutual Harmonies

I GREATLY WELCOME this opportunity to open a dialogue with representatives of Islam, as well as of Christianity, in this country. There has been far too much hostility and suffering between members of our three monotheistic communities and hopefully, this dialogue between the three branches of the one Covenant is a "sign of the times" marking the beginning of a more constructive and humane relationship between our three faiths.

From the researches and studies of such eminent scholars as Professor S. D. Goitein and many others, we know how great and lasting a reciprocal influence Judaism and Islam have had on each other from the seventh century down to recent times. Nearly 1,400 years ago, Judaism and a segment of the Jewish people then living in Arabia stood beside the cradle of the Muslim religion and Arab statehood. Judaism played a decisive role in the development of the religious, moral, and legal conceptions in the Koran in early Islam and in the formulation of the young Muslim community and state.

Indeed prominent scholars have stressed that Islam was far more akin to Judaism in its basic ideas, as well as in the details regulating the lives of its believers, than to Christianity despite the closer "family relationship" between Christianity and Judaism. Reciprocally, Jewish thought and philosophy, even Jewish law and religious practices, were systematically and finally formulated under Islamic influences. The Hebrew language developed its

Statement before the Pakistani Council of Asia Society, February 16, 1972. Well before Jewish/Christian/Muslim dialogues had become an accepted part of the interfaith movement, Rabbi Tanenbaum addressed the Pakistani Council of Asia Society to "open a dialogue" between the three monotheistic communities. Despite "periods of mutual intolerance and oppression," he points to "periods of enormously creative Islamic-Jewish symbiosis."

grammar and vocabulary on the model of the Arab language, and the revival of Hebrew today is unthinkable without the influence of the Arab world some 1000 years ago. To phrase the relationship more directly, the Muslim religion and Arab nationhood took form under Jewish impact, while traditional Judaism received its final shape under Muslim-Arab influences. When the Arabs faded out from world history (roughly from 1300 to 1900), the Oriental Jews also virtually disappeared from Jewish history, thus demonstrating their interdependence.

To gain a truer perspective today of relationships between Judaism and Islam, it would be helpful to remind ourselves that Judaism and Islam, in distinction from the great civilizations that surrounded them, shared very definite common ideals, and common traits in social traditions and moral attitudes. It is clear that the uncompromising attitude on monotheism by the Prophet Mohammed is due to the very strong influences of Jewish monotheists. Mohammed declared in the Koran (Sura No. 7, 59), after proclaiming himself the Prophet of Gentiles, "Among the followers of Moses there is one people who lead others with the truth and with it they judge." The prophet never ceased to emphasize that these ideals came from Israel—the intrinsic values of the belief in one God, the creator of the world and the designer of human destiny, the god of justice and mercy. Before Him everyone, high and low, bears personal responsibility.

As there is a very close connection between the Koran and the religion of Israel, there is an even more amazing affinity between the fully developed systems of the two religions:

1. Both possess a tradition of revealed law—*halachah* in Judaism and *Shariyah* in Islam—that regulates worship, ethics, and social etiquette, and all aspects of life.
2. Both have an oral tradition—in Judaism, *Torah She'beal Peh* and in Islam, *Hadith*—that authoritatively interprets and supplements the written law.
3. Both rely on a completely free and unorganized republic of scholars rather than on a hierarchy of religious dignitaries who make decisions.
4. The study even of purely legal matters is regarded in both religions as worship. The holy men of Islam and Judaism are not priests or monks, but students of the divinely revealed law.

In addition, both Judaism and Islam were "primitive democracies" characterized by the absence of privileged castes and classes, the absence of forced obedience to a strong authority, a high respect of freedom of speech, for human life, dignity, and freedom. Overriding these common features is the extraordinary and unique fact that both Judaism and Islam are basically national religions that are essentially universal in character. Much more could be said about the historical aspect of the Jewish people under Islam. Suffice it to say that there have been both periods of enormously creative Islamic-Jewish symbiosis, as well as periods of mutual intolerance and oppression. The moral and spiritual challenge posed to Muslims, Christians, and Jews today is essentially that of George Santanyana, "Those who will not learn from history are doomed to repeat it."

As Christians, Muslims, and Jews begin to dialogue together in mutual respect, hopefully they will recover those common features of their religious beliefs and ways of life that will enable them to make a genuine contribution to the building of a unified human community which respects the diversity of religious, ethnic, and racial groups as a source of positive enrichment.

16

Some Issues Raised by Forthcoming Evangelism Campaigns: A Background Memorandum

RECENT ANNOUNCEMENTS of a forthcoming series of nationwide campaigns of Christian evangelism have begun to raise concern in the Jewish community about the potential of these programs for intergroup tension and misunderstanding. The intensification of Christian evangelism raises two different questions for Jews:

1. How much of this forthcoming activity will be specifically directed to the conversion of individual Jews or the Jewish community?

2. Assuming that Jews are not singled out as special objects for conversion in these forthcoming campaigns, what are the implications of this "new evangelism" for the pluralist character of Amer-

---

In 1972, the AJC confronted "Key 73," a Protestant evangelical outreach, announced with great ceremony as influencing every area of American society and endorsed by numerous political leaders as well. Its theme was "Calling Our Continent to Christ in 1973." Rabbi Tanenbaum's response was not alarmist. Rather, he established direct, personal relations with evangelical Christians, such as the Rev. Billy Graham. But in June 1972, Rabbi Tanenbaum and his staff at the AJC put out a "background" memorandum on Key 73 and other evangelical phenomena of the period such as "Explo '72" (which aimed at an evangelized student population by 1976), Catholic Pentecostals, and Jews for Jesus. The memorandum lays the foundation for further work Rabbi Tanenbaum would contribute in a constructive encounter with evangelicals. Later, in a creative and positive response to Jewish concerns on resurgent Christian evangelism, Rabbis Tanenbaum and A. James Rudin, his colleague in AJC's Interreligious Affairs Department, launched a remarkable series of "conversations" with Marvin R. Wilson of Gordon College. These dialogues between evangelical and Jewish scholars have so far produced three volumes.

ican society, as well as for the unfolding nature of Jewish-Christian relations?

In response to the first question, it should be emphasized that none of the nationwide campaigns described below is specifically directed to Jews or the Jewish community. Nevertheless, those specialized groups and organizations that are committed to winning Jews for Christ have recently stepped up their activities. The American Board of Missions to the Jews (Beth Sar Shalom Fellowship)—a "Hebrew-Christian movement"—has mounted a direct conversion effort at the Jewish people through well-financed nationwide television programs and full-page ads in major daily newspapers ("So Many Jews Are Wearing 'That Smile' Nowadays").

The "Jews for Jesus" movement and the Young Hebrew Christian Alliance (YHCA) have concentrated their missionary attention on Jewish youth on college campuses, apparently riding on the wave of popularity of "the Jesus movement." The Broadway rock musical "Jesus Christ Superstar" contributed to and is a by-product of this movement.

The answer to the second question will depend largely on how these campaigns develop, how effective they are, and in part, how the Jewish community, and others, respond to them.

Both the general evangelism campaigns and the specific Hebrew-Christian missionary efforts will confront the Jewish community and others during the coming months—and perhaps the next several years—with one of the most complicated and challenging intergroup and interreligious problems. How to assure freedom of religion and at the same time preserve the diverse, pluralist character of American society in the face of tendencies to act as though Christianity and America were one and the same; how to preserve the substantial gains that have been made in recent years in Jewish-Christian understanding, and at the same time to communicate to Christian evangelists that the Jewish people reject any theological views that require that the Jews be "saved" by ceasing to exist as members of the historic Jewish faith and people, are at the heart of this task of interpretation.

In response to requests for guidelines and suggestions from the Jewish community—especially from rabbis, Hillel directors, and

Jewish parents—the AJC Interreligious Affairs Department has prepared this background memorandum[1] for the purpose of providing information about the various projected evangelism campaigns and "Hebrew-Christian" movements and suggesting approaches for articulating a Jewish response to these efforts insofar as they affect the Jewish community.

CURRENT EVANGELISTIC CAMPAIGNS

One of the most striking phenomena in recent American religious life has been the renaissance of evangelical Christianity. The period since the end of World War II has witnessed an extraordinary advance by evangelical groups. These groups are today growing at a rate that exceeds the expansion of the mainline denominations and the rise of the general population.

The contemporary evangelical movement continues to articulate the traditional theological concepts of fundamentalist Christianity but with increasing intellectual acumen. The message of evangelicalism is communicated through a highly skilled and effective utilization of the mass media.

Although evangelist activity has chiefly been the concern of conservative Protestants, there are growing indications that mainline Protestant bodies as well as Roman Catholics are being influenced by the intensified interest in evangelism.

Perhaps the two most outstanding evangelistic events planned for the next eighteen months are the International Student Congress on Evangelism (known as Explo '72) to be held in Dallas in June, and Key '73, a year-long effort that will undoubtedly attract immense interest in the general as well as religious media.

Bill Bright, the President of Campus Crusade, in discussing the purpose of Explo said, "Explo is a spring board to train thousands of college students and generate a movement for Christ which will sweep our country and the world. We are seeking to saturate the entire nation with the claims of Jesus Christ in 1976." Explo

---

[1] The factual information in this document is based on research by Gerald Strober, Consultant on Religious Curricula and specialist in Evangelical Relations for the AJC.

gained national visibility through nightly television services from the Cotton Bowl. The event closed on June 17 with an all-day festival keynoted by Billy Graham, and attended by an estimated 250,000 people.[2]

An indication of the surfacing of the ideology of "America as a Christian nation" at Explo '72 is to be seen in a recent statement by one of the most prominent leaders of the "Jesus People," the Rev. Arthur Blessitt of the Children of God. The 30-year-old evangelist said he "hopes to get President Nixon to make a public statement as to whether he is personally committed to Jesus Christ as his Lord and Savior." Mr. Blessitt observed, according to Religious News Service (March 29, 1972), that Explo '72 plans, among other things, to send teams of Christians to witness during the national political conventions this summer and spoke of his hope "for a man who has a personal commitment to Jesus Christ as Savior and Lord who will arise on the national political scene."

Even more important for its potential impact is the Key '73 evangelistic effort to be launched early next year. This program, which has the active support of over 100 Protestant denominations, cites its aim to "blitz" the continent next year with an evangelistic crusade, "to share with every person in North America more fully and more forcefully the claims and message of the gospel of Jesus Christ, to confront people with the gospel of Jesus Christ by proclamation and demonstration—by witness and ministry, by word and deed."

Evangelism and "Jews for Jesus"

One aspect of the significant increase in evangelistic activity has been the intensification of efforts aimed at converting Jews to Christianity. Most of these efforts have been conducted by long-established organizations involved with Jewish evangelism (Ameri-

---

[2] Other movements in the "Jesus Revolution" include the Inter-Varsity Christian Fellowship; Young Life (1,300 club affiliates); Youth for Christ (represented in 2,000 American high schools); Teen Challenge; The Pentecostal (estimated 10,000 members); and the Catholic Pentecostal (who are committed to the Catholic Church). There are an estimated 600 Christian communes across the country.

can Board of Missions to the Jews; Hebrew-Christian Alliance) but there have been indications of independent or offshoot groups formed to evangelize young people, i.e., "Jews for Jesus." To date there has been no evidence to suggest that the major evangelical groups or personalities are directly involved in the campaign to win Jews to Christ, although the possibility exists that such activity could occur, especially if the Jewish mission groups should succeed in attaching themselves to the major evangelistic events scheduled for the next several years.

There are an estimated 100–150 local and national organizations of "Hebrew Christians." According to *Christianity Today* ("Turning on to Jeshua," December 17, 1971), "Most mainline denominations have now quietly closed their Jewish evangelism offices, but independent agencies continue to proliferate, and Jewish evangelism departments are still operated by Chicago's Moody Bible Institute and the Bible Institute of Los Angeles."

According to *Newsweek* magazine (April 17, 1972), there are "5,000 or so 'Hebrew Christians' who worship at the American Board of Missions to the Jews' two dozen 'outposts' throughout the U.S.; it is estimated that perhaps as many as 100,000 other converts attend Sunday services at Protestant churches." Together with some 60 other similar organizations, the American Board operates almost entirely with money and ministers supplied by evangelical Protestants, *Newsweek* reports.

INTERGROUP AND INTERRELIGIOUS IMPLICATIONS

A number of basic issues are raised for Jews—both as American citizens and as adherents of Judaism—by these developments which call for the most careful consideration:

1. Does the revival of "the new evangelism" pose a real threat of regression to the early "Evangelical Empire" stage of American history which equated the Kingdom of God with Protestant republicanism (see Martin E. Marty, *The Righteous Empire: The Protestant Experience in America* [New York: Dial Press, 1970]), and supported a Christian theocratic conception of American institutions? Do these tendencies threaten to erode the ground of plu-

ralism, which made possible the liberal Christian understanding that the Jews are full partners in the American republic?

2. Can the "Hebrew-Christian" notions of "Messianic Judaism" and "completed Jews through Christ" reverse the recently emerging Christian "theologies of Judaism" that view the Jewish religion as a living, permanent faith, a source of truth and value to its adherents? For Jews to speak of the Jewish roots of Christianity is to contribute to the enrichment of Christian self-understanding. For Christians to see their relationship to Judaism solely as one of fulfillment and supersession is in fact an act of negation of Judaism, for the daughter faith denies the mother the right to an independent, self-determined existence by totally absorbing Judaism within Christianity. A number of major Christian theologians[3] have clearly affirmed that, on the basis of the New Testament, the believing Christian must acknowledge the continuing validity of Judaism. At the heart of the Hebrew-Christian claim is the fundamental issue of Christology which Hebrew-Christians do not appear to comprehend at all from the perspective of Judaism. The issue has been stated forthrightly by Rabbi Jakob Petuchowski in his book, *Heirs of the Pharisees* (Lanham, Maryland: University Press of America, 1970):

> To consider Jesus as the Messiah may have been, from the point of view of the Synagogue, a factual mistake (in light of the absence of a fundamental change in the elimination of evil in history and other signs of the Messianic Age—MT). But it was not a religious sin. To consider Jesus as part of a divine trinity was another matter altogether. A "Son of Noah" could believe that the one God had divine *shittuph* (associates) and still qualify as one of "the righteous men among the nations." A "Son of Israel," however, was bound to such a radical form of monotheism that he was unable to distinguish between a monotheistic trinitarianism and a polytheistic tritheism . . . A Jew who believed in divine "associates" was simply considered an idolater, and could not enjoy, in the eyes of the Synagogue, the status accorded the Gentile Christian.

---

[3] Professors Krister Stendahl, W. D. Davies, Markus Barth, J. Coert Rylaarsdam, Franklin Littell, Roy Eckardt, the late Reinhold Niebuhr and Paul Tillich, Revs. Edward A. Flannery, Gregory Baum, Cornelius Rijk, Msgr. John M. Oesterreicher, Rosemary Ruether, Monika Hellwig, Dr. Albert Outler, Dr. James Parkes, Dr. Johan Snoek, Rev. Joseph Fitzmeyer, Rev. Bruce Vawter, Rev. John Pawlikowski, Dr. Jaroslav Pelikan, Rev. William Harter, among others.

3. Should Jews oppose conversion campaigns by Christians directed at Jews, and vice versa? Here, too, the views of Rabbi Petuchowski are instructive:

> We admit that the wholehearted Jew and the wholehearted Christian have no need to convert each other to their respective faiths; they would, indeed, be untrue to their divine calling were they to do so. But our world is not populated by wholehearted Jews and Christians. It is inhabited by the religiously uprooted, the spiritually destitute. Not every offspring of Jewish parents actualizes his Jewish potential. Not every pagan born into a Christian household does, in fact, become a Christian. The world is full of only nominal Christians and nominal Jews. The Synagogue has a primary obligation to win over the nominal Jew to a full acceptance of the "yoke of the commandments," just as the Church has a primary obligation to lead the nominal Christian to Jesus, and through Jesus, to the Father. But addressing himself to the mass of agnostics, atheists, and religiously uprooted, one cannot always discriminate and distinguish between those of Jewish and those of Gentile origin. Church and Synagogue, in entering the marketplace of ideas, must offer and describe their wares to all comers, and must answer the queries of all questioners. And it may well happen that, here and there, the Jewish answer will appeal to the nominal Christian, just as the Christian answer may appeal to the nominal Jew. Of course, Jews consider a wide occurrence of the latter alternative as highly unlikely. Why should the twentieth century be more propitious for the Christian mission to the Jew than the last nineteen centuries have been? But theoretically the possibility of a limited kind of "two-way traffic" must be granted . . . But this possibility must never be more than a peripheral concern. It must be granted and openly faced in order to make a true and honest "dialogue" possible. It cannot, however, be the sole content of that "dialogue" itself. That can only be concerned with the tasks and the challenges which confront us in common.

4. Is there a possibility that the evangelism campaigns with their emphasis on the life, death, and resurrection of Jesus may provide new occasions for negative and hostile portrayals of Jews in the Crucifixion of Jesus? That such a possibility exists is evidenced by the constant cry over the stereotyped views of the role of the Jewish people and the high priests of Israel in the Broadway rock musical Jesus Christ Superstar. Writing in a recent issue of

The Christian Century, Dr. Richard Gelwick, Chairman of the Religion and Philosophy Department at Stephens College, Columbia, Mo., stated that he sees the "threat of anti-Semitism emanating from the Jesus revolution" on the basis of a "dogmatism stemming from biblical literalism—including the charge of Jewish guilt."

5. On March 1, 1972, the Rabbinical Court of Justice of the Association of Synagogues of Massachusetts issued an official decree declaring, *inter alia,* that "a person born of Jewish parents, when he joins the so called 'Hebrew-Christian' movement, abdicates his rights as a member of the Jewish faith." This is an understandable response on a juridical level, but raises the question of a more adequate response to the conversion of young Jews to Jesus on the part of the Jewish community. Do not such conversions constitute a judgment on the failure of our organized religious institutions and our homes to communicate meaningfully Jewish ideals, values, and experience to our own young people?

We would caution against overreactions, against baseless suspicion of all Christian motivations in approaching Jews for dialogue or interreligious programming, and against withdrawal from the arena of interreligious activity. Jews have benefited greatly and substantially from increased Jewish-Christian cooperation in recent years; in revised and improved Christian textbooks, in training programs for Christian teachers, in massive Christian support for Soviet Jewry, and in increasing sympathy for the cause of Israel. These gains must not be lost through an irrational reaction to movements that rely on persuasion and not coercion.

17

Judaism, Ecumenism, and Pluralism

IN HIS PERCEPTIVE STUDY, *The Social Sources of Denominationalism* (New York: Henry Holt, 1929), H. Richard Niebuhr argued that the religious diversity in American society during the first half of the twentieth century represented not so much theological differences as the accommodation of Christianity to "the caste system" of human society. He declared that social factors played a decisive, negative role and were largely responsible for the disunity of American Christendom. Elaborating his thesis, Professor Niebuhr asserted that the religious proliferation of the denominations and sects closely followed the division of men and women into castes of national origins, race, class, and sectional groups that constitute the American society. In short, the pluralism of America undergirded and reinforced the diversity of religious behavior.

Three decades later, quite paradoxically, another Christian analyst employed the identical categories of Professor Niebuhr and arrived at opposite conclusions. Robert Lee wrote in his book, *The Social Sources of Church Unity* (New York: Abingdon Press, 1960), that during the decade of the 1950s and thereafter, social factors made a positive contribution to the rise of ecumenism and Christian unity. He observed that church unity springs from the growing cultural unity within American society (p. 17). Dr. Lee posited the emergence of a *homo americanus*—a "consensus American"

Reprinted from *Speaking of God Today: Jews and Lutherans in Conversation* [Philadelphia: Fortress Press, 1974]. From 1969–1973, the American Jewish Committee and the Division of Theological Studies of the Lutheran Council in the U.S.A. co-sponsored four scholarly colloquia, the papers from which were published in the 1974 volume co-edited by Rabbi Marc Tanenbaum and Paul D. Opsahl, *Speaking of God Today*. The conversations probed such topics as Law-Grace-Election, Land-People-State, and Speaking of God after Auschwitz in a Pluralistic World. To the last exchange, Rabbi Tanenbaum contributed a presentation on "Judaism, Ecumenism, and Pluralism."

(p. 23). There was an increased awareness of a common frame of reference in which Americans tended to see things from a similar perspective. Dr. Lee cited the social changes in race, class, sectionalism, and nationalism as factors contributing to the emergent cultural unity. There was now "a common culture" based on a shared universal education, a common language, economic well-being, growing intermarriage between members of denominations and faiths, the establishment of national cultural symbols through the influence of the culture-producing mass media, and an evolving network of mutual dependence through the organizational revolution which is the basis of our urban, industrialized civilization. Cementing this social and cultural unity, Dr. Lee wrote, were the unifying influences of "common value themes," most notably, a shared belief in individualism, freedom, democracy, and success.

Whether or not social forces advance or inhibit unity between religious groups is a subject worthy of continued examination and reflection. One conclusion emerges inescapably, however, from the studies of Professors Niebuhr and Lee, and that is the basic fact than neither ecumenism, nor interreligious relations, nor pluralism can be adequately comprehended solely on "spiritual" or "doctrinal" grounds. A comprehension of "extra-theological" factors is critical for a genuine understanding of the complex reality of such vital relationships.

What are some of the extra-theological realities that constitute the matrix of the current ecumenical and interreligious scene? A portrait of that matrix has been sharply sketched by Professor Zbigniew Brenzinski of Columbia University, who writes in his study, *Between Two Ages: America's Role in the Technetronic Era* (New York: Viking Press, 1970):

> The paradox of our time is that humanity is becoming simultaneously more unified and more fragmented. That is the principal thrust of contemporary change. Time and space have become so compressed that global politics manifest a tendency toward larger, more interwoven forms of cooperation, as well as toward the dissolution of established and ideological loyalties. Humanity is becoming more integral and intimate even as the differences in the condition of the separate societies are widening. Under these circumstances, proximity, instead of promoting unity, gives rise to tension prompted by a new sense of global congestion (p. 3).

Another preeminent feature of current extra-theological reality that influences in decisive ways ecumenical and interreligious relationships is depicted by the Dutch theologian and social scientist, Dr. Anton C. Zijderveld, who writes in his book, *The Abstract Society: A Cultural Analysis of Our Time* (New York: Doubleday and Co., 1970):

> The structures of modern society have grown increasingly pluralistic and independent of man. Through an ever-enlarging process of differentiation, modern society acquired a rather autonomous and abstract nature confronting the individual with strong but strange forms of control. It demands the attitudes of obedient functionaries from its inhabitants who experience its control as an unfamiliar kind of authority. That means societal control is no longer characterized by a family-like authority but dominated by bureaucratic neutrality and unresponsiveness. The individual seems to be doomed to endure this situation passively, since the structures of society vanish in abstract air if he tries to grasp their very forces of control. No wonder that many seek refuge in one or another form of retreat (p. 11).

He adds:

> Modern society has become abstract in the experience and consciousness of man! Modern man, that is, does not "live society," he faces it as an often-strange phenomenon. This society has lost more and more of its reality and meaning and seems to be hardly able to function as the holder of human freedom. As a result, many modern men are turning away from the institutions of society and are searching for *meaning, reality,* and *freedom* elsewhere. These three coordinates of human existence have become the scarce value of a continuous existential demand (p. 54).

These two authors reinforce a shared conviction about what is the paradoxical and contradictory predicament in which the contemporary person finds himself and herself. The planetization of the human family through electronics, automation, instant mobility, and satellite communications has made mandatory that everybody adjust to the vast global environment as if it were a global city. At the same time, that globalization of the human consciousness has led to the undermining of dependencies on the more limited local loyalties, such as the nation-state. The effects of that are to be seen especially among our young people, many of whom feel a weakened sense of national patriotism and have little emotional fervor about national sancta and rituals, while feeling very much at home roaming Europe, Asia, Africa, and Latin America as if they were born as natural citizens of the world. To many of them, the global city is already a dominant fact of contemporary life.

The human situation is complicated by the fact, however, that those of us who live in the advanced Western societies based on scientific and technological foundations confront bureaucracies and vast organizations as the crucial and all-pervasive structures through which we sustain all the material conditions of our existence. And as Zijderveld indicates, the dominance of these bureaucracies in our lives has resulted in a profound identity crisis. By and large we do not dominate these structures, rather they control us. We have very limited roles in decision-making in these vast systems. Our functions are generally partial, fragmentary, frequently frustrating, leaving most of us with little sense of mastery or control or direction over this large segment of our lives. In the pursuit of personal meaning, a desire for wholeness, and for clarity about one's identity, it is no accident that here has emerged in recent years such a spontaneous growth of youth communes, encounter and human potential movements. On another level, this search for identity is also reflected in the growth of ethnic group self-assertion, and in the support of denominationalism rather than inter-denominationalism, which is perceived as abstract and distant from personal and direct communal needs. This identity quest is also a factor in the movement of peoplehood among blacks, *la Raza* among Spanish-speaking groups, "red power" among American Indians, and the mystique of peoplehood and mutual interdependence among Jews throughout the diaspora and in Israel. There is evidently a vast yearning for human-size communities in which the individual can relate to another person on a face-to-face basis, in an environment of caring, shared concern, and mutual confirmation (see "Do You Know What Hurts Me?" by this writer, *Event* [12 February 1972], pp. 4–8, published by the American Lutheran Church).

If this analysis of our situation is reasonably accurate, albeit sketchy, what then are some of its implications for ecumenism and interreligious relations today and tomorrow? I suggest that the following issues are involved and deserve our priority attention.

The emerging transformation of the planet into a global city makes it mandatory that we establish some living connections for ourselves and for our young people between our theologies, our religious teachings, and the realities of the emerging unity of the human family as well as its pluralism. Never before in human history, in my judgment, have Judaism and Christianity had an opportunity such as the present one to translate their biblical theologies of creation—the unity of mankind under the fatherhood of God—into actual experience.

This extraordinary, indeed unprecedented, moment of potential fulfillment of biblical ideals and values has become obscured for us by the dominance of uncritical tendencies to sloganize that we live in a "post Judeo-Christian era," a "post-Western age," a "postmodern era." The effect of such doom-and-gloom slogans is that they tend to become self-fulfilling prophecies, contributing to the paralysis of insight and will. If we would penetrate to the reality beneath slogans, we could justifiably conclude, in fact, that we are in a "*pre-*Judeo-Christian era." There are evidences supporting such a conclusion all around us if we will insist on careful analysis rather than allow ourselves to be seduced by faddist catchwords.

It is no accident that the most dramatic advances in science and technology have taken place in the Western world. The decisive impact of the biblical world view on Western civilization, in particular the Genesis teachings on creation, have resulted in the "disenchantment" of nature—to use Max Weber's concept—which enabled biblical man to subdue and master nature for human purposes, an absolute precondition for scientific and technological experiment. Further, the biblical theology of redemption contributed to a messianic conception of history, which conditioned biblical man to responsibility for the events of history. For a fuller discussion of this issues, see my essay, "Some Current Mythologies and World Community," *Theology Digest* 19 (winter 1971), p. 325.

In non-biblical cultures, religions, and societies, this linear view of history leading to messianic redemption does not prevail. Rather the cyclical views of history have by and large resulted in passivity and quietism, preconditions for indifference to poverty, illness, and illiteracy. If history is fated to repeat itself as an endless cycle, what reason exists for seeking to alter the course of history?

As nations in the Third World have begun to come to grips with the magnitude of human suffering and depravation in their midst, and to embark on economic development and nation-building, it is evident that they will have to appropriate science and technology as the instruments for producing the food, clothing, medicine, and shelter for meeting their basic human needs. The Third World nations will be able to mediate the benefits of Western scientific-technological technics, I contend, only if they make some fundamental accommodations to the Western, hence Judeo-Christian, assumptions and categories regarding nature and history, as well as toward man, society, and God. That means that a genuine convergence must perforce take place in which the Jewish and Christian *Weltanschauung* becomes central and formative in the construction of a universal technetronic civilization.

The moral and spiritual challenge to Judaism and Christianity in the convergence process will be as acute as the culture shock for Oriental religions and civilizations will inevitably be. The temptations to repeat triumphalisms, imperialisms, and monopolies of truth will have to be resisted mightily by the bearers of Western scientific cultures into the Third World. The need to help preserve the integrity of non-Western cultures and religions, their rich inheritances of mankind to become obliterated by the machines of science and technology becomes all the more evident with every passing day. Thus, a primary issue on the agenda of the human family is that of helping build a united human community that respects diversity and difference as a permanent good, quite clearly as a God-given good. We must confess, however, that based on present evidence we are far from adequately prepared either theologically or humanly to realize this delicate and essential balance of unity in the midst of diversity.

To the development of such a theology of human unity and pluralism I would hope that Judaism, in dialogue with Christianity and Islam and other world religions, would make a special and distinctive contribution. It is not widely known that there is available a substantial body of Jewish doctrine and teaching that, though composed over the past three thousand years, contains ideas, conceptual models, spiritual and human values of surpassing insight and meaning for our present situation. Let us review briefly some of the highlights of what is called "the Jewish doctrine of the nations of the world" *(ummot ha olam)*, which today we might well call the Jewish doctrine of pluralism, and world community.

The relationship of the people of Israel to mankind takes as its first and foremost principle the fact that, according to the Torah, all men are descended from one father. All of them, not as races or nation, but as men, are brothers in Adam, and therefore are called *bene Adam,* sons of Adam.

From the time of the occupation of the promised land of Canaan down to the present day, treatment of every stranger living in the midst of an Israelite community has been determined by the commandments of Mount Sinai as recorded in the book of Exodus: "And a stranger shalt thou not oppress, for ye know the heart of a stranger, seeing ye were strangers in the land of Egypt" (Exod. 23:9). In the extensive biblical legislation dealing with the stranger, the *ger* (sojourner or resident alien) or the *nokhri* (foreigner)—whom you are to love as yourselves (Deut. 10:19)—are equated legally and politically with the Israelite.

From the first century of the present era and thereafter, the "stranger within the gate" in the diaspora who joined in the Jewish form of worship but without observing the ceremonial laws became known as a *yire adonay*—a God-fearer. A God-fearer was one who kept the Noachian principles, that is, the moral principles known to Noah and to pre-Israelite mankind. As described in the Babylonian Talmud (*Sanhedrin* 56), the seven commandments of the sons of Noah are these: the prohibition of idolatry, of blasphemy, of sexual immorality, of murder, of theft, of cruelty to animals, together with the positive commandment to establish courts of justice.

The great twelfth-century Jewish philosopher, Maimonides, formulated the normative Jewish conception, held to and affirmed by all periods of Judaism (in *Mishnah Torah* 4, *Hilkot Melakhim,* Section 10, *Halachah* 2), in these words: "Whoever professes to obey the seven Noachian laws and strives to keep them is classed with the righteous among the nations and has a share in the world to come." Thus every individual who lives by the principles of morality of Noah is set on a par with the Jews. Indeed, a statement made by Rabbi Meir (ca. 150 C.E.) is recorded three times in the Talmud, "The pagan who concerns himself with the teaching of God is like unto the High Priest of Israel" (*Sanhedrin* 59A; *Baba Kamma* 38a, and *Aboda Zara* 36a).

Thus, this Rabbinic doctrine about "the righteous men among the nations" who will be saved made it unnecessary, from the point of view of the synagogue, to convert them to Judaism. At the same time, it should be acknowledged that Jews pray daily in the synagogue for what appears to be the ultimate conversion of the Gentiles, not to the cult of Israel but rather to the God of Israel: "Let all the inhabitants of the world perceive and know that unto thee every knee must bend and every tongue give homage. Before thee, O Lord our God, let them bow down and worship, and unto thy glorious name let them give honor."

While there is no unanimity in Judaism regarding the ultimate conversion of the Gentiles, there can be no doubt that, theologically speaking, Judaism does expect a redeemed mankind to be strict monotheists—in the Jewish sense. It is the duty, therefore, of every Jew to encourage both by teaching and personal example in the universal acceptance of the "Seven Principles of the Sons of Noah." The ultimate conversion of the world is understood by Judaism to be one of the "messianic" events. We will know that the messianic age has come when we realize a change—a conversion—in the kind of life being lived on earth, and not just in the inner life of the individual. Wars and persecutions must cease, and justice and peace must reign for all mankind.

Translating this religious language into contemporary terms, Judaism affirms that salvation exists outside the synagogue for all who are God-fearers, that is, all who affirm a transcendental reality as a source of meaning for human existence, and who live by the moral code of the sons of Noah. This Jewish theological view also perceives and undergirds world pluralism as a positive good. Thus, Judaism advocates a unity of mankind that encourages diversity of cult and culture as a source of enrichment, and that conception of unity in the midst of diversity makes possible the building of human community without compromise of essential differences.

The central issue of teaching about the unity of mankind raises
the pedagogical problem: How do we teach commitment and loyalty on the part of our youth and adults to one's own faith, and at
the same time recognize, respect, and even reverence the claims
to truth and value of religious tradition outside our own?

Critical for the management of that vital task is the need to face
the inadequacy of much of our current theological and philosophical understanding of the meaning of "unity" and the implications of such understandings for religious liberty and freedom
of conscience in a pluralistic world. The weight of much Western
ideological and religious thinking and experience is shaped by
the imperial theologies and ideologies that governed Europe
from the fourth until the early nineteenth century. At the request
of his friend Emperor Constantine, Bishop Eusebius of Caesarea
conceptualized perhaps the earliest Western version of "imperial
theology" when he linked monotheism with the concept of the
Roman emperor: "one God, one empire, one church." That led
Walter Ullmann to observe in his *History of Political Thought: The
Middle Ages* (Baltimore: Penguin Books, 1965), "The ancient
pagan idea of the Emperor as 'Lord of the World' reappeared in
the Christian universal idea of rulership. It was not only his right
but also his duty to spread Christianity and hold together the Eku-
mene, the totality of all cultured people, by means of the Christian faith (pp. 32–33)."

In the sixteenth-century Reformation, the enforced unity of
faith and nationalism was manifested in the imperial doctrine of
cuius regio eius religio ("whose the region, his the religion"). By his
act of uniformity and supremacy, Henry VIII brought the church
and commonwealth under his civil power, thus realizing in the
English Reformation the medieval philosophy of unity. In the
United States, Martin Marty has described in his book, *The Righteous Empire: The Protestant Experience in America* (New York: Dial
Press, 1970), how the first half century of American national life
saw the development of evangelicalism, which "set out consciously to create an empire, to attract the allegiance of all people,
to develop a spiritual kingdom, and to shape the nation's ethos,
mores, manners, and often its laws (p. 17)."

Two British churchmen, whom Marty cites, after their visit to
America in 1836 declared, "Blot out Britain and America from

the map of the world, and you destroy all those great institutions which almost exclusively promise the world's renovation." On the positive side, they added, "Unite Britain and America in energetic and resolute cooperation for the world's salvation, and the world is saved." This evangelical and Anglo-Saxon tradition equated the American way of life, the defense of laissez-faire capitalism, and the crusade against Communism with the Christian mission to the world. "So close was the fusion between the American republic with evangelicalism," Marty writes, "that a basic attack on American institutions meant an attack on Protestant Christianity itself. Positively, the defense of America meant a defense of the evangelical empire."

In the second, more recent, period of American history, the ecumenical moderates tried to extricate the Protestant churches from identification with the American way of life, from a single economic pattern, and from a crusading spirit. They tried to break away from the provincialism and chauvinism of their fathers who equated the kingdom of God with the evangelical empire. They sought to become an experiencing agent in the nation and not merely the dominant molder of symbols. They reached back to other elements in the American constitutional tradition and supported a pluralism whose ground rules were that "no religion was to have a monopoly or a privileged position and none should be a basis for second class status for others" (ibid., p. 253). That tradition of liberal Protestant pluralism has made possible the Christian ecumenical dialogue and the Jewish-Christian dialogue. The dialogue means that people could have exposure to each other across the lines of differing faiths without attempting to convert in every encounter, without being a threat, and with the hope that new understanding would result. The goal would be a richer participation in the city of man, the republic, or the human family.

The presuppositions of that ecumenical approach to pluralism and to Jewish-Christian relations involved at its deepest levels a fundamental theological and philosophical reconceptualization of unity. One of the clearest formulations of the revised rethinking of unity is reflected in the words of the Protestant theologian Herbert Richardson, who wrote in his book, *Towards An American Theology* (New York: Harper & Row, 1967):

By direct henological analysis, we can attain to the conclusion that the unity of everything that exists is (1) the unity of any denumerable individual or individuality; or (2) the unity of any two or more individuals when taken together, or considered as one thing—i.e., relationality; or (3) the unity of any or all possible relationalities considered as complete or wholeness. From this analysis, it seems that every unity (whether it be an individual, a relation, or a whole) is as real as any other unity. This means not only that each individual is, from the metaphysical point of view, as real as any other individual, but that any individual is as real as any relation, or any whole, including the whole which encompasses all things. Or, to say it another way, "the universe" is no more real than any individual within the universe—for the characteristic of reality is unity, and it is as real to be an individual as to be a whole. While a "whole" is "bigger" than certain individuals, it is not ontologically of a higher grade, i.e., not better. Moreover, a whole does not add to or subtract from the reality of the individuals existing within it. These have their own independent principle of being (their unity of individuality) and so they are *a se* and not from the whole . . . Individuals have their own being within the whole, but from themselves, for individuality does not originate in, nor derive from wholeness, nor the reverse. Wholeness, individuality, and relationality are therefore three distinct hypotheses of unity. As such, each is capable of being the principle of an independent system of categories (p. 82).

That recasting of a philosophical understanding of unity is experienced in our awareness of the many languages of mankind. The many languages and varieties of humankind are not something to overcome in a quixotic pursuit to bring mankind to speak one language. That does not mean that the many languages do not influence and change each other; they do. The multiplicity of languages points to the many-sided conversation that is required. That conversation distributes the varieties of human gifts and types; and it is as we gain the capacity to listen and speak, to hear and respond even though we will be changed, that our one humanity comes into existence.

The conception of the unity of the whole as not being ontologically "better" than the unity of the parts which compose it also has implications for the Jewish-Christian relationship. Rosemary Ruether, the Catholic theologian, has noted that "Christianity, as the fulfilled universalism of a particularism, could not tolerate the continued contrary particularism (i.e., the individuality) of the Jew" (Rosemary Ruether, "Christian Anti-Semitism and the Dilemma of Zionism," *Christianity and Crisis,* 17 April 1972, pp. 91–92). She further elaborates that "gentile attitudes toward Jews are unalterably fixed by the totalistic universalism of a Christian fulfilled messianism. Such a Christian theological stance demands, in some form, the drawing of a mental ghetto of negation around those who reject this fundamental Christian self-affirmation" (ibid., p. 94). "A Christian assertion," Dr. Ruether adds, "that Jesus is 'the Messiah of Israel,' which contradicts the fundamental meaning of what Israel means by 'Messiah,' is and always has been fundamentally questionable."

> The questionableness must now be clarified and unambiguously applied to the historic sin of its translation into the negation of the Jews. This demands a relativizing of the identification of Jesus as the Christ. Contextually, we can speak of Jesus as the "messianic experience for us," but that way of speaking doesn't make this experience self-enclosed: it points beyond itself to a liberation still to come. Both the original roots of Christian faith and the dilemma of modern Christology will make it evident that such an affirmation of the messianic event in Jesus in a contextual and open-ended rather than a "once-for-all" and absolutistic way, is demanded by the existence of Christian theology itself. In this way the Christian experience can parallel rather than negate the liberation experiences that are the community symbols of other faiths. For the Jews, the Exodus experience is also a very actuality of liberation that is, at the same time, a hope for liberation still to come. In this way the Jew and Christian stand in parallel traditions, each having tasted grace, each looking for a fulfillment that is "beyond" (ibid.).

In effect, Dr. Ruether employs the Jewish-Christian relationship as a microcosmic illustration of the macrocosmic theological problematic. The reality and urgency of reconceptualizing inherited categories whose exclusivistic and imperial tendencies paralyze Western religious communities in an effort to respect the claims to truth and value of the non-Western world's religions is graphically illustrated in the writings by Father Tissa Balasuriya, O.M.I., of Colombo, who declared in "The Church and Change in Asia" (*Commonweal,* 29 June 1973, p. 354):

In the last eight to ten years the concept of the salvific value of these religions (of Asia and Africa) also is gaining ground. It is now admitted that Christians too can learn something regarding God and salvation from the other religions. In the last 3–4 years the concept of salvation of individuals and even nations is giving way to the idea of a world mission in which every people has to learn and can teach something to others. Salvation is being understood as more closely related to justice and the building of the fraternal community of man on earth. This is the Kingdom of God, of which institutional churches are signs and means—sacramental expressions. Though the theory of the mission has changed among the more advanced Christian groups, the old mentality still largely prevails in practice.

In summary, there are two opposing conceptions of world community that are now being contested on the global scene. In a world in which two-thirds of the human family is neither white, nor Jewish, nor Christian, a refurbished Western evangelicalism, reinforced by Anglo-Saxon *hubris,* can be the surest way of leading to disaster on a global scale. If we have learned anything worthwhile from the American experiment, and particularly from the Jewish-Christian dialogue, it is the knowledge that Jews and Christians are learning to celebrate the wisdom that unity in the midst of diversity may after all be the will of God.

If Judaism and Christianity can grant the validity of each other's covenants, and seek to affirm the best in each other rather than deny it, there need be no reservation about their fruitful coexistence. Indeed the two covenants could be seen in the divine scheme of things as mutually complementary, not mutually exclusive. The very concept of the "covenant of the sons of Noah" demonstrates that Judaism did not limit God's covenanting to the Jews. The new covenant, as I understand St. Paul in Romans 9 to 11, does not revoke the old. Both covenanted communities have, after all, for some two thousand years uttered the same prayer, "Thy kingdom come." And when the kingdom comes, when the Jew sees the fulfillment of the prophecy, "The Lord shall be king over all the earth; in that day the Lord shall be one, and His name one" (Zech. 14:9), the Christian, too, will see the fulfillment of prophecy. "Then comes the end, when he delivers the kingdom to God the Father . . . the Son himself will also be subjected to

Him who put all things under him, that God may be everything to every one" (1 Cor. 15:24, 28).

Thus, perhaps, the most important export that Americans and Westerners have yet to contribute to the building of world community is the knowledge that we are called by God as children of his covenant, not to build a super-church nor a super-synagogue but to search together for the true service to God's own people gathered from all the nations on the mountain of the Lord.

18

Holy Year 1975 and Its Origins in the Jewish Jubilee Year

MY INTENTION in this paper is simply to set forth an understanding of the Jubilee Year in Judaism and Jewish history, and to leave it to Catholic—and other Christian—authorities to draw any implications from this background study that may be appropriate for Christian observances of the Holy Year. My hope is that such reflection on the Jewish origins of the Jubilee Year might contribute to advancing understanding and mutual respect between Christians and Jews, especially throughout the Holy Year.

Holy Year 1975, proclaimed by Pope Paul VI for observance by the Catholic faithful as a year of renewal and reconciliation, has been frequently characterized as the *Jubilaeus Christianorum*, the Christian Jubilee Year. That reference is to the Jubilee Year, which has its origins in Biblical Judaism, and it may therefore be helpful to understand something of the practice and meaning of the Jubilee Year as it was developed and experienced in about 3,000 years of Jewish history.

The word "jubilee" derives from the Hebrew term *yobel*, which means "jubilating" or "exulting." It refers to the sounding of the shofar—the ram's horn—on the Day of Atonement announcing the inauguration of the jubilee year. (Joshua 6:4 speaks of *Shofrot ha-yoblim*, trumpets of the ram's horn.) Yom Kippur, the Day of Atonement, and the Jubilee had much in common. The central intention of both was a "new birth." The Day of Atonement provided an opportunity to free the person from slavery to sin and

---

In 1975, the Roman Catholic Church celebrated a "Holy Year." Since the concept of the jubilee is rooted in Judaism, Rabbi Tanenbaum was asked during 1974 to address the issue of what Catholics can learn from Judaism about the origins of their liturgical tradition of a Holy Year. His response was published in the official journal of the Holy See's Council for Celebrating the Holy Year and is reprinted here from *Jubilaem: Consilium Primarium Anno Sancto Celebrando* (Vatican City: Libreria Editrice, 1974).

enabled him/her to start life anew, at one with God and with one's fellow human being. (Atonement is understood by the rabbis to be a precondition for at-one-ment.) The Jubilee had for its aim the emancipation of the individual from the shackles of poverty, and the elimination of the various economic inequalities in the Jewish Commonwealth in accordance with the demands of social justice. Since Yom Kippur involved the preparation of the hearts of all members of the community for the self-discipline and sacrifices required for such spiritual rectification, it was deemed by Jewish tradition to be the most appropriate day for inauguration of such a year of communal and interpersonal rectification, especially in the social and economic order.

So important was the law regarding the Jubilee that, like the Decalogue, it was ascribed to the divinely inspired legislation revealed on Mount Sinai (Lev. 25:1).

There could be no more stirring call to the conscience for inaugurating the Jubilee than the blowing of the shofar, which heralded the revelation of the Ten Commandments. The Prophetic portion of the Torah, which is read to this day in synagogue services throughout the world, is taken from Isaiah 58 which seems to have been recited on a Yom Kippur inaugurating a Jubilee Year. Isaiah scorns the hypocrisy and worthlessness of ritual without righteousness. On the most solemn Fast Day in the year, he reminds his people that prayer and fasting alone are not enough, "doing justice" and "loving mercy" must go hand in hand with "walking humbly with your God."

What objectives were to be served through the observance of the Jubilee Year? The Bible sets forth four-fold obligations, all of which focus on realizing liberation in the actual life of the people of God as basic preconditions, or corollaries, to their spiritual liberation:

1. Human—liberation of the slaves.
2. Economic—the moralization of the use of property and material goods.
3. Ecological—liberation of the land.
4. Educational—the creation of a spiritual democracy by devoting the Jubilee Year to intensive education of all men, women, children and "resident aliens" in the teachings of the Torah.

A few words of elaboration on each of these themes of the Jubilee Year. After proclaiming the observance of the Sabbatical Year *(Shemittah)*, the Bible ordains the Jubilee Year *(Yobel)* in these words:

> And you shall number seven Sabbaths of years unto you, seven times seven years; and there shall be unto you the days of seven Sabbaths of years, even forty and nine years. Then shall you make proclamation with the blast of the horn on the tenth day of the seventh month; in the day of atonement shall you make proclamation with the horn throughout all our land. *And you shall hallow the fiftieth year, and proclaim liberty throughout the land unto all the inhabitants thereof. It shall be a jubilee unto you; and you shall return every man unto his possession; and you shall return every man unto his family* (Lev. 25:8 ff.).

HUMAN LIBERATION

The proclamation of liberty was not a declaration of abstract rights, of philosophical or theological principles. As conceived and lived in Jewish life, it opposed the enslavement of one person by another and required the actual emancipation of slaves with their families. Slavery was a universal—and generally cruel—institution in the ancient world. While the Biblical and Rabbinic law were unable to abolish the deeply-rooted slave system, the Jewish legislation did seek to expose the evils of slavery, to curb its brutalities, and to ameliorate the hard lot of the slaves. By according the unfortunate the protection of the religious-civil law, it endowed him with human stature and human rights—something virtually unprovided elsewhere for the slave in ancient society.

Later on in the text, Lev. 25:39 ff., in a section that Rabbinic commentators call "practical love of neighbor," the Bible insists upon humane and equalitarian treatment of indentured servants—one who out of his own free will had sold himself to a master in order to escape the despair of his poverty.

> And if your brother be waxen poor with you, and sell himself to you, you shall not make him to serve as a bond-servant. As a hired servant, and as a settler, he shall be with you, he shall serve with you unto the year of Jubilee: Then shall he go out from you, he

and his children with him, and shall return to his own family, and unto the possession of his fathers shall he return. For they are my servants, whom I brought forth out of the land of Egypt; they shall not be sold as bondsmen.

The rabbis observe that the poor remains your brother and is to be treated in a brotherly and compassionate manner. You are not to allow him to come down into the depths of misery for then it is difficult to raise him, but come to his support and "uphold him"—at the time when his means begin to fail. Though he be a "stranger" or "an alien settler," he is to be included in the term "your brother" and is to be helped by timely loans, free of interest.[1] The expression that "your brother may live with you" means that it is the Israelite's personal and communal duty to see to it that his fellow man does not die of starvation. The great principle of "you shall love your neighbor as yourself" must be a reality in Jewish society, the rabbis insisted.

When a person's ill fortune forces him to sell himself into bondage, the dignity of the laborer was to be safeguarded. As a "hired servant" he was not to be given any menial or degrading work, but only agricultural tasks or skilled labor, such as would be performed by a free laborer who is hired for a season. Should the poor be the father of a family when he sells himself into slavery, the master has to take the children into his care and maintain them. The rabbis taught that the freed slave must be received with cordiality and friendliness by his relatives, and no slight shown him because of his former servitude.

Since the people of God are His servants whom he brought forth out of the land of Egypt, an Israelite therefore can never be more than nominally a slave to any human master.[2] "For unto me the children of Israel are servants; they are my servants"—and they shall not be servants to mortal servants, as God's bond has

---

[1] The prohibition of charging interest on loans led to the establishment in every organized Jewish community of *Gemilut Chasadim* Society for making available loans free of interest to the poor (see Deut. 23:19).

[2] According to Exodus 21:2 f. and Deut. 15:12 f., the Hebrew who sells himself into slavery serves his master for six years, and goes free in the seventh. Should the Jubilee occur before his six years of service are over, the servant regains his personal freedom at the same time that his inheritance returns to him in the year of Jubilee.

the priority (*Sifra, Behar Sinai* 7:1). The rabbis ruled that a Hebrew is not to be sold publicly in the slave market, but the sale is to be privately arranged to avoid any possible humiliation. In Rabbinic law, the rules that should regulate the relationship between a master and his slave are given in full detail and are based on the principle that master and man are kinsmen, e.g., the slave must not be given inferior food or accommodations to that of the master. Kindness and consideration are to characterize the bearing of the Israelite towards his less fortunate brothers and sisters.

The humane treatment demanded by the Biblical and Rabbinic laws for the pagan (i.e., non-Jewish) slave was identical with that for the Jewish slave. Philo, the Alexandrian philosophical moralist who lived in the generation of Jesus and whose teachings and reflections, mirroring the moral climate of Jewish life in that tumultuous age, were reflected in the gospels—in his role as rabbi counseled the Jewish faithful: "Behave well to your slaves, as you pray to God that he should behave toward you. For as we hear them so shall we be heard, and as we treat them, so shall we be treated. Let us show compassion, so that we may receive like for like in return."

ECONOMIC LIBERATION

"In this year of Jubilee, you shall return every man unto his possession" (Lev. 25:13). This enactment of the Jubilee Year required the compulsory restoration of all purchased land to the original owner and provided for the equal division of property. The permanent accumulation of land in the hands of a few was prevented, and those whom fate or misfortune had thrown into poverty were given a "second chance."

The Jubilee institution was an extraordinary safeguard against the moral and spiritual degradation of poverty. By keeping house and lands from accumulating in the hands of the few, pauperism was prevented, and generations of independent freeholders assured.[3] It represented a rare, even revolutionary breakthrough in

---

[3] The law regarding dwellings in a walled city was different from that pertaining to the sale of a field, in that the dwelling cannot be repurchased by its owner any later than one year from the sale, and it does not revert to its original owner

the introduction of morals into economics in the experience of mankind. According to the Torah, "the earth is the Lord's" and all land was acknowledged to be held from God on lease. "And the land shall not be sold in perpetuity: for the land is mine, for you are strangers and settlers with me.[4] And in all the land of your possession you shall grant a redemption for the land" (Lev. 25:23 ff.).

The Israelite who voluntarily or through some compulsion sold his land to another sold not the ownership of the land, but the remainder of the lease—until the next year of Jubilee, when the leases expired simultaneously. The land then came back to his family, all contracts of sale to the contrary notwithstanding. His children thus enjoyed the same advantage of a "fair start" as their father had had before them.

Scripture sets forth the laws of land-tenure in these words: "If you sell to your neighbor, or buy of your neighbor's land, you shall not wrong one another. According to the number of years after the Jubilee you shall buy of your neighbor, and according to the number of years of the crops he shall sell to you" (Lev. 25:15, 16). The Rabbinic commentaries state this passage forbade rent gouging ("you shall not wrong one another"). As the land itself belongs to God, the ground itself was not a proper object for sale, but only the result of a person's labor on the ground; i.e., only

---

in the Jubilee Year (Lev. 25:29). The reason for this difference is that special conditions obtained in the walled city. According to the Rabbinic commentary, *Meshekh Hakhmah*, the "walled cities" were fortresses, disguised to protect the inhabitants in case of enemy attack. It was imperative therefore that all the inhabitants be familiar with every secret passageway, cave, or shelter in the city. Moreover, it was virtually necessary that they be well acquainted with one another in order to be able to act together for purposes of mutual defense and protection.

[4] Commenting on the phrase "for you are strangers and settlers with me," the *Ohel Yaakov* (The Tents of Jacob) declares, "The Lord said to Israel, 'The relationship between yourselves and me is always that of strangers and settlers.' If you will live in the world like strangers, remembering that you are here but temporarily, then I will be a settler in your midst in that My Presence (the *shekhinah*) will dwell with you permanently. But if you will regard yourselves as settlers, as permanent owners of the land on which you live, when the land is actually not yours but mine, my Presence will be a stranger in that it will not dwell in your midst. In any case, you, O Israel, and I cannot be strangers and settlers at the same time. If you act the stranger, then I will be the settler, and if you act the settler, I must be the stranger." The rabbis applied this instruction to ownership of land in the diaspora as in the Holy Land.

the produce could be a matter for sale. Therefore, what is conveyed to the purchaser is not the land, but the number of harvests which the incoming tenant would enjoy.

The regulations of the Sabbatical year include also the annulment of all monetary obligations *(Shemittat Kesafim)* between Israelites, the creditor being equally barred from making any attempt to collect his debt (Deut. 15:1 ff.). While the law for the Jubilee Year does not have this provision, it operates in the same spirit by serving as the year of liberation of servants whose poverty had forced them into employment by others. This law of the Sabbatical year acts as a statute of limitations or a bankruptcy law for the poor debtor, in discharging his liability for debts contracted, and in enabling him to start life anew on an equal footing with his neighbor, without fear that his future earnings will be seized by his former creditors.

Significantly, the rabbis extended the laws of money-release *(Shemittat Kesafim)* to countries other than Palestine, but confined land-release *(Shemittat Karka-ot)* to Palestine during the period of the Second Temple. The money-release was obviously independent of the Holy Land and was included to free from his debts the poor in every land, and at a certain period of time. On the other hand, this bankruptcy law checked all business enterprises that the Jews reengaged in after they had largely abandoned agricultural pursuits. Hillel the Elder (first century of this era) then amended the law by the institution of the Prosbul, a document circumventing remission of debts in the sabbatical year as a means of encouraging people to supply necessary small loans. The money-release was undoubtedly intended for the poor debtor, though the rich person also might take advantage of the general law.

Heinrich Heine remarked, according to a citation quoted by chief Rabbi Joseph Hertz in his commentary on the Pentateuch (p. 533), that the Torah does not aim at the impossible—the abolition of property, but at the moralization of property, seeking to bring it into harmony with equity and justice by means of the Jubilee Year. "It is not the protection of property, but the protection of humanity, that is the aim of the Mosaic Code," Henry George has written. "Its Sabbath day and Sabbath year secure even to the lowliest, rest and leisure. With the blast of the jubilee trumpets, the slave goes free, and a redivision of the land secures again to the poorest his fair share in the bounty of the common Creator."

ECOLOGICAL LIBERATION

"A Jubilee shall that fiftieth year be unto you; you shall not sow, neither reap that which growth of itself in it, nor gather the grapes in it of the undressed vines. For it is a Jubilee, it shall be holy unto you; you shall eat the increase thereof out of the field" (Lev. 25:12). The Jubilee Year shares the features of the Sabbatical Year. It comes into force in this world, the real world, and becomes possible only after the Israelites take possession of the land of Palestine. "When you come into the land which I give you" (Lev. 25:2). The Bible provides that one may cultivate his field and vineyard six years, but during the Sabbath-year the land was to lie fallow (Exod. 23:10) and was to be "released" from cultivation. "In the seventh year shall be a Sabbath of solemn rest for the land, a Sabbath unto the Lord; you shall neither sow your field, nor prune your vineyard. That which groweth of itself of your harvest you shall not reap, and the grapes of your undressed vine you shall not gather; it shall be a year of solemn rest for the land" (Lev. 25:4–6).

Significantly, the Torah personifies the land, implying that it is due the respect and care that is owed to a person. "When you come unto the land which I give you, then shall the land keep a Sabbath unto the Lord" (Lev. 25:2). The land should rest in the seventh year, as the human being rests on the seventh day. The Israelite may not during that year till it himself or allow anyone to do so on his behalf. Just as the freedom of the individual was a fundamental principle of the Torah, so was the freedom of the land for the absolute ownership of man. The land belongs to God, and is to be in trust for His purposes. The meaning of this unique law was, among other purposes, to save the soil from the danger of exhaustion.

As the Sabbath day was more than a cessation of labor and was a day dedicated to God, similarly during the Sabbatical Year, the soil was to be devoted to Him by being placed at the service of the

poor and the animal creation (Exod. 23:10–11). This dedication
is stipulated by the Torah in the following manner: "And the Sabbath-produce of the land shall be for food for you; for you, and
for your servant and for your ward, and for you hired servant, and
for the settler by your side that sojourn with you; and for your
cattle, and for the beasts that are in your land, shall all the increase thereof be for food" (Lev. 25:6, 7).

The fruit and grain that grew of itself, spontaneously, in the
Sabbatical year might be plucked and eaten, but not stored. The
reference to the "Sabbath-produce—shall be for food *for you*" is
stated in Hebrew in the plural form *(la-chem)* to comprehend all
those who are to benefit by this provision, including the non-
Israelites *(Sifra)*. What hitherto had been sown for the private
gain, is now to be shared with all members of the community—
the owner, his servants, and strangers who are equal in the right
to consume the natural or spontaneous yield of the soil. The provision also includes the feeding of domestic animals and the free
beasts of the field or forest who are uniformly regarded with
tender concern throughout Scripture. They are part of God's creation and as such are comprehended in His pity and love. "A
righteous man regardeth the life of his beast" (Prov. 12:10).

Educational Liberation

According to Deuteronomy 31:9–13, we learn:

> And Moses wrote this law, and delivered it unto the priests, the sons
> of Levi, that bore the ark of the Covenant of the Lord, and unto all
> the elders of Israel. And Moses commanded them, saying: "At the
> end of every seven years, in the set time of the year of release, in
> the feast of *aberusdes,* when all Israel is come to appear before the
> Lord your God in the place which He shall choose, you shall read
> this law before all Israel in their hearing. Assemble the people, the
> men and the women and the little ones, and the stranger that is
> within your gates, that they may hear, and that they may learn, and
> fear the Lord our God, and observe to do all the words of this law;
> and that children who have not known, may hear, and learn to fear
> the Lord your God as long as you live in the land wither you go
> over the Jordan to possess it."

The Seventh Year and the Jubilee Year were to be utilized for national educational purposes. Special measures were to be taken to acquaint the men and the women, the children as well as the resident aliens, with the moral and spiritual teachings and duties of the Torah. Josephus rightly claims that while the best knowledge of ancient times was usually treated as a secret doctrine, and confined to the few, it was the glory of Moses that he inaugurated universal education of the entire People of Israel. Having committed the Torah to writing, Moses delivers it into the hands of the priests and elders—the religious and secular heads of the people—and enjoins them to have it read periodically to the assembled people. Religion in Judaism was not to be the concern of the priests only; the whole body of religious truth is intended to be the everlasting possession of the entire people. This commandment is the keynote of the spiritual democracy established by Moses. The Torah is the heritage of the Congregation of Jacob (Deut. 33:4).

"To place within the reach of the (modern) worker, once in every seven years, a year's course at a University in science and law and literature and theology, would be something like the modern equivalent for one of the advantages which the Sabbath year offered to the ancient Hebrew." (F. Verinder, *Short Studies in Bible Land Laws,* quoted in Chief Rabbi Hertz's *Pentateuch and Haftorahs* [New York: Soncino Press, 1960], p. 531).

Merely "to hear" the Torah read once every seven years in a public assembly would not be sufficient. It was to be "learned"; i.e., made an object of study. Further, the Torah must be made the rule of life, and its teachings "observed." The rabbis worked in the spirit of Moses the lawgiver when they determined to make the Torah the Book of the People by translating it into the vernacular, and expounding it for the masses. They went far beyond the requirement of reading to the people a portion of Deuteronomy every seven years. They divided the Torah into 156 portions, and had a portion read on each Sabbath in the synagogue, so as to make possible the reading of the whole Torah in three years. In the large and influential Jewish community in Babylon, there prevailed the custom of completing the whole Torah in one year, and this eventually became the rule throughout the diaspora.

History of Jubilee Year

A number of scholars have questioned whether the institution of the Jubilee Year was ever in actual force. According to the biblical scholar, Professor Heinrich Ewald, "nothing is more certain than that the Jubilee was once for centuries a reality in the national life of Israel." The prophet Ezekiel speaks of its non-observance as one of the signs that "the end is come" upon the nation for its misdoings. He mentions "the year of liberty," when a gift of land must return to the original owner. Professor S. R. Driver observes, "It is impossible to think that, as it has sometimes been supposed, the institution of the Jubilee is a mere paper-law; at least as far as concerns the land, it must date from ancient times in Israel."

The authoritative *Jewish Encyclopedia* states that "the Jubilee was instituted primarily to keep intact the original allotment of the Holy Land among the (Israelite) tribes, and to discountenance the idea of servitude to men." Evidence for this fact is derived from the knowledge that the Sabbatical Year and the Jubilee were not inaugurated before the Holy Land had been conquered and apportioned among the Israelite tribes and their families. The first Sabbatical Year is said to have occurred twenty-one years after the arrival of the Hebrews in Palestine, and the first Jubilee thirty-three years later. Only when all the tribes were in possession of Palestine was the Jubilee observed, but not after the tribes of Reuben and Gad and the half-tribe of Manasseh had been exiled. Nor was it observed more than nominally during the existence of the Second Temple. After the conquest of Samaria by Shalmanesser, the Jubilee was observed nominally in the expectation of the return of the tribes, and until the final exile by Nebuchadnezzar (586 B.C.).

In post-exilic times, the Jubilee was entirely ignored though the strict observance of the Sabbatical Year was insisted upon. This, however, is only according to a rabbinical enactment, but by the Mosaic law, according to Rabbi Judah (170–210 A.D.), the Sabbatical Year is dependent on the Jubilee and ceases to exist when there is no Jubilee.

The area of the Holy Land over which the Sabbatical Year was in force included, in the time of the First Temple, all the possessions of the Egyptian emigrants *(Ole Mizrayim)*, which territory extended south to Gaza, east to the Euphrates, and north to the Lebanon Mountains. Ammon and Moab in the Southeast were excluded. In the period of the Second Temple, the area of the Babylon emigrants *(Ole Babel),* headed by Ezra, was restricted to the territory west of the Jordan and northward as far as Acre. The area of Palestine was divided into three parts, Judea, Galilee, and the Transjordan districts, where the Sabbatical Year existed in more or less rigorous observance.

As indicated earlier, the Rabbinical enactment extended the money-release *(Shemittat Kesafim)* to countries other than Palestine, but confined the land-release *(Shemittat Karka-ot)* to Palestine within Ezra's boundary lines of occupation during the period of the Second Temple. The money-lease was obviously independent of the Holy Land and was intended to free from his debts the poor in every land, and at a specified period of time. The problem of encouraging the granting of loans was met by establishing the legal fiction of the Prosbul by Hillel the Elder, which circumvented the remission of debts in the Sabbatical Year by placing debts in the hands of a court, which are not released by the advent of the Seventh Year. The Mishnah plainly expresses the rabbis' satisfaction with the debtor who does not make use of the Sabbatical Year in order to be relieved of his obligations. The rabbis nevertheless desired that "the law of the *shemittah* shall not be forgotten." (Talmud, *Gittin* 36b).

In the diaspora, throughout the centuries following the destruction of the Temple in Jerusalem in 70 A.D., the Sabbatical Year was unevenly observed and was mainly nominal in performance. The land-release *(Shemittat Karka-ot),* however, has been generally observed in Palestine where settled Jewish communities were to be found in every century. "During the Sabbatical Year," the *Jewish Encyclopedia* states, "the Jews of the Holy Land eat only of the products grown in the transjordanian districts."

When in 1888–89 the Sabbatical Year 5649 (dated from the symbolic Year of Creation) approached, the Ashkenazic Rabbis in Jerusalem opposed any compromise or modification of the Sabbatical Year obligations. On October 26, 1888, Rabbis J. L. Diskin and Samuel Salant issued the following declaration: "As the year of the *shemittah,* 5649, is drawing nigh, we inform our brethren the colonists that, according to our religion, they are not permitted to plow or sow or reap, or allow Gentiles to perform these agricultural operations on their fields (except such work as may be necessary to keep the trees in a healthy state, which is legally permitted). Inasmuch as the colonists have hitherto endeavored to obey God's law, they will, we trust, not violate this Biblical Command. By the *omer* of the Bet Din of the Ashkenazim at Jerusalem."

At the end of the nineteenth century, an appeal, issued by prominent Jews in Jerusalem for funds to enable the colonists to observe the Sabbatical Year, was directed to Jews outside the Holy Land. Dr. Hildesheim, president of the Society *Lema'an Zion* (For the Sake of Zion) in Frankfurt, Germany, collected donations for this purpose. Baron Edmond de Rothschild, on being informed by Rabbi Diskin that the laws of the Sabbatical Year were valid, ordered the colonists laboring on the farm settlements under his protection in Palestine to cease work during the Sabbatical Year.

DATING THE JUBILEE YEAR

According to Talmudic calculations, the entrance of the Israelites into Palestine occurred in the year of Creation 2489, and 850 years, or seventeen jubilees, passed between that date and the destruction of the First Temple. For the first jubilee cycle commenced after the acquisition of the land and its distribution, among the Israelite tribes, which took fourteen years, and the last jubilee occurred on the "tenth day of the month (Tishri) in the fourteenth year after that the city was smitten" (Ezek. 40:1), which was the New Year's Day of the Jubilee. Joshua celebrated the first jubilee, and died just before the second.

The Babylonian captivity lasted seventy years. Ezra sanctified Palestine in the seventh year of the second entrance, after the sixth year of Darius when the Temple of Jerusalem was dedicated (Ezra 6:15, 16; 7:7), The first cycle of the Sabbatical Year *(shemittah)* began with the sanctification of Ezra.

The Talmud gives as a rule for finding the year of *shemittah* to add one year and divide by seven the number of years since the destruction of the Second Temple, or to add 2 for every 100 years and divide the sum by seven (Talmud *Abodah Zarah* 96).

Jewish authorities differ as to the correct Sabbatical Year owing to varied interpretations of the words "closing of *Shebi'it*" as meaning either the last year of the cycle or the year after the cycle; also as to the beginning of the Sabbatical Year in exile from the year when the destruction of the Temple occurred, or from the year after. Maimonides (1135–1204 A.D.) began the cycle with the year following that of the destruction of the Temple. A conference of rabbis called in Jerusalem, who concurred in the opinion expressed by the rabbis from Safad, Damascus (Syria), Salonica (Greece), and Constantinople, fixed the Sabbatical Year of their time as 1532 (3313 since Creation) in accordance with the view of Maimonides and also with the practice of the oldest members of the Jewish communities in the Orient by whom the Sabbatical years were observed. By that reckoning 1974 would constitute the twentieth year of the present Jubilee Cycle.

THE SIGNIFICANCE OF "SEVEN"

The cycle of sacred seasons in Judaism revolves about the system of Sabbaths—the Sabbath at the end of the week; Pentecost *(Shavuoth)* at the end of seven weeks; the seventh month, *Tishri*, as the sacred month featuring the holy days of Rosh Hashanah and Yom Kippur. The cycle is completed by the Sabbatical Year and by the Jubilee, which came after a "week" of Sabbatical years.

In the Kabbalah, the number seven is a symbolic division of time, and is sacred to God. This mystical tradition holds that the duration of the World is 7,000 years, the seven thousandth year being the millennium, the Great Sabbath of the Lord (*Sanhedrin* 97a). In his classic depiction of the Messiah, the great philosopher and Rabbinic sage, Maimonides, links the Sabbatical Year and the Jubilee with the Messianic Era. Writing in the eleventh and twelfth paragraphs of his code of "Laws Concerning the Installation of Kings," Maimonides declares:

> The Messiah will arise and restore the Kingdom of David to its former might. He will rebuild the sanctuary and gather the dispersed of Israel. All the laws will be reinstituted in his days as of old. Sacrifices will be offered and the Sabbatical and Jubilee Years will be

observed exactly in accordance with the commandments of the Torah. But whoever does not believe in him or does not await his coming denies not only the rest of the prophets, but also the Torah and our teacher, Moses (cited in Gershon Scholem, *The Messianic Idea in Judaism* [New York: Schocken Books, 1972], pp. 28–29).

19

The Maccabees and Martyrdom: Their Meaning for Today

THE SPIRITUAL AND HUMAN INTERDEPENDENCE of Christians and Jews as biblically covenanted is perhaps nowhere more decisively illustrated than in the struggle and martyrdom of the Maccabbees for religious freedom.

When Antiochus IV Epiphanes gained control over the Syrian kingdom, he worked vigorously to strengthen the power of his kingdom through political and military activity, focusing especially in recovering land from Ptolmeic Egypt through armed conflict in 169–168 B.C. Palestine was at the crossroads of Syria and Egypt, and as the main base for Antiochus's military campaigns in the Nile Valley, the Syrian emperor was particularly determined to assimilate the Jewish population of Judea and of all Palestine to Hellenistic culture, religion, and ways of life as a means of forging loyalty to his regime.

The Syrian monarch set about transforming Jerusalem, the Jewish capital, into a pagan, polytheistic Greek "polis" by introducing into the holy city foreign heathen settlers and their idol worship. In 167 B.C., Antiochus issued royal decrees that outlawed the Jewish religion. Anyone found in possession of a Torah scroll—the Bible—was executed. Mothers who circumcised their infant sons (as Mary and Joseph were to do with Jesus) were killed and the babies hung by the neck. Others were burned to death in caves where they had gathered in order to observe the Sabbath or the feast days. In addition, Antiochus demanded that the Jewish people take part in pagan worship and venerate the Syrian emperor as god.

All these practices were deeply offensive to believing Jews in

Rabbi Tanenbaum was an occasional contributor to a variety of publications. This brief reflection for the *Catholic Sentinel,* March 12, 1976, lifts up the importance of conscience.

Judea, where for hundreds of years after Prophetic agitation and protest, polytheism and idolatry had been uprooted from Judean soil. The priestly family of Mattathias and his son, Judah (the Maccabee or "hammer"), profoundly loyal to the Jewish religion, launched a rebellion of the "few against the many," which finally resulted in the repulsion of Antiochus's generals and his armies. Judea, historians tell us, was the first to succeed among many nations in the Syrian empire in freeing itself from foreign subjugation, thereby contributing decisively to the disintegration of totalitarian rule.

The achievements of the Maccabees in both the spiritual and human realms were tremendous and hold many implications for us, Christians and Jews, today. As indicated in the books of the Maccabees (1:64; 3:8), it was due to the military genius of the Maccabees "under the favoring guidance of God" that the Jewish people and Judaism are saved from the danger of extermination. The Christian scholar R. B. Townshend acknowledges that the blood of the Maccabean martyrs who saved Judaism ultimately saved Christianity, for "had Judaism as a religion perished under the Antiochian persecution, the seed bed of Christianity would have been lacking" (cf., Donald F. Winslow, "Maccabean Martyrs: Early Christian Attitudes," *Judaism* [winter 1974]).

In short, the Maccabees were the first fighters for freedom of conscience in the ancient world. In their victory over the forces that sought to establish by totalitarian power a single religion or ideology for all peoples in the Syrian empire, they helped establish the right of freedom of conscience for every group, as well as the principle of religious and cultural pluralism. It is no accident that the Feast of Hanukkah, which commemorates the victory of the Maccabees, has assumed such importance as a source of inspiration and hope for Jews in every period of persecution. Today, Hanukkah is such a parable of hope in the face of threat and suffering among millions of Jews in Israel, the Soviet Union, in Arab countries, and elsewhere where the right to existence and human rights is being threatened or denied.

"It is within the literature of the ancient Christian Church," Rev. Winslow writes, "that we find the most persistent and deeply felt recognition of the heroic deeds of the Maccabean martyrs." Such church fathers as Cyprian, Origen, Augustine, and Gregory of Nazianzus honored the Maccabees "because of their patient endurance for the sake of the tradition of their Fathers." When Christians observe the Feast Day of the Maccabees on August 1, they might do well to join with Jews in pondering what obligations the example of sacrifice and struggle of the Maccabees imposes on us today in securing the rights to freedom of conscience, human rights in the context of world pluralism for all of God's children who are suffering from persecution and injustice.

20

Major Issues in the Jewish-Christian Situation Today

IN THE FIRST CENTURY, Rabbi Hillel, a contemporary of Jesus of Nazareth, was asked by a pagan to instruct him about the entire Torah while standing on one foot. Being asked to write an article of about 2,000 words on the world of Catholic-Jewish relations involves something of the same order of *chutzpah* (impertinence) and hazard of distortion. Hillel's reply has become a classic model not only of epigrammatic rabbinic wisdom, but of literary brevity as well. "That which is hateful to you," Hillel instructed the pagan, "do not inflict on your fellow human being. All the rest is commentary." No 2,000 words about anything could improve very much on that insight!

But if I cannot improve on Hillel's wisdom, I will defer to him and borrow from his method. If I were asked therefore to summarize the present state of Catholic-Jewish relations, the generalization that keeps coming to mind is that "Catholics and Jews are out of phase." And now let me try to explain, not on one foot, but in some 2,000 words, which in themselves are inadequate when you consider seriously the intense complexity of both the Catholic and Jewish communities and traditions.

The Roman Catholic and Jewish communities possess both universal and national religious-ethnic dimensions, and in these senses they have very much in common. They are not simply creedal fellowships, but have rich social substance in which their

Reprinted from *New Catholic World*, 217:1279 (Jan.-Feb., 1979). This essay formed part of a special issue devoted to Jewish-Christian relations. Rabbi Tanenbaum comments that the shift in metaphor in the documents of the Second Vatican Council from "the mystical body of Christ" to "pilgrim Church" and "people of God," renders Catholicism more "understandable" to Jews because "those reformulations were essentially biblical and, forgive the triumphalism, essentially Jewish." This new way of understanding allowed for a rapprochement for the mutual setting of political agendas.

religious and moral ideals and values are incarnated in the very lives of their peoples. When Vatican Council II shifted the metaphor of Catholic self-understanding from the "mystical body of Christ" to "the pilgrim Church" and the "people of God," those reformulations were instantly understandable to Jewish theologians. Those reconceptualizations were essentially biblical, and forgive the triumphalism, essentially Jewish. Those Catholic affirmations have equivalencies in traditional Jewish categories of self-definition: by divine action at Sinai, the Jews emerged into history as a covenanted people, a "kingdom of priests and a holy nation" obligated to carry out a task of messianic redemption in the world until the coming of the kingdom. Thus, from their very origins, Jews have understood themselves as "a holy people of God" on pilgrimage. That growing commonality in the biblical worldview is decisive for understanding everything else that is happening between Catholics and Jews!

As human societies with universal and national aspects, Catholics and Jews have both "foreign" and "domestic" agendas. Each of these agendas reflects the life interests of our respective peoples, interests of survival and continuity, and the time is past due for either Catholics or Jews to feel apologetic or defensive about articulating or pressing for the realization of their legitimate group interests. But shaped by substantially different historical experiences, these "foreign" and "domestic" agendas are in some ways "out of phase" and it is important that we try to understand how we got this way, and what might be done to synchronize these interests where humanly possible. And if we cannot synchronize interests where differences of principle or faith are involved, at the very least we should try to understand the real reasons behind the different positions, and learn how to respect the difference, rather than deal with the other through caricatures and stereotypes, which are a violation of truth, justice, and charity.

I begin with the "Jewish agenda" which, for obvious reasons, I know best. Both the "foreign" and "domestic" sides of the Jewish agenda are determined decisively by the two watershed events of contemporary Jewish life—the Nazi Holocaust and the rebirth of the State of Israel. Nazi Germany's mass slaughter of six million Jewish men, women, and children destroyed one-third of the body of the Jewish people. Every Jewish person born in the shadow of Dachau and Auschwitz has learned from that trauma at least three permanent, universal lessons.

First, when your enemy says he is going to destroy you, you take him with absolute seriousness. In Germany in the 1930s, many Jews, inured by their middle-class comforts and deceived about the permanence of sin and evil by German *kultur* and *gemutlichkeit,* dismissed Hitler as "a monkey" and as "insane." Jews can no longer afford such delusions and faulty diagnoses.

Second, Jews can no longer tolerate for a moment the luxury of standing by while the blood of their brothers and sisters cries out from the earth. That is why Jews in such disproportionately large numbers marched in Selma and in the civil rights march on Washington; that is why they also joined with Catholics and Protestants in seeking to bring relief for the victims of massacres in the Nigerian-Biafran civil conflict. These were in many ways acts of delayed atonement for the sin of spectatorship during the Nazi genocide when there were few Jewish marches on Berlin and on Washington which could have made some difference; and even if not, there was a moral obligation to try to make a difference that was faulted.

Third, the fact that in our lifetime two out of five Jewish lives were destroyed has filled every Jewish life with heightened value and preciousness. Indeed, it has heightened the Jewish appreciation of the dignity and infinite worth of every human life, but in all candor there is a special intensity in the value attached to a Jewish life. For Jews are a minority people, and the very survival of this people depends on the preservation of "a critical mass" of Jewish persons who can make the sustaining of Jewishness and Judaism meaningful and worthwhile.

These three "lessons"—among others—inform critically the consciousness of the vast majority of Jews today. The overwhelming and unprecedented response of American and world Jewry in solidarity with Israel when attacked by unprovoked Arab aggression on Yom Kippur, the Day of Atonement, cannot be understood apart from these lessons of recent Jewish history. Spiritually, psychologically, and existentially, the Jewish people simply cannot afford another single attempt by Arab leaders or anyone else at their "final solution" of the Jewish problem through aggression and mass destruction. Virtually every Jewish person in the world—

whether religious, agnostic, or atheist—knew in his or her bones that the destruction of Israel, God forbid, would be the lethal blow that would end all meaning for the Jewish presence in history. Auschwitz epitomized the total vulnerability of Jews as defenseless victims in the scenario wrought demonically by others. Israel, the resurrection of Jews after their death, signified that for the first time in 2,000 years Jews finally were restored to mastery over their own fate and destiny. The universal determination of the Jewish people to try to preserve Israel against attack and aggression meant nothing less, symbolically and actually, than a supreme effort to close once and for always the Auschwitz chapter in Jewish history, with its nightmare images of Jews perennially led as victim sheep to the slaughter.

Animating these human and historical considerations has been the powerful spiritual and moral motif of Judaism that affirms that "he who saves one human life" is regarded as if "he had saved an entire world." Thus, sacrificial giving to the United Jewish Appeal, 35,000 young Jews volunteering their services for *kibbutzim* and other non-military services, and the giving of blood in vast quantities were all part of acting out the supreme *mitzvah* (religious commandment)—saving life.

On the graph of Jewish priorities, therefore, "foreign" concerns have predominated since the end of the Second World War. In addition to the massive undertaking of saving Jewish refugees from the wreckage of Nazi Germany and of helping to build a safe haven in Israel, the foreign agendum of Jewry has been preoccupied with concerns for assuring the human rights of the three million Jews in the Soviet Union, with the oppressed and persecuted Jews in Arab countries, especially in Syria and Iraq, and with combating the massive anti-Israeli and anti-Semitic propaganda waged on every continent by the Arab countries and the Communist nations, led by the Soviet Union.

These inescapable "foreign" obligations of preserving as many lives as humanly possible have in many ways overwhelmed the "domestic" needs of American Jewish life. And there are plenty of problems of Jewish survival, continuity, and renewal in America. The impact of the "American way of life"—its powerful assimilative forces, common culture, paganism, hedonism, consumerism, self-indulgence—is having the same corrosive effect on

Jewish traditions and group loyalties as it is on the Catholic community. The most pressing issues on the "domestic" Jewish agendum are those that deal with strengthening the religious and cultural identity of Jews, especially our youth: shoring up Jewish family life, which is beginning to erode under the impact of mobility, intermarriage, and zero population growth; enhancing the role of women in the synagogue and Jewish community life; making Jewish education more relevant to the ethical and value needs of our people; reinvigorating synagogue liturgy and ritual in ways that make connections between the tradition and the real needs of our people today.

During recent years, as I have observed relationships between Catholics and Jews, members of the Jewish community have approached their Catholic friends and neighbors for support of causes on the Jewish "foreign" agendum, and here is where the "out of phase" awareness begins to register. There is a Catholic "foreign" and "domestic" agendum that is frequently not well known by Jews.

My impression is that most Catholics are content to leave "foreign" questions to the disposition of the pope, the Holy See, the national Catholic hierarchy, or the impressive Catholic relief and welfare agencies. Except for the vigorous public anti-war activity of Catholic left groups, mainstream Catholics seem to be far more concerned about "domestic" issues involving personal faith and family life. The intensity of passion and conviction that many Jews exercise over the welfare and security of their brothers and sisters in Israel, the Soviet Union, and the Arab countries finds its parallel in similar intensity of Catholic feelings invested in right-to-life issues—abortion, birth control, involuntary sterilization, and euthanasia. The social dimension of parish Catholic concern seems to be located mainly in such issues of public morality as censorship and combating pornography.

An almost weird kind of "parallel play" seems to be developing between Catholics and Jews on the neighborhood level, and I worry about it. Increasingly, I am inclined to believe that it is not good for the "wholeness" of either Catholic or Jewish morality or spirituality for such "out of phaseness" to continue without correction. Surely it does not advance the cause of seeking to preserve the dignity of the human person created in the image of

God for the right-to-life issues to have become publicly identified as solely a "Catholic" issue, allegedly being imposed on the public by "Catholic power." In fact, the right-to-life issues are supremely issues of biblical morality, and it would have far better served our common spiritual purposes had Catholics, Jews, and Protestants found a way very early in the debate to clear a common ground. The Catholic Church and the Catholic people are to be applauded for having raised to public consciousness the centrality of the dignity of human life issue, but their strategy for building a domestic coalition leaves much to be desired. It is not too late to try to win broad support and understanding for these crucial spiritual and moral issues, and I for one propose to do what I can to bring Jews, Catholics, and others together in alliance for preventing the further erosion of the divine image of God in man.

Similarly, it is not good for the "wholeness" of the Jewish spirit and psyche for Jews to find themselves struggling almost alone for the human rights of Jews in the Soviet Union or for the right of the people and state of Israel to live a peaceful existence with secure, defensible borders. While it is now self-evident that in the pluralism of America, and of the world community, every religious-ethnic community has its own agendum and its own legitimate priorities for which the group itself is expected to be the foremost advocate, for the group to become the sole advocate of the cause invariably casts upon it the cloud of marginality.

I have not the slightest hesitation in saying that had not the Jews of America and elsewhere committed themselves heart and soul to the cause of emigration of Soviet Jews, very few of the 70,000 who were allowed to leave since 1971 would have been liberated. At the same time, the cause of the human rights of Soviet Jews is the identical cause of the human rights of Catholics in Russia, Lithuania, Poland, Latvia, and elsewhere. Jews, Catholics, Baptists, and others have very similar problems in Russia and elsewhere in terms of overcoming restrictions that prevent religious education of children, and the conducting of a significant religious life in houses of worship and homes. What great spiritual and political power could be released if Catholics were to join their Jewish neighbors in national and international efforts to compel the Communist countries to conform to the human rights obligations they committed themselves to when they signed the United Nations Charter! It is not enough to leave this to the Holy See, in my judgment. American Catholics, precisely because they are Americans, have an enormous leverage to exercise at this moment in history precisely because the Soviet Union is desperate for American wheat, trade, and technology. No one should underestimate the impact that George Meany of the AFL-CIO and Thomas Gleason of the Maritime Union had in prodding the Soviet Union to play a constructive role in helping bring about a cease-fire in the Middle East when they announced that longshoremen simply would refuse to load the wheat bought by the Soviet Union unless the Russians stopped arming and goading Arab nations to war against Israel. Similar actions in support of the human rights of Catholics, Jews, and other deprived communities in the Soviet Union might produce interesting results not otherwise obtained.

The right-to-life issue on the domestic agendum of Catholics, and the Soviet Jewry and Israel issues on the foreign agendum of Jews, are simply illustrative of the need to find more effective ways for synchronizing the priority issues of both communities and of replacing much unnecessary polarization by mutual understanding and mutual support. Both Jews and Catholics have got to find a constructive way of meeting the educational needs of their children in non-public schools. The quality education of nearly six million children in parochial and all-day schools is first and foremost an American education issue, rather than a religious issue. If we can send Skylab to the moon, we certainly must have enough ingenuity to find a formula for aiding our school children without violating the Constitution.

Jews and Catholics have a vital stake in seeking to overcome the widespread religious illiteracy in America, and the counterculture of paganism and hedonism that threatens all the religiously-based values of self-restraint, civility, and respect for the rights of others. And obviously there are other issues that should be calling Catholics and Jews together—America's national priorities of overcoming poverty, providing jobs, housing, education, improved courts of justice, prison reform, health care, aid to the elderly, affirmative action for the disadvantaged, etc. There are also the more elusive but nonetheless significant questions for theologians, scholars, and clergy to engage in together—the moral and ethical challenges of biomedical research, which threaten to make man in the image of man rather than in the image of God; the laissez-faire model of doing science and technology, which is leading to such devastating corruption and pollution of the environment. Catholics and Jews must begin to play some effective role in the decision-making process in these areas which shape the life of all of us.

How to go about it? I suggest that the time is ripe for Catholics and Jews to begin organizing national, regional, and local "Catholic-Jewish Agenda Meetings" that would enable each group to take inventory, in a careful, precise way, of all the problems and issues that are of real concern to each community and to place these on a common table for reciprocal consideration. By replacing vague impressions and stereotyped notions and images about what it is that genuinely concerns our respective communities, and by working out joint and parallel approaches to our common religious and societal problems, we will have gone a long way to implementing the spirit of the Vatican Council *Declaration on Non-Christian Religions,* which called for "mutual knowledge and reciprocal respect."

3

The 1980s: The Interreligious Agenda and Selected Texts

Important developments in Jewish-Protestant and Jewish-Catholic relations took place in the 1980s. The five hundredth anniversary of the birth of Martin Luther (1983) provided an opportunity for Lutherans and Jews together to examine Luther's vitriolic writings about Jews and Judaism, and to question the relationship of that hostile legacy to German anti-Semitism up to the modern period. The 1980 and 1984 productions of the Bavarian-based Oberammergau Passion Play, a crucifixion drama based on a medieval model that is usually performed every decade, were strongly criticized by Rabbi Tanenbaum and the American Jewish Committee. The Roman Catholic Church issued a set of catechetical "Notes" intended to help educators teach about Jews and Judaism in accordance with *Nostra Aetate* and subsequent guidelines. As with previous documents, these were both welcomed and criticized by Jewish religious and community leaders, often in the same response. Evangelical political clout was demonstrated in the growing activism of the Moral Majority, and Marc Tanenbaum sought to address the Jewish concerns about religious liberty and efforts to define America as a "Christian nation," at the same time affirming the need for Jews to understand, rather than demonize, Christian evangelicals.

Always the educator, he interpreted the elements of Jewish faith to a gathering of Christians from every corner of the world at the Sixth Assembly of the World Council of Churches in Vancouver, and to conferences of evangelical Christians and Jews at Gordon and Wheaton Colleges. He explored moral challenges to Jews and Christians at the Chicago Sunday Evening Club, continuously underscored the importance of religious freedom as a basic human right, and worked assiduously to maintain a Black/Jewish coalition in the face of increasing strains between the communities.

In the late 1980s, Rabbi Tanenbaum also became deeply involved in the painful controversy surrounding the establishment of a Carmelite convent at the Auschwitz concentration camp in Poland. Like other Jewish leaders, he was deeply distressed by what he saw as an inappropriate Christian intrusion into the site whose very name had come to represent the destruction of European Jewry—and where 90 percent of the murdered victims were Jews. He and others believed that, inadvertently or deliberately, the effect was to turn Auschwitz into a Christian "holy place." However, he also empathized with the feelings of Polish Christians, and he sought to resolve this very explosive issue through quiet, but intensive, advocacy and interreligious diplomacy, with a minimum of confrontation.

These were not easy times. Yet Rabbi Tanebaum looked always to the future. He imagined the possibilities of the future with the memory of a visit with Liv Ullman to a camp in Thailand for Cambodian refugees the year before. "There we understood the meaning of Jewish and Christian solidarity and cooperation in the kind of world we live in today . . . In one corner there was a Catholic intensive feeding center, with Catholic nuns bringing back from the brink of death infant children . . . Next to that there was a group of Israeli doctors and nurses [who] within a matter of three to four weeks [had] put an end to an epidemic of cholera and typhus."

In November of 1988, Rabbi Tanenbaum and Eugene J. Fisher, among others, participated by invitation in a symposium on "Jews and Christians in a Pluralistic World" sponsored by the Institut für die Wissenschaften von Menschen in Vienna, Austria. Rabbi Tanenbaum spoke of the "Achievements and Unfinished Agendas" of Jewish-Christian relations. Basing his analysis on the description by Dr. Eric Fromm, Rabbi Tanenbaum discussed the "pathological dynamic" at work in religious-political conflicts. He noted two vital corollaries to this process. First, "physical violence against a human person or group is invariably preceded by verbal violence," leading to "dehumanization" or even "monitoring" of the prospective victim and a "psychic numbing" of the victimizer that makes violence easier. Second, Rabbi Tanenbaum pointed to the fact that underlying "practically every major religious, racial, and tribal conflict" is a lack of "a religious ideology or political doctrine of coexistence in a pluralistic society."

Authentic pluralism rests on civility and tolerance. This is typified when, on March 11, 1987, Rabbi Tanenbaum shared a platform at Queens College in New York with the Rev. Jesse Jackson. They addressed an assembly gathered by the Queens Black-Jewish People to People Project established by Professors Alan Hevesi and Ernest Schwarcz of Queens College. It was a difficult time for the relationship, especially in New York. Rabbi Tanenbaum felt the need to open with a disclaimer. He was not, he said, speaking officially for the American Jewish Committee, or "certainly" for the diverse Jewish community-at-large. There had been opposition in both communities to holding the meeting: "The fact that Jesse Jackson and I made our own separate decisions to share this platform in the face of threats, slanders, and intimidations is a statement of our determination to reject hatred, bigotry, and verbal violence from whatever quarter it is issued . . . Our purpose tonight . . . is to try to find a better way, a more constructive way, for Blacks and Jews to live and work together, as they have done—we must not forget—for much of their history."

He brought his message to international audiences as well. Rabbi Tanenbaum sketched the troubling world of conflicts between religious, ethnic, and racial groups in Africa and the Middle East, and some of his own experiences in South Africa in 1985. "America is different," he said. "The true genius of America rests on the reality that each religious, racial, and ethnic group comes to the common American table by right, as first-class citizens, and not by sufferance. Each group has, appropriately, its own agenda, (but we) share the same table." He stressed a shared history of oppression between Jews and Blacks in America with extremist groups such as the Klan, Aryan Brotherhoods, the Posse Comitatis, and the farm belt militias. "Black-Jewish relations are bigger than Louis Farrakhan or Meir Kahane . . . they are addressing a common agenda."

Underlying this position was a pervasive Jewish ethic. This was made explicit in the summer of 1983 when Rabbi Tanenbaum was asked to make a presentation before the Sixth Assembly of the World Council of Churches in Vancouver, British Columbia. There he spoke on the "Moral and Ethical Values of Judaism" and suggested several practical areas for joint efforts by Jews and Christians: affirming the biblical value of human life; engendering an "international attitude of scorn and contempt for those who use violence" or advocate its use; curtailing "inflammatory propaganda" from international forums; developing pluralistic models of education and a theology of pluralism; and adjusting the international economy away from "billions wasted on arms" and toward "making the economy of each nation as self-sufficient and stable as possible." We include in this volume the final version of this paper as published in the second collection of papers from the Evangelical-Jewish dialogue, co-edited with Marvin Wilson and A. James

Rudin, *Evangelicals and Jews in an Age of Pluralism* (Grand Rapids, MI: Baker Book House, 1984).

There were, at times, shades of gray in the dialogues. For example, in 1985 the College of St. Thomas in St. Paul/Minneapolis celebrated its centennial. Linked with that celebration, the college launched a Center for Jewish-Christian Learning directed by Rabbi Max Shapiro. Rabbi Tanenbaum, along with Father Michael Mc-Garry, C.S.P., and Dr. Paul M. Van Buren, spoke in the Center's Inaugural Lecture Series. Rabbi Tanenbaum spoke on the twenty years of dialogue since the Council and the challenges that lay ahead. The 1985 *Notes on the Correct Way to Present the Jews and Judaism in Preaching and Catechesis in the Roman Catholic Church* had just been issued from the Holy See and a Jewish response was very much on Rabbi Tanenbaum's mind. One phrase in the document had asserted that Judaism had "prepared the way" for the coming of Christ. Was this chronological or theological? Was it only one of Judaism's many spiritual contributions over the centuries down to our own, as another section of the document clearly and strongly asserted; or would it be read by Catholics as reducing Judaism's role to that of a mere precursor to Christianity? Such concerns are both appropriate to and essential for the success of any mature dialogue. A vital lesson is derived from this, of course: questions help clarify dialogue and can lead to authentic understanding of the realities that challenge us all to act as partners in God's work on earth.

Judith H. Banki and Eugene J. Fisher

21

The Moral Legacy of Martin Luther King Jr.

DR. MARTIN LUTHER KING JR. lives on in our consciousness today as one of the greatest moral prophets of this century. Cast in the mold of Isaiah, he was, at one and the same time, an outstanding religious teacher and thinker, a great statesman, and a spiritual inspiration for ages yet unborn, whose central mission to his people and to the world was the establishment of justice and universal peace. Like Isaiah, Dr. King called upon the American nation to "cease to do evil, learn to do right, seek justice, relieve the oppressed, judge the fatherless, plead for the widow." And like Isaiah, he called upon the human race to turn away from war.

Long years have elapsed since April 4, 1968, when this American prophet of non-violence became a supreme victim of bloodthirsty violence. Why do so many Americans continue to feel such pain, such a deep sense of loss at his death? What was there about the life and work, the voice and the vision of this man that made him such a compelling, towering figure of our century? At least part of the answer lies in his capacity to tap the best instincts of every man and woman in his ever-expanding orbit.

In January 1963, a National Conference on Religion and Race convened in Chicago. It was the first time in American history that some seventy national organizations, representing Catholics, Protestants, and Jews, blacks and whites, came together to examine the role of religious institutions in ending racial discrimination in the United States. It was my privilege to serve as one of the three organizers of that historic meeting; and as its program chairman, it was my pleasure to invite Dr. King to address a na-

Excerpted from an Address at the Ecumenical Service Marking the Fifty-first Birthday of the Rev. Dr. Martin Luther King Jr. at the Ebenezer Baptist Church, Atlanta, Georgia, January 15, 1980.

tional ecumenical gathering commemorating the centennial of President Abraham Lincoln's Emancipation Proclamation.

At that conference, which many historians consider the starting point of a new coalition of conscience in our nation, Dr. King told a respectful audience of 1,700 religious and civic leaders: "Through our scientific genius, we have made of our nation— and even the world—a neighborhood, but we have failed to employ our moral and spiritual genius to make of it a brotherhood. The problem of race and color prejudice remains America's chief moral dilemma."

And in words as ringing today as when he first uttered them, Martin Luther King Jr. enunciated five challenges to America's churches and synagogues, and to all the nation's Christian and Jewish communities. What were these challenges?

1. To enhance the dignity of the human person;
2. To uproot prejudice;
3. To support social justice;
4. To encourage non-violent direct action;
5. To promote universal love.

The themes Martin Luther King Jr. sounded in 1963 are equally critical for human survival today: respect for the dignity of every human being; an end to racial, religious, and ethnic prejudice; a deepened commitment to social and economic justice; non-violent direct action as the truest expression of love and justice; the invisible inner law of universal love, which binds all men and women of the human family together as brothers and sisters. There is an epidemic of dehumanization in the world today. Every continent is shaken by violence, terrorism, massacre, and torture. And where are the voices of conscience to speak out against these acts? The Bible tells us that each human being is created in the sacred image of God and is therefore of ultimate worth and preciousness. Yet the meaning and value of human life is being ignored the world over. How can the world put a stop to this terrorism and violence?

We honor the moral legacy of Martin Luther King Jr. by joining in a national and international determination to reject violence and those who advocate violence. We must work to de-romanticize all appeals to the use of violence and terrorism as a means of liberation, for from a moral standpoint, no end can justify such anti-human means. "That which is hateful to you, do not inflict on others" was the first formulation of the Golden Rule, uttered by Rabbi Hillel, a contemporary of Jesus of Nazareth in first-century Palestine. We honor the moral legacy of Dr. King by working to curtail racial, religious, and ethnic prejudice in our nation and throughout the world.

Martin Luther King Jr. understood deeply and intuitively the destructive effects of racism and anti-Semitism. He knew that human rights are indivisible; that attitudes and actions that diminish respect for one branch of the human family are easily turned against another, and that no one is safe from the scourge of hatred. Dr. King made this point explicitly, in an address to a Jewish audience in May 1958: ". . . the segregationist makes no fine distinctions between the Negro and Jew. The racists of America fly blindly at both of us, caring not at all which of us fails. Their aim is to maintain, through crude segregation, groups whose uses as scapegoats can facilitate their potential and social rule over all people." Our common fight is against these deadly enemies of democracy, and our glory is that we are chosen to prove that courage is a characteristic of oppressed people, however cynically and brutally they are denied full equality and freedom.

Because he knew deep in his soul that the demeaning of any group's heritage diminished him and his people, Dr. King was an outspoken foe of Soviet anti-Semitism. Speaking to the American Jewish Conference on Soviet Jewry in 1966, Dr. King denounced the Soviet government's efforts to destroy the Jewish culture and heritage of Soviet Jews:

> While Jews in Russia may not be physically murdered as they were in Nazi Germany, they are facing every day a kind of spiritual and cultural genocide. The absence of opportunity to associate as Jews in the enjoyment of Jewish culture and religious experience becomes a severe limitation upon the individual. These deprivations are part of a person's emotional and intellectual life. They determine whether he is fulfilled as a human being. Negroes can well understand and sympathize with this problem. When you are written out of history as a people, when you are given no choice but to accept the majority culture, you are denied an aspect of your own identity. Ultimately you suffer a corrosion of your self-understanding and your self-respect.

The same sense of justice that motivated Dr. King to speak out against Soviet anti-Semitism led him to speak out in support of Israel, and to urge his country to work for peace in the Middle East. In an address to the Rabbinical Assembly of America, just ten days before his shocking, untimely death, he declared: "I see Israel, and never mind saying it, as one of the great outposts of democracy in the world, and a marvelous example of what can be done, how desert land almost can be transformed into an oasis of brotherhood and democracy. Peace for Israel means security and that security must be a reality."

As long as he lived, Martin Luther King Jr. held fast to his vision. In the same speech to the Rabbinical Assembly, he offered this ringing reaffirmation of the universal struggle to overcome prejudice: "We have made it clear that we cannot be the victims of the notion that you deal with one evil in society by substituting another evil. We cannot substitute one tyranny for another, and for the Black man to be struggling for justice and then turn around and be anti-Semitic is not only a very irrational course but it is a very immoral course, and wherever we have seen anti-Semitism we have condemned it with all of our might."

On April 5, 1968, the day after Martin Luther King Jr. was assassinated, Morris B. Abram, then president of the American Jewish Committee and a collaborator of Dr. King's from their earliest days in the civil rights movement, issued a statement that movingly expressed a Jewish appreciation of Dr. King's moral legacy: "When the pain and bewilderment is somewhat diminished, those of us who believed with him that the course of America could somehow be changed, that despair could be replaced by hope, and that peaceful solutions can be found to the profound problems that tear our communities apart and perplex us all—all of us who so believe must reassess our action and our participation in rebuilding the country in which we live. From this reassessment must come bold and practical steps that will demonstrate that we care deeply about the conditions of our fellow citizens, and that we are prepared to do more than we are now doing to help heal the wounds in the souls of America—black and white."

We all know that the corrosive poverty that afflicts 50 million citizens must be eliminated and that the insurance of a sense of dignity and well-being must be achieved. I urge you to go forth and act in your capacities as an individual citizen, in the traditions of Judaism and in the best interests of the whole country. Let us speak for a segment of white America in declaring our dedication to the principles for which Martin Luther King died.

Zecher Tzaddik L'vrachah. May the memory of this righteous man continue to be a blessing for us all.

22

The Moral Majority: Threat or Challenge?

THE FIRST AND MOST IMPORTANT ISSUE to understand about the Moral Majority phenomenon, I believe, is that it is a symbol, a metaphor, for a much larger, more complex social-political development that most Americans, and most American Jews, have not yet begun to confront. The Rev. Jerry Falwell first organized the Moral Majority in June 1979. In less than two years, it has, thanks to the pervasive cultural power of the mass media, caught the national fancy and fears of much of America.

That media blitz, however, has tended to obscure a far more significant, if less dramatic, reality; namely, the gradual but growing emergence of 40 to 50 million evangelical Christians into the mainstream of American life—economic, social, cultural, religious, as well as political. If the Moral Majority were to collapse tomorrow, and if Jerry Falwell were to disappear magically from the TV tube and the front covers of *Newsweek* and *Penthouse* magazines we, thoughtful American citizens, would still need to deepen our understanding of the facts and the meaning of the rise of the New South and the entry of evangelical Christians into the public stream of American religious-cultural pluralism. That historic development is of a magnitude comparable to that of the emergences into first-class citizenship of the Roman Catholic community in 1960 when the election of John F. Kennedy as the first "Catholic" president ratified the rite of passage of 50 million Catholics into American public life. Not incidentally, the Catholic religious-ethnic succession was attended by the same ambivalence. Would "a Catholic president" undermine the separation of church and state? Except then, evangelical Christians were in the forefront of expressing public anxieties, most notably when

Reprinted from *Hadassah* Magazine, March 3, 1981.

John F. Kennedy was compelled to assure Southern Baptist pastors at that famous encounter in Houston that his first loyalty would be to America and not to the pope and the Vatican.

Much of our national literary culture and popular folklore still perceives evangelical Christians through the stereotypes of crackers, red necks, Bible-thumpers, illiterates, and poor white trash. Anyone who has traveled through the South since the end of World War II knows that those are caricatures that have no relation to present-day realities. The South has become, during the past thirty-five years, the fastest growing economic region in America. (Houston today has the largest gross national product per capita of any city in the United States.) That economic growth has resulted in the massive movement of population to the South from the rest of America, so that today, the 80 million people in the eleven sun-belt states constitute the largest concentration of population in our country.

Those developments in turn have affected every other aspect of life in the South. Today, the New South is urbanized, industrialized, and its citizenry is overwhelmingly middle-class, white-collar workers, with income and educational levels comparable to the rest of the nation's population. The combination of economic wealth and widespread literacy has supported the growth of evangelical Christians as the fastest growing religious group in America.

That consciousness of newly acquired power—dollars and knowledge power—has transformed the formerly sleepy, magnolia-scented South into a rising political force on every level of government and society. Americans, and American Jews, will need to relate constructively to that new social-political-religious reality, long after Jerry Falwell and the Moral Majority disappear from the scene.

The second most important reality that needs to be understood is the extraordinary diversity and pluralism within the evangelical community. All fundamentalists are evangelicals but not all evangelicals are fundamentalists. More than one-half of the 40–50 million evangelicals are affiliated with the "mainstream" Southern Baptists, Southern Methodists, and Southern Presbyterians. The enlightened leadership of these 20–30 million evangelical Christians is proudly conscious of the fact that their forbears—the

Southern Baptist farmer-preachers, the Methodist circuit-riders, and the "dissident" Presbyterians in Virginia—fought and bled to disestablish the Anglican Church. We owe to those evangelical Christians both the doctrine and the institutionalization of religious liberty, freedom of conscience, and religious pluralism. With the assistance of James Madison and Thomas Jefferson, these evangelical Christians are responsible for the Virginia Statute for Religious Liberty, which became the basis for the First Amendment separating church from state.

It is no accident that when fundamentalist preachers in unholy alliance with ultra-conservative political organizers began advocating the establishment of a "Christian America" (a mythical idea with no substantial precedent in American history) and were urging their followers to "vote for born-again Christians only," that the first Americans to oppose that Constantian view were Southern Baptist leaders, foremost among them the Rev. Dr. Jimmy Allen, the Rev. James Dunn, among many others.

Similarly, when the fundamentalist preachers and politicians began advocating single issue politics and were urging their followers to vote for candidates solely on the basis of how they stood on pro-family and pro-life issues, mainstream evangelical leaders were in the forefront of condemning that reductionism of American domestic and foreign policy concerns. Indeed, the leading evangelical journal, *Christianity Today*, wrote a sharp editorial warning the fundamentalists that their single politics approach "could lead to the election of a moron who holds the right view on abortion" (September 19, 1980).

And, most significantly for Jews, when the Rev. Bailey Smith uttered his obscenities about "God not hearing the prayer of a Jew" and that "Jews have funny hooked noses," of far more enduring importance than this display of cultural anti-Semitism is the fact that Rev. Smith received literally thousands of letters, telegrams, telephone calls, and resolutions sent him by Baptist and other evangelical pastors and leaders condemning him for his anti-Semitism. Many quoted an official resolution adopted by the Southern Baptist Convention in 1972 which read in part: "Whereas, Baptists share with Jews a heritage of persecution and suffering for conscience's sake . . . Southern Baptists covenant to work positively to replace all anti-Semitic bias with the Christian attitude and practice of love for Jews, who along with all other persons, are equally beloved of God."

Since my first meeting with the Rev. Billy Graham in 1965, I have become increasingly persuaded that the mainstream evangelical Christians were potentially among the most stalwart friends of the Jewish people and of Israel. The record has borne that out. While many liberal Protestant church bureaucrats have become the willing instrument for PLO politics and propaganda, the vast majority of evangelical Christians have remained steadfast in their support of Israel as a Jewish state and of a united Jerusalem under Israeli sovereignty. American Jewry would be foolish to take that for granted, and it is just plain self-destructive to alienate that support by engaging in theological casuistry over why evangelicals and fundamentalists really support Israel. It is wise Rabbinic teaching that "even though the intention may not be pure (for the sake of heaven), the effects can be pure."

Much more could also be written about the wide support we have enjoyed among evangelical Christians in behalf of Soviet Jewry, and their collaborative programs with us to uproot the sources of anti-Semitism in Southern Baptist and other textbooks. And on the touchiest issue of proselytization, we have also begun to make progress, including the writing of evangelical essays that appreciate Judaism as a complete religion for Jews who do not require salvation by becoming Christians. We are in fact at a stage with evangelicals theologically not unlike the early stage we were at with Roman Catholics just prior to Vatican Council II. Those positive seeds need to be nurtured if they are ever to grow into sturdy plants, and they should not be poisoned by reckless polemics and noisy headline charges that suggest that all evangelicals are anti-Semites. That route seems predestined to snatch defeat from possible victory.

I do not want to suggest for a moment that there are not serious problems, especially with some fundamentalists. When they advocate views that we perceive to be a threat to democracy, to pluralism, to social justice, and to a reasoned foreign policy, we have an obligation to stand against those views.

But Jewish statesmanship requires that we seek to create an environment where it is possible to oppose, in a civil manner, those things with which we disagree and yet affirm those values with which we agree. And that method of how to disagree and yet affirm those values with which we agree, and that method of how to disagree agreeably holds for our relationships not only with evangelicals, but with Catholics, liberal Protestants, as well as other Jews. Ultimately, to cite Talleyrand, we do not have permanent friends, but we do have permanent interests.

23

Address on the Seventy-fifth Anniversary of the American Jewish Committee

IT IS A VERY GREAT PRIVILEGE to be invited to speak from this august pulpit and to be invited by the distinguished rabbi of this congregation, Rabbi Joshua Haberman, who is one of the foremost rabbis in this country, and who has made, in his own person, some of the historic contributions to the advancement of understanding between Christians and Jews as well as between Christians, Jews, and Muslims. It is particularly gratifying to be here and to share in his friendship, which is symbolized in a very special way this evening by the fact that this is the first time in thirty years of public service that I have come to a synagogue where a rabbi has bestowed upon me a tallis that is absolutely color-matched to my tie. You think of everything here! I am happy to renew my acquaintanceship with Rabbi Joshua Weinberg and the Cantor and other friends in this congregation.

It is deeply symbolic and profoundly important that the American Jewish Committee comes together at the gracious invitation of this synagogue and this congregation, to mark in a spirit of awe and reverence and gratitude the observance, in this way, around this theme this evening, of the seventy-fifth anniversary of the founding of this great American and great Jewish organization.

Address to the Washington Hebrew Congregation, May 15, 1981, during the celebration of the American Jewish Committee's seventy-fifth anniversary. The service was hosted by Rabbi Joshua Haberman, who himself had been a major leader in interreligious relations over the years in the nation's capital. Rabbi Tanenbaum was preceded at the pulpit by the Reverend Edward A. Flannery, then Director of Catholic-Jewish Relations for the National Conference of Catholic Bishops, who like Rabbi Tanenbaum was one of the great pioneers of what might be called, in retrospect, "the first golden age of Jewish-Christian relations" in this country.

The symbolism rests, in part, in the fact that we cannot begin to comprehend the historic power of what we have heard not just from the lips but from the heart of Father Edward A. Flannery, one of the great pioneers in advancing understanding between the Catholic community and the Jewish people who, thank God, increasingly finds larger and larger numbers of Catholic priests and nuns and Protestant ministers and evangelical Christians sharing the views that he has set forth with such clarity and feeling this evening.

We cannot begin to comprehend the significance of this moment—indeed, we dare not risk the sin of taking it for granted—unless we locate what is happening here this evening and what has been happening increasingly in every city in the United States, especially since the end of Vatican Council II in 1965, against the background of the founding of the American Jewish Committee.

As many of you know, the American Jewish Committee came into being in 1906, in response to a pogrom that began in Kishinev, Bessarabia, and spread throughout Russia and Eastern Europe. The Kishinev pogrom was inconceivable and could not have taken place without decades and centuries of Russian Orthodox Christian teaching about Jews and Judaism, which taught, century after century, all of the classic themes of contempt of the Jewish people: they are a deicide people; the Jews murdered God; they are the enemies of God and humanity; they are a wandering people because God has repudiated them for not accepting Jesus as the Messiah; they hold to a religion which has become moribund, which has been superseded by the emergence of Christianity.

All those centuries of teaching about Jews and Judaism, denying its legitimacy and its validity, began a process of dehumanization that made it possible for Russian Cossacks to tear through a village and rip Jews up as if they were tree saplings because they were not human beings. Jews had become in the eyes of too many of their fellow citizens some kind of inorganic matter without purpose, without dignity, and without honor.

The Second Vatican Council brought together 2,500 cardinals, archbishops and bishops, with Catholic theological experts from the entire inhabited world, from all of the continents of the earth. In addition to the other major issues they dealt with, the assembly concentrated on facing, for the first time in 2,000 years, the sources of anti-Semitism in certain traditions of Christian teaching, and made a decision once and for always to uproot the sources of anti-Semitism in Christian teaching. That was the greatest seminar in Christian-Jewish relations in 2,000 years.

Now its fruits are all about us. Father Flannery has referred to the fact that there have been a number of significant events since that time—official implementation of guidelines coming from the Catholic Bishops of the United States, France, Holland, Belgium, and Germany; an array of books and new catechisms; and new teachings about the Holocaust and Israel all over the Catholic world. One evidence of the power of what has been happening is that this Easter past, a Roman Catholic priest in Cincinnati picked up a document issued by the National Conference of Catholic Bishops through its Secretariat for Catholic-Jewish Relations on the eve of Holy Week and sent it to every Catholic priest in his diocese and to every Catholic parish. The document establishes guidelines for preachers on how to proclaim the Passion and death of Jesus without prejudice. It was written by Dr. Eugene J. Fisher, now the inheritor of the mantle of Father Flannery as Director of that Secretariat. In his covering letter to this document, this priest wrote to all of the priests in his diocese:

> Often in the past, Lent and especially Holy Week, have been times of fear for Jews living in Christian societies. In Eastern Europe this was the season for pogroms—anti-Jewish riots and massacres. Almost anywhere Jews and Jewish children might be subjected to insults and the spiteful cruelty of Christians. What can we as Christians, and especially of proclaimers of the Gospel, do to insure that never again will the proclamation of the Lord's Passion become a message of hate rather than redeeming love? At the very least we can purge our preaching and prayer of every way of speaking and every idea which might nurture the false notion that the Jews are in some particular way responsible for the death of Jesus.

That is an omen for the future and there are now, thank God, thousands of omens like that all over the United States, in Germany, in Italy, in France, in Belgium, and beginning in Latin America. It is not only a matter of the Roman Catholic community. This past December we held our second national conference with evangelical Christians—all of those people who are involved in the discussion of the Moral Majority today. There are the fundamentalists like Bailey Smith who, in their incredible cultural and spiritual illiteracy about Jews and Judaism, have the arrogance to declare God does not hear the prayers of the Jews. They are involved in the mainstream evangelical movement and include among them Southern Baptists, Presbyterians, Methodists, and others. In our conference in Deerfield, Illinois, this past December, we discussed everything—anti-Semitism, conversion, proselytization, Jews for Jesus, Messianism, covenant theories, and Israel. At the final session, the editor of a leading evangelical journal in America, *Christianity Today,* got up and read what he called "the Evangelical Manifesto on Jews and Judaism." When he came away from that meeting he decided to devote the major part of the issue of the magazine to be published on Yom Hashoah, Holocaust Remembrance Day, as an act of identification with the Jewish people. In his editorial, which occupied four pages of the journal and which was read by almost every evangelical pastor in America, he wrote the following: "As Evangelicals demonstrate in tangible ways, there are parts of the Evangelical community that will have nothing to do with anti-Semitic actions. They will declare a crucial truth to the Gentile world at large: to attack Jews is to attack Evangelicals, and such attacks will be resisted by Evangelicals as attacks against themselves."

Can you imagine such words as these? Can you imagine what would have happened in Germany had there been Father Flannerys and Vatican Council Declarations and statements on Passion Plays saying that it is impermissible to teach the deicide charge—the dehumanization of Jews that has been part of the teaching of contempt. What might have happened, what might have been the course of history in Germany had this gone on 300, 400, or 500 years ago?

It is not inconceivable that many if not most of the six million Jewish men, women, and children might be with us tonight. We have hardly begun to comprehend the extraordinary developments of recent decades because they are such a reversal from our past experience with Christians. In the minds of a great many Jews today, especially those of us who are sons and daughters of Eastern European immigrant parents (my parents came from the

Ukraine, after a pogrom in which my uncle was destroyed before the eyes of an entire Jewish village), in the minds of most Jews out of that historic experience, Christians and the Catholic Church have been the enemy. For 2,000 years pogroms, inquisitions, and crusades have made that our dominant perception of the Christian world. You may find the contemporary reversal difficult to believe but listen to it, because the case is unfolding before our eyes.

In this world in which there is so much violence; in which Jews are so vulnerable; and in which even Israel is so vulnerable—an Israel which was to bring about the end of the exile existence of the Jews; and which is so isolated in the United Nations—in this world the greatest allies of the Jewish people today in combating anti-Semitism are the Roman Catholic Church and Christian people of good will in every city and state of the United States and most of Western European civilization.

It will take time for that new image to set in for us. But I can tell you today that for the first time in 1,900 years we are engaged in dialogue, not only in formal relationships, but in deep friendship and collaboration and mutual respect, with Catholics and Protestants and Evangelicals and Greek Orthodox. It is a whole new reality in our experience. Part of our difficulty in sorting out the imagery is that for a great many Jews the past is present. This may be especially true of those who have lived through the 1930s and 1940s periods and were themselves caught up in the fever of Marxist, messianic, and utopian apocalypse. Given the history of the past, the hoped-for Marxist future was to represent the redemption of the Jews. Marxism would save us in that future utopian classless society and in that society prejudice and anti-Semitism were to disappear.

But everything today has turned upside down. Today the greatest sources of anti-Semitism, not only in the formulation of anti-Semitic ideological doctrines, but as the greatest distributors and purveyors of anti-Jewish hatred in the world, are the Marxist "utopia" of the Soviet Union, its allies in Eastern European countries, the PLO, and the Third World nations of the Arab League. See how dramatic the shift has become in our lifetime. Sheik Yamani made a speech two weeks ago in New York City before 800 oil executives, bankers, and captains of industry. He literally used the pattern, the scenario of the Christian Passion Play, and secularized it. And in that Passion Play, he described how there could be a millennium of peace between Saudi Arabia and the United States. All that stands in the way of that redemption is the State of Israel. If Israel can be isolated from the mainstream of human society somehow, peace will prevail and all that stands in the way in terms of the United States and Saudi Arabia having the optimum relationship is the Zionist lobby and Jewish power in America. That is to say, that Jews are collectively responsible for the absence of peace in the Middle East and the rest of the world. These people, the Jews, Yamani declared, crucified peace and stand in the way of universal redemption.

Idi Amin, the butcher of 400,000 to 500,000 Christians, was able to bring that off without a single word of reprimand at the United Nations. Indeed, he was invited to come to the United Nations to sit in a chair of honor, and to get a standing ovation from the representatives of 157 nations of the earth, which is to say that this man who is engaged systematically in violence and the terroristic destruction of human life, became legitimized as a hero. Do you think it is an accident that in this city, in March, a president of the United States can be shot down in an assassination attempt, and now this past week the pope, the sacred symbol of the conscience of Christendom, can be felled by a terrorist bullet?

There is a major challenge facing Jews and Christians beyond the issues that we have talked about tonight: the central moral and spiritual challenge that faces Jews and Christians today is the growing epidemic of dehumanization in the world; the growing sense that human life has become increasingly worthless; that human beings are expendable; that violence and terrorism can be normalized, can be legitimized, can be considered routine. At their deepest level, as we attack the problems associated with attitudes towards one another, as we begin to understand those essential differences which in fact make us distinctively Jews and Christians, we will need at the same time to acknowledge that there are ideals and values which bind us together in ways that cannot be compared to relationships between Jews, Christians, and any other people in the world. Jews and Christians, by virtue of their adherence to the Torah that Rabbi Haberman held before us tonight, affirm the dignity of every human life as an essential affirmation of the biblical tradition. Together we affirm that every human life is sacred; is of infinite preciousness; that no human being can be used for anyone else's program, or violence, or ideology, or for terrorism. Jews and Christians affirm, based on the biblical tradition, a sense of profound responsibility for the quality of life, for society, for the events of history, for which we have responsibility to bring about justice and equality and liberty. Together we anticipate a kingdom at the end of time where there will be a universal peace and fraternity and justice.

Liv Ullmann and I walked together in February of last year in a refugee camp in Thailand. It was filled with some 300,000 Cambodian refugees. We walked into a camp and there we understood the meaning of Jewish and Christian solidarity and cooperation in the kind of world in which we live today. In one corner of their camp there was a Catholic intensive feeding center with Catholic nuns bringing back from the brink of death infant children by intensive feeding. Next to that camp there was a group of Israeli doctors and nurses, the fourth medical team of Israelis who had come to Southeast Asia. They were seasoned physicians and nurses who came from Sinai and who had engaged in Bedouin medicine of an emergency kind. These Israeli doctors and nurses put an end to an epidemic of cholera and typhus within a matter of three to four weeks. They became heroes all over the country. Liv Ullmann and I looked at each other and we said, "That is what Jewish-Christian relations and its ultimate meaning is all about."

This recalls the words of Emerson: "What you are speaks out so loud I cannot hear what you say." Jews faithful to the Torah, Christians faithful to the gospel, both of them affirming that at the heart of the covenant is a conviction about the sanctity of every human life; that together we have a task in the world of standing against dehumanization to help bring about the rehumanization of the human family. Jews and Christians are the frontiers, at their best, of a community of conscience that can yet help make the world sane and civil and humane for all the members of God's human family.

24

Luther and the Jews: From the Past, A Present Challenge

WHEN THE U.S. POSTAL SERVICE recently announced approval of a commemorative stamp honoring the five hundredth anniversary of the birth of Martin Luther, the respective responses of Lutherans and Jews disclosed what profoundly contrary places Luther holds in Lutheran and Jewish history and in contemporary perceptions. Lutherans tended to feel a sense of pride, an appropriateness, in the honor bestowed by that commemorative stamp. Jews reacted with either disbelief or outrage.

The German Catholic scholar Joseph Lortz in his book, *The Reformation in Germany* (New York: Herder and Herder, 1968), writes of an analogous problem in Catholic-Lutheran relations. He uses the-term "bilateral confessionalism" to describe the existence of a Luther legend among Lutherans and many Protestants, "the preconceived sympathy for the hero of the Reformation" expressed in "sentimental and uncritical praise of Luther," and a Catholic legend of Luther which has assumed in the past "an antagonistic and adversary position" expressed in "hatred of the disrupter of church unity and a condemned arch-heretic."

"It was from the first Luther legend that Reformed polemic, as well as the Catholic reaction to it, acquired its churlish tone throughout the centuries," Lortz adds. "And for the same cause,

Published in pamphlet form in 1983, with essay by Eric Gritsch, by Lutheran Council in the U.S.A., and reprinted by the Evangelical Lutheran Church in America, 1988. The pamphlet exposed many in the Lutheran community to the later and darker views of the great Reformer on Jews and Judaism. When the reunited Evangelical Lutheran Church in America put out its major statement acknowledging and repudiating these later writings of Martin Luther on the Jews, Rabbi Tanenbaum's now posthumous and classic piece was included. The willingness of the ELCA and its predecessor Lutheran bodies to publish and republish such a hard-hitting article attests both to the courage of Lutheran leadership today and to the effectiveness of the Jewish-Lutheran dialogue that laid the groundwork for the statement.

for 400 years right down to the present day, historical study of the Reformation has been largely unable to arrive at accepted conclusions. Here as everywhere, bilateral confessionalism—i.e., a one-sided attitude of antagonism—has proved its fundamental fruitlessness."

If bilateral confessionalism has been a problem in the Catholic-Lutheran encounter, it has nothing less than bedeviled the Jewish-Lutheran encounter over the past 400 years. Only since the end of World War II, in the wake of the Nazi Holocaust, have Lutheran leaders begun to confront the dark anti-Jewish side of the Luther legend and have undertaken significant efforts to purge Lutheran teaching and culture of that destructive inheritance.

Welcome as has been the progress in Lutheran-Jewish relations in the past four decades, no person of conscience can rest content with such efforts in the face of the magnitude of the religious and moral challenge that the anti-Jewish writings of Martin Luther continue to represent. But if we concentrate our entire attention on Luther's anti-Judaic polemic alone, we could be diverted from the far more fundamental spiritual and human threat. Put simply, that threat is the pervasive tradition of the demonizing of Jews and Judaism that has existed in Christendom from the first century until our present age.

What have been the major features of that Christian tradition for Jews and Judaism? In what ways have Martin Luther's teachings been related to that 1,500-year-old legacy he inherited? What was Luther's "contribution" to that anti-Judaic culture? What was its impact on the response of German Lutherans in the face of the Nazis' barbarous assault against the Jewish people? And finally, what can we learn from this soul-searching for our life together today?

THE MIDDLE AGES AND THE JEWS

The problem of understanding the medieval attitude toward the Jew is necessarily complex. Just as today, a variety of factors operated during the Middle Ages to complicate Christian-Jewish relations. These included the anti-Jewish tradition stemming from the gospels themselves; the dogmatic enmity of the church fathers and the Constantinian Church, underscored by the religious and cultural non-conformity of the Jewish people within an essentially unified and totalitarian civilization; economic rivalry and the sometimes strategic economic position of Jews spread throughout the diaspora; the gradual evolution of new social balances of power and the political struggle it entailed, especially in Germany, where the Holy Roman Empire ceaselessly sought to impose imperial domination over the fiercely independent princes; and the emergence of a national spirit which eventually dissolved the medieval unity of European Christendom.

Christendom's hostility toward the Jews reached its apogee in the period of the Crusades. The rising menace of Islam with the Turkish conquest of Constantinople in 1453 and the spread of heresies—scriptural, anti-sacramental, and anti-clerical—that marked the eleventh and twelfth centuries called forth the greatest energies of the church to combat its enemies from within and without. Crusades and inquisitions were among the most powerful instruments for preserving the threatened unity of Christendom. Inevitably such a period of social and religious stress, especially noteworthy for a marked intensification of zealotry and fanaticism, also witnessed a heightened antagonism for the Jews, the most notoriously "heretical" and non-Christian force in Europe living in the midst of a citadel whose security was being threatened from every side. The antagonism was not new, but the form and intensity it assumed as a result of the stressful circumstances of the period were.

The peculiarly intense and unremitting hatred directed against Jewry in Christendom—and only in Christendom—can be accounted for, according to Christian and Jewish scholars, by the wholly fantastic image of the Jews which gripped the imagination of the masses at the time of the first Crusade in 1095–99. The Crusade began and ended with a massacre. "The men who took the cross, after receiving Communion, heartily devoted the [first] day to extermination of the Jews," wrote the historian and philosopher Lord Acton. They killed about 10,000 Jewish people.

When Godfrey of Bouillon, in the summer of 1099, succeeded after a heroic assault in capturing Jerusalem, he spent the first week slaughtering its inhabitants. The Jews were shut up in their synagogue, which was then set on fire. According to the Roman

Catholic historian Malcolm Hay, in his book, *Europe and the Jews* (published originally as *The Foot of Pride: The Pressure of Christendom on the People of Israel for 1900 Years* [Boston: Beacon Press, 1950]), Godfrey wrote to the pope, "Learn that in the Porch and in the Temple of Solomon, our people had the vile blood of the Saracens up to the knees of their horses." And then, said Hay, "when they thought the Savior had been sufficiently revenged, that is to say, when there was hardly anyone left alive in the town, they went with tears to worship at the Holy Sepulcher."

In the eyes of crusading people, Professor Norman Cohn of Britain's University of Essex writes in his landmark study, *The Pursuit of the Millennium: Revolutionary Messianism in Medieval and Reformation Europe and Its Bearing on Modern Totalitarian Movements* (New York: Oxford University Press, 1970), the smiting of the Muslims and the Jews was to be the first act in that final battle with the prince of evil himself. Above these desperate hordes as they moved about their work of massacre there loomed the figure of the Antichrist. As the infidels were allotted their roles in the eschatological drama, popular imagination transformed them into demons.

But if the Saracen long retained in the popular imagination a certain demonic quality, the Jew was portrayed as an even more horrifying figure. Jews and Saracens were generally regarded as closely akin, if not identical. But since Jews had been scattered throughout Christian Europe, they came to occupy by far the larger part in popular demonology; and for much longer—with consequences, Cohn states, that have extended down the generations to include the massacre of millions of European Jews in the twentieth century.

Based on his detailed historic and theological studies, Cohn asserts that official Catholic teaching had prepared the way for establishing the demonic image of the Jew which dominated the imagination of large parts of the Christian masses in the Middle Ages and beyond. Malcolm Hay similarly declares:

> The machinery of propaganda was entirely in the hands of the church officials. Preaching, chronicles, mystery plays and even ecclesiastical ceremonies were the principal agencies available for the dissemination of hate. Preachers dwelt with a morbid and some-

times sadistic realism upon the sufferings of Christ, for which they blamed all Jews of the time and all their descendants. For many centuries the bishops of Beziers preached a series of sermons during Holy Week, urging their congregations to take vengeance on the Jews who lived in the district. Stoning them became a regular part of the Holy Week ceremonial.

Even in the second and third centuries theologians were foretelling the Antichrist would be a Jew of the tribe of Dan. Born at Babylon, he would grow up in Palestine and would love the Jews above all peoples. He would rebuild the Temple for them and gather them together from their dispersion. The Jews, for their part, would be his most faithful followers, accepting him as the Messiah who was to restore the nation. And if some theologians looked forward to a general conversion of the Jews, others maintained that their blindness would endure to the end and that at the Last Judgment they would be sent, along with the Antichrist himself, to suffer the torments of hell for all eternity.

In the compendium of Antichrist lore which Adso of Montier-en-Der produced in the tenth century and which remained the stock authority throughout the Middle Ages, the Antichrist remained a Jew of the tribe of Dan, but became more uncanny and sinister. Now he is to be the offspring of a harlot and a worthless wretch. Moreover, at the moment of his conception the devil is to enter the harlot's womb as a spirit, thereby ensuring that the child will be the very incarnation of evil. Later his education in Palestine is to be carried out by sorcerers and magicians.

When the old eschatological prophecies were taken up by the masses of the later Middle Ages, all their fantasies were treated with deadly seriousness and were elaborated into a weird mythology. Just as the human figure of the Antichrist tended to merge into the wholly demonic figure of Satan, so the Jews came to be seen as demons attendant on Satan. In medieval dramas and passion plays they were shown as devils with a beard and the horns of a goat, while in real life, ecclesiastical and secular authorities alike tried to make Jews wear horns on their hats. Like other demons, they were imagined and portrayed in close association with creatures that symbolize lust and dirt—horned beasts, pigs, frogs, worms, snakes, and scorpions.

Conversely Satan himself was commonly given Jewish features

and was referred to as "the father of the Jews." The populace was convinced that in the synagogue, Jews worshiped Satan in the form of a cat or a toad, invoking his animal black magic. Like their supposed master, Jews were thought of as demons of destruction whose one object was the ruin of Christians and Christendom.

Hatred of the Jews has often been attributed to their role as moneylenders and usurers. But the fantasy of the demonic Jew existed before the reality of the Jewish moneylender, which Christendom helped produce by refusing to allow Jews to engage in any gainful economic, civil, or military functions.

LUTHER'S PLACE IN MEDIEVAL ANTI-SEMITISM

That demonology, which had fixed the image of the Jew as Antichrist, dominated the medieval world into which Martin Luther was born in 1483. As Joshua Trachtenburg says in his study, *The Devil and the Jews* (New Haven, CT: Yale University Press, 1943), to the medieval mind in which Luther was nurtured "the Jew was not human, not in the sense that the Christian was." He was the devil's creature, a demonic and diabolic beast "fighting the forces of truth and salvation with Satan's weapons . . . And against such a foe, no well of hatred was too deep, no war of extermination effective enough, until the world was rid of the menace."

Given that reality, that Luther, as an orthodox Christian, a former Augustinian monk, could have passed through a period of philo-Semitic sympathy for Jews is all the more remarkable. Earlier in 1510, during the controversy over the banning of Hebrew books that rocked Europe, young Martin Luther had sided with the great Christian Hebraist, John Reuchlin, uncle of Philip Melanchthon, over against the fanatic Dominican and former Jew, John Pfefferkorn. Luther's treatise, *That Jesus Christ Was Born a Jew*, was greeted in 1523 with enthusiasm by Jewish readers throughout Europe. In it he hoped that he might "entice some Jews to the Christian faith" and wrote the following:

> For our fools, the popes, bishops, sophists, and monks—the crude asses' heads—have hitherto so treated the Jews that anyone who wished to be a good Christian would almost have to become a Jew.

> If I had been a Jew and had seen such dolts and blockheads govern and teach the Christian faith, I would sooner have become a hog than a Christian. . . . For they have dealt with the Jews as if they were dogs and not men. They were able to do nothing but curse them and take their goods. When they were baptized, no Christian teaching or life was demonstrated to them. Rather they were only subjected to papistry and monkery. When they saw that Judaism had such strong scriptural support and that Christianity was nothing but twaddle, without any scriptural support, how could they quiet their hearts and become true good Christians?

Luther concluded the treatise with the following comments and recommendations:

> Therefore, I would request and advise that one deal gently with them and instruct them from Scripture. Then some of them may come along. Instead of this we are trying only to drive them by force, slandering them, accusing them of having Christian blood if they don't stink, and know not what other foolishness. So long as we thus treat them like dogs, how can we expect to work any good among them? Again, when we forbid them to labor and do business and have any human fellowship with us, thereby forcing them into usury, how is that supposed to do them any good? If we really want to help them, we must be guided in our dealings with them not by papal law but by the law of Christian love. . . . If some of them should prove stiff-necked, what of it? After all, we ourselves are not all good Christians either.

To understand why Jewish leaders in Germany and elsewhere perceived this Luther as a thunderbolt of light illuminating their otherwise darkened medieval landscape is not difficult. In light of this essay and for other more fundamental reasons, both Christian and Jewish scholars have observed that the Protestant Reformation has had Judaic inclinations: the zeal of Christian scholars for the study and use of the Hebrew language, a revolt from the complex system of Catholic Scholasticism to the seeming simplicity of Jewish teaching and dogma, and the effort to recover for the Bible its former centrality in Christian life, to name a few.

The enemies of Luther lost no opportunity to brand him as a Jew and as a Jewish patron. His doctrines, especially with reference to his polemics against idolatrous images and the worship of relics, won for him the title of "semi-Judaeus" or "half-Jew." In one instance he said of the Jews: "They are blood relations of our Lord; therefore, if it were proper to boast of flesh and blood, the Jews belong to Christ more than we. I beg, therefore, my dear papist, if you become tired of abusing me as a heretic, that you begin to revile me as a Jew."

By the 1530s the central issue for Luther was the proper interpretation of the Messianic passages in the Old Testament. Highly concerned about the impact of rabbinic exegesis that denied Christological interpretations, Luther appropriated all of the Old Testament in the service of the New. He left us nothing. The Jews, Luther asserts in his first lectures on the Psalms given during 1513–15, suffer continually under God's wrath and are paying the penalty for the rejection of Christ. They spend all their efforts in self-justification, but God will not hear their prayers. Neither kindness nor severity will improve them. They become constantly more stubborn and more vain. Moreover, they are the active enemies of Christ. They blaspheme and defame him, spreading their evil influence even into Christian hearts. As for Jewish efforts to interpret Scripture, these, Luther asserts, are simply lies. They forsake the Word of God and follow the imaginations of their hearts. He concludes that to extend tolerance to those who hold such views would be quite wrong for Christians.

LUTHER'S IMPACT ON MODERN ANTI-SEMITISM

In his 1543 treatise, *On the Jews and Their Lies,* Luther rails against the Jews for nearly 200 pages in his powerful, lusty style, with a torrential outpouring of passion and hatred that makes the diatribes of his predecessors seem languid. "Know, O adored Christ," he writes, "and make no mistake, that aside from the devil you have no enemy more venomous, more desperate, more bitter than a true Jew who truly seeks to be a Jew." Luther concludes his treatise with a series of recommendations to secular authorities on how to deal with the Jews. The duty of the secular authorities was to implement his recommendations, he insisted, and the duty of ecclesiastical authorities was to warn and instruct their congregations about the Jews and their lies.

As has been noted by Lutheran theologian Mark Edwards, neither the vulgarity nor the violence of these remarks is unique, comparable to his attacks on papal opponents and Turks. What is unique is the relative helplessness of these particular targets of Luther's wrath. Catholics could take care of themselves and give as well as they got. The Jews were at the mercy of their Catholic or evangelical rulers and could do precious little to protect themselves. Although Luther's savage texts enjoyed only a limited circulation during his lifetime and the next few centuries, his protective authority was invoked by the Nazis when they came to power, and his anti-Semitic writings enjoyed a revival of popularity. "A line of anti-Semitic descent from Martin Luther to Adolf Hitler is easy to draw," writes scholar Lucy Dawidowicz in her classic study, *The War Against the Jews, 1939–1945* (New York: Holt, Rinehart, and Winston, 1975). "Both Luther and Hitler were obsessed by a demonologized universe inhabited by Jews. Hitler himself, in that early dialogue with Dietrich Eckhart, asserted that the later Luther—that is, the violently anti-Semitic Luther—was the genuine Luther." Dawidowicz continues:

> To be sure, the similarities of Luther's anti-Jewish exhortations with modern racial anti-Semitism and even with Hitler's racial policies are not merely coincidental. They all derive from a common historic tradition of Jew-hatred whose provenance can be traced back to Haman's advice to Ahasuerus. But modern German anti-Semitism had more recent roots than Luther and grew out of a different soil—not that German anti-Semitism was new. It drew part of its sustenance from Christian anti-Semitism, whose foundation had been laid by the Catholic Church and upon which Luther built. It was equally a product of German nationalism. . . . Modern German anti-Semitism was the bastard child of the union of Christian anti-Semitism with German nationalism.

This union had corrosive effects on the conscience of millions of German Christians, leading the majority of the German nation into blind obedience to a murderous state.

Although the church could have influenced Hitler in the first months of 1933 while he "had still to feel his way with care," writes Richard Gutteridge in an essay on "German Protestantism and the Jews in the Third Reich,"

[the] vast majority of the church leaders and the clergy serving under them was eager to enter into the new order and to make their positive contribution there. On Easter Day, to give an example, Protestant churchgoers throughout Bavaria were told from the pulpit that the new state was reintroducing government according to God's laws and that the glad and active cooperation of the church was advocated in the task of creating a genuine *Volksgemeinschaft* in which the cause of the needy and oppressed would be promoted. There was a paucity of concern as to what would be the fate of the Jews and others who would be treated as outsiders. It was widely felt that if certain Jews found themselves at a disadvantage, it was a fair readjustment of balance. It would be regrettable if there were cases of violent and cruel treatment, but after all, a revolution had taken place. Excesses were unavoidable, but things would surely settle down.

Gutteridge documents a number of protests from individual church leaders and then states:

The church as a whole kept silent. No bishop, church government, or synod spoke out in public at this time on behalf of the persecuted Jews. Hitler and his associates had good reason to be satisfied that the church would not make overmuch trouble.

OUR PRESENT CHALLENGE

Forty years after the Nazi Holocaust, many church leaders have begun to confront this past in all its awfulness and face its moral challenge. It is a positive and hopeful sign. We might all take heart from the messages issued in recent months by major Lutheran bodies. The Lutheran World Federation's Fourth Consultation on the Church and the Jewish People called for a purging by Christians among themselves "of any hatred of the Jews and any sort of teaching of contempt for Judaism." The consultation further stated, "In his later years, [Luther] made certain vitriolic statements about the Jews that Lutheran churches today universally reject. We regret the way in which Luther wrote has been used to further anti-Semitism. This matter will be the subject of considerable attention . . ." Among themes suggested for such discussions are: the Christian understanding of the validity of the

Old Covenant and the implications of such understanding for the theology of mission; the question of mission-dialogue; the Torah and its relation to the New Testament; what Christians and Jews can do together in service to the world; the meaning of the Messiah for Jews and Christians; and the meaning of *dikaiosune* (justice or righteousness) for Christians and Jews.

We might find especially moving these words from a statement issued by the Evangelical Church in Germany (EKD), a group of regional Lutheran, Reformed, and United churches in West Germany, on the occasion of the fiftieth anniversary of Adolf Hitler's assumption of power, January 30, 1933:

> We cannot simply dismiss our history and forget about it. Things which are repressed are bound sooner or later to reassert their power. . . . Today we again repeat, unreservedly, the confession of guilt made immediately after the war by the members of the EKD council then in office: 'Through us endless suffering has been brought to many peoples and countries. We accuse ourselves for not witnessing more courageously, for not praying more faithfully, for not believing more joyously and for not loving more ardently. . . . To the older people in our midst we say: Please do not close your minds to the truth of what happened. To the younger generation we say: Do not stop facing up to this truth. You are not responsible for what happened then, but you are responsible for how these events affect our further history . . . To the politicians we add a word of warning: Be mindful of your responsibility. Injustice and want, the burden of unemployment and an unjust peace settlement were the breeding ground in which the National Socialist Party thrived. The selfishness and disunity of the democratic parties brought Hitler to power. This is why it is essential to preserve social peace and also why the common commitment to a democratic, constitutional state must stand above all argument, however necessary. To all our fellow citizens we say: Do not allow yourselves to be persuaded again into a new hate. Hitler's rule was based on hate. This is why hatred must have no place among us, whether it be of external enemies, foreigners or other classes, groups or minorities. Lastly, to our own parishes and congregations we say: Resist the heresy of believing in salvation of this world. Hitler's victory was also a victory for heresy . . . In the words of our predecessors at the end of the war we, too, acknowledge that our hope is in the God of grace and mercy that he will use our churches as his instruments

to proclaim his Word and to make his will obeyed among ourselves and among our whole people.

Martin Luther was a deeply committed Christian seized by a vision of God trying to bring about salvation. In the process he manifested his many gifts as a man of no small achievement: translator of the Bible, even helping to establish the German language; writer of magnificent essays; fighter against the domination of the papacy and an arid scholasticism in a freeing of conscience with which Jews identified. The task for us in this irenic time, this age of pluralism and growing dialogue, is to try to approach the issue of Luther and his teachings with something of the same method by which many Christians and Jews today approach the cumbersomeness of their inherited tradition. Our task always is to separate out the essential teachings of the faith which are healing and redemptive, productive of love and mutual respect, and simply to repudiate that of the past which is no longer relevant or appropriate and was a historical response for another time.

A fundamental principle of the Lutheran Reformation was that papal infallibility was not a Lutheran doctrine. And if the pope in Rome is not to be infallible, should infallibility then be transferred to Martin Luther? If there's anything that should characterize the observance of the five hundredth birthday of Luther, I feel it should be the determination to face the bad in past tradition and to replace it by building a culture filled with caring, understanding and above all—knowledge of one another, not as caricatures and stereotypes, but as we are, committed Jews and Christians.

25

The Role of the Passion Play in Fostering Anti-Semitism Throughout History

ACCORDING TO *The New Catholic Encyclopedia* (published under the Imprimatur of His Eminence Patrick Cardinal O'Boyle, Washington, D.C., 1967), the Passion Play was a genre of medieval religious drama, of relatively late and slow development, which concentrated on the suffering, death, and resurrection of Christ, and was thus distinguished from the Corpus Christi cycles narrating the entire biblical story from creation to judgment.

In their major study, *A History of the Theater* (New York: Crown, 1955), George Freedley and John A. Reeves assert that the ecclesiastical drama began with the elaboration of the Mass itself and seems to have come about first in France. There liturgical dramas were called *mysteres* (mysteries); in Italy they were the *sacre rappresentazioni;* in England, miracle plays (sometimes called mystery plays); in Germany, *Geistspiele*. The dramas of the period were based on "the holy mysteries of the Bible," hence their names, mystery plays. The miracles were taken from the events in the lives of the saints, though by the fourteenth century the two were used interchangeably in ordinary speech.

Alongside the mysteries and miracles there existed the moralities, which contrary to popular belief were contemporaries and not successors of the already described forms. Though the word "morality" was not in use at the time, this form was generally

Excerpted from *Good Friday Worship: Jewish Concerns—Christian Response,* Ecumenical Institute for Jewish-Christian Studies, Detroit, 1983. This long essay may be viewed in two parts. The first situates the nature of Passion Plays in their historical context. The second is an analysis of the implications of two modern versions, the Daisenberger and Rosner texts. This analysis of Passion Plays is a challenge to the organizers of the Oberammergau Passion Play in revising their production which is seen by hundreds of thousands each decade.

termed "moral," "goodly," or "pithy interlude." The first of which we have knowledge is the *Play of the Lord's Prayer*, which was performed in York before 1384 and until 1582. The seven vices of Pride, Lust, Sloth, Gluttony, Hatred, Avarice, and Anger were portrayed for the instruction of the auditors. The characters in these plays were allegorical and in some instances derived from miracles though they existed along with the liturgical drama.

It is held by scholars that there were no dramatic representations of Christ's death until the early thirteenth century, when all other types of liturgical play had long been performed. That may very well mean that there was a reluctance in the medieval Catholic Church to imitate in a fictive manner "the awesome mystery of Christ's sacrifice, especially since the Mass as the central act of liturgy was itself the actual continuation of that sacrifice" (*NCE*, p. 1062).

During the twelfth century, however, the custom of chanting a long, lyrical *planctus,* or lament, of the Blessed Virgin became attached to the Good Friday veneration of the cross. The latter ceremony already included the choral singing of the *Improperia,* or *Reproaches* of Jesus, (to which references in terms of attitudes toward Jews, Judaism, and the synagogue will be made later in this paper) and the uncovering of a veiled crucifix with the words *Ecce lignum crucis*. In addition to impersonations by clerics of the voices of the Sorrowful Mother, of Christ, or of John, chanting and rubrics of stylized gestures eventually appeared, and such activity was regarded by Karl Jung as "genuine Passion drama."

The only extant texts of Passion plays in Latin are the two in the Benediktbeuern manuscript from the thirteenth century, and their form suggests a development rather by elaboration of the already existing liturgical plays than by accretion to dramatic lyric, sermon, or narrative poem. The early vernacular Passion plays belong to the turn of the fourteenth century in both Germany and France. The typical plan of the vernacular Passion drama is a threefold design: The Fall (of the Angels and of Man), the suffering of Christ, and finally the Resurrection.

This plan omits virtually all of the Old Testament history except the original sin of Adam and Eve and ordinarily does not include the nativity of Jesus. The life of Christ is taken up at the beginning of his public ministry or at his triumphal entry into Jerusalem.

The earliest surviving German Passion play is found in a St. Gall manuscript, undated but probably of the early fourteenth century. Its span of sacred history extends from the marriage feast of Cana to the Resurrection. Of comparable date is the Vienna play, which adds to the St. Gall pattern the narrative of Adam's fall, thus presenting for the first time the triptych effect of the usual Passion play. Perhaps the most notable feature of the St. Gall text is the presence of a prologue in the voice of St. Augustine, a trace thus appearing of the famous Prophet plays, in which the church father summoned a procession of witnesses to the Messiah. Augustine also serves as a commentator in the play, at times interrupting to give a brief outline of coming action and at other times to give a little homily based on a scene just concluded, such as an exhortation to humility after Jesus washed the feet of the Disciples.

The flowering of German Passion plays occurred in the fifteenth and sixteenth centuries, which witnessed the expansion of the texts to many thousands of lines and thus to an action requiring three days for performance. Among the group of plays that survived this period are the Frankfurt and the Tyrol texts. The nucleus of the Frankfurt group of plays is the *Dirigierrolle,* which reveals in skeletal form a very extensive undertaking, from a Prophet play to an Ascension scene, climaxed by an epilogue debate between the allegorical figures *Ecclesia* and *Synagoga.* The Frankfurt Passion Play in its turn has served as a point of departure for other Passion plays performed in the same general area, of which the best known are the *Alsfeld* and the *Heidelberg* texts. These texts exist in manuscripts written shortly after 1500, and the great length of the scenes is attributed to "the loquacity of the characters, which has grown immeasurably from the cryptic speeches in the early plays, and also to the lavish use of comic motifs" (*NCE,* p. 1063).

The presence of buffoonery is quite marked in these southwestern German plays, notably in the scenes of merry devils, of Mary Magdalene's worldly life, and even of the counting out and quarreling over Judas's thirty silver coins. Allegory also is used, sparingly but effectively, for example, in the Heidelberg personification of Death as summoner of Lazarus. Death boasts ironically of his unlimited power and then suffers humiliation in his defeat by Christ's miracle at Lazarus's tomb (John 11:1–46). Also noteworthy in this text is the juxtaposition of prefigurative scenes from the Old Testament immediately before the corresponding events of the New Testament related typologically to them. (Thus the acquittal of Susanna by Daniel [Dan. 13] is staged as a prelude to Christ's encounter with the woman taken in adultery [John 8:1–11].) This method of structuring type and anti-type in sacred history is not widespread in drama. The much later Oberammergau play has something akin to this arrangement in a series of *tableaux vivants* from prefigurative Old Testament events preceding each New Testament scene.

The Tyrol Passion plays from the Eastern Alpine region are distinguished from other German texts by a greater selectivity of incident and by a uniformly elevated tone. Omitting Old Testament material, they begin late in the life of Jesus, with the council of "the Jews" plotting his death. The most characteristic plays of the German stage were the Shrovetide plays, *Fastnachtspiele,* which centered in Nuremberg, the center of learning and industry throughout the medieval period as well as during the Renaissance. The subject matter was similar to the French farces except for the representation of the peasants in a coarse and ugly light, their virtue and bravery always being subject to crude questioning. The fact that these plays were always written by townsfolk may explain the dislike, distrust, and ridicule heaped upon the country people.

Passion plays on French soil reveal much the same history as do those in Germany. The early vernacular texts are of Burgundian provenance and are all related ultimately to the nondramatic narrative poem, *Passion des Jongleurs,* written ca. 1200. The really great French Passion plays are those of Eustache Mercade and Arnoui Greban, both fifteenth-century dramatists, whose gigantic plays were subject to revision and adaptation by later writers, most skillfully by Jean Michel. These French mysteries show divergence from the standard German design; although they omit most of the Old Testament narrative, they do include the Nativity and the early life of Jesus. Moreover, they envelop the titanic serial narrative in a unifying framework known as the *Proces de Paradis,* quite different from the German forms of prophetic prologue and Augustinian commentary. The *Proces De Paradis* is a dramatization of the debate among Righteousness, Mercy, Truth, and Peace at the throne of God, allegorizing the conflict between his justice and his mercy.

The allegorized virtues, known in homiletic literature as the Four Daughters of God, are reconciled only when the Second Person of the Trinity undertakes to expiate man's sin; they reappear at intervals in the long cycle, most notably at the return of Christ to heaven, when Justice (Righteousness) at first sulks in a corner but then in a dramatic capitulation accepts the satisfaction made by Jesus.

Performances of Passion plays continued long into modern times. *The New Catholic Encyclopedia* describes the Oberammergau Passion Play as "one of the German dramas still flourishing in a regular presentation every tenth year." The origin of this custom is a well-known series of events related to the Thirty Years' War of the early seventeenth century. During the devastation of the Bavarian countryside by Swedish troops in 1632, a severe outbreak of the plague occurred, first in the lowlands, spreading gradually to the upland villages, including Oberammergau. After months of such disaster, the town council of this devout Catholic village decided upon a vow; they would sacrifice a year in every decade to the presentation of a Passion play. This promise was made by all the villagers for themselves and their descendants, as an act of penance and petition for deliverance. It is the Oberammergau tradition that no one died of the plague after this solemn religious act.

All surveys of the historic evolution of Passion plays that we have consulted suggest a number of conclusions that affect our approach to the 1980 version of the Oberammergau Passion Play. From the twelfth century *planctus Mariae* and the simple Latin plays of the Benediktbeuern manuscript, to the huge spectacles of the German and French cycles, there has been a very wide diversity of texts of Passion plays, reflecting para-liturgical expressions of popular devotion in a variety of cultural forms. From the earliest surviving German Passion Play found in the St. Gall manuscript of the early fourteenth century, there exists a tradition of structuring into the Passion Play a commentary, such as that in the St. Gall text which includes a prologue and commentary by St. Augustine, whose purpose is to lift up the spiritual message of the Passion. The relationship of Christianity to Judaism, the New Testament to the "Old Testament" (which Jews prefer to identify as "Hebrew Scriptures"), Christian attitudes to Jews and the synagogue are a persistent problematic in the majority of the diverse traditions of Passion Plays. As we shall elaborate, this polemical tradition of negative and at times hostile portrayal of the synagogue, the Jewish people, and Judaism begins already in the twelfth century in the inclusion of the *Improperia* (*Reproaches*), the dejudaization of the historic Jesus by omitting "virtually all Old Testament history" in the thirteenth century Benedicktbeuern manuscript, the arraigning of the *Ecclesia* in sharp and hostile opposition to the *Synagoga* through the literary method of "type" versus "antitype" found in the Frankfurt group of plays, but especially in the *tableaux vivants* of the Oberammergau Passion Play.

As *The New Catholic Encyclopedia* indicates, this method of casting the church in opposition to the synagogue and of using the "Old Testament" as prefigurement and antitype to the New Testament "is not widespread" in passion dramas, but is a special characteristic of the Oberammergau Passion Play and those derived from it. There are models of other Passion plays historically, such as those of Tyrol, which show "a greater selectivity of incident and a uniformly elevated tone." *The New Catholic Encyclopedia's* scholars describe the French mysteries as "the really great French Passion plays which show divergence from the standard German design" in that the *Prodis de Paradis* dramatizes the Passion of Jesus in the form of a debate among the allegorized virtues, Righteousness, Mercy, Truth, and Peace at the Throne of God, allegorizing the spiritual message of the Passion as the conflict between His Justice and His Mercy. Is the Daisenberger text or the Rosner text [both described below] of the Oberammergau Passion Play closer to this expression of authentic spirituality which precludes the singling out of "the Jews" as the enemies of God and the murderers of Christ collectively guilty as deicides, and therefore subject to eternal punishment?

The church, Professor Norman Cohn observed, had always tended to regard the synagogue as a dangerous influence and even as a potential rival and had never ceased to carry on a vigorous polemic against Judaism. For generations the laity had been accustomed to hear the Jews bitterly condemned from the pul-

pit—as perverse, stubborn and ungrateful because they refused
to admit the divinity of Christ, as bearers also of a monstrous he-
reditary guilt for the murder of Christ. Moreover, the eschatological tradition had long associated the Jews with the Antichrist
himself. The populace was convinced that in the synagogue Jews
worshiped Satan in the form of a cat or a toad, invoking his aid
in making black magic. Like their supposed master, Jews were
thought of as demons of destruction whose one object was the
ruin of Christians and Christendom, *"dyables d'enfer, enemys du
genre humain,"* as they were called in French miracle plays.

And if the power of the Jews seemed greater than ever, their
evildoing more outrageous, their sorceries more baleful, that was
but one more sign that the End was indeed at hand. Even the ten
lost tribes of Israel, whom Commodianus had seen as the future
army of Christ, became identified with those hosts of the Antichrist, the peoples of Gog and Magog, peoples whom the Pseudo-
Methodius described as living off human flesh, corpses, babes
ripped from their mothers' wombs, and also off scorpions, ser-
pents, and all the most disgusting reptiles. Medieval dramas were
written showing how the Jewish demons would help the Antichrist
to conquer the world until, on the eve of the Second Coming and
the beginning of the millennium, Antichrist and Jews would be
annihilated together amidst the rejoicings of the Christians. During the performance of such works, armed force was needed to
protect the Jewish quarter from the fury of the mob. Popes and
councils might insist that, although the Jews ought to be isolated
and degraded until the day of their conversion, they must certainly not be killed; subtleties such as these made little impression
on turbulent masses swept by eschatological hopes and fears and
already, as they thought, embarked on the prodigious struggles
of the Last Days.

Hatred of the Jews has so often been attributed to their role as
moneylenders that it is worth emphasizing how slight the connection really was. The fantasy of the demonic Jews existed before
the reality of the Jewish moneylender, whom indeed it helped to
produce by debarring Jews from any gainful economic, civil, or
military functions through exclusionary civic and ecclesiastical
laws.

When Bernard, Abbot of Clairvaux, was commissioned by Pope

Eugenius III in 1145 to preach the Second Crusade, he gained many recruits by announcing that the killing of an infidel would merit a place in heaven. Rudolph, or Ralph, a Cistercian monk who left his monastery at Clairvaux in order to enlist recruits in Germany for the rescue of the Holy Land, told the German masses it was their duty first to kill the enemies of Christ in their own country. Ralph told his congregations that these infidels, violent men and well armed, were a long way off, and that it was much safer, and equally meritorious, to kill unarmed Jews at home. The doctrine was readily accepted by the populace, whose minds for generations, says Malcolm Hay, had been prepared for such ideas by ecclesiastical propaganda. The massacre began, without regard to age or sex, at Speyer, Cologne, Mainz, and many other cities in Germany. "Many ecclesiastical historians," writes Malcolm Hay, "have treated the whole affair (of the massacre of the Jews in Germany) as if it had been merely an unfortunate incident, due to the ignorant fanaticism of single individuals and not, as in fact it was, characteristic and inevitable in the world of the twelfth century," and subsequent centuries.

That demonology which has fixed the image of the Jews as Antichrist in popular Christian eschatology has persisted to modern times in Germany and elsewhere. In her classic study, *The War Against the Jews, 1939–1945* (New York: Holt, Rinehart, and Winston, 1975), Dr. Lucy Dawidowicz observes (p. 9): "Between 1907 and 1910 Lanz van Liebenfels, an eccentric occultist-racist, published a series of pamphlets—which Adolf Hitler bought and read—called *Ostara: Briefbücherei der blonden Mannesrech tier* (Newsletter of the Blond Champions of Man's Rights) in which he depicted the struggle between blond Aryan heroes and the dark, hairy ape-men who represent the lower races. All human existence revolved around this struggle, whose central burden was to preserve the purity of Aryan women from the demonic sexuality of the ape-man." Dr. Dawidowicz continues (p. 10): "People living in an anti-Semitic milieu—as Hitler did—already viewed Jews as diseased and filthy creatures, degenerate and corrupting, outsiders beyond fraternity and compassion. Since the society had already branded the Jews as loathsome pariahs, the Jews could then serve the symbolic and pathological needs of the obsessed and guilt-ridden." The Daisenberger text of the Oberammergau Passion Play must be viewed against that background.

Of all the pageants that dramatize the crucifixion narrative, the most famous undoubtedly is the Passion Play performed every ten years at Oberammergau, in the solidly Roman Catholic region of Upper Bavaria, in West Germany. Over the centuries, it has been performed in at least five different versions. In modern times, the play and the picturesque mountain village in which it is performed have become a major international tourist attraction, and since the end of World War II, some 1.5 million people have come to Oberammergau performances. In 1970, according to village officials, some 530,000 people from 113 countries came to Oberammergau to view 102 performances. This indicates that despite its origins as a local village production, Oberammergau's Passion Play now has assumed an unprecedented international importance, influencing the image of German Catholicism, of Western Christianity, and of Germany itself in many parts of the world.

A prominent feature of most Passion plays, past and present, has been a strong anti-Jewish component, focused not only on Jesus's individual Jewish antagonists, but by implication or explicit statement on the Jewish people as a whole. A prominent Protestant scholar, Dr. Bernhard E. Olson, author of the landmark study, *Faith and Prejudice* (New Haven: Yale University Press, 1963), commented on this genre of pageants: "The crucifixion drama is . . . regarded not without reason as having played a prominent part in Jewish disabilities through the centuries as well as providing a major cause of negative attitudes toward Jews today" (p. 195). Similarly, a respected Catholic, Father John T. Pawlikowski, O.S.M., writes in his study, *Catechetics and Prejudice* (New York: Paulist Press, 1973):

> A major problem in Christian-Jewish relations . . . was the blame frequently placed upon the Jewish people as a whole for the death of Jesus. Historians have found that the doctrine of deicide was never officially proclaimed by a church council or by a papal decree. Yet it was widespread among the Christian masses since the time of the early church and church authorities rarely took any steps to curb its influence. This charge has led to a history of bitter persecution of Jews by Christians. Most of this terrible history does not appear in textbooks dealing with the history of the church.

Thus, most Catholics are simply uninformed about the long tradition of Christian anti-Semitism, while most Jews are well aware of it (p. 100).

The Oberammergau Passion Play is no exception to this rule of "providing a major cause of negative attitudes towards Jews today," a fact fully recognized by the enemies of the Jews. One of Oberammergau's strongest admirers in modern times was Adolf Hitler, who stated at the height of the Second World War (*Adolf Hitler, Secret Conversations, 1941–1944* [New York: Farrar, Straus and Young, 1953]): "It is vital that the Passion Play be continued at Oberammergau; for never has the menace of Jewry been so convincingly portrayed" (p. 457). Under the Nazi government, the Oberammergau Passion Play was classified as "a racially important cultural document," and on the occasion of the pageant's tercentennial, in 1934, a Nazified special performance represented Jesus and his disciples as Aryan heroes.

The performance, in 1950 and 1960 went back to the version used before the Nazi era, a text originally written by a priest named Joseph Alois Daisenberger for the 1860 season. Daisenberger's text is free from the nineteenth- and twentieth-century-style racism; but it abounds with anti-Jewish religious prejudices and misstatements, as well as demonological and satanic images of Jews as being in league with the Antichrist, long established in the popular tradition described earlier in this paper. Until recent decades, the anti-Jewish tenor of the Daisenberger text does not appear to have troubled many Christian consciences. Attention was focused on this critical concern only after the Second World War, when in the wake of the Nazi horror the Christian world began to reappraise its attitudes toward Jews and Judaism. That spirit is well reflected in the book, *Christology After Auschwitz,* by Father Michael B. McGarry, C.S.P. (New York: Paulist Press, 1977):

> On the Christian side, theologians and church leaders, in moments of contrition and bewilderment, wonder how such a catastrophe as the holocaust could have happened in a Christian country, in a nation nurtured and steeped in the Christian tradition. Anti-Semitism, to be sure, predates Christianity, but never before have men focused such a genocidal fury on the Jews with such an unambigu-

ous goal—the annihilation of the Jewish people. In an effort to eradicate every form of, and justification for, anti-Semitism from Christianity, church theologians and leaders have tried to investigate what could have laid the groundwork for such an expression of hate and utter disregard for human dignity. Some, ashamed at their own church's silence during the attempt at the "final solution" have pointed to the "unChristian behavior" of the Christian Church. That is, if Christians had been more truly faithful to the teachings of Christ, they never could have given in to the evils of anti-Semitism (p. 1).

Others have suggested that the answer is deeper and more radical than a matter of moral behavior: the basis for anti-Semitism is to be found in the Scriptures themselves, or, if not in the New Testament, in the content of church teaching and doctrine. Jesus's dispute with Jewish leaders, the caricature of Jewish ritual and synagogue, the "infidelity" of the formerly chosen; these and other anti-Judaism themes run through the Holy Book of Christians. In recent years, numerous studies have looked carefully at the New Testament to glean from it whether, in fact, the very Scriptures are anti-Semitic. These investigations come to different conclusions, but at least it can be said, Christianity (especially the New Testament) wrongly understood offers a constant temptation for hostility against the Jews and the synagogue.

In this reappraisal, the decisive influence has been Vatican Council II's Declaration on Non-Christian Religions, *Nostra Aetate*. Most important, the Vatican Declaration asserts: "Although the Jewish authorities and those who followed their lead pressed for the death of Christ, nevertheless what happened to Christ in His Passion cannot be attributed to all Jews without distinction, then alive, nor to the Jews of today . . . Besides, as the church has always held and holds now, Christ underwent His Passion and death freely, because of the sins of men and out of infinite love, in order that all may reach salvation." For these reasons, the Vatican Declaration calls on those who teach and preach not to utter "anything that is inconsistent with the truth of the gospel and with the spirit of Christ," and states that the Catholic Church "deplores hatred, persecutions, displays of anti-Semitism directed against Jews at any time and by any one."

In 1968, Pope Paul VI personally appointed a Vatican Secretariat on Religious Relations with Judaism, which, in elaboration of *Nostra Aetate,* issued in 1974 a set of *Guidelines and Suggestions for Implementing the Conciliar Declaration* Nostra Aetate. These *Guidelines* declared "the spiritual bonds and historical links binding the Church to Judaism condemn (as opposed to the very spirit of Christianity) all forms of anti-Semitism and discrimination, which in any case the dignity of the human person alone would suffice to condemn."

The Vatican *Guidelines* specify that "these links and relationships render obligatory a better mutual understanding and renewed mutual esteem" in the areas of dialogue, liturgy, teaching, and education, "at all levels of Christian instruction and education," including catechisms and religious textbooks, the mass media (press, radio, cinema, television), and joint social action. "With respect to liturgical readings," the *Guidelines* declare, "care will be taken to see that homilies based on them will not distort their meaning, especially when it is a question of passages which seem to show the Jewish people as such in an unfavorable light. Efforts will be made so to instruct the Christian people that they will understand the true interpretations of all the texts and their meaning for the contemporary believer." The *Guidelines* add:

> Commissions entrusted with the task of liturgical translation will pay particular attention to the way in which they express those phrases and passages which Christians, if not well informed, might misunderstand because of prejudice. Obviously, one cannot alter the text of the Bible. The point is that, with a version destined for liturgical use, there should be an overriding preoccupation to bring out explicitly the meaning of a text while taking scriptural studies into account. (Thus the formula "the Jews" in St. John sometimes, according to the context, means "the leaders of the Jews" or "the adversaries of Jesus," terms which express better the thought of the Evangelist and avoid appearing to arraign the Jewish people as such. Another example is the use of the words "Pharisee" and "Pharisaism," which have taken on a largely pejorative meaning.)

The preceding remarks apply to introductions to biblical readings, to the Prayer of the Faithful and to commentaries printed in missals used by the laity.

The new interest in the Oberammergau Passion Play created

by the Vatican Declaration (and the Vatican *Guidelines*) have led to demands for revision by Christians and Jews. The municipal authorities of Oberammergau, who exercise sole control over the production, have announced that a revision of the Daisenberger text was undertaken for use in the 1970 performance. The authors of this revision have not been publicly identified.

According to statements by Oberammergau spokesmen, the latest text of the Passion Play no longer contains anti-Jewish elements, except where dictated by the need to follow the biblical accounts faithfully. Thus, the director of the 1970 production, Anton Preisinger, has stated, "The text has been thoroughly overhauled, but we cannot change what the Bible says; at times the Bible does use hard words about the Jews." (Reported in the London *Daily Telegraph,* November 17, 1969.) Similarly, Ernst Zwink, Presiding Mayor of Oberammergau and Chairman of the Passion Play Committee, wrote on February 26, 1970, to the Upper Bavarian Government that the Committee had seriously and honestly striven to "attempt changes and to purge the text of all passages which can be misunderstood, in order to take into account the spirit of the times." In his letter, the Mayor rejected the imputation that the revised text might still be anti-Jewish in some degree: "The question whether the text is in harmony with the thoughts and wishes of the Vatican Council II, and whether it has anti-Semitic dispositions must be considered as a tendentious distortion." Indeed, he suggested that there was not much that could have been revised. The Daisenberger text (1860) is close to the obligatory basis of the Passion reports in the New Testament and to the views expressed by responsible experts in the field. These experts were not named.

To assess the validity of the claim that the current version of the Oberammergau Passion Play no longer contains anti-Jewish elements, the American Jewish Committee, long concerned with the effect of Passion Plays on Christians' attitudes toward Jews and Judaism, undertook a comparative content analysis of the 1960 and 1970 scripts. Published in German and English under the title, *Oberammergau 1960 and 1970: A Study in Religious anti-Semitism,* the analysis compared line by line the Daisenberger text in the original German, as performed in 1960, with the official German script prepared for 1970. To our knowledge, it is the first line-by-line analysis of the 1960 and 1970 scripts.

The analysis deals solely with text passages, deletions, and modifications that bear on the representation of Jews and Judaism. Changes that were clearly made for dramatic or stylistic reasons only—such as the removal of repetitions, or modernization of out-of-date expressions—have been disregarded. A copy of this analysis in German is being made available to each of the members of this Symposium for detailed study.

The American Jewish Committee analysis came to these conclusions. Taken all in all, the 1970 revision of the Passion Play text falls far short of removing all gratuitous anti-Jewish elements. However well-intentioned those responsible for the updating may have been in their desire to purge the text of all passages which can be misunderstood, the attempt has not succeeded. Except for one excision of some length (the prologue and the tableau opening Act II which, revealingly, associated Jesus's antagonists with "all the spirits, up from nethermost Hell/Which from Creation's dawn stubbornly have rebelled/And forever have discord/Sowed against the Divine," images of the Antichrist), the revisions are limited to deletions and modifications of emotionally charged individual words or brief phrases. Even this editing has been so inconsistently carried out that not one of the objectionable themes or ideas in the earlier version has wholly disappeared. Indeed, the characters as well as the story line and its implications are quite unchanged.

1. The 1970 "revised" text, like its predecessor, still draws Jesus's antagonists as fiendish, almost subhuman, creatures, thus perpetuating the medieval images of the Jews as "demons of destruction," *"dyables d'enfer, enemys du genre humain."*

2. It misrepresents Jewish religion in Jesus's time as harsh, corrupt, and worthless, thereby violating the Vatican *Guidelines'* instruction that "The Old Testament and the Jewish tradition founded upon it must not be set against the New Testament in such a way that the former seems to constitute a religion of only Justice, fear, and legalism, with no appeal to the love of God and neighbor (cf. Deut. 6:15; Lev. 19:18; Matt. 22:34–40)."

3. It falsely turns Jesus and his disciples into renegades from Judaism, concealing their roots in the Jewish past and their com-

mitment to Jewish religion and ethics. That historical caricature
is in opposition to the statement of the Vatican *Guidelines:* "Jesus
was born of the Jewish people, as were the Apostles and a large
number of His first Disciples . . . And although His teaching had a
profoundly new character, Christ, nevertheless, in many instances
took His stand on the teaching of the Old Testament. The New
Testament is profoundly marked by its relation to the Old. . . .
Jesus also used teaching methods similar to those employed by
the rabbis of His time."

4. It presents all Jews as enemies of Jesus, asserts they knowingly
accepted the guilt in his death for themselves and their descendants, and maintains that they have been permanently rejected by
God for this reason, contradicting the explicit teaching of Vatican
Council II and the Vatican *Guidelines.*

Reflecting major trends in contemporary Christian scholarship
that unambiguously reject the "deicide" canard against the Jewish people, Dr. Eugene J. Fisher, a noted Catholic educator who
is the executive secretary of the Secretariat for Catholic-Jewish
Relations of the United States Conference of Catholic Bishops,
writes in his book, *Faith Without Prejudice* (New York: Paulist Press,
1977) under the chapter heading, "Who Killed Jesus?" the following:

> The Catechism of the Council of Trent, Article IV, as promulgated
> in the sixteenth century, shows clearly what has always been essen-
> tial Christian teaching on responsibility for the death of Christ.
> Theologically, all humanity bears the blame. It is not one particular
> group, but the sins of us all that are responsible for his death. The
> same Council of Trent also declared that the crucifixion was
> Christ's true decision: "It was the peculiar privilege of Christ the
> Lord to have died when He Himself decreed to die, and to have
> died not so much by external violence as by internal assent."

The New Testament does not present history in our sense of the
term. It reveals the meaning of history. As revelation, it is not
intended to give us merely a listing of facts and events. Rather it
aims to teach us the salvific will of God that underlines all human
events. Only in this way is it "relevant" to us: that it reveals to us
our sins and our own salvation. To the question "Who Killed
Jesus?" the Christian replies: "I did."

5) It falsifies the character and historic role of Pilate, and shifts the role of the crucifier from the Romans to the Jews.

This sympathetic portrayal of Pilate contradicts the findings of modern biblical scholarship which, as Father Pawlikowski wrote, "has shown quite convincingly that the death of Jesus was not a plot engineered by the general Jewish populace." As Father Bruce Vawter has insisted, "there seems to be no doubt that Jewish responsibility has been heightened at the expense of the Roman . . . In particular, the governor Pontius Pilate as portrayed in the gospels appears to be credited with a greater degree of disinterested justice in his makeup than other historical sources concerning him would cause us to suspect." Father Vawter also goes on to say that "a factual history of the trial and death of Jesus has to be reconstructed rather than read from the gospels. A great deal of vital background material is missing from the gospel narratives as they now stand. It must be supplied through auxiliary readings and commentaries" (cited in Pawlikowski, *Catechetics and Prejudice*, p. 107). Fisher, in his book, *Faith Without Prejudice*, states:

> Contemporary accounts of Pilate show another picture of him. Pilate was so brutal that even Rome could not take him for long, and he was eventually called back by Rome because of excessive cruelty. . . . A letter of the period reveals Pilate's true character. It charges him with "corruptibility, violence, robberies, ill treatment of the people, grievances, continuous executions without trial, endless and intolerable cruelties (p. 77)."

And Father Pawlikowski concludes, "This situation makes it almost impossible for even the very best of Passion Plays to entirely avoid a travesty of the gospel story. We cannot obtain a fully accurate picture of the trial and death of Jesus from reading the gospels alone. This is the clear conclusion of the vast majority of modern biblical scholars."

6) It fails to make clear the background of oppressive Roman rule against which the drama of Jesus's ministry was enacted, and without which the actions of Jesus's antagonists cannot be understood.

The United States Secretariat for Catholic-Jewish Relations has issued a statement on Passion Plays, with guidelines for improvement (February 28, 1968). It points out that in trying to heighten religious fervor, carelessly written or produced Passion plays can become a source of anti-Semitic reactions, contrary to the spirit of the Vatican Declaration on Non-Christian Religions. Writers and producers of such pageants are specifically warned to avoid the following exaggerations and misinterpretations:

> "To conceal the fact that Jesus is a Jew and that His friends as well as His enemies in the drama are Jews";
> "To create the impression that most Jews of Jesus's day willed his death, failing to show that the secrecy surrounding much of Jesus's trial was motivated by the large following He had in Jerusalem";
> "To change the 'crowd' before the governor's palace into a screaming 'mob,' as representing all Jerusalem, and indeed all Israel";
> "To depict Pilate, whom historiography has shown to have been a ruthless tyrant, as an innocent and kindly bystander";
> "To highlight those texts of the gospel narrative that are amenable to misinterpretation by uninformed audiences, such as, 'His blood upon us and upon our children' (Matt. 27:25)."

The Secretariat for Catholic-Jewish Relations has defined the true purpose of the Passion Plays as follows: "To increase in the hearts of their audiences a greater love of God and of men, reminding them that those who played a part in the Passion drama were, in the Christian view, representatives of all of us." One wishes the 1970 and the 1980 Oberammergau pageants had adhered to this definition instead of falling, as they do, into every one of the pitfalls the Secretariat has cautioned against. As it is, the summer of 1970 found half a million people viewing a spectacle that differed little, not only from its immediate predecessor, but also from what was performed on the same stage in the time of Hitler, who so acutely recognized the harmony between the pageant's anti-Jewish elements and his own anti-Semitic policies. Once more, the old lies, the medieval demonology indicating the Jews as the enemies of God and of mankind, backed by the prestige of the play and the fanfare attending its production, are being declaimed for the entire world to hear.

In sum, our study of the texts and those specific changes proposed for the 1970 version, convinces us that the central theme of the Daisenberger text is the collective guilt of all Jews in the death of Jesus. We wish it were possible to eliminate that hostile and defamatory theme from that text. We, and the Christian authorities and scholars who have studied the problem, believe that the removal of that and related themes from the Daisenberger text would be impossible without destroying the text itself.

We have seen the trial production of the Rosner text that we previewed in August 1977 as an honest effort to give artistic and emotional expression to Christian views of human sin, the possibility of human redemption and Jesus's teachings of love and faith. We, and most Christians who have studied the history of religious differences between Christianity and Judaism, agree that the central theme of the Daisenberger text contradicts all of these teachings while the central theme of the Rosner text does not. It is the right of the Oberammergau Town Council to nonetheless choose to perform Daisenberger. It would also be the right of both other Christians and Jews to draw their own conclusions about such a decision.

On November 9, 1978, the date of the fortieth anniversary of Kristallnacht, His Eminence Cardinal Hoeffner, president of the German Catholic Bishops Conference, issued a public statement in which he declared:

> Today, forty years after the horrible events, should be an occasion for every individual who was alive at that time to examine his conscience and ask himself: "What have I done then, and what have I failed to do since then?" And this day is posing to all Christians the question what they are doing today that these things should not happen again. In memory of all the victims among the Jewish people in the years 1933–45, I want to assure you that the Catholic Church in Germany, faithful to the *Guidelines* of Vatican Council II, will counteract in its preaching, instructions, and by all means, anti-Semitism and all racial hatred, and work for good neighborliness and friendship among Jews and Christians.

All over the world, people of goodwill await the decision of Oberammergau authorities to obey fully the mandate of their church, as enunciated by Vatican Council II and the German Catholic Conference of Bishops.

26

Jewish-Christian Relations: Heschel and Vatican Council II

THERE IS NO NEED to exaggerate, much less apotheosize, the role and impact of our beloved teacher, Rabbi Abraham Joshua Heschel, on Vatican Council II, and on Jewish-Christian relations generally. His contributions and achievements—intellectual, theological, and above all, the impact of his person—were so singular, profound, varied, and lasting that simply to try to record and evaluate them is in itself a monumental statement that requires no embellishment. Beyond that, much of Rabbi Heschel's influence derived from his charismatic personality, his sheer presence, and that forever defies the conventional methods of the social or religious historian.

Two events symbolize the extraordinary—indeed, unprecedented—nature of his spiritual influence on the course of Jewish-Christian relations in our generation. The first took place on January 31, 1973, just about one month after his untimely death. Pope Paul VI, addressing a general audience of thousands assembled at the Vatican, spoke about the nature of man's quest for God. Toward the end of his address, the Pope declared that "even before we have been moved in search of God, God has come in search of us." Those words did not catch the attention of the world's press. What did get reported in the international media was the fact that the subsequently published text of the papal talk quoted the writings of Rabbi Heschel as the source of the Pope's thoughts about God and man. Pope Paul's citation of the 1968 French edition of Heschel's *God in Search of Man* (reprinted in

---

Address to the Jewish Theological Seminary, February 21, 1983. Although Rabbi Tanenbaum attended only one session of the Second Vatican Council, he was instrumental in setting up the relationship between Rabbi Abraham Joshua Heschel and the future Cardinal Johannes Willebrands, who took charge of the conciliar commission in charge of drafting *Nostra Aetate*.

English [New York: Octagon Books, 1972]), was to the knowledge of experts on the Vatican and the papacy, an unprecedented public acknowledgment by a pope of a thinker and writer who was not a Christian.

The second event occurred on March 10, 1973. *America* magazine, the leading Jesuit journal in the United States, devoted its entire issue to the life, thought, and impact of Rabbi Heschel on Christian and Jewish communities. The then editor of *America*, the Rev. Donald R. Campion, wrote in his lead editorial:

> This may be the first time in history that a Christian magazine has devoted an entire issue to contemporary Jewish religious thought and life. The immediate inspiration for this innovation was Abraham Joshua Heschel's premature death . . . He was a dear friend and an informal—but most effective teacher to many of us. It is our hope that this issue will be not so much an elegy as a lively continuation of Rabbi Heschel's instructive and ecumenical spirit. As these pages testify, he was enormously energetic, both intellectually and spiritually. We Christians frequently say that the best Christian instruction is the life of a genuine Christian. Similarly, the best instruction we Christians may receive concerning the continuing vitality and richness of the Judaic tradition in which we providentially share is the life and example of a Jew like Professor Heschel. . . . May this special issue serve not only to introduce a Christian readership to the wisdom and holiness of a man and the sacred tradition that nourished him, but also promote the love among men in all troubled corners of the world that he strove mightily to inculcate. Each of you, our readers, will have his own lesson to learn from Abraham Heschel as he speaks to you of the living tradition of Judaism, in all its energy, holiness, and compassion. May the God whom Jews, Christians, and Muslims worship bring us to live together in peace and understanding and mutual appreciation.

The appreciation of Dr. Heschel's inspired life and work was no less among major Protestant personalities. In that same issue of *America* magazine, Dr. John C. Bennett, former president of Union Theological Seminary where in 1965, Dr. Heschel served as the Harry Emerson Fosdick Professor, wrote in an article entitled, "Agent of God's Compassion," the following:

> Abraham Heschel belonged to the whole American religious community. I know of no other person of whom this was so true. He

was profoundly Jewish in his spiritual and cultural roots, in his closeness to Jewish suffering, in his religious commitment, in his love for the nation and land of Israel, and in the quality of his prophetic presence. And yet he was religious inspiration to Christians and to many searching people beyond the familiar religious boundaries. Christians are nourished in their own faith by his vision and his words.

A volume could be written on the intellectual symbiosis and personal friendships that Rabbi Heschel enjoyed with such towering Christian personalities as Reinhold Niebuhr, Paul Tillich, W. D. Davies, Robert McAfee Brown, John Courtney Murray, Gustav Weigel, Raymond Brown, among literally hundreds of other seminal thinkers, scholars, and leaders in the Christian world in the United States and abroad.

On the occasion of the publication in 1951 of Dr. Heschel's first book in English, *The Earth is the Lord's: The Inner World of the Jew in Eastern Europe* (New York: H. Schuman, 1950),[1] Dr. Niebuhr wrote in a major book review that Dr. Heschel was a spiritual treasure snatched from the smoldering embers of Nazi Germany. Niebuhr, who subsequently referred affectionately to Dr. Heschel as "Father Abraham," predicted then that Heschel would soon become "a commanding and authoritative voice not only in the Jewish community, but in the religious life in America."

During the following decade, Dr. Heschel spoke from a series of national forums on critical issues facing the life of this nation: on children and youth, on the aging, on race relations, on war and peace. At the outset, he was reluctant to speak out on these issues, feeling perhaps the insecurity of not being American enough yet. My classmate and cherished friend, Rabbi Wolfe Kelman, and I, both students and disciples of Heschel, had to persuade him to address the 1960 White House Conference on Children and Youth, the 1961 White House Conference on Aging, and the 1963 National Conference on Religion and Race.[2]

---

[1] As editor and publicist with the publisher Henry Schuman Books, I had the privilege of helping prepare Dr. Heschel's first book and to gain attention for it in the intellectual world. Dr. Niebuhr enthusiastically agreed to write the first major review, which launched Dr. Heschel's career.

[2] In my capacity as Vice Chairman of the White House Conferences on Children and Youth and on Aging, and as Program Chairman on Religion and Race, I was in the fortunate position of being able to invite Dr. Heschel to be a keynote

In each instance, his papers became the rave of these large national conferences. Americans of all religions and races discovered in Heschel a rare religious genius of penetrating insight and compassion, whose prophetic words never failed to provide direction for helping all Americans to cope with the moral and spiritual malaise of the nation. (Copies of Dr. Heschel's addresses at these and other meetings are to be found in his book, *The Insecurity of Freedom—Essays on Human Existence* [New York: Schocken Books, 1972].)

Against this background, Dr. Heschel emerged as a national presence. He also became the natural ally and frequent spokesman of the American Jewish Committee in its efforts relating to Vatican Council II. In 1958, the late blessed Pope John XXIII ascended the throne of St. Peter, and one year later, he called into being the Second Vatican Council, 1962–1965, as a means for realizing *aggiornamento* or the reformation of the church. During the period of 1958–1960, Pope John entered into searching discussions with Professor Jules Isaac of France, noted for his writings on the religious roots of anti-Semitism. Professor Isaac's researches in this field were begun under the impact of the Nazi Holocaust, which took the lives of his wife and daughter.

Earlier in 1947, Prof. Isaac was a guiding light in convening the Seelisburg (Switzerland) conference on the persistence of anti-Semitism in Europe. My colleague, Zachariah Shuster, then European director of the AJC, played a leading role in that pioneering meeting, a role that he was to repeat with Rabbi Heschel and myself later on in Rome. The Seelisburg conference framed the agenda for the dawning of a new era in Jewish-Christian relations.

The conference, whose thinking stemmed largely from the work of Prof. Isaac, called on the churches to face these religious and historic facts: "that one God speaks to us all through the Old and New Testaments," and that "Jesus was born of a Jewish mother," as well as to avoid "disparaging Judaism with the object of extolling Christianity," "presenting the Passion in such a way as to bring the odium of the killing of Jesus upon Jews alone," or "promoting the superstitious notion that the Jewish people is

---

speaker. My Catholic and Protestant colleagues eagerly joined me in extending these invitations.

reprobate, accursed, reserved for a destiny of suffering." It was further suggested that the history of the Jews and Judaism be handled more sympathetically in teaching the young, and that Christian publications, especially educational ones, be revised in this spirit.

In accordance with the Seelisburg guidelines, efforts were made in a number of countries to revise harmful Christian teaching about Jews and Judaism. But the efforts were modest and the pace was uneven. It became clear that large-scale improvement was possible only if a revision of the traditional "teachings of contempt" for Jews and Judaism could be officially incorporated into the church's teaching.

Pope John gave repeated indications that the time might be ripe for such decisive action. He personally ordered certain phrases offensive to Jews, such as *Perfidi Judaei* ("perfidious" or "unbelieving Jews") stricken from the Holy Week liturgy. Most important, he felt the Second Vatican Council should provide an opportunity for the Catholic Church to clarify officially its attitude toward Jews and Judaism, and to repudiate traditions that too long perpetuated hatred and oppression. In keeping with its longstanding concern over uprooting the religious sources of anti-Semitism dating to the 1930s, as well as for the advancement of interreligious understanding, the American Jewish Committee wholeheartedly welcomed the opportunities afforded by the Ecumenical Council for reexamining relationships between Catholics and Jews.

During the preparatory phase of the Vatican Council, the AJC, at the request of church authorities, submitted detailed research data documenting the presence of anti-Jewish elements in Catholic teachings and liturgical writings, and suggesting steps toward better understanding between the two faiths. That such documentation would be useful was established through consultations with numerous advisors in the Americas, Europe, and Israel. Scholars representing Orthodox, Reform, and Conservative Judaism[3]—foremost among them, Rabbi Heschel—were continually

---

[3] Among the Jewish scholars AJC consulted were: Orthodox—Rabbi Joseph B. Soloveichik, Rabbi Samuel Belkin; Conservative—Rabbi Louis Finkelstein, Rabbi Heschel; and Reform—Rabbi Louis B. Freehof.

consulted before and during preparation, so that the memoranda in their final form reflected a wide range of responsible Jewish thought. At the same time, the views of many Catholic and Protestant experts were sought. These consultations impressively demonstrated the concern of leading churchmen with the problems to which the Committee was addressing itself.

The task of drafting a statement on Catholic-Jewish relations for action by the Vatican Council had been assigned to the Vatican's Secretariat for Promoting Christian Unity, presided over by the renowned Jesuit scholar, Augustin Cardinal Bea. From the outset, the venerable Cardinal, with his passion for justice and his keen sense of what anti-Semitism had led to in his native Germany, proved himself one of the great figures of the *aggiornamento*. The American Jewish Committee and Rabbi Heschel as its spiritual mentor soon entered a period of fruitful discussion with him, a working relationship which was to continue through the Council sessions.

During July 1961, in the first of a long series of audiences with AJC representatives, Cardinal Bea requested that a memorandum on anti-Jewish elements in present-day Catholic religious instruction be sent to him, to be followed by a similar presentation on passages derogatory to Jews in Catholic liturgical materials and literature. The desired documents were submitted in the summer and fall of that year.

The first memorandum, entitled *The Image of the Jew in Catholic Teaching,* drew heavily on the three Catholic textbook self-studies that the AJC had co-sponsored with the Jesuit St. Louis University. The document cited and analyzed hostile references to Jews as a group (e.g., "the bloodthirsty Jews," "the blind hatred of the Jews"); unfair comparisons between Judaism and Christianity ("The Jews believed that one should hate an enemy; but Christ taught the opposite"); failure to acknowledge the Jewish roots of the Christian religion ("The world must thank the Catholic Church for the Bible"); and partiality shown in identifying the enemies of Jesus as Jewish ("The Jews decided to kill him"), while ignoring the fact that his disciples and friends also were Jews ("Jesus was held in great admiration by *the people*"). Most important, the memorandum quoted numerous references to the Jews as an accursed nation of deicides ("Him also [Jesus] they put to death. Because of this fact, they were finally rejected by God . . .").

The companion memorandum, *Anti-Jewish Elements in Catholic Liturgy*, again focused mainly on the deicide accusation. It acknowledged the recent removal of anti-Jewish expressions from the liturgy, but went on to emphasize that prejudiced material remained in certain texts, particularly those read in churches during Holy Week, and in commentaries on the liturgy prepared for the use of the faithful. Passages cited described the Jews collectively as bloodthirsty killers of Jesus (e.g., "As if frenzied by a delirious fever . . . they hit upon the plan to do away with him"), or as rejected and deservedly persecuted ("A curse clings to them; Cain-like, they shall wander fugitives on the earth . . . Slavery, misery and contempt have been their portion"). After recalling the fate of European Jewry under Hitler, the document closed with the request that the church find ways of rectifying liturgical passages that "stimulate and reinforce the slanderous concept of the Jews as a cursed, despised, deicide people."

The American Jewish Committee felt that these critical studies should be supplemented with positive suggestions for the betterment of Catholic-Jewish understanding. In November 1961, an audience was arranged in the Vatican for Rabbi Heschel and AJC representatives with Cardinal Bea. Following a lengthy and cordial conversation, Cardinal Bea invited Rabbi Heschel and the AJC to draw up a set of recommendations for the use of the Cardinal and his secretariat. The offer was welcomed, and the proposed document was submitted in May 1962.

Zachariah Shuster, who accompanied Rabbi Heschel at the Cardinal Bea meeting, wrote to AJC's New York office on December 20, 1961, about the impact that Rabbi Heschel made in the Vatican:

> I should like to tell you that I found him to be outstanding in many respects, and primarily as a man of profound knowledge of Judaism, an excellent interpreter of Jewish lore in modern terms, and a man imbued with a spirit of enthusiasm about ultimate values . . .
> He was deeply impressed by his experiences in Rome, and with our approaches to the leaders of the Catholic Church. For my part, I can testify that he succeeded in creating a rapport with Christian religious leaders in a way few laymen and even Jewish religious leaders could have done.

This third memorandum, *On Improving Catholic-Jewish Relations,* prepared by Rabbi Heschel in cooperation with AJC's Interreligious Affairs Department, suggested that a start be made with a Vatican Council declaration recognizing the "integrity and permanent preciousness" of the Jews as Jews rather than as potential converts, condemning anti-Semitism and explicitly rejecting the deicide charge. This was not a conventional memorandum. It was pure Heschel, flaming with his Jewish spirituality and his prophetic passion against injustice. Space does not allow the inclusion of that document in its entirety in this paper, but this sampling is suggestive:

> This is the outstanding characteristic of the Prophets: openness to the historic situation, to the divine call and its demands. In their eyes the human situation may be a divine emergency. . . . It is such a situation that we face today when the survival of mankind, including its sacred legacy, is in balance. One wave of hatred, prejudice, or contempt may bring in its wake the destruction of all mankind. Vicious deeds are but an aftermath of what is conceived in the hearts and minds of man. It is from the inner life of men and from the articulation of evil thoughts that evil actions take their rise. It is therefore of extreme importance that the sinfulness of thoughts, of suspicion and hatred, and particularly the sinfulness of any contemptuous utterance, however flippantly it is meant, be made clear to all mankind. This applies in particular to such thoughts and utterances about individuals or groups of other religions, races, and nations. Speech has power and few men realize that words do not fade. What starts out as a sound ends in a deed.

Heschel went on to propose that the Vatican Council adopt an official declaration "which would be binding for Catholics and considered reasonably moral obligations by all men of good will," stating:

> Condemnation of the persecution of any man or group of men on account of the faith they hold or the race to which they belong by birth or by choice. . . . Affirmation that those who hold a faith other than the faith held by the Roman Catholic Church, are to be respected for their views and treated as people who are as bona fide as Roman Catholics are in their particular faith. . . . In view of the past historical events which brought great sacrifice and suffering to Jews on account of their faith as Jews and their race, and

particularly in view of the fact that anti-Semitism has in our time resulted in the greatest crime committed in the history of mankind, we consider it a matter of extreme importance that a strong declaration be issued by the Council stressing the grave nature of the sin of anti-Semitism. Anti-Semitism, one of the most grave and historically important sins of prejudice and contempt, is incompatible with Catholicism and in general with all morality.

Beyond these declarations, the Heschel-AJC memorandum proposed such measures as the creation of a permanent high-level commission at the Vatican to watch over Catholic-Jewish relations and take the lead in combating anti-Semitism; official Church encouragement for cooperation in civic and charitable endeavors; and joint research projects and publications to foster reciprocal knowledge between Catholics and Jews. Thus, during the Vatican Council's planning stage, Rabbi Heschel, in close cooperation with the AJC, documented the crucial points then under consideration by the Catholic Church.

Throughout 1962, Jewish-Christian relations became the object of increased public attention. Articles on deicide, anti-Semitism, and the history of Catholic-Jewish relations appeared widely in the Catholic press in the United States, Europe, and Latin America. A major *agape* was held in Rome in January 1962 in which Cardinal Bea and the AJC participated, during which the Cardinal called on "all groups of mankind to overcome the hatreds of the past."

In February 1962, three of Dr. Heschel's books—*God in Search of Man, Man is Not Alone,* and *The Sabbath*—were sent to Cardinal Bea which he warmly acknowledged "as a strong common spiritual bond between us." Meanwhile, vigorous opposition to the proposed Jewish declaration began to be heard from conservative-minded prelates, many of whom questioned the very idea of an Ecumenical Council. Similarly, strong opposition emerged in the Arab world on the grounds that any action taken by the Catholic Church favorable to the Jews might be interpreted as beneficial to Israel. There were warnings of possible reprisals against the church and Christians in certain Arab countries if it were enacted.

While Cardinal Bea and his secretariat went on with his work on the schema on the Jews and on religious liberty, procedural controversies took up most of the council's opening session during the fall of 1962, and the declaration on the Jews was postponed until the second session, scheduled to start in September 1963. In March 1963, Cardinal Bea visited Harvard University where he presided over a Catholic-Protestant colloquium. He then went on to New York for an unique civic interfaith *agape* in his honor attended by United Nations officials, noted political figures and leaders of the world's major faiths, including Rabbi Heschel.

While in Boston as the guest of Richard Cardinal Cushing, Cardinal Bea invited Rabbi Heschel and myself for a confidential conversation. Meeting alone with us in Cardinal Cushing's Chancery, Cardinal Bea told us that Pope John was exploring the possibility of establishing diplomatic relations with the State of Israel as a dramatic gesture of goodwill toward the Jewish people. He asked us for our reactions. We were literally stunned by the idea, but quickly recovered to tell him how welcome that action would be received by Jews throughout the world. The Cardinal was heartened by our enthusiastic responses and said he would report them to the pope. Three months later, Pope John died and his great-hearted gesture toward Israel and the Jews apparently was buried with him.

The afternoon before the *agape*, the Cardinal and two of his staff members, then Monsignor Johannes Willebrands and his personal secretary, Father Stephan Schmidt, met in private conference with a group of prominent Jewish religious and communal leaders to consider problems linked with the proposed declaration on the Jews. The meeting, held off-the-record and without publicity, was his only encounter with a representative group of Jewish spokesmen during his American tour.

Meeting at the AJC building in New York on March 31, 1963, the conferees, though attending as individuals, were connected with such organizations as the Jewish Theological Seminary, the Rabbinical Council of America, the Synagogue Council of America, the Central Conference of American Rabbis, and Yeshiva University. The President of Pro Deo University, a papal institution in Rome, and ranking officers of the AJC took part in the unprecedented meeting. At the request of the AJC, Rabbi Heschel served as chairman of the gathering. Among those attending were Rabbis Louis Finkelstein, Theodore Friedman, Joseph H. Lookstein, Julius Mark, and Albert Minda.

By prior agreement, a series of key questions had been prepared beforehand and answered by Cardinal Bea in writing. The agenda centered on the significance of the deicide concept; on the urgent need for combating anti-Semitism among Catholics; on the importance of having biased teachings officially rejected; and on the desirability of interreligious cooperation.

The Cardinal opened his statement with several theological arguments by which the deicide accusation might be refuted within the framework of Catholic dogma. First of all, he said, the death of Jesus was not the work of Jewry as a whole, but merely of certain Jewish individuals—and even they were forgiven by Jesus. Secondly, St. Paul had explicitly condemned the idea that God had rejected the Jews. And finally, the diaspora was by no means evidence of divine punishment, as had been held by some; on the contrary, it had served the divine purpose by helping to bring monotheism to the world. The Cardinal then turned to the first of the questions prepared for him: whether the Vatican Council could explicitly reject the idea that the Jews are an accursed people guilty of deicide. He assured our group that this issue figured large in the draft being prepared by his Secretariat, together with the recognition of Judaism as a living religion in its own right, and of Christianity's roots in the Old Testament.

Other points raised were whether the Council could condemn unjust allegations and imputations about religious, racial, or other groups generally; and whether dogmas and moral principles in this sphere might be translated into concrete regulations through Council action. Cardinal Bea stated that the Council could combat unjust generalizations by laying down guidelines enjoining justice, truth, and love toward all human groups; but practical applications of these principles would presumably be governed by the church's day-to-day teaching, preaching, and confessional practice, rather than by specific Council action. He closed with the observation that his views were endorsed by Pope John.

Rabbi Heschel and other Jewish participants felt that this meeting was of unusual, perhaps of historic significance, in that the essential content of the Vatican Declaration on Catholic-Jewish relations was contained in the written answers that Cardinal Bea had composed in response to our questions, subject now to refinement as a result of our dialogue with him.

Under the influence of Pope John XXIII and thanks to his quiet diplomacy, the tide continued to run strongly in favor of a clear, meaningful decree on the Jews. But on June 4, 1963, Pope John died, his work hardly begun. Even though his spirit continued to be felt under the new pontiff Paul VI, the decree was soon to face serious obstacles.

On September 29, 1963, the second session opened. It soon became apparent that, contrary to earlier expectations, no quick decisions were likely. Meanwhile, the contents of the prospective declaration on the Jews became public through the press. On October 17, a front-page article in *The New York Times* stated that the draft—part of a schema on ecumenism—would acknowledge the Jewish roots of the church, reject the idea that the Jews rather than all mankind were to blame for Jesus's death, and vigorously repudiate anti-Semitism. In effect, that text contained all the themes that Cardinal Bea had outlined in his March 31 meeting with Rabbi Heschel and other Jewish leaders. The AJC promptly voiced the hope that the proposed measure would "represent an historic breakthrough," and that the Council might "finally do away with the epithet 'Christ-killer,' which was hurled upon Jews in so many countries in the past and present."

By agreement, Rabbi Heschel issued his own statement in which he said: "The report about a Declaration to be introduced to the Ecumenical Council fills me with a sense of intense gratification. Such a Declaration, will, should it be adopted, open new sources of spiritual insight for the Western world. It is an expression of the integrity and ultimate earnestness of those who are inspired by the consciousness of living in the presence of God, the Lord and the Judge of history. May the spirit of God guide the work of the Council."

Objections soon came from conservative elements, especially the tradition-minded Italian bishops, and from prelates from the Arab world. President Gamal Nasser and the United Arab Republic diplomats also intervened.[4] As controversy mounted, the AJC

---

[4] While attending the Vatican Council, I found that a massive volume entitled *Il Complotto Contra La Chiesa (The Plot Against the Church)* had been distributed to the 2,500 Council Fathers. Its thesis was that an international Jewish conspiracy

took steps to underscore to appropriate church authorities in the United States, Europe, and South America the hopes and expectations aroused by the Council among Jews and others the world over.

When formally introduced to the Council on November 18, the proposed draft drew the session's loudest round of applause. The next day, Cardinal Bea was given a warm and attentive hearing when he stated that the document was drafted at the late Pope John's instructions, and that the history of the Nazi crimes made authoritative action by the church imperative. A majority of bishops plainly wished to see the measure adopted, foremost among them the American Catholic bishops. Passage seemed assured. But suddenly, in ways still not entirely clear, the tide turned. The progressive majority found itself unable to bring the matter to a vote. The opposition of Arab prelates and conservatives apparently was augmented at this juncture by churchmen who felt a statement on Jews did not belong in the context of a schema on Christian ecumenism, or who objected to the draft on religious freedom which was under consideration at the same time. Cardinal Bea remained confident of ultimate success. "What is put off is not put away," he observed. But the two controversial chapters on the Jews and on religious liberty were now subject to basic reconsideration.

During the spring and winter of 1964, the prospects took repeated turns for the worse. Proposals were made to shift the declaration from Cardinal Bea's jurisdiction to a new Secretariat for Non-Christian Religions. Even more significant, it was reported that a revised text then in process contained passages implying the expectation that the Jews would be converted to Christianity—a development that created consternation and anger in Jewish circles, and among a number of enlightened Christians. Persistent reports also indicated that efforts were afoot in Rome to empty the measure of meaning by weakening the condemnation of the deicide charge.

As throughout much of the Council, Dr. Heschel and I were

---

in collaboration with Catholics, such as Cardinal Bea, had undertaken to change Catholic teaching. Informed reports indicated that the Egyptian embassy in Rome was responsible for the book and that Nasser had spent an estimated $3 million in trying to subvert the "Jewish Declaration."

almost in daily contact, and we agreed that it was now important for him to express his views on these developments forcefully to Cardinal Bea. On November 22, 1963, as these negative trends began to unfold, Rabbi Heschel wrote to the Cardinal the following:

> I am informed of a few phrases which may not only mar the splendor of this magnificent document but may, God forbid, virtually nullify the abundance of blessing contained therein. I refer to the words: "Even though a great part of the Chosen People for the time being stand far from Christ yet it would be wrong . . ." This clause introduces a dissonant note of indulgence and a tentativeness incompatible with the spirit and intention of this momentous declaration. Those who are anxious to cast suspicion upon the ecumenical spirit will interpret this statement to mean that the friendship of the church for the Jews is contingent upon the Jews' willingness to accept the Christian faith. As your Eminence knows such an implication would deeply hurt the sensitivity of the Jewish people. The enemies of the church will spare no effort in maintaining that the whole document is intended to bring about the end of the Jewish faith. This document is a proclamation inspired by the love of God, a love which knows no conditions, no bounds, no qualifications. I respectfully suggest that the phrase quoted above be deleted.

Rabbi Heschel then objected to the proposed phrase, "The death of Christ was not brought about by all the (Jewish) people then living. . . ." Heschel wrote: "I respectfully suggest that the expression *non a tutto popolo* (not by all the people) may be misinterpreted to imply that the majority of Jewish people living at that time bears responsibility for the crucifixion. In a recent statement by yourself and others it was made clear that only a few individuals might have shared in the responsibility for that event, but that the Jewish people as a whole had nothing to do with it and are entirely free from any guilt."

In late November, at our request, Rabbi Heschel went to Rome where he met with Monsignor Willebrands. The pressure from the conservatives and the Arab prelates and diplomats was so great that at that time Cardinal Bea found it politically inexpedient to meet with Dr. Heschel. Nevertheless, Monsignor Willebrands, who had great respect for Dr. Heschel, received him

cordially and heard out attentively his objections to these passages. The monsignor agreed that there was a possibility of misunderstanding and he pledged to bring Heschel's views to Cardinal
Bea and the Secretariat. While in Rome, Dr. Heschel also met
with Cardinal Meyer of Chicago and with Protestant observers to
the Council who expressed sympathy and support of his positions.

On May 30, Pope Paul VI held an audience with the AJC during
which he issued a statement acknowledging the intimate links between Christianity and Judaism and deploring the suffering of
Jewry in the recent past. The AJC delegation raised the deicide
problem referring to a recent address of Cardinal Spellman before the AJC in New York in which he condemned anti-Semitism
and called the deicide charge "absurd." The pope responded, "I
have read Cardinal Spellman's speech, and Cardinal Spellman
spoke my sentiments." The pope gave permission for his expressed opinion—his first commitment on the subject—to be
publicly circulated, and the Vatican itself gave considerable publicity to the exchange of views in the *L'Osservatore Romano* and
other publications.

On September 3, 1964, on the eve of the third session that was
to be opened on September 16, the new version of the declaration became known to the public through a newspaper story.
There was no longer a forthright denial of the Jews' supposed
collective responsibility for the death of Jesus; it had been replaced by a vague warning "not to impute to the Jews of our time
that which was perpetrated in the Passion of Christ." Hatred of
Jews was reproved as one among many kinds of human wrong,
but the special nature of anti-Semitism and persecution of Jews
through centuries were not touched upon.

Moreover, the declaration in this version expressed the hope
for an "eventual union of the Jewish people with the Church," a
thought which could well be taken to mean that acceptance of
Jews was contingent on their conversion. No such idea was expressed with respect to Muslims, who were mentioned elsewhere
in the revised document, nor to non-Catholic Christians.

The changes in the text were received with exultation in the
Arab press, and with profound disappointment by Jews and others. In a widely-quoted statement, the AJC acknowledged the
church's right to hope for the eventual Christianization of man-

kind, but objected to the active conversionary implications. "Any declaration, no matter how well intended, whose effect would mean . . . the elimination of Judaism as a religion would be received with resentment," the AJC statement asserted. On September 3, 1964, Dr. Heschel issued a powerful statement condemning the revised draft. He said:

> Since this present draft document calls for "reciprocal understanding and appreciation, to be attained by theological study and fraternal discussion," between Jews and Catholics, it must be stated that *spiritual fratricide* is hardly a means for the attainment of "fraternal discussion" or "reciprocal understanding." A message that regards the Jew as a candidate for conversion and proclaims that the destiny of Judaism is to disappear will be abhorred by Jews all over the world and is bound to foster reciprocal distrust as well as bitterness and resentment. Throughout the centuries, our people have paid such a high price in suffering and martyrdom for preserving the Covenant and the legacy of holiness, faith, and devotion to the sacred Jewish tradition. To this day, we labor devotedly to educate our children in the ways of the Torah. As I have repeatedly stated to leading personalities of the Vatican, I am ready to go to Auschwitz any time, if faced with the alternative of conversion or death. Jews throughout the world will be dismayed by a call from the Vatican to abandon their faith in a generation which witnessed the massacre of six million Jews and the destruction of thousands of synagogues on a continent where the dominant religion was not Islam, Buddhism, or Shintoism.

Dr. Heschel concluded with "the profound hope that during the course of the forthcoming third session of the Vatican Council, the overwhelming majority of the Council Fathers who have courageously expressed their desire to eradicate sources of tensions between Catholics and Jews, will have an opportunity to vote on a statement which will express this sacred aspiration."

In light of the hostile forces that were bringing mounting pressure to subvert the declaration, the AJC felt it was important for Rabbi Heschel to meet with Pope Paul VI. An audience was arranged literally on the eve of Yom Kippur. Rabbi Heschel felt it was an act of *kiddush hashem* to go despite great personal inconvenience.

On September 14, Rabbi Heschel had an audience with the

pope that lasted some thirty-five minutes. Rabbi Heschel informed me that the following took place: he gave the pope a clear exposition of the four disputed points in the proposed declaration, but concentrated on the passage on conversion. The pope said that he considered the present document friendly to the Jews. He claimed it is primarily a religious document and cannot be ruled by people from the outside. He said the passage on conversion is based on the scriptures of the New Testament. It is what the church itself has expressed, and the Jews are not obliged to accept. The deicide statement is also based on the scriptures of the New Testament.

The pope added that many people within the church believe that the declaration is too favorable to the Jews. If there is too much pressure brought to bear, they may take the declaration off the agenda. Heschel said that the pope was very friendly and cordial and concluded that it is up to the Council to decide the matter. Dr. Heschel left an extensive theological memorandum with the pope that he promised to submit to Cardinal Bea's Commission. In that extraordinary 18-page document, Dr. Heschel wrote:

> Why is so much attention paid to what Vatican II is going to say about the Jews? Are we Jews in need of recognition? God himself has recognized us as a people. Are we in need of a "Chapter" acknowledging our right to exist as Jews? Nearly every chapter in the Bible expresses the promise of God's fidelity to His Covenant with our people. It is not gratitude that we ask for: it is the cure of a disease affecting so many minds that we pray for.

When the third session of the Council opened on September 16, 1964, it was evident that prelates supporting a stronger statement on the Jews would fight to get it on the floor of the Council. The liberals moved rapidly, denouncing the changes in the draft made, they said, without the approval of Cardinal Bea's secretariat. On September 17, 170 of the 240 bishops from the United States met in urgent conference and publicly called for a return to the sense of the original document.

The draft was introduced to the Council Fathers by Cardinal Bea on September 28 and was finally debated on September 28–29. Altogether no fewer than thirty-four Council members from twenty-two countries arose to speak. Only a small handful defended the weakened draft or objected to any Jewish declaration whatever. An overwhelming majority asked that the text be strengthened. At the end of the first day's debate, a *peritus* (theological expert) to the Council told the AJC with deep emotion in response to the near-unanimity and determination that was shown, "This was the Council's greatest day, and a great day for the church. On no issue have the fathers been so united; on none have they spoken so forthrightly."

In the wake of that historic debate—what I have called the greatest seminar in Catholic-Jewish relations—a final text was redrafted. Unlike earlier versions, it encompassed all the great non-Christian religions, but the passages concerning Jews and Judaism closely resembled what Cardinal Bea had proposed in the first place. Clearly and forcefully, the deicide accusation against Jews past and present was rejected; teachers and preachers were enjoined to spurn ideas that might foster hostility against Jews; increased mutual knowledge and respect among Christians and Jews were recommended; hatred and persecution of Jews, in former days and in our own, were condemned. Hope was voiced for mankind's ultimate religious unity but the time of such union was said to be "known to God alone." Nothing suggestive of proselytizing in the here and now was said; the permanence of Judaism was in effect acknowledged on the statement, that "even though a large part of the Jews did not accept the Gospel, they remain most dear to God."

On November 20, the last day of the Council's session, the text dealing with the Jews came up for a vote. It was ringingly approved by a vote of 1,770 to 185; the declaration as a whole on non-Christians was accepted by a similarly large majority. The Council's fourth session opened on September 14, 1965. Maneuverings and pressures continued throughout 1965 down through the opening days of the final session.[5]

On September 30, the Secretariat for Promoting Christian Unity distributed copies of the new statement on the Jews to the bishops and released it officially to the press. The text repudiated

---

[5] An excellent and authoritative account can be found in two articles on "The Church and the Jews: The Struggle At Vatican Council II," by my associate, Judith Hershcopf (now Banki) in the American Jewish Year Book, 1965 and 1966.

the idea of Jewish collective guilt for the death of Jesus: "What happened to Christ in His Passion cannot be attributed to all Jews, without distinction, then alive, nor to the Jews of today." Rather, it stressed, "Christ underwent His Passion and death freely, because of the sins of men and out of infinite love." The Jews, it was stressed, should not be presented as accursed or rejected by God. According to the document, "the church acknowledges that . . . the beginnings of her faith are already found among the Patriarchs, Moses, and the Prophets," and "recalls that Christ, the Virgin Mary, the Apostles, as well as most of the early Disciples sprang from the Jewish people." The declaration recommended theological studies and fraternal dialogues to foster mutual knowledge and respect between the two faiths. Finally, anti-Semitism was rejected explicitly, a step never before taken in any Conciliar document: "The church . . . moved not by political reasons but by the Gospel's spiritual love, deplores hatred, persecutions, displays of anti-Semitism directed against Jews at any time or by anyone."

At the same time, the new text contained negative elements that were disturbing to many. The term "deicide" no longer appeared. Moreover, the repudiation of the charge of the Jews' collective guilt for the death of Jesus was now prefaced with the qualification that "the Jewish authorities and those who followed their lead pressed for the death of Christ." A clause emphasizing that "Jerusalem did not recognize the time of her visitation" also was added. Where the earlier text had said the church "deplores, indeed condemns" hatred of the Jews, the new draft retained only the term "deplores." Again, where the older version, in denying that the Jews were a cursed people, had flatly forbidden any teaching "that could give rise to hatred or contempt for Jews in the hearts of Christians," the new text stated less emphatically that "the Jews should not be presented as rejected by God or accursed, as if this follows from Holy Scriptures," adding an injunction to teach nothing "inconsistent with the truth of the Gospel and with the spirit of Christ."

At a bishops' press conference, the American theological experts held that the new text was preferable to the old. Nevertheless, newspaper stories from Rome predicted heated debate over the new wording both at the Council sessions and behind the scenes.

The new version of the Jewish declaration evoked mixed feelings among many Jews and Christians alike. Together with satisfaction that the declaration had survived, there were regrets over the departures from the more vigorous 1964 version and misgivings about the new note of ambivalence. The American Jewish Committee's initial response was one of gratification tempered with disappointment. While acknowledging the "sharp and explicit condemnation of anti-Semitism" in the new draft, and its stress on "the common bonds between Jews and Christians," the AJC nevertheless noted that the older text had been more decisive and satisfactory.

On October 14, the declaration came before the Council for a vote. In a written summary and an address to the Council Fathers, Cardinal Bea called for adoption of the text as released and defended the revisions that had been made. The pressure for these changes, he explained, had come both from bishops in Arab Lands, who argued that Muslim states considered the earlier wording politically favorable to Israel, and from conservative theologians, who insisted that the exoneration of the Jews be qualified by Scriptural references to the role of Jewish leadership in the death of Jesus. The term "deicide" had been eliminated, the Cardinal stressed, because it had caused "difficulties and controversies," but the essential injunction to Catholics against the teaching of anything "inconsistent with the truth of the Gospel" remained intact. The word "condemned" in reference to anti-Semitism had been dropped, he added, because it was felt that this term should be reserved for heresies. (Observers pointed out, however, that as long ago as 1928, a Holy Office document had "condemned" anti-Semitism.)

The same afternoon, the Council Fathers voted, 1,875 to 188, in favor of the clause stating that responsibility for Jesus's death could not be attributed collectively to all Jews. The omission of the word "deicide" in this context was approved 1,821 to 245; the passage deploring anti-Semitism was accepted, 1,905 to 199. The entire schema on non-Christian religions was approved 1,763 to 250.

The American Jewish Committee characterized the Council's

vote as "an act of justice long overdue," but expressed keen regret over some of its assertions on the ground that they might "give rise to misunderstandings." The President of the Committee stated the hope that the declaration—especially its repudiation of the "invidious" charge of the collective guilt of the Jews for the death of Jesus and its rejection of anti-Semitism—would afford "new opportunities for improved interreligious understanding and cooperation throughout the world."

The ultimate significance of the step just taken, he went on, would depend on "the manner and vigor with which the affirmative principles embodied in this declaration will be carried out." In that connection, he said that the American Jewish Committee had been heartened to learn of the recent creation of a special Commission on Catholic-Jewish Relations by the American hierarchy.

The final text came to a public vote on October 28, 1965—a date chosen by Pope Paul VI because it was the anniversary of the late Pope John XXIII's election to the papacy. The vote was 2,221 in favor, 88 opposed, and 3 void. Immediately afterward, Pope Paul promulgated the declaration as the official teaching of the Church.

If the declaration falls short of its supporters' highest hopes, it nevertheless signals an historic turning point. For the first time in the history of the twenty-one Ecumenical Councils, the highest ecclesiastical authorities have committed the Catholic Church throughout the world to uprooting the charge of collective guilt against the Jews, eliminating anti-Semitism, and fostering mutual knowledge and respect between Catholics and Jews. Obviously, such deepened understanding will not spring up quickly or spontaneously. The antagonisms of centuries will not be swept away overnight. For people of goodwill on both sides, decades of massive work lie ahead.

Rabbi Heschel joined with the AJC in participating from the very beginning in this Catholic-Jewish encounter, the most significant of our time. He gave of himself freely, abundantly, even sacrificially. Whatever progress is made in growing mutual respect between Christians and Jews in generations to come will be immeasurably indebted to my beloved mentor, friend, and inspiration, Rabbi Abraham Joshua Heschel, *zecher tzaddik l'vrachah.*

27

The Concept of the Human Being in Jewish Thought: Some Ethical Implications

Moral and Ethical Values and Ideals in Judaism

Neither the Bible nor Rabbinic Judaism has a word for ethics. A small volume in the Mishnah, often referred to as the "Ethics of the Fathers" because it contains much ethical instruction, is titled in Hebrew merely "The Chapters of the Fathers." Ethics is not conceived apart from religion, so that it is included in whatever expression the Bible and the Talmud use for religion. Ethics is part and parcel of "the way of life" of Judaism. This conception is reflected in the following representative Rabbinic statements:

> The beginning and the end of Torah is the performance of loving kindness.
> Deeds of kindness weigh as much as all the commandments (*Sotah* 14a).
> When one's deeds are greater than one's knowledge, knowledge is effective, but when one's knowledge is greater than one's deed, then knowledge is futile (*Ethics of the Fathers* 3:14).

That Jewish "way of life" has its origins in the experience of the divine presence in the midst of the decisive events of the Exodus and of Sinai, events that have altered the entire course of human history. The children of Israel experienced the reality of the Lord of history through His involvement in their liberation from physical oppression, persecution, massacre, and injustices as "slaves unto Pharaoh in Egypt." To Pharaoh, who was worshiped as a divine emperor and who was the source of law, never its servant,

Reprinted from Marc H. Tanenbaum, Marvin Wilson, and A. James Rudin, eds., *Evangelicals and Jews in an Age of Pluralism* (Grand Rapids, MI: Baker Book House, 1984).

the Israelite slaves were regarded as chattel, "the untouchables" of ancient Egypt.

At Sinai, the Israelites had a transforming experience of divine revelation as moral will which was ratified by an everlasting covenant. Henceforth, the Israelites are perceived by God to be "a kingdom of priests and a holy nation." What an extraordinary divine-human scenario! Yesterday they were slaves, the outcasts of history. Now an entire people is stamped with the dignity of priesthood and holiness and are set on the course of history with a messianic task of redemption in society and through history until the coming of the kingdom.

Israel's religion, Professor David Flusser asserts, was a breakthrough in human consciousness. The God of Israel initiated a new era in the history of mankind, introducing a new concept of justice—which is the central message of His revelation—an uncompromising moral law, and an original social order to be established paradigmatically in the Holy Land of Palestine. This postulate of individual and social justice was not to be limited to Israel only. The Creator of the universe postulates this justice for all his human creatures; it is incumbent on all the peoples of the world.

The concept of justice that emerges from the Hebrew Bible is not just the regimen of mighty men. The Bible does not identify God on the side of Pharaoh and his imperium! It stresses that God cares for the poor and unprotected, for the orphan, the widow, and the stranger. The basis of social justice is not to be external power and might, but the reverence of God and obedience to his moral will.

THE SACREDNESS OF HUMAN LIFE

To understand the idea of justice in Israel, we must bear in mind the biblical teaching that the human being is created in the image of God, that each human life is sacred and of infinite worth. In consequence, a human being cannot be treated as chattel or an object to be disposed of for someone's program or project or ideology, but must be treated as a personality. Every human being possesses the right to life, dignity, and honor, and the fruits of his or her labor.

Justice is respect for the personality of others and their inalienable rights, even as injustice is the most flagrant manifestation of disrespect for the personality of others. Judaism requires that human personality be respected in every human being—in the female prisoner of war, in the delinquent, even in the criminal condemned to death. The supreme importance of the human being in the economy of the universe is expressed in this Rabbinic teaching: "Man (the human being) was first created as a single individual to teach the lesson that whoever destroys one life, Scripture ascribes it to him as though he had destroyed a whole world; and whoever saves one life, Scripture ascribes it to him as though he had saved a whole world" (*Sanhedrin* 4:5).

However, justice is more than mere abstention from injuring our fellow human beings. "The work of justice is peace, and the effect thereof quietness and confidence forever" (Isa. 32:17). It is a positive conception and includes economic well-being, intellectual and spiritual growth, philanthropy, and every endeavor that will enable human beings to realize the highest and best in their natures.

The conditions for that self-realization require active efforts to bring about the final disappearance of injustice and oppression, which, as represented in the Jewish high holiday liturgy, is the goal of human history. "And may all wickedness be consumed as a flame and may evil rule be removed from the earth," declare the *Rosh Hashanah* prayers.

Moral Duties of *Tzedakah*

Nothing is more fundamental in biblical and Rabbinic ethics than the moral obligation of *tzedakah,* a Hebrew term which means both "charity" and "to do justice." The Rabbinic sages of the Talmud declared that "Almsgiving, i.e., aiding the poor and feeding the hungry, weighs as heavily as all the other commandments of the Torah" (Talmud *Baba Batra* 9a).

In proclaiming the Jubilee year, which like the Ten Commandments was ascribed to divinely inspired legislation revealed on

Mount Sinai, the Bible ordained, "be kind if your brother waxes poor, and his means fail with you, then you shall uphold him; as a stranger and a settler shall he live with you" (Lev. 25:35). The rabbis observe that the expression, "your brother may live with you," means that it is our personal and communal duty to see to it that our fellow human beings do not die of starvation. Though the person be a stranger or an alien settler, he (or she) is to be included in the term your brother and is to be treated in a brotherly and compassionate manner.

To underscore the supreme virtue of humanitarian aid to the needy in the hierarchy of Jewish moral and spiritual values, the Rabbinic sages regarded such compassionate care of man as an act worthy of association with divinity itself: "God says to Israel, 'My sons whenever you give sustenance to the poor, I impute it to you as though you gave sustenance to me,' for it says, 'Command the children of Israel . . . my bread for my sacrifices . . . shall ye observe unto me.' Does, then, God eat and drink? No, but whenever you give food to the poor, God accounts it to you as if you gave food to Him" (*Numbers Rabbah* 28:2).

The virtue of such care for the poor and hungry is depicted in Jewish tradition as the salient attribute of the founding father of Judaism, the patriarch Abraham, who is called the archetype of the "Pharisee of love." In a Midrashic commentary that begins with the phrases, "Let your house be open; let the poor be members of your household. Let a man's house be open to the north and to the south, and to the east and to the west," the rabbis describe the humanitarianism of Abraham: "He went out and wandered about, and when he found wayfarers, he brought them to his house, and he gave wheaten bread to him whose wont it was not to eat wheaten bread, and so with meat and wine. And not only this, but he built large inns on the roads, and put food and drink within them, and all came and ate and drank and blessed God. Therefore, quiet of spirit was granted to him, and all that the mouth of man can ask for was found in his house" (*Abot de Rabbi Nathan* 7:17a, b). Elsewhere the Talmud admonishes, "He who has no pity upon his fellow creatures is assuredly not of the seed of Abraham our father" (*Bezah* 32b).

In Jewish communities from biblical times through the present, there was much free and generous giving of alms to all who asked.

Even to deceivers! There was also much systematic and careful relief through established institutions. Each Jewish community had a *tamhui* (public kitchen) from which the poor received two meals daily. There was also the *kupah* (alms box) for the disbursement of benevolent funds on Sabbath eve to provide three meals for the Sabbath (*Mishnah Peach* 8, 7). Additional care was exercised in respect to the itinerant poor who were provided with a loaf of bread which sufficed for two meals, and who were also entitled to the cost of lodging.

The biblical laws of charity in Palestine relating to "gleaning," the "forgotten sheaf," and "the comer of the field," implied the underlying idea that national territory belongs to the public as a whole. In accordance with Jewish law, landowners used to lay open fences surrounding their fields and vineyards, and during certain hours of the day the needy were allowed to eat from the produce of the harvest. There was also a three-yearly allocation of *Maaser Ani* (poor man's tithe) from the threshing floor. Thus, there arose the charitable traditions and institutions of the Jewish people which have remained a religious-communal characteristic ever since. These customs of charity, which were foreign to the pagan frame of mind of the Greeks and Romans, also had an abiding impact on the nature of the Christian *caritas*.

Peace and War

And finally, the stability, as well as the happiness of a community, can be assured only when it rests on a foundation of peace. In the absence of peace there can be neither prosperity nor well-being. "Peace is equal in worth to everything," declare the rabbis *(Sirra)*. And they add, "Beloved is peace since the benedictions conclude with the hope of peace," thus teaching that the blessings even of the high priest are of no avail unless accompanied by peace (*Numbers Rabbah* 11:7).

While the prophets of Israel and the rabbis believed that God intended the nations to be at peace with one another, war was not prohibited. Jewish ethics would admit the duty to defend the higher values in human life by war if necessary. If Isaiah or Jeremiah had thought that yielding to the foreign invader would mean destruction to the religion or the people they valued, they would have urged resistance with the same vigor that they demanded constantly the practice of righteousness in obedience to God's will. All the facts of biblical and post-biblical Judaism taken together lead to the conclusion that the ethical judgment on war, according to Judaism, is that it must be eradicated to make human life conform to the divine rule, that those guilty of causing it commit a crime against humanity and a sin against God. However, resistance is justified to defend the higher values in human life. The justification would extend to a nation's defense of its liberty. The spiritual values in the life of a nation, which include its historic distinctiveness, may justify defense when that nation is attacked and must engage in war to save its independent existence. (See Dr. Israel Mattuck in his study, *Jewish Ethics* [New York: Hutchinson, 1953], particularly his chapter on "The Judgment on War.")

SOME IMPLICATIONS OF MORAL VALUES FOR THE CURRENT HUMAN CONDITION

The deep concern for upholding and preserving the preciousness of human life and for building a just and peaceful world community has at no time in human history been more seriously threatened, in my judgment, than by the spread of violence and terrorism throughout the world, accompanied by the staggering increase in the international trade in arms and the insane proliferation of nuclear weapons.

The first volume of a comprehensive work on psychoanalytic theory written by the late Dr. Erich Fromm is titled, *The Anatomy of Human Destructiveness* (New York: Holt, Rinehart, and Winston, 1973). Dr. Fromm explains that he started with the study of aggression and destructiveness because, aside from being one of the fundamental theoretic problems in psychoanalysis, "the wave of destruction engulfing the world makes it also one of the most practically relevant ones." Noting that the preoccupation of professionals and the general public alike with the nature and causes of aggression is rather recent, dating in fact only to the middle of the 1960s, Dr. Fromm asserts that "one probable reason for this change was the fact that the level of violence and the fear of war had passed a certain threshold throughout the world."

As noted in a 1973 study of "Violence, Non-Violence and Struggle for Social Justice," prepared for the World Council of Churches, "violence today has become demonic in its hold on human life. In the life of some nations and among many severely oppressed peoples, it seems more like an addiction than like rational behavior."

Amnesty International, reporting on its worldwide study of the use of torture by individuals and governments, came to the conclusion that "torture can exist in any society," and indeed "the practice of torture is becoming internationalized." Although there are some exceptions, torture has been standard administrative practice in more than thirty countries and has occurred in more than sixty. From the perspective of an economic historian in post-Vietnam, post-Watergate America, Robert L. Heilbroner, author of the book *An Inquiry Into the Human Prospect* (New York: W. W. Norton, 1974), writes pessimistically of the "malaise of civilization." He states:

> There is a feeling that great troubles and changes loom for the future of civilization as we know it. Our age is one of profound turmoil, a time of deep change, and there is a widespread feeling that the world is coming apart at the seams. . . . We have gone through "a drubbing of history," and a barrage of confidence-shaking events have filled us with a sense of unease and foreboding during the past decade or so. No doubt foremost among these has been the experience of the Vietnam War, an experience that has undermined every aspect of American life—our belief in our own invincible power, our trust in government, our estimate of our private level of morality. But the Vietnam War was only one among many such confidence-shaking events. The explosion of violence in street crime, race riots, bombings, bizarre airplane hijackings, shocking assassinations have made a mockery of the TV image of middle class American gentility and brought home with terrible impact the recognition of a barbarism hidden behind the superficial amenities of life. . . . We switch on the evening TV and learn what's going to hit us next on the head—a hijacking, a murder, a rape, or some other daily terror. These things profoundly affect our outlook.

Social analysts report that ever since Hitler and the founding of the United Nations, more persons have been killed by massacre than by the traditional wars that have kept the world on edge. As Nathan Glazer has documented in his essay on "The Universalization of Ethnicity," (*Encounter,* February 1975), an epidemic of conflicts is taking place literally on every continent of the world in which race, religion, region, and nationality are involved, frequently resulting in practices of torture, mass aggression, and in some cases, near-genocide."

Among informed observers of the international scene, a mood of pessimism, even despair, has emerged over the human prospect in the face of these assaults against human life. This *kulturpessimisraus* is further compounded by a number of massive universal problems that show no signs of going away in the foreseeable future.

There is the enormous world refugee problem. A total of 12.6 million people were refugees from their homelands or displaced from their homes within their native countries ("internally displaced peoples") at the beginning of 1981. While the world's attention has been focused on the plight of southeast Asians—the Vietnamese boat people, the Cambodians, the ethnic Chinese, among others—the most tragic, "life-threatening" refugee problems today are to be found among the 6.3 million refugees and displaced persons on the African continent.

It should be here noted that the response of Catholic, Protestant, evangelical, and Jewish leaders and institutions to the Southeast Asian tragedy was one of the glorious chapters in the history of these religious bodies in this century. Since 1975, some 400,000 southeast Asians were resettled and rehabilitated in the United States alone, and 70 percent of these human beings were sponsored, resettled, and rehabilitated—restored to their human dignity—by groups such as Lutheran Relief Service, Catholic Relief Services, Church World Service, World Vision, and the American Jewish Joint Distribution Committee and the Hebrew Immigrant Aid Society.

These life-saving programs were a translation into human reality of the basic biblical affirmations of the dignity of human life and love of neighbor that is inspiring in itself. Equally important, however, is a paradigm for our future collaboration in seeking to humanize the conditions under which so many millions of fellow human beings are forced to exist, frequently through no fault of their own.

It should appropriately be acknowledged that Denmark, Norway, and Sweden are among the top contributors to the United Nations efforts to help refugees, when measured on a per capita basis. The United States accepted more refugees (677,000) than any other country but ranked fifth on a per capita basis. The United States also contributed more money than any other nation in refugee aid, but on a per capita basis, ranked twelfth in its financial contributions. Israel accepted one refugee for every thirty-seven residents, and Malaysia, Australia, and Canada also accepted more refugees per capita than the United States.

Asia and Oceania, 2 million
Africa, 6.3 million
Middle East, 3.5 million
Latin America, 240,000
Europe, 350,000

There is the world hunger and population problem, which is, of course, also part of the refugee complex of problems. Despite the recent heroic efforts to provide massive food supplies—in which Christian and Jewish institutions also played a leading role—some eight hundred million people in Asia, Africa, and Latin America continue to starve or suffer from severe malnutrition. It is estimated that in the developing countries several million people will die from hunger during the coming year.

The world's present economic condition, Robert L. Heilbroner writes, resembles an immense train, in which a few passengers, mainly in the advanced capitalist countries, ride in first-class coaches in conditions of comfort unimaginable to the enormously greater numbers crammed into cattle cars that make up the bulk of the train's carriages.

For Western civilization, with its liberal, humanitarian ideals, and for people with our unambiguous Jewish and Christian ethical heritages to temporize in the face of the greatest moral challenge in the last decades of the twentieth century is to risk the betrayal of everything morally meaningful that we profess to stand for. What is at stake in the way we respond during the coming months and years to this unparalleled world famine is our capacity to arrest the cycle of dehumanization and callousness to suffering that is abroad in the world, ultimately affecting all peoples. We need to set into motion forces of caring and compassion that are the singular qualities without which an emergent interdependent, and peaceful, world cannot be sustained.

The Christian and Jewish communities, I believe, in concert with other cultural forces in our societies, can make a distinctive contribution, namely, the definition and articulation of a new "Ethic of Scarcity" for peoples in our Western (and other) societies. The Western nations, in particular, have been blessed since their founding with what appears to be almost limitless natural resources and raw materials. We seem to have been living in a set of unexamined assumptions that constitute an "Ethic of Abundance" which has rationalized and justified endless consumption, self-indulgence, and permissive hedonism. The waste at our business and social functions—conferences, conventions, weddings, confirmations, bar mitzvahs, even funeral wakes—has verged on the scandalous, especially when seen against the background of the needs of the world's starving masses. We have in fact entered a new experience of growing scarcity of resources and energy supplies; and our nations require a definition of values and human priorities that will result in greater self-discipline, restraint, and a genuine motivation to share out of a more limited supply of the earth's goods.

There is the arms race and the nuclear weapons proliferation. Poor nations can be expected to obtain nuclear weapons as a by-product of the atomic power plants that many of them are now building or contemplating, and it is quite conceivable that some may use these as instruments of blackmail to force the developed world to undertake a massive transfer of wealth to the poverty-stricken world.

Five arms control experts, writing in the *Harvard* magazine of November 1975, predict that some nuclear wars are likely to occur before this century's end as a direct result of bombs spreading around the world like an "epidemic disease." The proliferation of "peaceful" nuclear power only aggravates the danger because as MIT political scientist George Rathjens (formerly of the U.S. Arms Control and Disarmament Agency) writes, "By the end of the century there will be several thousand reactors around the world, each producing enough material to build a weapon a week."

The peril is compounded by the knowledge disclosed by Dr. Theodore Taylor in his study, "Nuclear Theft," that an atomic weapon would not be impossible for a guerilla group to construct with just over thirteen pounds of plutonium. It is believed that more than four thousand pounds of plutonium were shipped in the United States last year and nobody knows exactly how much of that material was lost in transit or production.

I fully appreciate, and support in many ways, the argument made by Dr. Paul Nitze that "the United States take positive steps to maintain strategic stability and high-quality deterrence" to assure that the Soviet Union or some other enemy does not believe they could profit from seeking a nuclear-war-winning capability or effectively use pressure tactics to get their way in a crisis situation (*Foreign Affairs*, January 1976). Nor am I unmindful of the need and possibilities of controlling the defense budget through judicious pruning of waste (Barry M. Blechman and Edward R. Fried, "Controlling the Defense Budget," *Foreign Affairs*, January 1976).

Given the absolutely catastrophic nature of nuclear war, we must ask whether or not our government and its allies have done enough to restrict their sales of nuclear reactors to unstable countries and to countries of uncertain persuasion. The late Senator Hubert Humphrey introduced a bill calling for Congress to share systematically in shaping policies guiding arms exports. We sincerely trust that Congress will help America finally to develop a rational approach to arms sales as well as to the intensification of universal disarmament measures. The very survival of the human family depends on such measures taken vigorously here and in concert with other nations.

SOME IMPLICATIONS FOR CHRISTIANS AND JEWS

What are the implications of these facts for Christians and Jews today? It is evident that we live in an age of violence and terror. There is not a continent on the globe that is not despoiled by terror and violence, by barbarism, by a growing callousness to human suffering and pain, and by threat to human existence. At the center of the human crisis is the fundamental depreciation of the meaning and value of human life. The biblical affirmation that each human being is created in the sacred image of God and is therefore of ultimate worth and preciousness is being battered from every side.

It is my conviction that this erosion in the belief in the sanctity of human life is one of the decisive black legacies bequeathed by Nazi Germany to mankind. The overwhelming majority of citizens of the Western world, and their dominant institutions have avoided confronting the magnitude of evil incarnate in the Nazi Holocaust, and have therefore failed to learn how to cope with forces and structures of dehumanization that are being replicated in many parts of the globe.

The Nazi campaign against the Jewish people was unique and in many ways unprecedented. Yet the Nazi trauma must not be seen as "a Jewish obsession," for the fateful meaning of the Holocaust is of ultimate importance to the future capacity of mankind to understand itself and to acquire the resources to cope with the challenges to its survival.

Bleak as are the prospects for countering these forces of dehumanization in the world, "we need not complete the task," as Rabbi Tarphon admonished, "but neither are we free to desist therefrom." In concert, if we are to learn from the Nazi Holocaust and not be doomed to allow its repetition, we must attempt at the very least the following. First, Christians and Jews should engage in a massive, concerted effort to establish a "new humanism" on a global basis. They should seek to restore the biblical value of the infinite worth of each human life, life that must be appreciated as an end in itself and never as an object of somebody else's project, program, ideology, or revolution. Second, Christians and Jews must help engender a national and international attitude of scorn and contempt for those who use violence or who advocate the use of violence. We must work to deromanticize all appeals to use violence and terrorism as a means of liberation or of institutionalized oppression, since from a moral standpoint no ends can justify such antihuman means. Third, Christians and Jews must work to curtail inflammatory propaganda, especially from international forums that have psychological impact on an international scale. As Professor Gordon Allport of Harvard University demonstrated in his monumental study, *The Nature of Prejudice* (Cambridge, MA: Addison-Wesley Pub. Co., 1954), there is an inevitable progression from "verbal aggression to violence, from rumor to riot, from gossip to genocide." Fourth, Christians and Jews must work toward educational development and communication among peoples to reduce the abrasive effects of "differences." Differences, as we have learned in the pluralistic experiences of the Western world, can be a source of enrichment rather than a threat. Fifth, Christians and Jews should engage in an urgent educational effort to elaborate a theology and ideology of pluralism which presupposes the right of each religious, racial, and ethnic group to define itself in its own terms and to be accepted unconditionally. Group narcissism, as Dr. Erich Fromm observes, arouses intense hostility between groups, and "is one of the most important sources of human aggression." In helping establish a pluralist worldview, Christians and Jews have a decisive contribution to make to the building of the ideological foundations without which a stable world community cannot come into being. Sixth, Christians and Jews should work toward making the economy of each nation as self-sufficient and stable as possible, not perpetually requiring relief support. Inextricably linked with such an effort is the control of the arms race on an international scale, and a rational reordering of priorities that allows for adequate defense and yet at the same time reallocates some of the billions wasted on arms for the crying needs of the hungry, the diseased, and the homeless.

Central in such efforts is the need to raise international human consciousness to halt the irrational proliferation of nuclear weaponry and to bring about serious action for universal simultaneous disarmament. There is no higher priority for human survival at this moment in human history. Christians and Jews need to recognize the fundamental interdependence of all human rights and collaborate vigorously to assure that every nation implements fully the Universal Declaration on Human Rights. In particular, Christians and Jews should work for the completion of the judicial instrumentalities called for by Article 6 of the Genocide Convention in the form of an international penal tribunal for trying those who are accused of genocide attempts anywhere in the world. "The salvation of mankind," Alexander Solzhenitzyn reminds us, "will depend on everyone becoming concerned about the welfare of everybody everywhere."

28

On Black-Jewish Relations

PRESIDENT KENNEY, Rev. Jackson, Dr. Hevesi, Dr. Schwarcz, friends: Let me say at the outset that one of the most practical projects in Black-Jewish relations that Jesse Jackson and I could do would be to organize a Black-Jewish collection plate for an audience like this. I don't know about Jesse's experience in Baptist churches, where I have spent a good deal of time with many Baptist friends, but it began to look like Yom Kippur in a Baptist service tonight.

I want to pay tribute here to the respect for scholarship, especially biblical scholarship, that is implicit in the way in which this evening has been organized. There was a wonderful story told during the Second Vatican Council, at which I was honored to be present, while the Catholic Church was facing up for the first time in some 1,900 years to what has been its relationship to the Jewish people. Admirably, the church leaders faced what had to be faced, repented of what had to be repented, changed what had to be changed. During the course of the Council someone told me a story about the late blessed Pope John XXIII. It was his inspiration to summon the Second Vatican Council, which literally changed the course of the Catholic Church. Before he was elevated to the papacy, Archbishop Roncalli served as an Apostolic Delegate to the Balkans, in Istanbul. And then after that, he served as Apostolic Delegate to the French government, representing the pope in France. Monsignor Roncalli, as he was then called, developed a very warm and intimate friendship with the Chief Rabbi of France, Rabbi Jacob Kaplan. According to this account, Monsignor Roncalli and Chief Rabbi Kaplan had been invited by the President of France to a banquet. They came together into a large reception hall, and they were chatting, making small talk, exchanging pleasantries. Then someone rang the gong for

Address, with Rev. Jesse Jackson, Queens College, New York, March 11, 1987.

the banquet, for them to walk through the reception hall into the main dining hall. And, as this story has it, when the Chief Rabbi came to the door, before entering into the banquet, he turned to Monsignor Roncalli and said, "Your Excellency, after you. You first." Monsignor Roncalli, who was very fond of the Rabbi, turned to him and said, "No, Your Excellency, Chief Rabbi, you first." And this went on for perhaps five minutes, back and forth, a diplomatic Alfonse and Gaston routine. Meanwhile, people were piling up behind them, waiting to go through the door. Finally, Pope John—then Monsignor Roncalli—in his characteristic Italian, earthy, peasant way, grabbed hold of the arm of Chief Rabbi Kaplan, exclaiming, "No, Chief Rabbi, the Old Testament before the New Testament," and shoved him into the banquet hall. Well normally I would appear after Jesse Jackson, after he has, in his powerful, charismatic, mesmerizing way, taken over an audience, and I would feel like a *shlemiel* after that, trying somehow to take hold of what was left over of the audience. But I guess this is an act of pure academic scholarship, the Old Testament, the Hebrew Scriptures, before the New Testament.

The invitation to speak here was extended to me by the Honorable Alan Hevesi, Assistant Majority Leader of the New York State Assembly, and Professor of Political Science at Queens College. He noted in introducing me that we share wonderful memories of association with his late blessed father, who served the American Jewish Committee with distinction. The invitation from him and from Professor Ernest Schwarcz, Dean of Jewish Studies at the College, is deeply appreciated. Their establishment and support of the Queens Black-Jewish People-to-People Project is both a symbol and a substantive contribution to a vital, compelling goal that hopefully all of us here tonight share: the overcoming of misunderstanding and the advancement of knowledge, mutual respect, and cooperation between the Black and Jewish people and their communities, in the context of a profound common concern for the welfare of our beloved American democratic republic. Let me be clear at the outset about my mandate as I see it this evening. I speak here as an individual, only for myself, exercising my democratic right of free speech. While I believe that I may express the feelings and views of many in the Jewish community, what I am about to say does not represent the official positions of the American Jewish Committee, and certainly not those of the American Jewish community, which is characterized by diversity and a plurality of views, as is true of every other religious, racial or ethnic group in our democratic society.

Why are we here this evening? Why is there such an impressive turnout of people from this community coming together tonight at Queens College? This is not an easy evening, either for the Reverend Jesse Jackson or for myself. If the bigots and extremists in our society had their way, this evening would not have taken place. The fact that Jesse Jackson and I made our own separate decisions to share this platform in the face of threats, slanders, and intimidations is a statement of our determination to reject hatred, bigotry, and verbal violence from whatever quarter it is issued. We do not and we will not ignore the troublesome and disturbing episodes in Black-Jewish relations in the recent past. What our purpose is tonight, as I see it, is to try to find a better way, a more constructive way, for Blacks and Jews to live and work together, as they have done—we must not forget—for much of their history during the past twenty-five years. I asked, why are we here tonight? I want to try to answer that question out of my reflections and my experiences during the past quarter century or more.

In 1968, I became involved with Catholic and Protestant leaders in trying to relieve the suffering of the victims of the Nigerian-Biafran conflict. That exposure, day in and day out, to so much destruction of human lives, with tens of thousands of deaths of Muslims and Christians, and the incredible starvation of thousands of innocent children, transformed my life. While the Jewish agenda—the cause of Soviet Jews who suffer oppression still; the cause of Israel and of peace in the Middle East between Jews and Arabs; the Black Jews of Ethiopia, who still suffer incredible oppression and poverty among other Ethiopians—is constantly at the core of my consciousness, since that experience of 1968, I have been driven to dedicate much of my waking hours to the problem of world refugees, world hunger, and international human rights. There are some 12 million refugees in the world today, some six million of them in Africa, the largest refugee problem in the world, most of them living in desperate conditions. The searing fact is that most of these refugee tragedies to which I have been exposed, or have been involved, are the result of religious, racial, ethnic, and tribal conflicts. In the Sudan several years ago, nearly a million Black Christians and Animists were massacred by Arab Muslim tribes of the north. In Uganda, President Idi Amin and his tribesmen slaughtered some half million Black Christians, half of them Anglican, half of them Roman Catholic. In India, there are unending slaughters of Muslims, Hindus, and Sikhs; in Sri Lanka, Tamils and Sinhalese destroy each other—all in the name of God and nation. The Iran-Iraq war has resulted in the deaths of an estimated quarter million human beings, many of them children twelve to fourteen years of age, who are told that by their martyrdom they have assured themselves a certain ascent to Paradise. Lebanon, once the citadel of Arab Christendom; Lebanon, once to the Arab Christian world what Israel is to world Jewry; the model of pluralism in the Middle East as Lebanon has been, is now a daily abattoir. And who loses sleep over Ireland where, for more than decades, Protestants and Catholics have been destroying each other?

Religious, racial, and ethnic hatreds have become the engine of an epidemic of dehumanization in the world. Nowhere is that dehumanization more palpable and tragic than in South Africa. In October 1985, I went with an American Jewish Committee leadership mission to South Africa. We met with a great many representatives from every segment of that blighted society, Archbishop Desmond Tutu, Black union leaders, the leaders of the government, business, and the Jewish community. It is a nightmare, an abomination, to experience the chemistry of nationalist arrogance and religious bigotry. Two fundamental religious lies have dominated the vices of Western civilization, including that of South Africa, which is a Western country. Jews have suffered and have been destroyed by the 1,900-year-old religious lie of deicide, the absurd notion that the Jewish people collectively killed Christ, and therefore must endure unending punishment and exile. And some fundamentalist Christians even to this day preach the obscenity that the Nazi Holocaust was God's ultimate punishment of the Jews for having allegedly killed Christ. But apartheid is another such religious lie. In the Dutch Reform churches it has been taught for generations as gospel truth that the Black people have been cursed by God with the curse of Ham, the forebear of

Black people in the biblical story. Segregation and apartheid have thus been justified as doing God's will. I saw the demonic power of that religious lie as I watched from afar in Soweto. In 1985, dozens and dozens of young Afrikaans leaped out of their armored troop carriers, shooting Black youths at will. These young Afrikaans, fresh off the farms, their heads filled with their church lessons, have been raised in a culture of religious and racial hatred and bigotry that has been indulged without limit. Where were they to learn that the life of a Black child is as precious in the eyes of God as their own?

The late psychoanalyst, Dr. Erich Fromm, in his monumental last work, *The Anatomy of Human Destructiveness* (New York: Holt, Rinehart, and Winston, 1973), called such behavior "group narcissism." As in the dynamics of individual narcissism, a group attributes to itself all virtue and assigns to the "out" group all vice. Such a group becomes totally self-centered. It sees itself as naturally superior and sees the other as inferior, infidel, heretic, deserving of destruction. Dr. Fromm identified such group psychopathic behavior as being responsible for much of the group aggression, terrorism, and violence that pockmarks the world today. The cost in human lives that the human family is paying for such religious and racial hatred all over the world is staggering, beyond human comprehension. In a nuclear missile age, such psychopathology without control could conceivably, God forbid, trigger a nuclear holocaust.

Blacks and Jews, all Americans, need to acknowledge that America is different, has been different, is different. For the past 200 years our national and religious leaders have struggled mightily to establish an open, democratic, pluralist society. The true genius of America rests not on sending our automobiles and Coca-Cola around the world. The true genius of America rests in the reality that each religious, racial, and ethnic group comes to the common American table by right, as first-class citizens, and not by sufferance. Each group—religious, racial, ethnic—has its own agenda, appropriately; its own needs and priorities; and has a right to receive a fair and sympathetic hearing; has a share at the American table. While advocating our own agenda, at the same time, each of us has a simultaneous, a collateral and overarching obligation to serve the common welfare. American democracy is founded on a social compact that is a very fragile instrument. Watergate and Iran-gate have taught us how fragile that compact can become. That compact needs to be continuously nurtured by an intense commitment to civility and mutual respect. That does not prevent nor preclude constructive criticism of each other's positions, or holding different views. By indulging religious or racial bigotry, reckless and uninhibited racial epithets, or anti-Semitic defamations, we can beat this precious, fragile social compact into the ground, into dust. My friends, America is the only nation on earth that has not been despoiled by religious wars. We have not had a thirty-year war; we have not had one hundred-year wars of a religious character, as one finds all over the European landscape. We have had far too much of racism and anti-Semitism, of lynching and verbal violence, and let me tell you that the canard, the obscenity, that Zionism is racism is just such an expression of defamation and verbal violence.

At their height, and at their most productive, Black-Jewish relations in the 1960s and 1970s were a paradigm of democratic pluralism at its best. The essential reason for that extraordinary, indeed historic, cooperation was once formulated by our colleague, Albert Vorspan, who, in an op-ed piece in *The New York Times,* recalled how, in 1964, the late Doctor Martin Luther King Jr. was challenging, together with Jesse Jackson and Andrew Young and many others, racial discrimination in public accommodations. In Saint Augustine, Florida, where there was a fierce resistance from the sheriff and the police, as well as from the White Citizens' Council and the Ku Klux Klan, Martin Luther King sent a telegram to the Central Conference of American Rabbis—the association of Reform rabbis in the U.S.—then meeting in Atlantic City, appealing for their help. Within hours, that very day, sixteen rabbis came to Saint Augustine where they joined Dr. King and his brothers and sisters. They entered the Black church and joined in common prayer and mutual solidarity and then went off to try to integrate a lunch counter in the face of incredible hatred, contempt, anti-Semitist, and racial obloquies. All of them—Martin Luther King and the crowd around him, as well as the sixteen rabbis—were forced by electric cattle prods into a cell in the prison of Saint Augustine. A number of them had their lives threatened. Why did these rabbis engage in acts of civil dis-

obedience? Why were they prepared to go to jail, almost spontaneously, at once? Vorspan wrote the following:

> The answer is simple: Martin Luther King Jr. No other person
> could have evoked such an instantaneous and uncritical response
> from us. With Dr. King there was implicit trust, a profound bond
> and a mutual respect, and a deep sense of solidarity with his mis-
> sion and that of his people. We respected him because he was intel-
> lectually keen, and a powerful orator.

His disciple, Rev. Jackson, is not too bad, either! And, Vorspan
adds:

> We loved him because he cherished the glory of racial and religious
> diversity. He despised Black separatism as both wrong and counter-
> productive. He saw the Civil Rights revolution not as a Black rebel-
> lion, but as a covenant of White and Black, Christian and Jew,
> standing together for decency. To Doctor King, justice was a seam-
> less web. Anti-Semitism and anti-Catholic prejudice, like racial big-
> otry, were anathema. His goal was not only justice for America's
> Blacks, but human rights for all peoples everywhere. . . . If, as I
> believe, Meir Kahane is essentially a problem Jews must face and
> resolve, so the Reverend Louis Farrakhan is a central challenge to
> the integrity and the future of the Black community.

Black-Jewish relations are bigger than Louis Farrakhan or Meir
Kahane, and we still have much in common to transcend our
demagogues and our frictions. As Dr. King never tired of pointing
out, Blacks and Jews have common enemies—not just in the
1960s. Read *The New York Times* this week, on what is happening
on sixteen major campuses in America; the racism that has begun
to erupt again against Black students on college campuses. Read
what is happening in the Farm Belt of America, where the Aryan
Brotherhood, the Christian Identity Movement, and the Posse Co-
mitatus, joining together with the Klan, are now trying to create
the canard that the decline of farms in America, the breakdown
of the family farm—one of the great tragedies of this country—is
due to one reason only: the Jewish conspiracy has set out to buy
out the farm land of America. It is the Jewish conspiracy that is
responsible for the crisis in the farm belt. Racists and anti-Semites
have not gone away. They are always beneath the surface.

We have a shared history of oppression that gives us a shared vision of a compassionate and open society. And, my friends, we need each other. I spoke today to our Washington representative, Hyman Bookbinder, about problems relating to South Africa. And he talked to me about the incredible closeness, the incredible cooperation between congressmen who are Blacks and Jews, and he said, "No two other groups in the United States Congress vote together as consistently for their respective agendas as do the Jewish and Black congressmen in the United States Congress."

And they are addressing a common agenda: protecting the poor, the increasing poverty, especially among the underclass, from the social cuts which have taken place during the last four years; working together on the problems of unemployment, on family life, on education, on fair housing; drugs, crime, violence; resisting together the violations of the separation of church and state, which continue to mount, from the radical right, week after week; together working for the security of the State of Israel, speaking out for Soviet Jews and others denied their human rights; opposing together apartheid in South Africa and racism at home. Despite the irritation of the conflicts that cloud Black-Jewish relations, even on such anguished issues as affirmative action, where there can be legitimate and constructive criticism, there is still a bond that links Jews and Blacks together. Dr. Martin Luther King Jr. forged a Black-Jewish bond in love, devotion, blood, and dreams. The greatest homage we Jews can pay to his memory, that superb religious leader as political activist, is to nurture and strengthen that bond which was and must remain a blessing for America and for the world. I can only hope and pray that this shared evening with Jesse Jackson, whom I've known for many years, will mark a turning away from the aberration and the deviation from Black-Jewish relations of the past, and will return us to the highway of justice, mutual respect, mutual support, and solidarity, for the sake of the Black and Jewish people of our nation and, above all, for the well-being of this great American democratic society which we love. Thank you.

29

Response on Receiving the "Interfaith Award" of the International Council of Christians and Jews

THIS WOULD BE a meaningful and moving moment in my life under normal circumstances. Given my recent hospitalization, this event—the receiving of the prestigious "Interfaith Award" of the International Council of Christians and Jews in the midst of your presence—assumes a very special, even a rare quality of grace.

I must confess that an element of its specialness derives from the fact that this is one of the few events in my life that I did not have to arrange myself. That adds to why I am so touched and grateful for today. Sir Sigmund Sternberg, one of the most distinguished leaders of British Jewry and a statesman of the Jewish people, and the International Council of Christians and Jews, perhaps the most representative body devoted to the improvement of relationships between Christians and Jews internationally, quite spontaneously informed me several months ago that I had been selected for this distinction in recognition of my more than twenty-five years of service in the advancement of Jewish-Christian understanding. That spontaneity lends the luster of authenticity to this tribute.

With your permission, I should like to take just a few moments to reflect on some of the meaning of this occasion and Award to me. It is most effectively synthesized for me in the writings of Dr. Ernest Becker, a brilliant but neglected cultural anthropologist. In his book, *The Denial of Death* (New York: Free Press, 1973), Dr. Becker states that human beings do not in fact fear death. What

Remarks delivered May 11,1988.

people fear is dying in insignificance. That is the real terror of death. He proposes that all of us—at least most of us—have a need to live our lives in a way that makes a difference, significant lives that give meaning to human existence. That is our immortality, Becker writes.

All of our art, literature, music, culture, even religion are ways of making a statement, leaving a landmark that we have not simply endured as animal life endures, but that we have lived lives of purpose and meaning. In short, Becker asserts, each of us has a powerful need to make a difference through our living, to help ennoble the human condition. That, he says, is true immortality.

As I have thought about my past twenty-seven years with the American Jewish Committee, I experience feelings of deepest gratitude for AJC's having made possible opportunities for living a life of such high meaning, enabling contributions to be made in many areas of importance to the Jewish people and to society-at-large—in some cases contributions, I trust, of lasting, even transforming value.

In retrospect, it is remarkable that AJC's lay leaders and professional leadership supported activities literally in every decade during which I have been associated with AJC that helped change the course of history for the better.

In the 1960s, AJC made possible the participation of my beloved colleague and mentor, Zachariah Shuster, and my precious teacher, Rabbi Abraham Joshua Heschel, both of blessed memory, and myself, in Vatican Council II. The Council was a transforming event, which has radically changed the course of 1,900 years of Catholic-Jewish relations, much of it now for the better. In the 1970s, we were able to pioneer with Dr. Billy Graham and the Southern Baptist Convention in opening a new world of Evangelical-Jewish relations which continues to this day.

In the late 1970s and early 1980s, AJC enabled my taking part in four separate International Rescue Committee missions to Southeast Asia that literally resulted in the saving of thousands of lives of Vietnamese boat people and Cambodians, and led to the resettlement of a half-million refugees in the United States. Earlier in the mid-1960s, we were able to engage in similar lifesaving roles in the Nigerian-Biafran conflict, and then in Ethiopia, and in the drought-ridden Sahelian zone of West Africa.

In the 1980s, we were able to make significant gains with major European countries—both West and East—particularly in West Germany through the excellent work of William Trosten and his predecessors, as well as in Latin America, led by Jacobo Kovadloff and Sergio Nudelstejer, that require further serious, responsible cultivation. And now in 1988, we are beginning to explore the possible importance to Jews and Israel of Japan and the Pacific Rim in light of their powerful geopolitical and economic presence in America and in the world.

While these were the dramatic and historic highlights, we conjured with those challenges while concentrating much of our energies on the priorities of Israel, Soviet Jewry, endangered Jewish communities in Ethiopia, Iran, Syria, Yemen, Central America, and elsewhere. We visited Oberammergau several times to bring about changes in their Passion Play. We implemented religious textbook studies, and we sought to combat teaching of contempt against Jews and Judaism in cooperation with friends such as Mme. Claire Huchet-Bishop, a great Christian lady who graces us with her presence.

I will never be able to thank adequately Dr. John Slawson and Bert Gold, who put up with my idiosyncrasies and *mishigas,* my specialized *shtiks,* but also gave me the freedom and support to do what I thought had to be done in our common interest. They instilled in me one crucial motto, which is the motto of AJC at its best: be effective, know the facts, and do it right.

Ted Ellenoff, Leo Nevas, our AJC officers, our eminent former presidents, our professional colleagues—for me especially those in interreligious affairs and international relations—our chapter leaders, our area directors—that is, the moral and human framework without which none of this history could have been made, decade after decade. And I am confident that under Ira Silverman's leadership as Executive Vice President that tradition of significant accomplishment will continue and expand. In truth, I feel deeply that this Award is to be shared with the American Jewish Committee, the ICCJ, and those thousands of extraordinary Christian and Jewish leaders who collaborated with us throughout the United States and in other parts of the world to bring about this "revolution of mutual esteem." There are few greater personal satisfactions for me today than that of being embraced as friend and colleague by these Christian and Jewish leaders in virtually every major city in the United States and in many parts of the world.

There is a Hebrew phrase, *acharon, acharon chaviv,* "the last is the most beloved." My magnificent, beautiful, and brilliant wife, Georgette, has saved my life in many ways. It is difficult to imagine that any human being can give more to another than my wife has given to me. During our years together, Georgette has made me possible.

Sir Sigmund, ICCJ, AJC, and my family of friends, for this memorable day, I thank you from the bottom of my heart.

30

Jewish-Catholic Relations: Achievements and Unfinished Agenda

DURING THE 28 YEARS since the adoption of *Nostra Aetate* by Vatican Council II, the Catholic Church and the Jewish people have experienced what has rightly been called "a revolution in mutual esteem." That transformation of a 1,900 year-old encounter between Christians and Jews which had been characterized mainly by a culture of contempt into a radically new culture of "covenantal partnership" and growing mutual esteem, even of "love between us" (Pope John Paul II, February 15, 1985) is a momentous achievement in its own terms.

It is an achievement, even in its infancy, that also resonates with moral and spiritual meaning for enabling us to understand and cope constructively with the enormous challenges and threats that are posed by the immense diversity of religions, races, ethnic groups, and political ideologies in the pluralistic world which we inhabit.

Since 1968, I have devoted a large measure of my energies to working with Jewish and Christian groups seeking to bring relief to suffering refugees and starving peoples in Southeast Asia (the Vietnamese boat people, Cambodians, Laotians, ethnic Chinese); in Africa (Ethiopians, South Africans in the black homelands, Nigeria, Uganda, the Sahel, Sudan, Mozambique, etc.); in the Caribbean (Haitians, Cubans); in South America (Miskito Indians, descamisados in the favellas of Brazil, Venezuela, etc.); in India (Tibetans, Sikhs); Sri Lanka (Tamils, Sinhalese); and Soviet Jews and Polish refugees in the United States.

Excerpted remarks given at the Institut für die Wissenschaften von Menschen, Vienna, Austria, November 27–30, 1988. Together with Eugene J. Fisher, among others, Rabbi Tanenbaum participated in a symposium on "Jews and Christians in a Pluralistic World."

There are today about 12 million refugees scattered throughout the world, some 6 million of them in Africa alone. Through study and personal observation, it is now apparent that many, if not most of these refugees are victims of profound religious, racial, and tribal conflicts. In a large number of these tragedies, religious fanaticism and absolutistic, messianic nationalism have become the terrible chemistries that resulted in these explosions causing so much human devastation and pain.

The late psychoanalyst, Dr. Eric Fromm, a great humanist, became deeply disturbed by the growing pattern of violence and fanaticism throughout so many parts of the world. At the time of the strife between Hindus and Muslims in India, he carried out a clinical psychoanalytic study of that inter-group violence. In his last monumental publication, *The Anatomy of Human Destructiveness* (New York: Holt, Rinehart, and Winston, 1973), he concluded that there is "a pathological dynamic" at work in such religious-political conflicts which he termed "group narcissism." As is the case with individual narcissism, groups that are narcissistic attribute to themselves all virtue and ultimate value, while denying value to the outside group, "the other." The narcissistic group views itself as "superior" and regards the other as "inferior." This mentality leads to a process of "dehumanization" or "monsterizing" in which the so-called superior group feels justified in emptying the alleged inferior group of all human dignity and value. Such dehumanization becomes the precondition as well as the justification for destroying the other.

There are two vital corollaries to this process, which Dr. Fromm characterized as the engine of such vast destructiveness in the world. First, physical violence against the human person or group is invariably preceded by "verbal violence." White racist segregationists in the American South invariably abused blacks verbally before carrying out their lynchings. The Nazis engaged in systematic verbal violence against the Jews (and also the Polish people, gypsies, among others), reducing them to dehumanized *untermenschen* as a cultural precondition for their systematic pogroms. In every instance, it becomes easier to destroy human beings when they are reduced to caricatures filled with contempt and hostility. "Psychic numbing" (Dr. Robert Jay Lifton's concept) makes that possible.

Second, in practically every major religious, racial, and tribal conflict that I have studied in recent years, there is non-existent or seriously undeveloped religious ideology or political doctrine of coexistence in a pluralist society. There are simply no religious or ideological resources for living with differences. Difference invariably is experienced as a threat rather than a possible source of enrichment. What does all that have to do with "Jews and Christians in a Pluralistic World"? Since the adoption of *Nostra Aetate* by Vatican Council II, a great reversal of historic proportions has taken place in the Church's relationship to Judaism and the Jewish people. His Holiness Pope John Paul II expressed that new spirit powerfully during a February 15, 1985, audience with the American Jewish Committee:

> I am convinced and I am happy to state on this occasion, that the relationships between Jews and Christians have radically improved in these years. Where there was ignorance and therefore prejudice and stereotypes, there is now growing mutual knowledge, appreciation, and respect. There is, above all, love between us, that kind of love, I mean, which is for both of us a fundamental injunction of our religious traditions and which the New Testament has received from the Old (cf. Mark 12:38; Lev. 19:18).

And then, as if to suggest his idea of pluralism between Christians and Jews, he added, "Love involves understanding. It also involves frankness and the freedom to disagree in a brotherly way where there are reasons for it."

I wish to pause here and acknowledge with respect and appreciation the singular contribution that Pope John Paul II, building on the foundations laid by his predecessors, Pope John XXIII and Pope Paul VI, personally has made in redefining and advancing on deep theological, moral, and human levels improved understandings between the Catholic Church and the Jewish people. That assertion should not obscure the fact that there are significant differences regarding certain policies and actions relating mainly to some interpretations of the Nazi Holocaust and the State of Israel. But anyone who wishes to speak seriously about the role of the pope in his inspired commitment to fostering genuine solidarity and mutual respect between the Catholic Church and the Jewish people has a moral duty to study the texts of his numerous addresses and declarations contained in the booklet *On Jews and Judaism, 1979–1986,* edited by Dr. Eugene J. Fisher and Rabbi Leon Klenicki, and the pamphlet, *John Paul II—On the Holocaust,* also edited by Dr. Fisher.

His Eminence Cardinal Johannes Willebrands, President of the Holy See's Commission on Religious Relations with the Jews and a worthy bearer of the mantle of the late Cardinal Augustin Bea, has recently affirmed that the pope was consistent and untiring in his efforts to spread the teachings of the Second Vatican Council on Jews and Judaism elaborated in the foundation documents of *Nostra Aetate* of 1965, the *Guidelines and Suggestions for Implementing the Conciliar Declaration* Nostra Aetate of 1974, and *Notes on the Correct Way to Present the Jews and Judaism in Preaching and Catechesis in the Roman Catholic Church* of 1985. In their essence, these themes embody the central theological and practical achievements in Catholic-Jewish relations since Vatican Council II.

The spiritual bond with Jews is properly understood as "a sacred one; stemming as it does from the mysterious will of God." The relationship is not marginal to the church. It reaches to the very essence of the nature of Christian faith itself; so that to deny it is to deny something essential to the teaching of the church (cf., Vatican *Notes,* pp. 1–2). The dialogue between Catholics and Jews is not a dialogue between past (Judaism) and present (Christianity) realities; as if the former had been "superseded" or "displaced" by the latter. "On the contrary," the pope declared in his moving elocution to the Jewish community of Mainz, "it is a question rather of reciprocal enlightenment and explanation, just as is the relationship between the Scriptures themselves" (cf., *Dei Verbum,* 11). Instead of the traditional terms of "Old Testament" and "New Testament," which might be understood to imply that the "old has been abrogated in favor of the new," the pope in his address to the Jews of Australia (November 26, 1986) has suggested the use of the terms "the Hebrew Scriptures" and "the Christian Scriptures" as appropriate alternatives.

In his historic visit to the Great Synagogue of Rome (April 13, 1986), the first such visit since Apostolic times, the pope asserted, "The Jewish religion is not 'extrinsic' to us, but in a certain way is 'intrinsic' to our own religion. With Judaism, therefore, we have a relationship which we do not have with any other religion. You are dearly beloved brothers and in a certain way, it could be said that you are our elder brothers."

In his address to the Jewish community of Mainz, the pope spoke of "the spiritual heritage of Israel for the church" as "a living heritage, which must be understood and preserved in its depth and richness by us Catholic Christians." The "common spiritual patrimony" of Jews and Christians is not something of the past but of the present which includes an understanding of post-biblical Judaism and "the faith and religious life of the Jewish people as they are professed and practiced still today" (March 1982). "Jews and Christians are the trustees and witnesses of an ethic marked by the Ten Commandments in the observance of which man finds his truth and freedom" (Rome Synagogue, April 13, 1986).

The pope teaches that the Jews remain God's chosen people in the fullest sense ("most dear") and this in no way diminishes the church's own affirmation of its own standing as "the people of God." In Mainz, the Pope addressed the Jewish community as "the people of God of the Old Covenant, which has never been revoked by God," referring to Romans 11:29, and emphasized "the permanent value" of both the Hebrew Scriptures and the Jewish community that witnesses to those Scriptures as sacred texts (November 17, 1980).

In his very first audience with Jewish representatives in March 1979, the pope reaffirmed the Second Vatican Council's repudiation of anti-Semitism, "as opposed to the very spirit of Christianity," and which "in any case the dignity of the human person alone would suffice to condemn." The pope has repeated this message in country after country throughout the world. And despite the recent controversies, the record is clear that the pope, who lived under Nazism in Poland and experienced personally the ancient evil of anti-Semitism, has called on Catholics in country after country to remember "in particular, the memory of the people whose sons and daughters were intended for total extermination" (Homily at Auschwitz, June 7, 1979).

In Otranto, Italy, he linked for the first time the Holocaust and the rebirth of a Jewish state in the land of Israel: "The Jewish people, after tragic experiences connected with the extermination of so many sons and daughters, driven by the desire for security, set up the State of Israel" (October 5, 1980).

On the twentieth anniversary of *Nostra Aetate,* the pope stated "anti-Semitism, in its ugly and sometimes violent manifestations, should be completely eradicated." He called the attention of the whole church to the mandate given in the 1985 Vatican *Notes* to develop Holocaust curricula in Catholic schools and catechetical programs: "For Catholics, as the *Notes* (no. 25) have asked them to do, to fathom the depths of the extermination of many millions of Jews during World War II and the wounds thereby inflicted on the consciousness of the Jewish people, theological reflection is also needed" (October 28, 1985). On August 29, 1981, Pope John Paul II condemned a bomb-throwing attack on a synagogue in Vienna, Austria, as a "bloody and absurd act, which assails the Jewish community in Austria and the entire world," and warned against a "new wave of that same anti-Semitism that has provoked so much mourning through the centuries" (NC News, September 1, 1981).

The complexities of the Middle East situation and the differences between the Holy See and Israel on the issue of establishing full diplomatic relations are well known. Suffice it for these purposes in this limited space to cite the pope's generally positive views on a moral plane toward the State of Israel as disclosed in an Apostolic Letter of April 20, 1984:

> Jews ardently love her (Jerusalem) and in every age venerate her memory, abundant as she is in many remains and monuments from the time of David who chose her as the capital, and of Solomon who built the Temple there. Therefore, they turn their minds to her daily, one may say, and point to her as a sign of their nation. . . . For the Jewish people who live in the State of Israel and who preserve in that land such precious testimonies of their history and their faith, we must ask for the desired security and the due tranquility that is the prerogative of every nation and condition of life and of progress for every society.

Beyond the rethinking of the traditional understanding of Jews and Judaism, the pope has called upon Catholics to undertake a major effort: "We should aim in this field, that Catholic teaching at its different levels, in catechists to children and young people, presents Jews and Judaism, not only in an honest and objective manner, free from prejudices and without any offences, but also with full awareness of the (Jewish) heritage." He also said that the often tragic history of Christian-Jewish relations over the centuries needs to be made clear to Catholic youth: "The proper teaching of history is also the concern of yours. Such a concern is very understandable, given the sad and entangled common history of Jews and Christians—a history that is not always taught or transmitted correctly." During his Rome Synagogue address he urged the implementation of the Vatican *Guidelines* and *Notes:* "It is only a question of studying them carefully, of immersing oneself in their teachings, and of putting them into practice."

The pope repeatedly affirms his vision for Jews and Christians of joint social action and witness to the One God and the reality of the Kingdom of God as the defining point of human history. This way of collaboration "in service to humanity" as a means of preparing for God's Kingdom unites Jews and Christians on a level that, in a sense, can be said to be deeper than the doctrinal distinctions that divide us historically.

The pope's views have been reinforced by pronouncements issued by national bishops' conferences in the United States, Austria, Holland, Belgium, France, Switzerland, the Federal Republic of Germany, Colombia, and Brazil, which have promulgated their own statements on Catholic-Jewish Relations, on occasion advancing their teachings beyond those presented in the Vatican documents. Individual cardinals and bishops, as well as theologians, have made pronouncements on a variety of religious and moral issues relating to Catholic-Jewish bonds that have enlarged the culture of mutual esteem.

To appreciate the dramatic changes in Catholic teaching about Jews and Judaism inaugurated by Vatican Council II and significantly advanced by the *Guidelines and Suggestions for Implementing the Conciliar Declaration* Nostra Aetate of 1974 and the *Notes on the Correct Way to Present the Jews and Judaism in Preaching and Catechesis in the Roman Catholic Church,* issued in June 1985, one needs only to examine the contrasts in educational materials published since the Council with textbooks and teaching manuals in common use into the 1960s. The St. Louis University textbook studies conducted in the Unites States by three Catholic sisters, under the supervision of Jesuit Father Trafford Maher, revealed teachings of hostility and contempt that lent credence to Jewish concerns about Christian polemical traditions as a source of anti-Semitism.

In Europe, the Louvain and Pro Deo University studies—which examined Catholic teaching materials in a variety of languages: Italian, French, including materials from French-speaking countries (Belgium, France, Switzerland, and Canada), and Spanish—showed that teachings of contempt were widespread throughout the religious culture. In her study summarizing these findings, Mme. Claire Huchet-Bishop, a Catholic scholar, wrote in her book, *How Catholics Look at Jews* (New York: Paulist Press, 1974), that many young Catholics in these countries were still being instructed in the 1960s, twenty years after the Nazi Holocaust, the following teachings:

1. The Jews are collectively responsible for the crucifixion and they are a "deicide people";
2. The diaspora is the Jews' punishment for the crucifixion and for their cry, "His blood be upon us and upon our children";
3. Jesus predicted the punishment of his people: the Jews were and remained cursed by him, and by God; Jerusalem, as a city, is particularly guilty;
4. The Jewish people as a whole rejected Jesus during his lifetime because of their materialism;
5. The Jewish people have put themselves beyond salvation and are consigned to eternal damnation;
6. The Jewish people have been unfaithful to their mission and are guilty of apostasy;
7. Judaism was once a true religion, but then became ossified and ceased to exist with the coming of Jesus;
8. The Jews are no longer the chosen people, but have been superseded as such by the Christians.

Mme. Bishop noted that charges against the Jewish people were accompanied by a rhetoric of invective, "verbal violence," which attributed the most vicious motives to them. In citing these themes of negative theology toward the Jews, it is not my intention to obsess about the past or to seek to evoke guilt. Rather, my purpose is to underscore that the radical improvement in Catholic-Jewish relations, theologically and morally significant in itself, may also be a primordial model of how it is possible to transform a culture that once demonized and thereby dehumanized a people into a new culture of rehumanization. It also has something to teach us about the importance of overcoming verbal violence and toxic language, which destroy human dignity and family solidarity, and of replacing those invectives with healing language of respect and mutual affirmation. That lesson applies equally to Jews as well as Christians, and, I believe, to all groups who are afflicted by such dehumanizing tendencies.

One of the critical methods for bringing about the dismantling of the old negative culture and constructing a new culture of mutual esteem is to be seen in the dramatic effects in improved and enlightened education. Thus, both the Louvain and Pro Deo studies reported a sharp drop in negative statements in textbooks and other teaching materials issued after Vatican Council II. Mme. Bishop observed: "It seems reasonable to assume that these figures reflect the church's adoption of a new positive policy toward Jews and Judaism at the Second Vatican Council."

In the United States, Dr. Eugene J. Fisher published a study of post-Vatican Council II Catholic textbooks covering sixteen major religion series used in the elementary grades and high school levels. In his book, entitled *Faith Without Prejudice* (New York: Crossroad, 1977), Dr. Fisher found great improvement in the treatment of many of the past troublesome themes. For example, he found clear references to the Jewishness of Jesus, which had been mostly avoided in the past. He found the notion of Jewish suffering as an expression of divine retribution completely eliminated from the textbooks. References to the Holocaust were handled with great sensitivity. References to violence against Jews during the Crusades and the Inquisition and references to the modern State of Israel he found to be still "inadequate."

Here it may be appropriate to report that in the growing atmosphere of confidence and trust, the Jewish community has conducted its own self-studies of Jewish textbooks in terms of what Jewish schools teach about Christians and Christianity. As summarized by Mrs. Judith H. Banki, my former associate at the American Jewish Committee, which helped to sponsor the Dropsie University study, later followed by a study of Jewish seminary curricula, the Dropsie study reported the following:

While Judaism has been influenced in its development by interaction with Christianity more than is generally acknowledged (Maimonides and St. Thomas Aquinas, etc.), it does not define itself in contrast to or comparison with Christianity. The Jewish-Christian encounter as described in Jewish high-school textbooks is social and historical, not doctrinal or theological. On the one hand, this avoids the problem of polemical approaches to Christianity; on the other hand, recounting the episodes of persecution, expulsion, and massacres which Jews suffered at the hands of Christians for centuries, and which are among the realities of Jewish history, tends to leave a negative image, not so much of Christian faith, but of the church as temporal power. In fairness, it must be said that this negative image is somehow offset by attention paid to righteous Christians who shielded and protected Jews across the years, and to the high value assigned in Jewish textbooks to religious and cultural pluralism and human kinship.

Still, Ms. Banki observes, many Jews—like many Catholics—are not aware of the momentous changes in Catholic thinking about Jews and Judaism that have issued from the highest levels of the church since Vatican Council II. As part of the future agenda, Jewish students, as well as others in the general Jewish population, need to be informed of these developments both in formal education and through mass communications.

On the Jewish seminary level, briefly, Christianity and Jewish-Christian relations are taken seriously, and there are a number of courses dealing with the origins of Christianity, the intertestamental period, medieval, and contemporary relations. There are also a number of programs that bring Jewish and Christian seminarians together for study and dialogue.

It is important to record that a number of prominent Jewish theologians, scholars, and rabbis have been working to conceptualize systematically a Jewish theology or religious understanding of Christianity. As Orthodox Rabbi Irving Greenberg formulates the issue, "It is possible for Judaism to have a more affirmative model of Christianity, one that appreciates Christian spiritual life in all its manifest power. After the Holocaust, a model of the relation of Judaism and Christianity ideally should enable one to affirm the fullness of the faith claims of the other, not just offer tolerance."

UNFINISHED AGENDA

Education: While remarkable progress has been made since Vatican Council II, there is still much to be done to change habits of thinking. The self-definition-by-denigration model has not yet been fully replaced on the pedagogical level. Current scholarship which sets the conflict events described in the New Testament, particularly the Passion narratives and the portrayal of the Pharisees, into historical perspective should be reflected in textbooks, teacher's manuals, teacher training, seminary education, and homiletics to a much greater extent than at present.

Excellent basic reference materials, such as Dr. Eugene J. Fisher's publication, *Seminary Education and Christian-Jewish Relations* (Washington, D.C.: National Catholic Education Association, Seminary Dept., 1983), provide important perspectives on such areas as sacred scriptures, liturgy and homiletics, church history, catechetics, systematic and moral theology, spiritual formation and field education. In Jewish education, particularly the seminaries, there is need to overcome the little knowledge about Christian beliefs, history of present communities, as well as a longer view of the development of Christian thought and history.

Communications: There should be a concern that commitment to improved Jewish-Christian relations is progressing primarily among the "ecumenical generals," leaving a substantial gap in the vast number of "infantry troops." A thoughtful, creative, and systematic use of modern means of public education through mass communications would help close this gap and give depth to Jewish-Christian solidarity.

Joint Witness, Social Justice, and Human Rights: The epidemic of dehumanization at loose in large parts of the world is, I believe, one of the most profound challenges facing Christians and Jews. Fanaticism, resort to verbal and physical violence, torture, terrorism, violations of human rights and freedom of conscience are daily assaults on the dignity of human life created in the divine image. Close collaboration of Christians and Jews who share a common vision of biblical humanism could become a critical mass in stemming the forces of dehumanization and in upholding the preciousness of every human life in God's human family. There are models and structures in both the Christian and Jewish communities for advancing this fundamental objective of redemption. It requires moral will, commitment, and courageous leadership.

World Refugees, World Hunger: At a time when nations and peoples squander billions on arms races and weapons of death and destruction, it is scandalous that such modest resources are available to help relieve the staggering hunger, starvation, poverty, and disease in so many parts of the developing world. Wherever and whenever Christians and Jews join hands together and mobilize their common will and material resources, they make a crucial difference in relieving vast suffering and in saving human lives. There is no clearer moral and religious duty than *tikkun olam*, the repair and healing of a broken world. The "covenantal partnership" of the church and the Jewish people is the surest of God's instruments for realizing that work of the Kingdom.

Pluralism: If after two millennia of estrangement and hostility, Christians and Jews could create a genuine culture of mutual esteem and reciprocal caring, the Christian-Jewish dialogue could well become a sign and an inspiration of hope to other religions, races and ethnic groups to turn away from contempt to realizing authentic human fraternity. This pluralistic model of the Jewish-Christian symbiosis may be the most important service that we have to offer to our troubled world.

31

No One Has the Right to Turn Auschwitz into a Christian Holy Place

SINCE THE CLOSE of Vatican Council II in 1965, major strides have been made in overcoming misunderstanding and in fostering mutual respect between Catholics and Jews in many parts of the world.

The current furor over the Carmelite convent built on the grounds of the Auschwitz death camp is a dramatic sign of the deep miscomprehensions between both groups that are yet to be overcome. Blind spots exist in both the Catholic and Jewish communities. In the case of the Auschwitz convent, I believe the present Polish Catholic insensitivities are far more morally damaging and dangerous.

Let me say at the outset that I feel strongly that the Carmelite nuns—and all Catholics—have every moral right and religious duty to honor the memory of the Polish martyrs killed by the Nazis.

More than a million Polish people were murdered at Auschwitz. No thoughtful Jew I know criticizes or opposes the spiritual act of memorializing the Polish dead.

But 90 percent of those murdered at Auschwitz were Jews. The Carmelite nuns and the Polish Catholic Church do not have a right under the laws of God or man to transform Auschwitz into a Christian "holy place" that displaces or supersedes the uniqueness that the purgatory signifies to world Jewry.

For Jews, Auschwitz is the ultimate *Vernichtungs-lager* (annihilation camp). It is the permanent sign—the incarnation—of the Nazis' barbaric campaign to exterminate the entire Jewish people, simply because they were Jews.

Reprinted from the *New York Post* Opinion, August 18, 1989.

None of the descriptive brochures about the Carmelite convent published by a Catholic fundraising group in Belgium in 1985 contained a single reference to the systematic mass killings of European Jews at that death camp. Indeed, there were vague, mystical references to "the conversion of the strayed brothers from our countries" that resonated to many Jewish ears a triumphal appeal to pursue the dead even beyond the grave.

In subsequent months, a twenty-three-foot cross was erected next to the convent. It is now the dominating religious symbol over Auschwitz. Both the promotional brochures and the dramatic cross signify to many Jews—and to sympathetic Christians—who recently visited the convent that Auschwitz is now being commemorated as a site essentially of Christian martyrdom. Whether consciously intended or not, a revisionist scenario of history has been unfolding at the very gates of Auschwitz. Christians are being perceived as the victims, not Jews.

The silence over the destruction of three-quarters of European Jewry, ninety percent of Polish Jewry, suggests that Christians were victims only, never persecutors or murderers.

If this pattern were to continue, it is not inconceivable that in fifty years Auschwitz will be understood as having nothing to do with the planned extermination of the whole of European Jewry, nor with the demonological anti-Semitism—the deicide culture—which prepared the way for the Nazi Holocaust.

An eminent Catholic cardinal of France, who has been at the center of the controversy, has spoken to the core issue with utter clarity. Cardinal Albert Decourtray of Lyon, president of the French Conference of Catholic Bishops, has declared: "It is the attempt to totally exterminate the Jews, which we call the *Shoah,* of which Auschwitz is the symbol. Such affliction and suffering have conferred on the Jewish people through its martyrs a particular dignity that is quite properly its own. And to construct a convent at Auschwitz would, for me, impinge on that dignity."

Where are we now? Four European Catholic cardinals who share Cardinal Decourtray's convictions signed an agreement with European Jewish leaders in Geneva in 1987. They committed themselves and the Polish Catholic Church to build a new convent as the first structure in a new interreligious center 550 meters off the grounds of Auschwitz.

That is a major achievement in mutual comprehension. It must not be allowed to be sidetracked by provocative Jewish demonstrations or by violent Polish responses.

Pope John Paul II, I was told in Rome, recently met with the four cardinals on the Auschwitz convent issue and reportedly said to them in Latin, "An agreement entered into by the church must be implemented."

Patience and wisdom on the part of the authentic representatives of the church and the mainstream Jewish community will make that implementation possible, sooner rather than later. And Catholics and Jews will yet make another major step forward in mutual comprehension.

Epilogue

"More than Enough for Doing the Work the Lord Commanded" (Exodus 36:5)

Eugene J. Fisher

RABBI MARC TANENBAUM'S JOURNEY through life was sadly cut short with many miles still untraveled. Yet it is also needs to be said that what he and the other pioneers of dialogue in his generation together began has profoundly altered for the better the landscape of the present and future through which all of us who follow him will travel in our own journeys. I would like to give just a few examples here based upon my own experiences with him of some of the areas of Jewish-Christian relations that continue to be influenced by his work. Readers of this volume, I am sure, will be able to supply many more.

First, I would point to the field of Christian religious education. In the mid 1950s, the American Jewish Committee initiated a series of "self-studies" of the treatment of "the other" in school textbooks. Catholics, Protestants, and Jews were each to analyze their own curriculum materials using research designs suited to those materials. The studies took the form of doctoral dissertations for St. Louis University, Dropsie College, and Yale University. In the interreligious categories of the Catholic and Protestant studies, which began to be published in the early 1960s shortly before Rabbi Tanenbaum joined the AJC staff, a very dismal picture emerged. In the Catholic and Protestant textbooks, Jews and Judaism were regularly portrayed in a negative and even polemical fashion, while in the Jewish texts Christians and Christianity were scarcely treated at all. The problem with the latter situation, of course, was that Jewish students would be left to develop their understanding of their Christian neighbors solely on the basis of their portrayal in popular media and family anecdotes handed down from immigrant forebears. Neither of these sources, needless to say, would be likely to provide a nuanced or balanced perspective.

These studies and their implications might have languished on the bookshelves of university libraries had Rabbi Tanenbaum not moved so aggressively to spread awareness of the results among Christian and Jewish educators through further publications, conferences, and symposia, and even studies of textbooks published in Europe in the period. My own doctoral dissertation updated the Catholic self-study fifteen years later, for example, and Rabbi Tanenbaum opened up the AJC library for my research. Most spectacularly, perhaps, was the submission of the results of the studies to the Second Vatican Council, a project ably carried through by my co-editor, Judith H. Banki. The precision of the studies greatly aided the framers of *Nostra Aetate* in understanding where the real problems actually lay in Catholic teaching so that the document could go right to the source in rooting them out.

Results of follow-up studies such as my own *Faith Without Prejudice* (New York: Crossroad, 1976) and Philip Cunningham's *Education for Shalom* (Collegeville, Minn.: Liturgical Press, 1995) have also been shared with the Holy See's Commission for Religious Relations with the Jews and have influenced its statements, especially the 1985 *Notes on the Correct Way to Present the Jews and Judaism in Preaching and Catechesis in the Roman Catholic Church.* So it can safely be said that the vastly more positive and accurate portrait of Jews and Judaism that is to be found today in Catholic school, university, and seminary classrooms is in generous part due to the unflagging efforts of Rabbi Tanenbaum and his staff at AJC in this field over the years (along, of course, with complementary efforts by other Jewish leaders and agencies, most notably Rabbi Leon Klenicki of the Anti-Defamation League).

In the late 1960s, in the wake of the Second Vatican Council, Rabbi Tanenbaum was one of a small group of visionary Jewish leaders, including Dr. Gerhart Riegner of the World Jewish Congress and Dr. Joseph Lichten of the Anti-Defamation League of B'nai B'rith, both of blessed memory, who sought to bridge internal Jewish institutional boundaries in order to create a fully representative committee to engage in international dialogue with the Roman Catholic Church and the World Council of Churches ("Rome and Geneva"). In 1970, their delicate and diligent efforts paid off when six major Jewish groups came together to form the International Jewish Committee on Interreligious Consultations (IJCIC) with headquarters in New York and Geneva. The groups spanned the spectrum of religious and secular Jewish agencies. The original IJCIC members were the World Jewish Congress, the Synagogue Council of America (which then counted as its constituents the rabbinical and congregational associations of Reform, Conservative, and Orthodox Judaism), the American Jewish Committee, B'nai B'rith International, and the Jewish Council for Interreligious Consultations in Israel.

IJCIC has evolved over the years. The Anti-Defamation League is now separately listed from B'nai B'rith, and the Synagogue Council, now dissolved, is represented directly by its six former members. In addition to continuing relationships with the Holy See and the World Council of Churches, IJCIC has begun a series of direct, bilateral consultations with Christian Orthodox bodies worldwide. Such evolution, with its attending stresses, strains, and opportunities, reflects the ongoing creative vitality of the Jewish people as it meets the challenges of a post-Cold War world. The tectonic plates of Jewish institutional geography are today shifting radically in response. It is a mark of the care with which Jewish leaders such as Reigner, Lichten, and Tanenbaum built into Jewish life an awareness of the tremendous potential for interreligious cooperation that the vision of a new era of Jewish-Christian relations has perdured and even flourished in the midst of such fundamental changes in Jewish communities around the world.

On December 30, 1993, an event took place in Jerusalem that represented the fulfillment of one of Rabbi Tanenbaum's dearest dreams and the culmination of a long process that consumed much of his professional life. This was the signing of the Fundamental Agreement establishing diplomatic relations between the Holy See and the State of Israel. Though Rabbi Tanenbaum did not live to see the day for which he had worked so long, he would have agreed with the document's preamble in which the signers noted that the agreement represented not simply a diplomatic victory but was more fundamentally a reflection of "the unique nature of the relationship between the Catholic Church and the Jewish people, and of the historic process of reconciliation and growth in mutual understanding and friendship between Catholics and Jews." Rabbi Tanenbaum, along with the other key architects on the Jewish side of that "historic process of reconciliation," is here implicitly acknowledged by the framers of the accord (cf., Eugene J. Fisher and Leon Klenicki, eds., *A Challenge Long Delayed: The Diplomatic Exchange Between the Holy See and the State of Israel* [New York: Anti-Defamation League, 1996]).

On the national level within the U.S., a major ongoing forum for the dialogue that Rabbi Tanenbaum supported and nourished and which owes much to his leadership over the years is the National Workshop on Christian-Jewish Relations (NWCJR). Begun by the women of a local Catholic-Jewish dialogue group in Dayton, Ohio, the first NWCJR took place in November of 1973 with about 100 participants. Subsequent workshops, now averaging over 1,000 participants each, have been held in Memphis (1975), Detroit (1977), Los Angeles (1978), Dallas (1980), Milwaukee (1981), Boston (1983), St. Louis (1984), Baltimore (1986), Minneapolis (1987), Charleston (1989), Chicago (1990), Pittsburgh (1992), Tulsa (1994), Stamford, CT (1996), and Houston (1999).

The breadth of the NWCJR's national sponsorship reflects the wide range and scope of its agenda in which virtually every aspect of the Jewish-Christian relationship, religious, social, and cultural, may be addressed in a given workshop. These include on the Christian side the National Conference of Catholic Bishops, the National Council of Churches, and the Southern Baptist Convention, and on the Jewish side the American Jewish Committee, American Jewish Congress, the Anti-Defamation League, and the National Jewish Community Relations Advisory Council as well as the national rabbinical and congregational associations of Reform, Conservative, and Reconstructionist Judaism. The workshops not only recharge the energies of those long involved in the dialogue, but also serve to bring into the movement and train new folks in its issues and dynamics. The NWCJR can safely be said to be the oldest, largest, and most widely representative continuous forum for the dialogue between Jews and Christians in the world today.

Rabbi Tanenbaum worked hard at establishing and maintaining the personal relationships and trust upon which lasting institutional relationships may be built. The preceding pages detail numerous jointly-sponsored conferences and events that he developed together with Protestant, Catholic, and Orthodox Christian groups. Not detailed are the hundreds of meetings and thousands of hours of preparation and follow-up that went into their planning and execution. Much of this enormous amount of work in the dialogue has been done over the decades by a relatively small group of dedicated professionals and volunteers, among whom Rabbi Tanenbaum was almost always a key figure.

Then, too, there have been the crises: the 1973 war in the Middle East, Bitburg, Waldheim, the Auschwitz Convent, and the visit of Cardinal Glemp of Poland to the United States, among others. Behind the scenes and the fractious headlines in the media, Rabbi Tanenbaum worked with Christian leaders to hammer out solutions, such as the meetings with Pope John Paul II at Castel Gandolfo in 1987 and Cardinal Glemp in Washington in 1991, and then "selling" them to his own, understandably skeptical Jewish community. Successfully weathering such crises together leads to increased trust not only between the individuals involved but in the institutions represented by them. These relationships in turn can be called on in future crises. So it was that in 1996, when word of the burnings of mostly African-American churches began to spread, the American Jewish Committee, the National Conference of Catholic Bishops, and the National Council of Churches, with a few phone calls, were able to announce together a virtually unprecedented joint campaign to raise funds for rebuilding.

The spirit and energy of Marc Tanenbaum lives on today in the network of interreligious relations he devoted his life to building.

Sukkoth 5757

ANTHOLOGY SOURCES

Chapter 1: Paths to *Agape* (*AJC Reporter,* November 1962)

Chapter 2: What Is a Jew? (Conference Address, *Encounter: Catholic-Jewish Confrontation,* Rockhurst College, January 29, 1963)

Chapter 3: Pope John XXIII: "One of the Righteous Among the Peoples of the Earth" (*Ave Maria National Catholic Weekly,* June 15, 1963)

Chapter 4: An Interfaith Reexamination of Christian-Jewish Relations (Lecture, *Sister Formation Workshop,* Marquette University, August 1963)

Chapter 5: The American Negro: Myths and Realities (*Religious Education,* January-February 1964)

Chapter 6: The Role of the Church and Synagogue in Social Action (Philip Scharper, ed., *Torah and Gospel: Jewish and Catholic Theology in Dialogue* [New York: Sheed & Ward, 1966])

Chapter 7: Vatican II: An Interfaith Appraisal: A Jewish Viewpoint (Address, International Conference on Theological Issues of Vatican II, University of Notre Dame, March 20–26, 1966, published in John H. Miller, ed., *Vatican II: An Interfaith Appraisal* [Notre Dame, IN: University of Notre Dame Press, 1966])

Chapter 8: A Jewish Reaction to Catholic Positions in Vatican II (Address, Twenty-first Annual Convention of the Catholic Theological Society of America, Providence, Rhode Island, June 20–23, 1966)

Chapter 9: Israel's Hour of Need and the Jewish-Christian Dialogue (Excerpt, *Conservative Judaism* 22:2 [winter 1968])

Chapter 10: The Meaning of Israel: A Jewish View (Address, Southern Baptist-Jewish Scholars Conference, Louisville, August 18–20, 1969)

Chapter 11: Jewish-Christian Relations: Issues and Prospects (Excerpt, *Perkins Journal,* Perkins School of Theology, fall 1970)

Chapter 12: A Survey and Evaluation of Christian-Jewish Relationships since Vatican Council II (Address, "Toward a Theology

INDEX